How to Be an Investment Banker

Founded in 1807, John Wiley & Sons is the oldest independent publishing company in the United States. With offices in North America, Europe, Australia and Asia, Wiley is globally committed to developing and marketing print and electronic products and services for our customers' professional and personal knowledge and understanding.

The Wiley Finance series contains books written specifically for finance and investment professionals as well as sophisticated individual investors and their financial advisers. Book topics range from portfolio management to e-commerce, risk management, financial engineering, valuation and financial instrument analysis, as well as much more.

For a list of available titles, visit our web site at www.WileyFinance.com.

How to Be an Investment Banker

Recruiting, Interviewing, and Landing the Job

ANDREW GUTMANN

WILEY

Cover Design: Leiva-Sposato
Cover Images: columns, © Fuse / Getty Images; financial chart, © Danil Melekhin / Getty Images

Published by John Wiley & Sons, Inc., Hoboken, New Jersey.
Published simultaneously in Canada.

Library of Congress Cataloging-in-Publication Data:

Gutmann, Andrew.
How to be an investment banker : recruiting, interviewing, and landing the job / Andrew Gutmann.
pages cm. — (Wiley finance series)
Includes bibliographical references and index.
ISBN 978-1-118-48762-4 (cloth) — ISBN 978-1-118-49448-6 —
ISBN 978-1-118-49446-2 — ISBN 978-1-118-49436-3
1. Investment banking — Vocational guidance. 2. Investment bankers — Employment. I. Title.
HG4534.G88 2013
332.66023 — dc23

2012049841

Printed in the United States of America

10 9 8 7 6 5 4 3 2 1

To my wife, Julie, who reminds me daily that
she thought she married an investment banker.

Contents

Introduction

Some years ago, in the fall of my second year of business school, I had a final-round interview scheduled with a boutique investment bank. The night before the interviews all of the candidates from different schools were invited to dinner so that the firm could get to know us a little better. The dinner was held in a private room of a nice Italian restaurant in midtown Manhattan, and we were all assigned to a table. Each table consisted of six people, evenly split between bankers and students.

Toward the beginning of the evening, one of the other candidates at my table asked me if I was ready for the next day's interviews. Sure, I said, trying not to sound arrogant. After all, I considered myself to be a pretty good interviewer. "What resources did you use to prepare for the technical interview?" my friendly tablemate followed up with.

"Huh?"

"Don't you know that one of the interviews tomorrow will be solely technicals? This firm is known for its tough technical interviews." To be honest, I don't recall my response. But I do remember thinking that, well, at least I got a nice dinner out of the deal.

My interviews started at 9:00 AM the next day. The first one was a fit interview. It went fine. Piece of cake. The next one was the technical.

I recall walking into a small office and seeing this little guy sitting with his feet up on his desk, holding a sheet of paper, and trying his best to look intimidating. He looked pretty young. I figured he must have been an analyst, though I found out later he was a vice president. Anyway, one at a time, reading from the piece of paper in his hand, he started firing away with technical questions.

A question about calculating enterprise value. Something about the inputs to a Black-Scholes model. Something else about discounting net operating losses. I tried to remember what I could from the accounting and finance classes I had taken during my first semester of business school (not much). Being hung over from the previous night didn't help either. Finally it was over. I'm not sure if he reached the end of his questions, or if he just felt sorry for me and stopped.

I went on with the rest of my interviews that morning. They were easy. They're usually easy when you feel like you have nothing to lose. Lucky for me, it worked out. I wound up getting an offer from that firm, and I worked there as an associate for about three years.

Needless to say, I was somewhat unprepared for the investment banking recruiting process. My goal in writing this book is to make sure you won't be.

OVERVIEW OF THE BOOK

Competition for investment banking positions is fierce. To be successful in the recruiting process and to become an investment banker requires three types of knowledge. First, you need to be knowledgeable about the industry. You need to understand what it is that investment banks do and what it is that investment bankers do. If you come across as naive about investment banking, you have no shot.

Second, you need to possess a basic understanding of accounting and finance; have the core technical skills of financial statement analysis, valuation, and financial modeling; and be able to converse about mergers and acquisitions and leveraged buyouts. As part of the investment banking interview process, you will be evaluated on how well you answer technical interview questions. While you need to understand the theory and principles that underlie the work of a banker, what you need to know goes far beyond what is typically taught in school. You need to know how investment bankers apply this theory and these principles in order to advise clients and to execute transactions. That is, you need to understand how things are done in practice, in the real world, in the world of investment bankers.

Third, you need to be prepared for the recruiting and interview process itself. You need to understand what banks are looking for and how you will be evaluated. You need to know how to differentiate your resume and how to tell your story in a way that will make you an attractive candidate. And you need to know how to network your way into interviews and how to turn those interviews into job offers.

The purpose of this book is to introduce you to the basic technical skills required in investment banking and to help prepare you for the investment banking recruiting and interviewing process. We will start off with an in-depth discussion of the field of investment banking, and the work and lifestyle of an investment banker. The bulk of the book focuses on teaching you the technical skills you need to know, starting with the very foundations of accounting and finance and up through the advanced skills of valuation, financial modeling, mergers and acquisitions (M&A), and leveraged buyouts (LBOs). Understand these concepts and you will be able to answer nearly any technical interview question you will encounter. Finally, we will wrap up the book with an extensive overview of the investment banking recruiting and interviewing process, with an emphasis on the kind of very tactical advice that will help you to succeed and to become an investment banker.

WHO IS THE BOOK FOR?

First and foremost, this book is meant for undergraduate and MBA students and recent graduates interested in recruiting for investment banking analyst or associate positions. Because we start with the first principles of accounting and finance, you should be able to learn from this book even if you are a liberal arts, science, or engineering major, and have never before taken an accounting or finance class. However, business major and MBA students will find that we go far beyond what is typically taught in school and should find even the first few chapters helpful in preparing for technical interview questions.

This book is also intended to be a guide for anyone else looking to learn about investment banking and to brush up on the fundamental knowledge and skills used in the industry. This includes new and current bankers at any level. Different from many other available resources, we will actually explain the concepts behind the work that you do. So if you have ever wondered why certain formulas are the way they are, or why you do a particular analysis in Excel, this book will help you be a better banker.

Finally, while our core focus is investment banking, nearly everything we will discuss is applicable to other areas of finance, including equity research, asset management, hedge funds, private equity, corporate development, and corporate banking. So if you are recruiting for one of these areas, or are already a professional in one of these fields, this book is for you, too.

STRUCTURE OF THE BOOK

The book is structured as follows. Chapter 1 will provide an introduction to investment banking, and a general overview of the work and lifestyle of an investment banker. Then we get into the heart of the book, which is the technical content. Chapters 2–4 cover the fundamentals of accounting, finance, and financial statement analysis, which together from the foundation for everything that a banker does. Chapters 5 and 6 focus on the two most important core technical skills of investment bankers: valuation and financial modeling. Chapters 7 and 8 take those technical skills a step further and discuss the more advanced topics of mergers and acquisitions and leveraged buyouts. Finally, we conclude the book with Chapter 9, which contains a detailed account of the recruiting and interviewing process.

Except for the first and last chapters, at the end of each chapter is a list of technical questions. These questions serve two purposes. First, they are intended to test your knowledge of what we have covered in that chapter. However, much more importantly, these questions reflect the actual kinds of technical questions that you will be asked in investment banking interviews. In fact, the majority of technical interview questions that you will encounter will be found in these "end-of-chapter" questions.

Chapter 1: Introduction to Investment Banking

The first chapter of the book is meant to provide you with a broad overview of investment banking and of life as a junior investment banker. The chapter will start with an overview of the different roles and divisions of an investment bank and then move on to cover the specific function we call investment banking. We will discuss the various types of transactions that investment banks execute for their clients and the different types of investment banks that exist, including bulge bracket banks and boutiques. We will also talk about the different groups found in a typical large investment bank.

Then this chapter will turn its attention to the life of an investment banker. We will cover the hierarchy of job titles that exist in the industry and the day to day work that junior investment bankers perform. Then we will discuss the lifestyle of an investment banker, including typical work hours, culture, personalities and compensation. Finally, we will wrap up the chapter with a discussion of the common exit opportunities that exist from investment banking and try to clear up some of the common misconceptions held by many prospective bankers.

Chapter 2: Accounting Overview

Chapter 2 is meant to provide you with the basic accounting knowledge required of investment bankers. We will start with a brief overview of the different types of accounting and some important general accounting principles. Then we will move on to a discussion of the concept of accrual accounting and the basic line items of the income statement. Following that, we will cover the basic equation of the balance sheet and the significant line items found on that statement, as well as some additional balance sheet concepts. Then we will cover the third of the three key financial statements: the cash flow statement.

The final section of this chapter will discuss how the three financial statements are integrated and will include a number of numerical examples to help demonstrate these interactions. This section is meant to reinforce a real understanding of accounting principles and also to prepare you for some of the trickiest technical interview questions that you are likely to encounter.

Chapter 3: Finance Overview

Chapter 3 will present an overview of the core finance topics that form the foundation of a banker's work. We will start with an introduction to the financial system, including the important role that financial institutions play. Then we will cover the most fundamental principles of finance, time value of money, risk and reward, and discount rate. Next, we will apply those concepts to learn the basic present value formulas that underlie the pricing and analysis of nearly all financial securities.

We will then move on to the topic of corporate finance, where we will discuss how companies make decisions whether to invest in a project based on the concepts of internal rate of return (IRR) and net present value (NPV). After that, we will focus on the different types of funding that companies can use to finance an investment, including the different types of debt and equity. We will also discuss how companies make capital structure decisions and the various ways in which they can return money to investors if there are no worthy investments to make.

In the final section of this chapter, we will learn how to value and analyze important financial securities. We will start off with bonds, where we will cover valuing a bond, interest rates, and various metrics to analyze a bond's yield. Then we will move onto the theoretical techniques for valuing stocks. Lastly, we will cover the conceptual method for valuing options and warrants, including a discussion of the Black-Scholes model.

Chapter 4: Financial Statement Analysis

In Chapter 4 we will cover how investment bankers and other financial professionals analyze a company's financial statements. We will begin with a discussion of the sources of information used for this purpose. We will focus primarily on SEC documents, from where much of this information can be found. Next, we will discuss the two most important types of SEC documents: the 10-K and the 10-Q.

Then we will move on to the actual process of financial statement analysis. We will introduce some of the key metrics that investment bankers frequently calculate in order to analyze financial statements, namely various types of growth statistics, profitability ratios, return ratios, activity ratios, and credit ratios. We will also discuss several different types of time periods that are commonly used in financial statement analysis. We will conclude this chapter with a discussion of the adjustments that bankers often make to financial statements, a process known as "normalizing the financials."

Chapter 5: Valuation

Chapter 5 will cover the first of the two core technical skills required of junior investment bankers and the most common topic of technical interview questions: valuation. The chapter will start with an introduction to valuation, including a discussion of the crucial concept of enterprise value. Then we will cover in detail the three primary valuation methodologies used by all investment bankers to value companies: the comparable company analysis, the precedent transaction analysis, and the discounted cash flow analysis.

In the first two methods, comparable companies and precedent transactions, we will learn how to select appropriate comparables and how to spread their financial information. We will cover calculating various valuation multiples and learn how to understand, analyze, and apply those multiples to value a company.

For our discussion of the discounted cash flow analysis, we will talk about forecasting free cash flow and estimating a terminal value. We will also talk about estimating the weighted average cost of capital using the capital asset pricing model to approximate the cost of equity, as well as how to estimate the cost of debt and the appropriate capital structure. We will then discuss how to appropriately discount cash flows to determine value today and how to sensitize this value.

After discussing the various steps required to perform each methodology, we will talk about how we conclude the appropriate valuation range for a company or its stock based on a combination of the three techniques. We will discuss how the context of valuation affects a banker's analysis and how valuation differs between investment banking and buy-side roles. We will conclude the chapter with a brief discussion of several additional valuation methodologies that bankers sometimes employ.

Chapter 6: Financial Modeling

Chapter 6 will cover financial modeling, the second of the two core technical skills required of analysts and associates. This chapter will begin with a general overview of how to build an integrated cash flow model and a discussion of modeling "best practices." Then we will move on describe in detail how we forecast the income statement, balance sheet, cash flow statement, and an additional schedule, the debt schedule. We will also talk about the reasons our model is circular and the importance that the revolving credit facility plays in the model. We will wrap up the chapter with a discussion of how to check and analyze a model and some suggestions on how to practice your modeling skills.

Chapter 7: Mergers and Acquisitions

Chapter 7 will introduce you to mergers and acquisitions (M&A) and discuss the kind of work that investment bankers do when advising on an M&A transaction. The chapter will begin with a discussion of the various rationale for which companies make acquisitions. Then we will discuss the different methods by which companies effectuate transactions. Next, we will go through a typical M&A process that a banker uses when executing a sell-side M&A deal. We will also talk about the role of investment bankers on a buy-side transaction.

In the final section of the chapter, we will cover the specific M&A related analyses that bankers perform when analyzing and/or executing transactions. The most important such analysis is the accretion/dilution analysis, which we will discuss in some detail. We will also briefly cover additional M&A analysis, including the contribution analysis and the analysis at various prices.

Chapter 8: Leveraged Buyouts

Chapter 8 will cover leveraged buyouts (LBOs). The chapter will start with an explanation of why using substantial amounts of debt can be an advantage when making acquisitions. Next, we will discuss the main players in an LBO transaction, namely the private equity firms, the role of investment bankers, and the types of companies that make good LBO targets. We will also discuss how credit conditions have a large influence on LBO activity.

Following that, we will move on to the actual LBO analysis that investment bankers frequently perform. We will talk about how to build an LBO model and then, based on that model, we will discuss how to measure the investment returns to the private equity firm making the acquisition, how to perform credit analysis, and how to utilize an LBO model for purposes of valuation. We will conclude the chapter with a brief discussion of the various considerations that influence a private equity firm's investment decisions.

Chapter 9: Recruiting, Interviewing, and Landing the Job

The final chapter of the book will cover recruiting and interviewing. We will begin with a discussion of the various criteria that investment banks use to evaluate analyst and associate candidates, and how you can stand out in the recruiting process. Then we will give an overview of the recruiting process itself, whether you are a student from a target school participating in on-campus recruiting, a student at a non-target school, or someone trying to break into investment banking from another type of job or industry.

Next, we will discuss how to craft a resume and cover letter that are tailored for investment banking. We will talk about recruiting receptions, networking, and the importance of doing informational interviews with bankers. After that, we will move on to the interview process, where we will provide some general interview tips and then focus our attention on the two core types of interview questions that you will encounter: fit questions and technical questions. Finally we will wrap up the chapter with a discussion of what happens after the interview, how to choose among various investment banking offers, and how to start your career off as an investment banker the right way.

Acknowledgments

I want to thank my editors at Wiley, including Laura Walsh, Judy Howarth, Tula Batanchiev, and Stacey Fischkelta, for all of their efforts and contributions to this book.

I also want to thank the staff of the Columbia Business School Career Management Center, especially Gina Resnick, Mark Horney, Michael Malone (now at Northwestern's Kellogg School of Management), and Ronny Bernstein for putting up with me as a career coach over the past five years and allowing me to speak my mind to students.

Thanks to my friends Alex Yoo and Scott Lee, who introduced me to my first gig teaching investment banking classes.

A special thanks to all of the students I have taught and coached over the years, and to everyone who has written to me through my web site, www.ibankingfaq.com. You have all helped me to be a more effective teacher, and this book is a beneficiary of all of your questions, comments, and feedback.

Most of all to thanks to my parents, Susan and Ben, for your enormous support through all of my professional endeavors; to my in-laws, Noryne and Jack, for your generous time through this process; to my daughter, Lauren, for reminding me of what's really important in life; and to my wife, Julie, for your patience and encouragement, and for helping me find the time to write this book.

How to Be an Investment Banker

CHAPTER 1

Introduction to Investment Banking

Tell people that you are an investment banker and you will likely get varying responses. Some will be highly impressed and may ask if they can hitch a ride on your private jet. Others will blame you personally for nearly blowing up the global economy in 2008 and for all the ills of the world that have followed. But perhaps the most frequent reply goes something like this: "Oh, you're an investment banker. Do you have any good stock tips?"

One thing is pretty certain: Ask a random person from Main Street, not Wall Street, to describe what it is that an investment banker does, and he or she will likely have no idea.

Maybe you are trying to decide whether to recruit for investment banking. How will you decide? First, you need to know what you are getting into. Will your life as a junior banker be glamorous? Will the work be intellectually challenging? Will you be well paid for all of your sacrifices? What will you learn? And where can a foundation in banking take you over the longer term?

Now, let's suppose you decide to go for it. Full steam ahead with recruiting. What's the first thing you need to do? You need to be knowledgeable—or at least sound like you're knowledgeable. You need to be able to articulate what investment banks do and what investment bankers do. There is no more surefire way to fail at the recruiting and interviewing process than to come across as naïve about the industry.

Okay, so let's say you've successfully navigated the recruiting process. You have offers—good offers. You're going to be an investment banker. Now what? Go in with your eyes open, have realistic expectations, and understand what it takes to succeed. Know what you want out of it and, most importantly, do it for the right reasons. Take this advice and your career will flourish. Don't, and you will struggle and be miserable, and your time spent as an investment banker will likely be brief.

This chapter is meant to give you a broad overview of investment banking and of what life will be like as a junior investment banker. We will begin with a discussion of the various functions of a typical large investment bank, the kinds of transactions that investment banks execute, and the different types of investment banks that exist. Next we will cover the structure of an average investment banking division and the standard hierarchy of job titles. Following that, we will talk about the actual work that investment bankers perform, and the culture and lifestyle that you should expect as a junior banker. Finally, we will wrap up the chapter with a discussion of some of the common career paths that exist for bankers leaving the industry and clear up some frequently held misconceptions about investment banking.

OVERVIEW OF AN INVESTMENT BANK

Let's start with the basics. An investment bank is an institution that provides financial advice and raises money for three main sets of clients: companies, governments, and wealthy individuals.

However, the large investment banks of the world, the firms like Goldman Sachs and Morgan Stanley, do a lot more than just advise and raise money for their clients. In other words, they do much more than just investment banking. For example, they have departments that sell and trade various securities, provide research to institutions and individuals about such securities, manage the investments of institutions and wealthy individuals, and trade the bank's own capital.

Following is a brief list of the many of the significant functions and/or divisions of a typical large investment bank. These functional areas are considered to be part of the institution's front office. Loosely speaking, that means that they are client-facing and typically revenue-generating parts of the firm. Investment banks also have substantial middle-office and back-office roles. Middle-office areas of the bank encompass such things as risk management and treasury management, whereas back-office roles include operations and information technology (IT).

Key front-office functions include:

- Investment banking.
- Sales and trading.
- Proprietary trading.
- Research.
- Asset management.
- Private banking.

As you may be aware, not every investment bank is large, and not every investment bank provides all of these types of financial services. Some investment banks indeed only do investment banking, and not trading or research or asset management. We will discuss the different types of investment banks later in this chapter.

Moreover, even the large investment banks may be just one division of a larger financial institution. Some firms provide not only investment banking services to companies but also commercial banking services. Such services typically include bank lending, money market savings accounts, and cash management. A firm that contains both an investment bank and commercial bank is often referred to as a universal bank. And even universal banks may be just a small part of a larger retail bank with a retail branch network that offers banking services to individuals, including checking and savings accounts, credit cards, and mortgages.

Key Divisions of an Investment Bank

As mentioned earlier, large investment banks do many different things. This section includes a brief description of these divisions or functional areas, and a short discussion of the lifestyle of the types of finance professionals who work there.

Keep in mind that the various divisions of banks are often structured differently from one another, and banks frequently have different names (and sometimes acronyms) for the same functions. An example of such a difference is private banking, which might fall under the umbrella of asset management at some firms and be an independent division at others. Some more poorly run banks even go through the exercise of restructuring their divisions every few years.

Investment Banking Given that the remainder of this chapter is about the investment banking division, we will keep this section very short. Investment banking is the division within an investment bank that advises companies, sometimes governments, and occasionally wealthy individuals on two things:

1. Executing large financial transactions such as an acquisition, sale, or divestiture.
2. Raising substantial amounts of money both privately and publicly through the debt or equity markets.

Within a larger financial institution, the investment banking division is sometimes abbreviated IBD, or referred to as corporate finance or advisory.

There are also plenty of standalone firms that only do investment banking. From this point on in the book, when we use the term "investment banking," we are speaking specifically of this functional area or division.

Sales and Trading Sales and trading is the division within the investment bank that, as its name indicates, sells and trades various securities and financial instruments. The sales and trading division is often abbreviated S&T and is sometimes referred to as capital markets or just markets.

The sales and trading division earns revenue through trading commissions and trading profits. By being both a buyer and seller of securities, it also provides liquidity to the marketplace, often referred to as market making. Over the past decade or so, a large focus of the sales and trading division has also been on inventing and structuring complex financial products (derivatives) such as interest rate swaps, collateralized debt obligations (CDOs) and credit default swaps (CDSs).

Examples of securities and financial instruments that are sold and traded by this division include:

- Equities (i.e., stocks).
- Fixed income securities (i.e., government and corporate bonds).
- Currencies.
- Commodities.
- Derivatives.

Professionals who are employed in this division work on what is known as the trading floor, an often-cavernous room taking up entire physical floors of the buildings that house financial institutions. The trading floor is segregated by financial product into what are known as desks. Individuals sit on a desk depending on what financial product they sell or trade. For example, a trader might sit on an equity derivatives desk or a convertible bonds desk.

Each desk typically has three types of personnel: institutional salespeople, traders, and sales traders. Salespeople suggest trading ideas and take trading orders from clients. These clients include institutional investors such as hedge funds and other asset managers. Traders then execute those trades. Sales traders act as intermediaries between the sales people and the traders.

Over the past several decades, the sales and trading division has become the largest front-office division of a typical large investment bank, both in terms of headcount and revenue. However, at most firms, this division has shrunk significantly over the past several years as trading revenue has declined, as more trading has become automated, and as products that were once considered complex have become standardized and "plain vanilla."

These trends have had a negative impact on recruiting, especially among undergraduates and MBA students.

The sales and trading division of investment banks have placed a large focus on increasing revenue and profits by inventing highly complex financial instruments that are not standardized and cannot be traded on an exchange. However, the hiring needs to structure and trade these kinds of products have focused on those with highly quantitative skills such as PhDs in the hard sciences, mathematics, and finance.

In general, sales and trading tend to attract individuals who are interested in the markets, have aggressive personalities, and handle stress well. The trading floor tends to be a male-dominated, fraternity-like atmosphere. Women are underrepresented, even by the standards of the finance industry. The lifestyle is intense during market hours, with traders and salespeople glued to their multiple computer monitors and phones. However, compared with investment banking, there is much more predictability to the hours. Plus, traders rarely work nights or weekends, the exception being salespeople who entertain clients. Compensation in sales and trading can be very high, even at relatively junior levels, though the compensation can be very volatile as market conditions change. Exit opportunities from sales and trading are generally limited to doing similar work at a hedge fund or other asset manager.

Proprietary Trading One of the greatest sources of profits for some of the large investment banks over the past decade has been from trading securities with the firm's own capital, as opposed to trading on behalf of a client. This activity is known as proprietary trading, or prop trading for short. Essentially, proprietary trading is like an internal hedge fund within the sales and trading division. However, recently regulators have tried to put a stop to proprietary trading, arguing that it is too risky of an activity for regulated banks. It remains to be seen how successful regulators will be in curtailing proprietary trading since it is difficult for regulators to distinguish between trades made on behalf of a client and trades that are not.

Sell-Side Research Sell-side research departments produce the fundamental research and analysis of industries, companies, economies, and related securities such as stocks, bonds, and currencies. The largest division within the research department is typically equity research, where analysts are responsible for covering the stocks of companies within a specific industry. Research analysts produce reports with detailed analysis, earnings forecasts, and commentary about the companies that they cover. They also often issue buy and sell recommendations, and come out with price targets on the stocks of those companies.

Research departments have two main sets of clients: internal and external. Internal clients are those that are within the bank, such as the equity sales and trading department. External clients are those that are outside of the bank, namely institutional investors such as hedge funds, pension funds, and mutual fund companies. Individual investors are also considered to be external clients.

Historically, many research analysts acted as investment bankers, helping to market their firm's mergers and acquisitions (M&A) and capital raising services to senior management of the companies that they covered. However, after the dot-com bust of the early 2000s, regulators tried to put an end to that practice, citing the inherent conflict of interest between independent research and investment banking. This has resulted in shrinkage of the equity research departments at most large investment banks and generally lower compensation for research analysts. Now that analysts cannot act as investment bankers, research is thought of as more of a cost center than a revenue generator. Research analysts are under significant pressure to cover a great number of companies and have strong relationships with institutional investors who will place trades with the bank, an activity that does generate revenue.

Equity research analysts have a similar skillset to investment bankers, and, in fact, some research analysts do make the switch to banking and vice versa. Like investment banking, research requires finance, accounting, valuation, and financial modeling skills. However, research analysts generally have more in-depth knowledge of the industry and companies that they cover than do bankers. In addition to the reports that research analysts publish, and the financial models underlying those reports, analysts spend time meeting with management, attending industry conferences, and meeting with and talking to institutional investors such as hedge funds.

Equity research tends to attract individuals who like to follow the stock market, enjoy fundamental research, and have an interest in a particular industry. The stress level is high, though not at the level of trading, and hours are long, though not at the level of banking. However, life gets very challenging during earnings seasons, when there is intense pressure to publish reports following each covered company's earnings release.

Chinese Wall Before we move on from our discussion of equity research, there is one additional topic worth mentioning: that of the Chinese Wall. Within an investment bank, a Chinese Wall is a separation between individuals who possess non-public information about a company and those who should only have public information. The most significant of these Chinese Walls exists between research analysts and investment bankers. For example, a research analyst should not know about a potential M&A deal on which an investment banker is secretly working. The compliance departments of investment banks take this separation very seriously and typically limit or chaperone interaction between the research analysts and the bankers.

Asset Management and Private Banking The asset management division of an investment bank manages and administers the assets of institutions such as pension funds, endowments, foundations, corporations, governments, and individuals. This division may manage investments on behalf of clients in all sorts of financial assets, such as equities and fixed income, as well as alternative investments such as hedge funds and private equity. Within the asset management division there are many different types of job functions including buy-side research (which is similar to sell-side research), portfolio management, and risk management. Asset management is sometimes also referred to as investment management.

The private banking department advises and manages money for high net worth individuals, their families, and their estates. In addition to managing money, they might help with such things as tax planning and estate planning. Private banking is sometimes also referred to as private client services (PCS) or private wealth management (PWM). This division may be a standalone division of the investment bank, or it may fall under the asset management or investment management umbrella. Most large financial institutions that offer private banking have different tiers of service, depending on the wealth of the client and the amount of assets a client has under the firm's management.

As with equity research, individuals attracted to asset management tend to enjoy following the markets and have good fundamental analysis and valuation skills. Individuals in asset management tend to stay in asset management, though they may move from an investment bank to another type of institution such as a hedge fund or mutual fund company.

Private banking requires very strong sales and client management skills, in addition to a varying degree of finance knowledge. At the junior levels, cold-calling is often required, and at the senior levels, significant entertaining. Wealthy individuals are often demanding clients, and catering to them is not always easy. Private banking is one area of the bank that tends to attract a significant number of women.

OVERVIEW OF INVESTMENT BANKING

Now that we've introduced the larger entity known as the investment bank and many of its important divisions, it is time to turn our attention specifically to investment banking, which is the focus of the remainder of the book.

We will start with a discussion of the types of transactions that investment bankers execute for their clients, and how they market their services and pitch for new business. Then we will cover the different types of investment banks that exist, namely the bulge bracket firms and the boutiques. We will conclude this section by talking about the structure of the different groups within a typical investment bank.

Types of Investment Banking Transactions

The primary role of an investment banker is to execute financial transactions for their clients. When we talk about an investment banker advising a client, what we really mean is a banker is advising on the execution of a transaction or potential transaction. The most common types of transactions that bankers execute are mergers and acquisitions, leveraged buyouts, capital raises, and restructuring transactions. Before bankers are hired to execute a transaction for a client they typically have to market their services, a process known as pitching.

Mergers and Acquisitions (M&A) For a number of reasons, companies sometimes merge with or acquire other firms, or purchase divisions or assets of other firms. For all but the smallest of deals, firms hire investment banks to help execute these transactions. Companies also hire investment bankers when they want to sell their entire company or divest divisions or large amounts of assets. Together, these types of transactions are known as mergers and acquisitions or, for short, M&A.

For an investment bank, this kind of advisory work can be segregated into two types: sell-side M&A and buy-side M&A. Sell-side M&A refers to the work representing a company that seeks to sell itself or a portion of its assets. On the flip side, buy-side M&A refers to the work advising a company that seeks to buy another company or portion of a company. In any given M&A transaction, there are typically one or more investment banks advising each side of the deal.

We will discuss mergers and acquisitions in much greater detail in Chapter 7.

Leveraged Buyouts (LBOs) Leveraged buyouts (LBOs) refer to a type of transaction whereby a company is acquired using a substantial amount of debt to help finance the purchase. The companies that make these types of acquisitions are a special type of investment fund known as a private equity firm or financial sponsor. Investment banks advise private equity firms on the acquisition and help to raise the substantial amounts of funding required to complete the transaction.

We will discuss leveraged buyouts in more significant detail in Chapter 8.

Capital Raisings As we mentioned earlier in this chapter, one of the two primary roles of the investment banking division is to help raise money for companies. Companies often require money for many different reasons, such as to fund organic growth, for a product or geographic expansion, for an acquisition, or because they have to repay existing lenders or investors. As we will discuss in Chapter 3, there are many different types of funding available to most companies, but nearly all types of funding can be categorized as either debt or equity.

Investment bankers help companies raise debt and equity from both the private and public markets. Raising capital is a highly regulated process, especially when seeking funds through the public markets, such as issuing traded stocks or bonds. In the United States, investment banks and the investment bankers who work on fundraising transactions must be licensed by regulatory agencies. Even raising money privately from banks, hedge funds, or other accredited investors requires following regulatory processes.

Most fundraisings, whether public or private, and whether for debt or equity, follow a similar process. Perhaps the most talked-about of fundraising processes is when a private company issues new shares of common stock to public investors. This is known as an initial public offering, or IPO. Many investment banks (collectively known as the underwriters) are involved in selling the new securities to both institutional investors and individual investors (also referred to as retail investors). However, there are typically one or two investment banks that play the lead role in the fundraising process, known as the bookrunner, or lead manager (or joint bookrunners/lead managers, in the case of multiple investment banks).

The lead manager(s) does a substantial amount of work through the IPO process. Key tasks include doing substantial due diligence on the company, working with the company's management and lawyers to draft and revise the S-1 registration statement (which becomes the prospectus), and determining the appropriate valuation for which to issues shares. The lead manager also organizes what is known as the road show, where management markets the company and presents its investment case to prospective institutional investors. The lead investment bank also helps to coordinate with the other underwriters on the deal (the co-managers). After all of that work, shares are allocated to investors and the stock begins trading publicly. Generally for an IPO, the investments banks receive fees of up to 7 percent of the amount of money raised, with the lead manager receiving the largest share, though in recent years, IPO fees for large and high-profile IPOs, such as GM and Facebook, have been significantly lower.

In addition to helping private firms issue new shares to the public in an IPO (known also as a primary offering), investment banks often help public companies sell additional new shares to investors, which is known as a follow-on offering. There is typically much less work that needs to be done in a follow-on offering than for an IPO, and the time it takes to execute the transaction is much shorter. Sometimes investment banks also help institutional investors sell large blocks of existing public shares of a company in what is known as a secondary offering.

When investment banks help companies raise money privately, it is typically referred to as a private placement. These types of fundraises are generally, though not always, smaller in size than a public offering. They are also less regulated than a public offering, but the process and the work required of the investment bank are quite similar. The investment bank must perform due diligence and valuation, and help draft the marketing material known as a private placement memorandum (PPM) or offering memorandum, as well as seek out and negotiate with investors or lenders.

Restructuring When times are good, investment bankers are busy helping companies raise money and make acquisitions. When times are bad, sometimes companies get into trouble. Companies may find themselves in the position of not having enough funds on hand to pay the interest or principal on their debt, or even operate their business. Or they may be in breach of various financial requirements (known as covenants) that lenders have placed on them. Companies in such a precarious state are referred to as being distressed. In distressed situations such as these, investment bankers are frequently brought in to provide advice.

Just as M&A assignments can be bifurcated into two broad categories (buy-side and sell-side), so can restructuring work be split into two type types. In the case of restructuring, there are investment banks that advise the distressed company, which is known as being on the debtor-side. In a typical distressed situation, there are also investment banks hired to advise the lenders and/or investors of the company, known as being on the creditor-side.

Debtor-side work involves representing a distressed or bankrupt company through a financial reorganization or recapitalization. Often this restructuring takes place under the legal protection of a bankruptcy court (a Chapter 11 reorganization), though sometimes a restructuring transaction can be effectuated without the company having to file bankruptcy (an out-of-court restructuring). The general goal of the debtor-side adviser is to help negotiate a reduction or elimination of the company's debts so that the company can be healthy when it emerges from bankruptcy or from the restructuring transaction. Bankers also help distressed companies raise funds to allow them to operate while in bankruptcy (debtor-in-possession, or DIP financing) and raise funds to allow them to operate upon emerging from bankruptcy (exit financing). Debtor-side work also frequently involves the sale of assets or multiple sales of assets, as in a sell-side M&A transaction.

Creditor-side involves representing the creditors (or a certain group of creditors) of a distressed or bankrupt company to try to maximize recoveries to that constituent. In a large restructuring, there are often multiple classes of creditors, each represented by a different investment bank.

Generally restructuring work is very interesting, given the legal backdrop of the bankruptcy laws. Transactions are also often contentious given the highly sophisticated parties involved (i.e., distressed hedge funds) and the fact that these parties are fighting over a zero-sum pool of money (the value of which is typically declining the longer the company is distressed or in bankruptcy). Much of the work involved is similar to that in M&A and fundraising processes, involving due diligence, valuation, modeling, and the creation of marketing materials and other presentations. However, timetables are often much quicker than in healthy transactions, and the technical work of junior bankers such as valuation often plays a key role in determining recoveries to the various creditor classes.

Unlike M&A and capital raises for healthy companies, for which advisory work is generally dominated by the larger investment banks, most restructuring work is done by smaller, boutique banks. This is due to the fact that large institutions often have conflicts of interest in distressed situations because they had a role in previously raising funds for the now-distressed company. Moreover, given the contentious nature of most restructuring transactions, large banks are reluctant to negotiate against the interests of some of their best clients, namely hedge funds and large institutional investors that typically make up a sizable portion of a distressed company's bondholders or other class of lenders. Lastly, keep in mind that within the small community of investment banks that do have restructuring practices, some firms focus primarily on either debtor-side or creditor-side roles, and some firms will perform both functions (though obviously not on the same transaction).

Pitching

While investment banks get paid for executing transactions for clients, bankers spend much of their time marketing their firm's services to prospective clients. This marketing activity is known as pitching. In fact, in nearly all circumstances, before a bank is hired to execute a particular transaction, it will have pitched for the business first.

Broadly speaking, there are three different types of pitches. The first type of pitch is an introductory pitch, when the investment bank or a particular senior investment banker meets a new prospective client for the first time. In this type of pitch, the bankers are there to introduce the firm and the firm's services to the company, and to learn about the company and its anticipated need for future investment banking services. The goal of such a pitch is to begin a relationship with the company that will ultimately result in the bank being hired to execute one or more transactions down the round.

The second kind of pitch is what we will call an untargeted pitch. In an untargeted pitch, bankers will present a variety of different investment banking "ideas" to a client, such as possible acquisition targets. The bankers will also frequently use this opportunity to provide management with an update on current market conditions. These types of pitches are used by bankers to get in front of senior management periodically, sometimes as often as every month for large companies that execute lots of transactions and are frequently in the market for investment banking services. The goal of this kind of pitch is to continue to foster a relationship with the company and to demonstrate helpfulness so that when the client is ready to hire a bank to execute a transaction, the investment bank is considered. It is unusual for the "ideas" presented in these kinds of pitches to result in actionable transactions.

The third kind of pitch is a targeted pitch, where investment bankers meet with the management of a potential client to talk about one or more specific transactions. Frequently, this kind of meeting is initiated not by the investment banker but by the company. This is the case when the company is contemplating a transaction and wants to hire an investment bank to help execute it. Often the company will invite a number of investment banks to pitch for the business in what is commonly referred to as a bake-off or beauty contest. Occasionally, such contests will go through multiple rounds of pitching, something that is difficult for bankers because, in each round, they will have to come up with additional material to present to management.

Pitchbooks In nearly every single meeting in which bankers pitch clients, junior investment bankers assigned to the pitch will create what is known as a pitchbook. A pitchbook is a PowerPoint presentation that gets printed in color, bound with a fancy cover, and presented to potential clients in the actual pitch meeting. Enormous work often goes into the process of creating these pitchbooks. In fact, junior bankers can routinely expect to spend half of their time or more working on pitchbooks, as opposed to working on live transactions.

A typical pitchbook contains a number of different sections. One of the first tasks of the deal team assigned to a new pitch is to decide what sections should be in the pitchbook. The list of sections is also often referred to as the pitchbook's table of contents, or TOC. Pitchbooks can run from a couple dozen pages to a hundred pages or more, the length of which will often vary, depending on the type of pitch but also on the senior investment banker running the pitch. Some senior bankers are notorious for demanding "fat pitchbooks." Many junior bankers believe there is an inverse relationship that exists between the size of the pitchbook and the quality of the senior banker.

Following are examples of some of the key sections contained in a typical investment banking pitchbook.

Credentials and Experience The goal of the credentials and experience section is to impress a prospective client with the vast experience and range of services that the investment bank can offer. In addition to providing an overview of the firm, this section will highlight the bank's (or group's) experience working with similar types of companies and/or executing similar types of transactions. For example, a pitchbook created for a sell-side M&A pitch will naturally highlight the firm's vast experience executing sale transactions. This section contains little analysis and is mostly boilerplate material that is periodically updated. Usually each group within the investment bank has its own set of materials for this section. In an introductory type of pitch, this section might be the only one contained in the pitchbook, whereas if the bank is pitching a client it knows well, this section may be relegated to the back of the pitchbook in an appendix.

The credentials section will typically include a grid of "tombstones" highlighting relevant deals with which the bank has been involved. It may also include one or more case studies, containing more detailed information about a previous transaction and its successful outcome.

League Tables One additional set of information nearly always contained in the credentials and experience section is known as the league tables. League tables are rankings of investment banks compiled by various services and grouped by type of investment banking activity. The most commonly used source for investment banking league tables is Thomson Reuters.

The goal of including league tables in a pitchbook is to make the investment bank appear to be the top-ranked adviser for relevant transactions. It is often up to the junior bankers putting the pitch together to "slice and dice" the league table data to make their employer be ranked first, or at least in the top three, of the league tables.

As an example of this often-silly exercise, suppose a number of investment banks are pitching to provide advice to a $1 billion European technology company that is contemplating selling itself. One bank might present the league tables showing that is ranked number one for all global M&A transactions. A second firm might show being ranked number one for European M&A transactions. A third bank might be ranked number one for European M&A transactions in the technology sector, and a fourth bank might show being ranked number one for European technology M&A for deal sizes of $750–$1.25 billion (for which there might only have been one recent deal!).

Situation Overview/Market Overview Another common section included in pitchbooks is a situation overview, or market overview. The section might include commentary and/or analysis about the company, its industry and industry trends, and the company's current positioning within its industry. Typically, a positive spin is put on company information and recent performance so as not to offend management. This type of section might also include information about the current M&A or financing environments, and any other relevant data that will help encourage the client to consider doing a deal.

Strategic Alternatives Even if an investment bank has been invited to pitch regarding a specific transaction, the bank will typically include a strategic alternatives section highlighting other possible transactions the company may want to consider. Alternatives might include a sale of the company, a sale of a division, a capital raise, or doing nothing at all. However, since bankers only get paid for doing deals, doing nothing is usually not recommended.

Bankers will typically list the pros and cons (or advantages and disadvantages) of each strategic alternative. However, as one of the unspoken rules of investment banking, words with negative connotations like "cons" or "disadvantages" are not used. "Cons" become "issues," and "disadvantages" turn into "risks." After all, issues can be dealt with and risks can be mitigated.

Valuation As we will discuss in Chapter 5, a valuation exercise is performed for nearly all investment banking transactions. Since the majority of pitches discuss one or more possible transactions, a section on valuation is common in most pitchbooks. Generally, the pitchbook will include a summary page showing a range of concluded values, as well as summary pages for each of the different methodologies utilized. Sometimes the detailed work supporting the summary valuation exhibits are included in an appendix to the pitchbook.

Depending on the type of transaction being contemplated, bankers may skew the valuation higher or lower. When pitching a sell-side assignment, the valuation is likely to be on the aggressive side. In other words, hire us and we will get you a top price. On the other hand, for a buy-side pitch, valuation is more likely to be conservative. Sophisticated clients that deal frequently with investment bankers understand these types of games that bankers play and know to temper expectations accordingly. However, less sophisticated clients can become upset when transaction value winds up being substantially different from a banker's initial valuation. In a pitchbook, bankers always label valuation and other analysis as preliminary so as not be held legally or reputationally responsible for analyses that later gets revised, or for mistakes or inaccuracies. In addition, presentation pages containing analysis typically have very detailed footnotes describing the sources of information that have been used and the assumptions that have been made.

Potential Buyers/Investors/Targets A pitch for a sell-side assignment will typically contain a list of potential buyers that the investment bankers think might be interested in acquiring the company or assets being sold. Most of the time this list will be segregated into two categories of buyers: strategic buyers and financial buyers. Strategic buyers are usually companies in the same or a related industry as the seller and would be interested in making the acquisition for "strategic" reasons. Financial buyers are typically private equity firms that might be interested in acquiring the firm in a leveraged buyout.

Some background information is frequently included for each possible buyer, along with some commentary specifying the rationale for the buyer being interested and the likelihood of success for each buyer. For some pitchbooks, a couple of bullet points are sufficient to describe each potential buyer; other times the pitchbook will contain a slide for each buyer. If the list is sufficiently targeted, bankers may even perform some preliminary analysis for a transaction with each possible buyer, such as an accretion/dilution analysis (which we will discuss in Chapter 7).

Similar to the buyer's list contained in a sell-side M&A pitch, a list of potential investors will be compiled for a fundraising transaction. In a pitchbook for an untargeted buy-side pitch, this section will often contain detailed profiles of possible acquisition targets that the company may (or, more likely, may not) be interested in purchasing. These are usually among the most painful types of pitches to put together for junior bankers, especially when the number of profiles reaches into the dozens.

Summary Conclusions Most pitchbooks will contain a summary or conclusion section detailing the investment bank's recommendations based on its understanding of the situation and on its preliminary analysis. Depending on the type of pitch, recommendations may include pursuing a particular transaction or using a certain financing structure.

Bios At the end of nearly every pitchbook is a section containing bios. Of all the sections contained in the pitchbook, the bios are typically the only section actually read by the potential client. Bios are usually a paragraph or two of information about each member of the team who will work on the engagement should the investment bank be hired. The bios of the bankers in attendance at the actual meeting are often highlighted, and bios are typically listed in the order of each banker's job title. However, between bankers of the same rank (especially managing directors), the order is sometimes highly contested. It is not enjoyable for the junior investment bankers putting the pitchbook together to get caught in the middle of such a political squabble.

Winning the Pitch Given how much work goes into creating pitchbooks, it would be reasonable to think that the investment bank that creates the best pitchbook will get hired. Alas, this is rarely the case. The quality of the pitchbook (or the analysis contained therein) rarely decides which investment bank will get hired. Since bankers typically have access to the same information and perform the exact same types of analysis, pitchbooks from different investment banks tend to be very similar.

For the most part, investment bankers are hired based on the quality of their relationships with the potential client and their experience executing similar transactions. Some large companies that frequently engage investment bankers like to spread the work around multiple banks; other companies tend to stick with one investment bank for all of their transactions. Except for very small transactions, the decision to hire a bank is almost never based on the fees that the bank will charge. Investment banking fees tend to be very comparable from bank to bank.

Types of Investment Banks

The universe of investment banks can be segregated into two types: bulge bracket banks and boutiques. On one hand, this is a gross simplification of the world, since as we will see there is a lot of diversity within the boutique landscape. On the other hand, this is pretty much the way people who work in the industry think.

In this section, we will describe the two different types of investment banks, in terms of the type of work they do, the types of transactions they execute, and the clients they advise. Later in this chapter, when we talk about the lifestyle of a junior investment banker, we will discuss some of the cultural differences between bulge bracket and boutique banks.

Bulge Bracket Investment Banks The term bulge bracket is used very frequently within the finance community to describe a certain subset of investment banks. In light of that fact, it may be surprising to you to learn that there is no technical definition of what bulge bracket means, and there is no official list of which investment banks should indeed be considered as members of the bulge bracket.

When we speak of the bulge bracket, we are referring to the large investment banks that (1) market to and advise the biggest clients in most, if not all industries, and (2) execute a variety of types of large-cap investment banking transactions. Bulge bracket banks also tend to operate globally, having offices across the world, something that is important given the ever-increasing number of cross-border transactions.

As of 2012, most professionals in the industry would consider the following investment banks to be within the bulge bracket:

- Bank of America Merrill Lynch (BAML).
- Barclays.
- Credit Suisse.
- Citigroup.
- Deutsche Bank.
- Goldman Sachs.
- J.P.Morgan.
- Morgan Stanley.
- UBS.

Keep in mind that this list is not forever static. For a variety of reasons, over time, banks have dropped off the list and others have been added. The most recent changes to the bulge bracket community occurred during the tumultuous period of 2008 and 2009, with the bankruptcy of one bulge bracket bank, Lehman Brothers (much of its U.S. investment banking assets acquired by Barclays) and the distressed sales of two others, Bear Stearns (acquired by J.P.Morgan) and Merrill Lynch (acquired by Bank of America). In addition, over the past decade other large financial institutions have attempted to break into the bulge bracket. HSBC tried and failed in the mid-2000s, and Nomura has made an effort in recent years.

Boutique Investment Banks So, if you are not a bulge bracket bank then you are a boutique investment bank. Admittedly, some of the larger financial institutions that are not considered bulge bracket might find this classification a touch insulting. However, within the context of our discussion, the term boutique does not necessarily mean that a firm is small, but that its investment banking presence and/or the type of its investment banking activity is more limited than that of the bulge bracket.

Some boutique investment banks are actually quite large, with multiple offices in multiple countries.

We will classify the boutique investment banks into four categories:

1. Investment banks that focus on one or more investment banking products (product focus).
2. Investment banks that focus on one or more industries (industry focus).
3. Investment banks that focus on smaller deal sizes and smaller clients (middle market focus).
4. Large domestic or international financial institutions that have limited investment banking capabilities or dealflow (bulge bracket lite).

Product Focus Some boutiques focus on advising clients on one or more particular types of financial transactions. Some of the most prestigious and sought-after boutiques among job seekers specialize in providing advice on mergers and acquisitions. These investment banks often compete with the bulge brackets for M&A deals, but they do not offer their clients a full range of investment banking services. For example, boutiques may not have the capital markets capabilities to help execute an IPO, and they may not have the balance sheets necessary to be a lender to a client in connection with an acquisition. For these reasons, sometimes boutiques will pair up with a bulge bracket bank when executing a large transaction.

Following are a few examples of boutiques that are known for having a strong M&A focus. Note, however, that some of these firms are large and do much more than solely provide M&A advice. Also keep in mind that M&A is not the only type of transaction on which boutiques focus. For instance, there are boutique banks that specialize in restructuring transactions.

- Evercore.
- Greenhill.
- Lazard.
- Moelis.
- Perella Weinberg.

Industry Focus A second type of boutique investment bank encompasses firms that focus not on a product like M&A, but on providing services to clients in one or more specific industries. Some boutiques that fit this bill specialize in smaller clients and smaller transactions. Others, like the product-focused banks, will compete with the bulge bracket banks for larger deals. Some industry-focused boutiques also concentrate on products such as M&A while others provide a broader range of investment banking services, including executing IPOs and private placements, and have capital markets and equity research divisions. Often industry-focused banks are small but their senior-level bankers tend to have a high degree of industry knowledge and strong industry relationships.

Following are three examples of well-regarded boutiques that focus on a specific industry, with the industry in parentheses.

- Allen & Company (media).
- Qatalyst Partners (technology).
- Simmons & Company (energy).

Middle Market Focus The next category of boutique investment bank to discuss is those firms that focus on middle market clients and middle market transactions. Like with the term bulge bracket, there is no correct definition of what constitutes the middle market. Most people think of the term middle market as generally referring to companies or transactions valued at less than $500 million. However, some of the bulge bracket banks define the middle market as starting higher—say, at $1 billion.

Many of the middle market firms offer the broad range of investment banking services and also have sales and trading, asset management, and equity research arms. However, unlike bulge bracket banks, which operate nationally or internationally, many of the middle market boutiques are regionally focused. At the upper end of the middle market, these boutiques do compete for deals with the bulge bracket banks. This is especially the case during periods when investment banking activity is slow, as the bulge bracket firms tend to move down market to try to keep busy.

Several examples of middle market banks include:

- Jefferies.
- Oppenheimer.
- Piper Jaffray.
- Raymond James.
- Stifel Nicolaus.

"Bulge Bracket Lite" The final category of boutique investment bank is a little bit harder to categorize than the product-focused, industry-focused, and middle market shops. This last grouping encompasses large financial institutions that do some investment banking activity but not enough to be considered bulge bracket. For lack of a better term, we will call these firms bulge bracket lite. These institutions are certainly not boutiques from the standpoint of their entire operations (many are huge firms!), but their investment banking divisions are considered boutique because of the limited investment banking services they provide, their limited deal flow, or their limited scope of clients.

Often, these firms pursue middle market deals where they have prior corporate banking or private banking relationships. Because these firms are often very large, with significant balance sheets, they are sometimes co-advisers on M&A transactions or co-managers on equity raises, but they much less frequently play the lead advisory role on a large deal. As we discussed in the section on bulge bracket banks, sometimes these firms do attempt to build their investment banking divisions, either organically or through acquisition, and break into the bulge brackets. However, history has time and time again shown this to be an expensive and difficult undertaking.

A few examples of large financial institutions that do a limited amount of investment banking activity include:

- HSBC.
- Macquarie.
- Nomura.
- Wells Fargo.

Structure of the Investment Banking Division

The investment banking division of a bulge bracket bank is generally divided into two types of groups: product groups and industry groups. Industry groups are sometimes also referred to as sector groups or coverage groups. Some of the larger boutique banks have a similar structure, while smaller boutiques tend to have fewer, if any, groups. At boutique banks, bankers are more likely to be product and/or industry generalists rather than specialists.

Investment bankers in product groups typically have product expertise and execute transactions, while bankers in industry groups do more marketing of the firm's services by building and maintaining relationships with companies within the industry they cover. However, the division of labor between marketing and execution does vary from bank to bank. For example, some of the bulge bracket banks do not have M&A product groups. Instead, bankers in industry groups execute deals. It also varies firm to firm whether junior bankers are hired directly into a group, do a rotation in different groups, or are hired as generalists. We will talk more about group selection from a career perspective in Chapter 9.

Product Groups The three most well-known product groups are mergers and acquisitions (M&A), leveraged finance, and restructuring. These three groups in particular are desirable by many junior investment bankers because they are perceived to offer more experience on live transactions, more modeling experience, and better exit opportunities. The tradeoff is often longer hours and a tougher lifestyle. There is a degree of truth to this perception, though how much really depends on the particular bank, on the level of deal flow, and on general market conditions.

Equity capital markets (ECM) and debt capital markets (DCM), which are sometimes grouped together as capital markets, are specialized product groups within the investment bank. In fact, they are really a hybrid group situated between the investment banking division and the sales and trading division. Professionals in these groups sit on or near the trading floor, rather than near the investment bankers. However, they are technically on the investment banking side of the Chinese Wall. The ECM group helps execute equity raises such as IPOs while the DCM group typically helps to raise investment-grade debt for clients. These groups tend to be less analytical than the other investment banking groups and generally offer fewer exit opportunities. However, the lifestyle and hours tend to be significantly better.

Following is a list of many of the product groups of a typical bulge bracket investment bank:

- Mergers and acquisitions (M&A).
- Leveraged finance.
- Restructuring.
- Project finance/public finance.
- Equity capital markets (ECM).
- Debt capital markets (DCM).

Industry Groups As we stated, bankers in industry groups market the bank's investment banking services to companies in specific industries. At the senior levels, bankers in industry groups tend to have relationships with the senior management teams of the companies they cover. In fact one significant advantage of industry groups over product groups is that you are more likely to start making valuable client relationships earlier in your career. Also keep in mind that at a bulge bracket bank, there are generally far more investment bankers working in industry groups than are working in product groups. Finally, it is also worth mentioning that being in an industry group does not require an enormous amount of industry knowledge—in fact, certainly less so than working in equity research.

Some of the larger groups are sometimes further segregated into subgroups. For example, healthcare might be divided into biotechnology, medical devices, managed care, and pharmaceuticals, while the financial institutions group (FIG) might be separated into asset managers, banks, financial technology companies, and insurance.

The last group in this list, financial sponsors, does not technically refer to an industry like all the other groups. Bankers in a financial sponsors group cover private equity firms that make leveraged buyouts (which we will talk about in Chapter 8). However, since they typically operate like the other industry groups, marketing the bank's services and having relationships with clients, they are typically classified as such.

Following is a list of many of the common industry groups to be found in a typical bulge bracket bank:

- Consumer/retail.
- Financial institutions (FIG).
- Healthcare.
- Industrials and transportation.
- Natural resources.
- Power and utilities.
- Real estate, gaming, and lodging.
- Technology, media, and telecom (TMT).
- Financial sponsors.

THE LIFE OF AN INVESTMENT BANKER

So far in this chapter, we have talked about the institution we call an investment bank. Now it is time to turn our attention to the professionals who work there: the investment bankers.

We will start this section with a discussion of the various job titles and hierarchy that are mainstays of nearly all investment banks worldwide. Next, we will talk about the actual work that investment bankers perform on a day-to-day basis. Then we will discuss the lifestyles of both junior and senior bankers, and the compensation structure that exists in the industry. We will also examine some of the cultural differences that exist between bulge bracket and boutique banks, between different geographies, and between different groups. Finally, we will wrap up this section by talking about some of the common exit opportunities that exist for investment bankers.

Investment Banking Hierarchy

Like the military, investment banks typically have a very strict hierarchy of job titles and career progression. From junior to senior, the career ladder or hierarchy in a typical investment bank is as follows:

- Analyst.
- Associate.

- Vice president (VP).
- Senior vice president (SVP) or director.
- Managing director (MD).

Some investment banks do deviate from this hierarchy a bit (e.g., having the senior vice president and director titles be separate positions). Moreover, other firms, especially some of the non-U.S. banks, have the same five-tiered structure but use different names for each position as follows:

- Analyst.
- Associate director (AD).
- Director.
- Executive director (ED).
- Managing director (MD).

Bear Stearns, before it was acquired by J.P.Morgan, used to refer to the second most senior position as a managing director and the most senior position as a senior managing director, confusing job seekers and industry professionals alike.

Finally, keep in mind that in equity research, the titles of analyst and associate are reversed. Equity research associates are the most junior level position, and analysts can have anywhere from several years to several decades of experience.

Regardless of the job titles used by any given investment bank, the general job functions of each position tend to be very consistent. Over the next few pages, we will provide an overview of each role, including a discussion of the traits and skills that can help make one successful at each level.

Analyst Analysts are typically men and women directly out of top undergraduate institutions who join an investment bank for a two-year program.[1]

[1]In September 2012, Goldman Sachs announced a change to their analyst program: The firm is no longer giving two-year contracts to analysts. This is thought to be the result of the firm tiring of analysts beginning to recruit for private equity and hedge fund positions well within their first year of employment. Likely, this change is just a way to keep analysts motivated for two full years, since their bonuses are no longer essentially guaranteed. However, it remains to be seen if other investment banks will follow Goldman's lead and if this will indeed represent a major change to the typical investment banking analyst program.

Top-performing analysts are sometimes offered the chance to stay for a third year, and the most successful analysts can be promoted after three years to the associate level.

As analysts are the bottom rung on the investment banking ladder, they do the vast majority of the actual work, which we will discuss later in this chapter. Analysts are the grunts of the investment bank. They are sometimes derogatorily referred to by the higher ups as the Excel monkeys or the widget monkeys.

What Makes a Good Analyst? If valuable real estate is due to "location, location, location," then a valuable analyst is because of "attitude, attitude, attitude." Attitude is really what separates the top-performing analysts from the middle of the pack. Strong analysts have a proactive, can-do mindset. They volunteer for work and they never bitch or complain. Good analysts never have to be asked twice to do something. Great analysts never have to be asked once to do something.

Analysts need to be smart, to be able to learn quickly, and to have strong analytical skills. In fact, analysts tend to be the brightest rung on the investment banking ladder. Basic accounting and finance skills are obviously helpful and generally necessary to get through the interview process. However, some of the best analysts that I've personally worked with have been liberal arts or engineering majors, not business or finance majors.

Analysts also need to have a very strong attention to detail. It goes without saying that they need the ability to work extremely hard and be able to handle having little sleep. People skills and a pleasant personality are also helpful. However, since most analysts have limited interaction with clients, analytical skills and attitude generally trump people skills. People skills do help you make friends internally, which, given the political nature of all investment banks, can be beneficial for getting staffed on deals, come bonus time, and for being considered for a third year and/or associate promotion.

Associate Associates are typically men or women recruited directly out of top MBA programs. A handful of associates are also investment bankers who have been promoted after having worked three years as an analyst. The typical investment banking track is to be an associate for three and a half years before being promoted to the next position, which is vice president. Associates are also typically categorized into class years as in first years, second years, and third years (or for example, class of 2012, 2013, and 2014).

The associate generally has two primary roles. The first is, along with the analyst, to do the work. The associate's second function is to check the work of the analyst. The associate is directly responsible for making sure that the analyst's work is accurate, correct, and perfect. In reality, whether the associate actually performs this second role varies. Often, checking the analyst's work takes the following form:

Analyst: "I'm finished with the analysis."
Associate: "Is it correct?"
Analyst: "I think so."
Associate: "Well, check it again and don't come back until you are 100 percent *sure* it is correct."

What Makes a Good Associate to the Firm? Many of the same traits that make a good analyst also make a good associate, including a great attitude, the ability to work hard, strong attention to detail, and competent finance and accounting knowledge. Analytical skills are also important, though less so than at the analyst level. More important to the associate is possessing a solid communication and management skillset. The associate needs to be able to manage the analyst as well as manage the expectations of senior bankers. Since the associate also typically begins to have significant exposure to clients, he or she needs to be able to represent the firm in a positive manner and be generally presentable.

What Makes a Good Associate to the Analyst? The analyst works directly for the associate. Given this strict hierarchy, what makes a good associate in the eyes of the firm is not always the same as what makes a good associate in the eyes of the analyst. To an analyst, a good associate is technically strong, can answer questions, and can be a mentor and teacher. Well regarded associates take responsibility for errors, help to protect the analyst from the wrath of the VP or MD, and can even push back at times, given unreasonable demands.

On the other hand, there are the associates that analysts hate to work for. These associates tend to create unneeded work, either out of ignorance or spite. They are quick to blame analysts for mistakes and have the tendency to throw analysts under the proverbial bus in front of senior bankers. They are too high and mighty (or lazy) to hit the print button, constantly calling analysts to ask for things to be printed out for them. Finally, they think what they learned in business school is correct (it usually isn't) and refuse to consider deferring to experienced analysts who frequently know more than they do.

Vice President (VP) The primary role of the vice president is to be to the project manager on pitches and live transactions. Bankers generally spend about three years as a VP, though it can vary by a year or so based on performance. The vice president position is the most junior of the senior bankers, and many in the industry regard the VP as the first "real" investment banking position.

The vice president is frequently the intermediary between the senior banker (the managing director) and the junior bankers (the analysts and associates), and typically has the most day-to-day client contact on a deal. The VP is also responsible for all work product, and for supervising and directing the analysts and associates. However, the VP very rarely does any of the actual work.

The VP typically decides the structure (i.e., the table of contents) of presentations and pitchbooks. On live engagements, the VP is typically the banker running the deal. The VP must manage the client, manage the senior bankers, and manage the analysts and associates who are actually doing the work. It is often at the VP level that bankers begin to form valuable relationships with clients. Depending on the individual and also the bank, some VPs will start to play a role in client development and marketing.

What Makes a Good Vice President to the Firm? Given that the primary role of the vice president is as a project manager, the most important skillset of a VP is naturally someone with strong project management skills. Specifically, the VP needs to manage three constituencies: the analysts and associates who do the actual work, the senior banker to whom the VP reports, and the client. Managing all three is no easy task. Like the associate but more so, the VP needs strong communication and client skills to able to manage up and manage down. A good VP is also someone who is beginning to develop strong relationships with the firm's clients.

What Makes a Good Vice President to the Analyst and Associate? Ask many a junior banker about the vice president role and they will tell you that VPs are often useless. VPs don't do any of the real work (that's not their job anymore), they don't yet have client relationships, and they are not all that good at managing—or worse: VPs actually slow things down. They demand unnecessary work in order to ingratiate themselves with senior bankers and clients, and they are frequently guilty of excessive red-penned comments on presentations that wind up being reversed or excised by the more senior bankers.

It is not without reason that many a vice president has been informally labeled by those above and below as a bag carrier or a bag-carrying VP. That is to say, the VP's true utility begins and ends with the task of carrying to meetings and pitches the heavy bag containing the copies of printed presentations.

Of course, not all VPs warrant such negative association. To the analysts and associates, a good VP is efficient, does not create excessive and unnecessary work, and does not keep the junior bankers waiting around for no reason. Helpful vice presidents act as buffers to, and interpreters of, the wishes and whims of senior bankers and difficult clients.

Senior Vice President (SVP)/Director Depending on a variety of considerations, the senior vice president or director will either play the role of project manager, like the vice president, or a client-development and relationship-building role, like the managing director. The factors determining whether the SVP/director will act more like the VP or more like the MD may include the skills, experiences, and maturity of the individual, the structure of the investment bank, the particulars of the transaction or project, and the makeup of the other investment bankers involved. Bankers typically spend two to four years at the SVP or director level before being promoted to managing director, a promotion that is often predicated on the banker demonstrating an ability to form client relationships, to market the firm's services, and to successfully bring in new business.

What Makes a Good SVP/Director? Given the dichotomy of roles, a strong SVP/director will possess many of the skills required of a vice president and managing director. From the firm's perspective, the SVP or director is often viewed as a budding managing director and is typically evaluated (and compensated) accordingly.

Managing Director (MD) As the most senior-level investment banker, the role of the managing director is mostly one of client development, especially in the industry coverage groups. The MD is typically the banker with the senior-level relationships with a company's CEO, CFO, head of corporate development, and sometimes board of directors. The MD is most frequently responsible for spearheading marketing efforts to a set of current and/or potential clients. On a live transaction, once the investment bank is engaged, the MD often plays only a minor role, getting involved when difficulties arise during the deal and for high level negotiations.

In addition to marketing, client-relationship, and deal-execution duties, some MDs also have broader managerial responsibilities. Especially at the bulge bracket banks, more senior managing directors are often tapped to be the head (or co-head) of their particular product or industry group. MDs that are group heads have responsibility for setting and forecasting the group's budget and profit and loss (P&L), making hiring and firing decisions, setting compensation, and deciding on promotions. Group heads also tend to have strong influences on the culture of their group.

What Makes a Good Managing Director to the Firm? From the investment bank's perspective, a good managing director (at least on the coverage side) is someone who brings in business—lots of business. To bring in business, it certainly helps to have strong client relationships (most MDs don't) and be good at marketing and pitching (most MD's aren't). Developing valuable relationships takes time and often involves months or years of meetings, pitches, and entertaining.

The best managing directors do add real value to their clients. By maintaining a high-level network throughout an industry, an MD can have insight into, for example, what companies might be considering selling divisions and what companies might be in acquisitive moods. A well connected MD may even occasionally help broker a high-profile merger between two competitors. However, in today's oversupplied world of investment bankers and given the short-term-focused compensation structures that exist, the days of MDs being long-term trusted advisers to CEOs are mostly behind us. Managing directors need to bring in revenue each and every year or risk disappointing bonuses or worse.

What Makes a Good Managing Director to the Analyst and Associate? At the junior levels of investment banking, getting strong deal experience is imperative toward building one's skillset and moving one's career forward. From that perspective, an MD that is effective at originating deals is obviously highly valued by analysts and associates. However, a number of other factors contribute to make a managing director desirable (or undesirable) to work for.

The highest-regarded MDs by junior bankers are often demanding but also fair. They hold everyone to the same high standards, treat analysts and associates with respect, and take an interest in junior bankers' career development. Effective managing directors do not overpromise to clients and do not set unrealistic expectations. Nor do they micromanage. But they are decisive and available to answer questions when needed. The best managing directors also make sure to keep the team informed of high-level discussions and the big picture, and invite junior bankers to meetings whenever possible. The worst MDs to work for are those who forget (or just don't bother) to tell you that a meeting or pitch was cancelled, forcing you to pull consecutive all-nighters for no reason whatsoever. Yes, this happens.

Deal Teams Now that we have reviewed each of the various ranks within the investment bank, let us discuss how they come together to form a deal team. On nearly every investment banking project, whether a pitch or live transaction, a deal team will be assigned to the engagement.

A typical deal team is made up of four bankers: an analyst, an associate, a VP or SVP/director, and an SVP/director or MD. Deal teams for large or high-profile transactions can be larger, with multiple personnel at any given level. In some transactions, multiple deal teams may be assigned. For example, an M&A assignment for a healthcare company might consist of a deal team from the M&A group and a separate deal team from the healthcare group.

While we always use the word "team" to describe the group working on the project, "team" is somewhat of a misnomer. Unlike in other industries, in investment banking the deal team is nearly perfectly hierarchical, not collegial. That is to say, it rarely feels like a team in the conventional sense. The analyst reports to the associate, the associate reports to the VP, and the VP reports to the MD. The senior bankers normally want nothing to do with the junior bankers, so as long as the work is getting done, this chain of command is rarely broken.

The "Work" of an Investment Banker

We have already talked about what investment bankers do in very general terms. Investment bankers execute various types of financial transactions for their firm's clients. They also expend considerable amounts of time and effort marketing their firm's services to prospective clients in the hopes of executing lots more transactions. But what exactly is the work involved in executing transactions and pitching prospective clients? In other words, what will you actually be doing on a daily basis as an analyst or associate?

Broadly speaking, we can categorize the work done by junior investment bankers into four types:

1. Analysis.
2. Creating presentations and other documents.
3. Administrative tasks.
4. Recruiting and other firm-building activities.

The highly attentive reader among you may have noticed that we prefaced this list as the work of *junior* investment bankers and not all investment bankers. Why? Because generally, only the analysts and associates actually do the work. Once you get to the vice president level, you no longer have to get your hands dirty. So, when we talk about the work of an investment banker, we really mean the work of a junior investment banker. We will talk about how senior-level bankers spend their days later in this chapter when we discuss lifestyle.

Analysis The first type of work performed by analysts and associates that we will discuss is analysis. Basically, if a banker is using Microsoft Excel, then we will consider their work to be analysis. Common examples of work done in Excel include entering historic company data from public documents and calculating various statistics using that data (which we will discuss in Chapter 4), estimating the fair market value of a company or its stock (to be covered in Chapter 5), and projecting a company's financial statements (discussed in Chapter 6). Other varieties of analysis include examining and charting historical stock performance, and evaluating and sensitizing the impact of various potential deal structures or financing arrangements.

Analysts spend a significant amount of their time using Excel, performing various types of analysis. In fact, most of this type of work is performed by the analysts. However, associates do sometimes help, especially with the creation of financial models. And as we discussed earlier, associates are responsible for checking and verifying all of the work done by the analysts.

Creating Presentations and Other Documents The second significant type of work performed by junior bankers is drafting and editing presentations and other types of documents. This type of work typically involves the use of Microsoft PowerPoint or Microsoft Word to put together such materials. Probably the most common examples of such documents are the pitchbooks that are used for marketing purposes.

Various types of documents are also created by bankers for use on live transactions. Examples include materials presented to a company's management or board of directors that provide the deal team's recommendations on strategic alternatives or financing strategies, or give updates on a particular transaction's process or timing. On sell-side M&A transactions and capital raises, presentations are created to help management present important information to prospective lenders, investors, or buyers.

Junior investment bankers also create various types of Word documents, many of which are used to aid with the marketing of new securities or the sale of a company or division. Common examples of these documents include offering memorandums and private placement memorandums used for equity raises, credit memorandums relating to debt financings, and teasers and selling memorandums utilized on sell-side M&A assignments.

Most presentations and Word documents created by investment bankers contain two types of content. They contain descriptive, textual information such as company, industry, and situation overviews. This type of content is typically in bullet form when in PowerPoint presentations and in paragraph form when in Word documents. The second type of content is analysis. In fact, the vast majority of the analysis performed by junior bankers gets inserted into presentations and other documents, at least in summary form.

Analysts and associates often share the workload of authoring and creating documents. In situations where there are time constraints, the work is often split up between analysts and associates. Most frequently in these circumstances, analysts do the Excel work and associates do the writing. This makes sense since associates tend to have better writing and communication skills and more advanced business knowledge, given their MBA degrees and professional work experience.

While the analysts and associates create the documents, the more senior bankers act as editors. Typically each member of the deal team from the associate on up will take out his or her red pen in turn, and make comments or changes. As is often the frustrating case, each member of the deal team has a tendency to contradict the edits of the previous reviewer. The most senior banker, typically the MD, has the final say.

This editing process helps teach the junior bankers two important skills. The first is patience. Analysts and associates are often left sitting around for hours waiting for comments to be faxed from VPs who are traveling visiting clients, or from MDs who are vacationing at their beach house or ski lodge. The second skill is one that is shared with Egyptian scholars: that of translating hieroglyphics. Many an analyst has wasted hours trying to decipher the illegible handwriting of senior bankers.

Most of the larger boutique banks and all of the bulge bracket banks have professionals on staff (non-investment bankers) to aid with the creation of these documents and presentations. Such departments have various names, depending on the bank, but are commonly referred to as graphics or word processing or document presentation services. These groups do not do analysis or writing but provide help creating graphics, charts, and tables, and with formatting.

As we discussed earlier in this chapter in the section on pitchbooks, most of the work product of a banker gets printed in color and bound with fancy-looking covers for use in client meetings. The vast majority of banks have copy centers that help with printing and binding, and at many banks, these centers operate 24 hours a day, as does the graphics/word processing department. However, it is ultimately the responsibility of the junior bankers to make sure that presentations and other documents are printed perfectly and ready in time for the meeting or the deal team's flight. Analysts typically examine each page of each copy, a process known as flipping the books.

Administrative Tasks One of the analyst's first tasks on a new engagement is to create what is commonly known as a working group list, which is a list of the names and contact information for everyone working on the deal, including the investment banking team, company management, lawyers, accountants, and so forth. It is also the analyst's job to keep this document up to date for the duration of the transaction. Needless to say, creating working group lists is not one of the more stimulating tasks required of investment bankers, and it is for good reason that analysts sometimes refer to themselves as glorified admins.

Creating working group lists is an example of the third type of work performed by junior bankers. Other administrative tasks frequently performed by analysts and associates include scheduling conference calls, organizing meetings, making travel arrangements, and coordinating due diligence and information exchanges with clients and with the investment bankers on the other side of the deal. These kinds of tasks arise most frequently when working on live transactions, especially during the latter stages of a deal, after most of the analytical and presentation work has been completed.

Moreover, scheduling large meetings for due diligence sessions, investor meetings, or negotiation sessions often requires dozens of e-mails and phone calls to ensure all parties are available, a tedious process often referred to as herding cats. Many an associate has questioned the value of their MBA degree, having spent hours trying to reschedule a meeting for the third or fourth time.

Recruiting and Other Firm-Building Activities In addition to the day-to-day work of Excel and PowerPoint, analysts and associates also spend a portion of their time on various firm-building activities. In fact, these types of activities are often required of investment bankers at all levels, and a banker's level of participation and enthusiasm is often taken into consideration in one's annual performance review.

The activity on which bankers typically spend the most time is recruiting. Given that an investment bank's core asset is intellectual capital (i.e., its bankers), firms take recruiting very seriously, and they spend significant time and money on it. For a banker, recruiting activities involve such things as attending receptions at undergraduate and/or graduate business schools, meeting candidates for coffee for what are known as informational interviews, reviewing resumes, interviewing prospective candidates, and attending sell-day events with candidates who have received offers. Other firm-building activities include being involved with the firm's training of new analysts and associates, mentoring junior bankers, and participating on various committees.

The Lifestyle of an Investment Banker

There is no such thing as work-life balance in investment banking. As an investment banker your life *is* work. To be an investment banker requires significant sacrifice, whether those sacrifices are sleep or health, or friendships or family, or hobbies or holidays. Of course, those costs must have some benefits, too. Otherwise being an investment banker wouldn't be the sought-after job that it is. Those benefits include a level of compensation unusual to most jobs inside or outside of the finance world, as well as a foundation and skillset that can lead to careers even more sought-after than investment banking.

In this section, we will talk about the culture of an investment bank and what the lifestyle is like for both junior and senior bankers. We will also discuss what kind of people and personalities tend to do well in this industry.

Investment Banking Culture Shortly, we will discuss the work hours and lifestyle of a typical investment banker at both the junior and senior levels of banking. First, let's turn our attention to the culture of an investment bank. In reality, culture is a tricky thing to describe. You really have to live it to truly understand and appreciate it, but I'll give it my best shot at describing what the investment banking culture is really like. As you read this section, keep in mind something that is probably obvious to you: Culture and lifestyle are very much related, since the culture of an institution will often play a large role in dictating the lifestyle of the professionals who work there.

I think that there are four key points you need to know to try to comprehend the culture of investment banking:

1. Junior bankers are commodities.
2. Only the work matters.
3. The firm owns you.
4. Everything you do is life or death.

Junior Bankers Are Commodities The first thing to understand is that junior investment bankers are treated like commodities. Being a commodity means that you are easily replaceable, and replaceable you are. You will frequently be reminded that there are hundreds of undergraduates or MBA students who would die to be in your position.

You are replaceable because of the nature of the work. It is not very hard intellectually, and it requires little thought and virtually no creativity. In other words, as long as you are smart enough, have a great attitude, and are capable of putting in the requisite hours, you can be an analyst or associate. Moreover, you are there to do the work assigned to you, not to come up with brilliant ideas. Junior bankers, and especially analysts, are supposed to be seen but not heard.

Since you are replaceable, you can be worked until you burn out. This is especially true for analysts, who are typically employees for only two years, anyway. Even junior bankers who do manage to differentiate themselves positively, so-called rock stars, wind up being worked even harder since senior bankers always want them on their team. This culture helps result in the "sweatshop mentality" investment banking is famous for, and the hours and work schedule (which we will discuss in the next section).

Only the Work Matters The next thing about investment banking culture to understand is that only the work matters, which is another way of saying that the ends justify the means. From a senior banker's perspective, as long as the work gets done and gets done correctly, that the analyst hasn't slept in two days or that the associate had to cancel a spouse's birthday dinner is inconsequential. This attitude is exacerbated by the fact that a managing director rarely interacts with the analysts and associates. There is almost always one or more layers of bankers, such as a VP, in between.

A secondary consequence is that a junior banker's career development also takes a backseat. As a junior banker, you are there to do work, not to learn. Senior bankers do not typically have the time or inclination to be mentors or to answer questions. It is simply not a high priority for them.

The Firm Owns You Many an analyst has referred to their lives as one of indentured servitude. It is understood that when you become a junior investment banker that your life now belongs to the firm. Any free time that you do have away from the office is because the firm allowed you to have it. An analyst going home at only 10 PM? A gift from her associate. An associate being able to attend a friend's out-of-town wedding? The result of a magnanimous VP.

Everything You Do Is Life or Death The final thing point I want to make about the investment banking culture is that, as a junior banker, you are made to feel like that with everything you do, your life, and indeed the fate of the world, is on the line. Typo in an e-mail? Mistake in a model? Didn't finish your assignment? Your life is over. The world will end.

The result is twofold. First, an enormous amount of stress is embedded in every task and in every interaction you have with your superiors. Even a simple chore like sending an e-mail becomes an exercise in fear. It is not uncommon for grown men and women to break down crying at times from a combination of this stress and the lack of sleep.

Second, since the bar is set at perfection for everything that you do, there is really no way to exceed it, only to fall short. Do not expect pats on the back for exceptional work. Exceptional work is expected. Do expect to be yelled at if you make a mistake, even if that mistake is inconsequential to the big picture. Generally speaking, as a junior banker, you know you are doing a good job if you are not being yelled at.

The reality is that the instant you realize that investment banking is just a job and not a life-or-death situation, you have a hard time doing it anymore.

The Lifestyle of a Junior Banker In case you have not figured it out already, the life of a junior investment banker is miserable. I'm not trying to scare you off, or to be provocative or overly dramatic. I just want to be as honest as possible about what you have to look forward to so that you can set appropriate expectations.

There are 168 hours in a week. As an analyst at a bulge bracket banks or well-regarded boutique, you should expect to work 90 to 100 of those hours. A typical weekday might have you arrive at the office around 10:00 AM and leave around 2:00 AM. Be prepared to work Saturday and Sunday, too. Have a big pitchbook due this week? You will probably pull one or more all-nighters. Maybe even two in a row. For everyone's sake, hopefully you will have time to go home to take a quick shower and change clothes. Sometimes you won't. Occasionally, a workweek will be lighter, but not by much.

Associates generally have a slightly better schedule and might average 80–90 hours per week. A typical schedule for an associate might be weekdays from 9:00 AM until perhaps 11:00 PM, and working on either Saturday or (more likely) Sunday. Associates will sometimes also find themselves pulling all-nighters. The first year of an associate's life is especially tough, and most first-year associates work similar hours to analysts. Hours in the second and third years do tend to improve a bit.

While we are on the subject of hours, a few additional things are worth mentioning. The first is that even if you are in the office for those 16-hour days, you are not necessarily always doing actual work that entire time. Sometimes you will be cranking on a model or presentation for literally days on end, but often a fair amount of time is spent waiting around for comments from your senior bankers or for information from your client. If you are lucky, you might even have the chance to duck out of the office to go the gym or grab a quick coffee with your compatriots.

Investment banking also tends to have a pretty strong face-time component. That is to say, even if you do not have work to do, you are pretty much required to be in the office the same hours as the other analysts or associates. You need to look busy. Consistently leaving early or disappearing for extended periods of time during the day is a quick way to find yourself staffed on a new project or to be given extraneous work on a current project by your associate or VP as punishment. When market conditions are tough, deal flow is soft, and layoffs are a risk, face time is even more important.

The third thing to note regarding hours is that, especially among analysts, there does tend to be a degree of competitiveness over who works the most hours, with all-nighters earning a special badge of honor. This tendency naturally results in some exaggeration of how many hours people say they work.

Believe it or not, most analysts and associates quickly become acclimated to working these kind of hours. You tend to surprise yourself by how productive you can still be with only a few hours of sleep. Somehow models get built and pitchbooks get created even when you are too tired to speak coherent thoughts—though, not surprisingly in these instances, the quality of your work product often suffers.

Nearly all junior bankers will agree that the long hours themselves do not actually represent the worst thing about the investment banking lifestyle. The worst thing is the total lack of control you have over your life. As an analyst or associate, you could be assigned a new project or given a new task at a moment's notice. You are completely tied to the office and are expected to be reachable at all times day and night, including weekends and holidays. Even in the infrequent instances when you are able to take a vacation, you will still be checking in to the office and expected to be working.

This lack of control makes it extremely difficult to schedule time to see friends and family, to date, and to generally make any plans whatsoever. For a typical new analyst or associate, the first few months on the job will be those of consistently canceling dinner plans, weekend plans, and even vacations at the last minute. You will miss birthday parties, weddings, and even funerals. The hours and minutes leading up to the evening, especially on a Friday, are fraught with anxiety, with bankers praying that their phone doesn't ring. For most junior bankers, after a few months, the combination of this apprehension and the fatigue of having to apologize over and over to friends and family are too much to take. Most analysts and associates stop making advanced plans altogether.

The upshot of not ever leaving the office and not being able to make plans is that you tend to lose touch with your classmates from school and other friends because you just do not have time to see them. Few people outside of investment banking really understand your lifestyle, including girlfriends/boyfriends and spouses. So for better or worse, most of your friends will be fellow bankers. You don't have to apologize to them when you cancel on them. They will understand.

Within the firm, analysts do typically find some camaraderie among their fellow analysts. On most days, groups of analysts will take a short break from work in the evening to eat dinner together in a conference room.

It is an opportunity to relax, share some firm gossip, and complain about life. Since analysts will likely be at the office late anyway, a few minutes spent socializing are worth it. This is less true for associates, however. Associates more often have boyfriends or girlfriends or spouses, and prefer to eat at their desks while working so they can get home as early as possible.

Finally, it is worth mentioning that at both the analyst and associate level, the first six to nine months are especially difficult, since you tend to be clueless about what you are doing and add little value to the deal team. You are constantly scared of making mistakes but also scared to ask questions. It generally takes about two years before you really feel comfortable. This is one of the reasons why analysts who stay for a third year are so valuable. Not only have they built up their knowledge base, but they often act as mentors to the first-year analysts and sometimes even the first-year associates.

Travel Before we move on to talk about the lifestyle of senior bankers, let us discuss one last aspect of a junior banker's work life: travel. The majority of a junior banker's time will be spent in the office. However, sometimes analysts and especially associates will be invited to travel to go to pitches and other meetings. In fact, going to meetings can occasionally be a reward for good work.

On the other hand, junior bankers may have a significant opportunity to travel when they are working on live deals. For example, during the early stages of a sell-side M&A transaction, the analysts and associates will often spend a significant amount of time at the client's headquarters doing due diligence and gathering information. Later in the transaction, junior bankers may continue to travel to the client's headquarters to babysit management presentations and to accompany prospective buyers and their bankers on due diligence trips and site visits. If you are lucky, you may even get to fly on your client's private jet—a definite perk!

Other than racking up frequent-flier miles and hotel points, there are at least three things that junior bankers like about traveling. The first is that you usually don't get staffed on a new project when you are on the road. Second, traveling is a respite from the daily grind of the office. The third benefit is that you might actually get a chance to catch up on some much-needed sleep on the plane. Just pray that you are not sitting next to your MD on the plane, as he or she, reading your presentation for the first time, points out every single typo.

The Lifestyle of a Senior Banker At the vice president level, the hours start to improve significantly. At bulge bracket banks, VPs might work 60–80 hour weeks on average. However, even more importantly, VPs start to have much more control over their lives. They can make dinner plans during the week, go away for a weekend, and even take an occasional week-long vacation. If they have to work weekends or late nights, which they often do, VPs can usually do so from home. And since VPs are usually the project managers on a deal or pitch, they frequently get to select the time of internal meetings and conference calls.

On the flip side, there is a lot of pressure on VPs to show that they are adding value, especially since the average vice president is not actually doing the work and does not yet have strong industry and client relationships. Especially insecure VPs tend to require analysts and associates to do a lot of unnecessary work and analysis in order to try to ingratiate themselves with both managing directors and clients.

The work of a vice president, as project manager, is to set the direction for presentations and analysis, to make edits, and to be the point person to the client or opposing investment bank on a deal. At many investment banks, some VPs also act as the staffer or resource manager, with the job of assigning projects analysts and associates.

The role of the staffer is a thankless one. Junior bankers hate you for assigning them to a new project at 5:00 PM on a Friday. Senior bankers hate you for assigning a weaker analyst or brand-new associate to their transaction. Moreover, the staffer must always be reachable, as new pitches or deals can come in at any time, day or night, weekday or weekend. Luckily, most investment banks allow the staffer to cut down on (or even eliminate) the amount of deals he or she is expected to work on while playing this role, and rotate the job of staffer once a year.

Compared with the rest of the investment banking hierarchy, managing directors have a much more normal work schedule, at least when they are not traveling. MDs tend to come in early in the morning (often between 7:00 AM and 9:00 AM) and leave relatively early, by banking standards (between 6:00 PM and 7:00 PM). However, MDs are often on the road visiting clients and prospective clients, traveling on average perhaps three out of every five days. When they are in the office, MDs tend to spend a lot of time on the phone and in meetings. They also often participate in various managerial duties, such as being a part of recruiting and compensation committees.

While the hours of a managing director aren't too bad aside from the travel, the lifestyle of an MD is not an easy one. MDs are under intense pressure to pitch clients and bring in deals, year after year. Given the amount of money involved, there are often internal politics at play, with MDs fighting over clients, over credit for deals, over compensation, and over resources for their staff or group. This is especially true when market conditions are difficult.

The People Now let's turn our attention to the types of people that are both attracted to and excel at investment banking careers.

Analysts Analysts tend to be smart and tend to be very high achievers. Most analysts come in to investment banking having worked exceptionally hard in school to get very high grades and have filled their free time with extracurricular activities and internships. This makes sense, since working hard and being able to juggle many things at once while excelling in all are the same traits that make a strong analyst.

With regard to personality, there is generally more diversity among analysts than among any of the other more senior positions of banking. Some analysts are more personable and outgoing, some more shy and reserved. Some are nerdy and analytical, and some are very social and gregarious. As long as you are not at the extreme of personality and are willing to work hard, you can do well as an analyst. Having said that, among the very top-rated analysts, there is probably a bias for those who have more sociable qualities.

Even though most analyst have Type A personalities and are high achievers, within an analyst class there tends to be much more camaraderie than competition. Since analysts rarely work together on the same project or deal, there isn't much reason to be competitive. And even given the fact that analysts are ranked against each other each year, the tough lifestyle of banking and the sheer number of hours they spend together in the office tend to bring them together. Of course, in nearly every analyst (and associate) class, there is always the one outlier who is cutthroat and political.

Associates–MDs At the associate level, individuals in investment banking tend to be more homogeneous. They are still smart and high-achieving but generally somewhat less so than the analysts. Whereas analysts are typically bankers for only two years, associates are viewed as people who could be MDs someday. Therefore, they tend to have better social and communication skills than analysts, traits they will need to move forward on the track toward being a senior-level banker.

Most senior investment bankers are assholes.[2] As we discussed earlier, the culture inherent to the industry is one in which you have to be willing to treat other people poorly, especially the junior staff. There is simply no other way to get all of the work done under the time frames and circumstances required by clients and transactions alike. Moreover, as a senior-level banker you need to have the sharp elbows and ruthlessness necessary to win at the political games that your compensation and career advancement will require.

Associates attracted to investment banking as a long-term career tend to possess many of these personality traits, but these kinds of traits are also

[2]Yes, asshole is the technical term.

reinforced and further developed as associates become more senior investment bankers.

In addition, senior investment bankers and aspiring senior bankers also must share a love of money. As we will discuss when we get to compensation later in this chapter, there is simply no other reason to put up with the long-term sacrifices required of banking other than for the compensation. For a typical banker, this pursuit of money and all things related will have a much higher priority than most other things. In other words, if you are not interested in talking about fancy cars, exotic vacations, expensive clothes, and trophy wives, it is best to avoid inviting investment bankers to your next cocktail party. And of course, the arrogance and self-importance that often accompany high levels of compensation in any industry, tend to reinforce the view of bankers as "difficult" people.

Lifestyle and Culture Differences For the most part, banking is banking. In other words, regardless of the type of investment bank, the location of the office, or the particular group, you should expect the work to be similar, and the lifestyle and the culture to be similar. However, there are some relatively minor differences between different banks and different groups. (Note that we will return to this subject in Chapter 9 when we discuss how to choose between multiple job offers.)

Differences among the Bulge Bracket Banks There are very few differences between the culture and lifestyle of the various bulge bracket banks. This is reinforced by the fact that senior bankers tend to switch banks with some frequency, thus stirring up the cultural pot. In fact, there is considerable more variability between the various groups within a bank than among the large banks. That the bulge bracket banks are difficult to differentiate actually presents a challenge when recruiting and interviewing, which we will discuss in Chapter 9.

The one outlier amongst the bulge bracket is Goldman Sachs. Different from the other large financial institutions, Goldman does have its own unique and very strong culture. Since entire books have been written about the firm, its history, and its culture, we can only scratch the surface. Briefly, the culture is one of the firm first and the individual second. This is the opposite of most other investment banks, where individuality is the rule and loyalty is virtually nonexistent. Goldman invests more in its recruiting process to ensure its employees are the right fit for the firm, and it invests more in its training and mentoring to ensure employees continue to uphold its values. One obvious benefit is that employees tend to have much longer tenures than at the other bulge bracket banks.

Differences between Bulge Bracket and Boutique Banks Many of the name-brand boutiques have cultures that are similar to that of the bulge brackets. There are also boutiques, often smaller firms, where the lifestyle is considerably better (i.e., fewer work hours). There are even a handful of boutiques where you will likely work even harder than at a bulge bracket. One thing to keep in mind that it is much tougher to generalize about boutiques given how many there are and how broad is the range of different types. Having said that, there are some generalizations that can be made that will hold true much of the time.

Analysts and associates at boutiques frequently have the opportunity to take more responsibility than their bulge bracket equivalents, as deal teams are often smaller. Junior bankers at boutiques also tend to have more interaction with senior bankers, as well as with clients, and are more likely to be invited to attend pitches and meetings. There also tends to be less face time at boutiques than at bulge bracket banks, meaning fewer wasted hours and fewer total hours spent in the office.

Differences among Geographies Discussing the cultural and lifestyle differences between different geographies always carries the risk of offending people. Bankers tend to be very possessive of their home office location and often take pride in the "toughness" of their culture and lifestyle vis-à-vis offices in other geographies. As with boutiques, it is difficult to generalize here, too.

Having said all that, though, generally, the life of an investment banker is more difficult in New York than anywhere else. Even though other major financial markets have grown enormously in recent decades, New York is still the central hub of investment banking activity and will likely remain so for some time. The other big international banking centers, London and Hong Kong, come next.

In any of the major regions of the globe, offices in secondary financial cities tend to be a bit more relaxed, and bankers tend to work fewer hours. This is especially true of regional offices, which we often refer to as satellite offices. However, there are always exceptions. In fact, not all regional offices are truly satellite offices since some industries get covered outside of the major financial centers. For example, an M&A banker in San Francisco probably has a better lifestyle than an M&A banker in New York. The same might not be true for a technology banker, given that an investment bank's technology group is often headed out of San Francisco.

One additional geographic difference worth mentioning is that of investment banking in emerging markets such as Latin America, Eastern Europe, and China, Southeast Asia, and India. These areas have seen enormous growth in investment banking activity over the past decade. However, given the less-developed capital markets in these regions, investment banking tends to be more relationship-driven and less of a commodity. The result is that people often have the opportunity to become relationship bankers much earlier in their careers than in regions with more mature markets. In these markets, it is not unusual for even associates to be calling on clients and to perform marketing activities.

Differences among Groups Once again, I preface this section with the warning that generalizations are difficult to make and fraught with risk. Alas, some groups, especially within bulge bracket banks do have reputations for having better or worse lifestyles. Bankers in product groups such as M&A, leveraged finance, and restructuring, on average, probably work more hours than bankers in industry groups. However, this will not necessary hold true if there is little deal flow for that product due to market conditions. For example, if the credit markets are shut down, leveraged finance bankers will be twiddling their thumbs. Similarly, if the markets are booming and bankruptcies are few, restructuring bankers might be seen leaving the office at 7 PM.

The same can be said for industry groups. Often the lifestyle of a particular coverage group depends mostly on the level of deal flow in that sector. For instance, if there are a lot of deals in industrials but few in healthcare, then the analysts and associates in the industrials group will likely be busier and work more hours. However, group culture is also highly dependent on the MD or MDs running that group. If the head of the group head is laid back, face time will likely be limited. If the MDs are more typical bankers and are aggressive about marketing and pitching, then the junior staff will likely be working long hours, even if deal flow is light.

Lastly, recall from earlier in this chapter that both equity capital markets (ECM) and debt capital markets (DCM) tend to offer significantly better lifestyles (and lower compensation) than most of the other groups within investment banking.

Being a Female Investment Banker Like most areas of finance, investment banking is very much a male-dominated culture (though nowhere near as extreme as trading). While certain groups tend to have more women (the consumer/retail coverage group is a typical example), overall the male/female ratio is heavily skewed male. While the industry has made progress in recent years in recruiting and retaining women, this fact alone leads to a number of consequences.

Given that most analysts and associate are men, it tends to be more difficult for the women to make strong friendships and to feel a true sense of camaraderie with their peers. Furthermore, female junior bankers are routinely forced to put up with the often-tasteless, inappropriate, and chauvinistic jokes of 22-year-old analysts (and 40-year-old managing directors). It is also much harder for female bankers to find mentors, given the limited number of senior female bankers at a typical investment bank.

In addition, the investment banking lifestyle presents different challenges for women than for men. For better or worse, most societies have different expectations for men and women when it comes to physical appearance. The lack of time available to junior bankers to meet such basic needs as eating healthy, exercising, and even getting one's hair cut tends to take a tougher toll on most women than it does on most men.

At the senior levels of banking, the differences are even more pronounced. As is the case in any high-powered industry, when it comes to having a family, the obvious sacrifices and tradeoffs that women must make tend to dwarf those of men. Moreover, female bankers tend to miss out on certain opportunities to build or strengthen relationships with both clients and colleagues. As much as the finance industry likes to hide it, a fair amount of networking and client entertaining still involves heavy consumption of alcohol and visits to strip clubs. Finally, it is a fact of the world in which we live, especially in certain cultures, that female bankers are often taken less seriously by the senior management of clients.

Compensation In any industry or job, if you are going to work very long hours in a very stressful environment then you better get paid well for your efforts. This is certainly true for investment banking. Long-term, the chief rationale for being an investment banker is for the money. And even though there are a handful of other reasons to be a banker at the analyst or associate level, you still need to be highly compensated for making the sacrifices that you are required to make. In this section, we will talk about every banker and prospective banker's favorite topic: compensation. Before we get to actual figures, we need to first discuss a few things.

Compensation in investment banking is nearly always made up of two components: a base salary and a bonus. In addition, new analysts and associates straight out of school typically receive a signing bonus. The base salary is fixed each year and is paid throughout the year like a normal paycheck. The bonus is completely discretionary and is paid at the end of a bank's fiscal year, except for analysts at most banks, who are paid their bonuses in the middle of the year. The annual bonus typically makes up a significant portion of a junior banker's compensation and is often the vast majority of a senior banker's compensation.

Total compensation can vary significantly from year to year, depending on market conditions. While base salaries sometimes move up or down each year, most of the variability comes from bonuses. Recent difficult economic conditions have seen a number of trends in banking compensation. Total compensation has declined since the beginning of the financial crises given that the industry has shrunk in headcount. Individual compensation has also declined, but less so. The percentage of compensation attributed to base salaries has risen as regulators, especially in Europe, have made efforts to curtail bonuses.

In addition, an increasing portion of bankers' bonuses are being paid in company stock or special illiquid securities, beginning at the associate level. This reflects the desire of investment banks both to better align the incentives of bankers and also to limit cash payments, given declining revenues. Some investment banks have even put a cap on cash bonuses as little as $150,000. Depending on the bank, the portion of one's bonus paid in company stock cannot be converted into cash for up to five years. A banker typically loses the value of these shares if he or she leaves the firm before the stock has vested.

The compensation figures that follow are merely estimates and are representative of average compensation at bulge bracket banks in major markets such as New York. Pay in smaller geographic markets is often, though not always, less. Some boutique banks pay at scales or even above the bulge bracket, though most, especially middle market banks, pay somewhat less. One final thing to keep in mind is that compensation tends to be commensurate with hours and lifestyle.

Both analysts and associates are grouped into classes (first-year, second-year, and third-year), and are also ranked by performance and grouped into tiers or buckets. The figures discussed here are generally for top-ranked analysts and associates, which typically make up no more than 20 percent of a class. However, there tends not to be significant variability to bonuses in different buckets, except for poorly ranked bankers who might receive no bonus and/or be terminated. For analysts, for example, bonuses might be lower by around $5–10K by tier.

Analyst Compensation In 2012, compensation for the average top-ranked first-year analyst at a bulge bracket bank included a base salary of approximately $70,000 and a bonus of $40,000–$60,000, for total compensation of $110,000–$130,000. First-year analysts also frequently receive one-time signing bonuses of $15,000–$20,000.

Pay for second-year analysts consisted of a base salary of $80,000 and a bonus of $60,000 – $80,000, for total compensation of $140,000–$160,000. Third-year analyst saw base salaries of about $90,000 and bonuses of $80,000–$100,000, for total compensation of $170,000–$190,000. Consider that few other jobs pay nearly $200,000 to 24-year-olds, three years out of college!

Associate Compensation Base salaries for top-ranked first-year associates have ranged from $100,000 to $125,000 in recent years. Bonuses for first-year associates have ranged from $75,000 to $150,000, for total compensation of $175,000–$275,000. Associates in their first half-year (often referred to as the stub year) recruited out of business school also typically receive a signing bonus of $40,000–$45,000.

For second- and third-year associates, base salaries generally increase approximately $15,000–$20,000 for each year, and bonuses tend to increase $50,000–$75,000 per year. Total compensation for a highly regarded third-year associate can approach or possibly even exceed $400,000.

VP Compensation At the vice president level and above, there tends to be much more variability of compensation than at the analyst or associate level. Bonuses can vary significantly with title, class year, and especially performance. Base salaries at the VP level tend to start around $175,000, with total compensation of perhaps between $400,000 and $700,000. Note that salaries for SVP/directors will be somewhere in between those of VPs and MDs.

MD Compensation Base salaries for managing directors have risen significantly over recent years and often range from anywhere from $250,000 to $600,000. Bonuses for MDs are the most variable of any level of investment banker, ranging from zero (be lucky you have a job) to several million dollars or more.

Exit Opportunities

In the previous section, we stated that the primary reason to consider investment banking as a long-term career is for the compensation. However, over the shorter term, investment banking can often represent a bridge or stepping-stone to another job or industry. We typically refer to these other jobs or industries as the potential exit opportunities of investment banking.

For many investment bankers, the most desirable exit from banking is to a career on the buy side. Investment banking is considered part of the sell side, since bankers sell their services to clients. The buy side is when you are the client and you make the investment decisions. When bankers speak of moving to the buy-side, they are most frequently referring to two types of investment firms: private equity and hedge funds.

As we will discuss in Chapter 8 when we cover leveraged buyouts, private equity refers to firms that make control investments in companies. Bankers are attracted to private equity partly because the compensation can be significantly higher than investment banking, but also because it seems cool to buy and sell companies, to sit on boards of directors, and to be able to give advice without having to do any of the work. Of course, the grass is sometimes greener, and many private equity professionals work just as hard as bankers.

Hedge funds refer to firms that invest in different types of securities and employ different strategies in the hopes of achieving high-risk adjusted returns for their investors. The types of hedge funds that attract ex–investment bankers are typically those that do fundamental analyst of companies, such as long/short equity funds or funds that take activist roles in the companies in which they invest. Other types of hedge funds that appeal to bankers are special situation funds, such as those that focus on merger arbitrage or distressed companies. As with private equity, the compensation at a hedge fund can sometimes dwarf that of investment banking.

Now, let's discuss some of the common exit opportunities for analysts, associates and for senior bankers. Keep in mind one very important point: Of all the levels of investment banking, analysts have by far the most exit opportunities. In fact, the more senior an investment banker you become, the more limited your exit opportunities tend to be.

Analysts Probably the most common exit for analysts after their two-year program is to private equity. In fact, historically there was a very common track of two years as an investment banking analyst, two years as a private equity associate, off to business school to get an MBA, and then back to private equity at either the same firm or a different firm. In recent years, however, the growth of hedge funds has altered this path somewhat. Many analysts go directly to hedge funds after their two-year analyst program or after spending two years in private equity. As opposed to private equity, once in a hedge fund, it is somewhat less common to leave to get an MBA.

Other exit opportunities include going to work for a medium or large company in its corporate development group. Sometimes analysts wind up joining companies that they worked with on one or more transactions while a banker. Some bankers leave to be an entrepreneur and start a business, while others join their family business. It is not altogether uncommon for certain analysts to find that they strongly dislike business and finance altogether and do something totally different, like go to law school or medical school, or become a teacher.

Finally, as we discussed earlier in this chapter, some analysts do stay on for a third year and then get promoted to associate. A handful of bankers also go directly to business school. Once in business school, a few typically wind up going back into investment banking, but the vast majority do not.

Associates As we already stated in the introduction to this section, the exit opportunities for associates are significantly more limited than they are for analysts. In fact, it is a very common misconception among MBA students that investment banking at the associate level is a bridge job to private equity. It is not. While not completely unheard of, few associates are successful making that transaction. Hedge funds represent a somewhat higher probability but, again, certainly less so than for analysts. More common are corporate development jobs, entrepreneurial ventures, and family businesses. Occasionally, associates will switch to other areas of finance, such as equity research or asset management. And just like with analysts, many associates leave the finance world altogether.

Senior Bankers The exit opportunities for VPs, SVPs/directors, and MDs are more limited still. Corporate development jobs represent the most common transition, especially going to work for a client to execute internal M&A transactions. Occasionally, a senior banker (most likely an MD) will make the switch into private equity. This tends only to be case if the MD has very strong relationships in an industry and can help the private equity firm with deal flow.

Truth be told, the real exit for a senior banker is retirement. It is the goal of many an investment banker to make a lot of money and then retire at a young age, perhaps in his or her 40s. Retirement might mean playing golf all day or investing one's own money or opening a restaurant or doing any number of other things that the person did not have time to do when hard at work as an investment banker.

A discussion of exit opportunities for senior bankers does beg a certain question: Once you have made it as a banker to the vice president level or above, other than for retirement, why leave? Chances are, you have put in the hard work and hours, and are now reaping the benefits in terms of compensation. Few jobs will pay anywhere near what banking will. Of course, many senior bankers do leave the industry—but more often than not, the choice to leave was not theirs.

FREQUENTLY ASKED QUESTIONS

In the introduction to this chapter, we talked about the need to be knowledgeable about investment banking in order to be successful at the recruiting process. We also cited the importance of knowing what you are getting into and of having realistic expectations. In my experience teaching and mentoring prospective investment bankers, most undergraduate and MBA students share many of the same misconceptions about the industry. In the spirit of helping you to understand what investment banking really is, and what being an investment banker really is like, let's conclude this chapter by answering some frequently asked questions.

1. Is investment banking right for me if I love to follow and invest in the stock market?

This is an easy one. No. The day-to-day work of an investment banking actually has very little to do with the stock market. Yes, the stock market has an influence on investment banking activity, and yes, as an analyst or associate you will perform analysis that values a company's stock. However, if you are interested in the stock market and investing in general, you are much better off pursuing asset management, trading, or equity research.

2. Do investment bankers really advise companies?

We mentioned early on in this chapter that one of the alternatives names used for the investment banking division is advisory. It would therefore seem obvious that the answer must be yes. However, the reality is much less clear.

In a very narrow sense, investment bankers do provide advice on certain aspects of a transaction on such things as valuation and financing structure. In reality, what bankers are paid by clients to do is not to give advice but to execute transactions. In fact, it is rare that a transaction occurs because a banker suggested it. Most of the time, a client wants to do a deal and then hires the banker. If you are interested in providing strategic advice to companies, you are much better off working for a strategic consulting firm like McKinsey & Company.

3. Will investment banking teach me about business?

Investment banking will teach you a lot about a small subset of finance, which is in turn only a narrow aspect of business. Investment banking will not teach you much about sales or marketing or operations or product development—topics that are usually much more important to running or growing a business.

It is a fact of life that investment bankers, given their levels of compensation and inherent personalities, often take the view that finance is paramount, that companies are easy to run, and that most CEOs are dumb. Yes, some CEOs are dumb, but running a successful business is much harder than executing an M&A transaction. Long story short, if what you really want to do is learn about business then seek out a management trainee program at a large company. Rotate through different divisions. Run a factory. Become a CEO. You can always hire a banker to execute your transactions.

4. Is the work of an investment banker challenging? Is it intellectually challenging?

The work of a banker is challenging in certain respects. Dealing with difficult people can be challenging. Debugging a model at 3:00 AM can be challenging. Writing a coherent industry overview after you've been up for 36 hours straight can be challenging. Not falling asleep at a pitch in front of a CEO of a Fortune 500 company after you've barely slept in a week can be challenging.

Getting up the learning curve can be intellectually challenging, especially given that the typical new analyst or associate is "thrown into the fire" and is not given much guidance. But what you are really learning during this process is not the accounting or the finance theory or the valuation techniques or the various deal structures. What you are really learning is how to be an investment banker: how to have the proper attention to detail, how to format a presentation, how to craft a professional e-mail.

Once you know what you are doing, there isn't much that most bankers find intellectually challenging. People like to say all the time that banking isn't rocket science. It's true. You will never use more than about fourth-grade math. For junior bankers, occasionally a detailed, complicated financial model can be stimulating to build. But that's about it. In summary, what is challenging about investment banking is the lifestyle, not really the work itself.

5. Why don't investment banks just hire more people and pay them less?

The answer is threefold. For one, it's just the culture of banking to work really hard. And if people are working really hard, being put under a lot of stress, and making significant sacrifices, then they need to be paid accordingly.

The second answer is that the nature of investment banking transactions is that they are often extremely fast-paced and often require work to be done at a moment's notice with very quick turnaround. The implication of that is you need a small number of people who are intimately knowledgeable about the deal to be able to complete the work in a timely manner. There isn't usually time for new people to get up to speed. Plus some of the work, like building financial models, cannot easily be handed back and forth from one banker to another.

Finally, if I'm a senior banker, I want one person that is responsible for doing the work so if something isn't finished or isn't correct, I know who to yell at.

6. Is banking a work hard, play hard environment?

A lot of people who work in finance, especially in trading, refer to their jobs as work hard, play hard. It really isn't the case in investment banking. You may work hard, but you rarely play hard or indeed play at all. Some analysts do get out of work at 3:00 AM and go to clubs. They are the exception. Most bankers just want to go home and go to sleep.

7. Is investment banking compensation really that great?

Yes and no. Even taking into account recent trends, compensation in investment banking is higher than nearly all other jobs available to undergraduates and MBA students, both at the junior levels and senior levels of banking. However, the upside is nowhere near as high as it could be in private equity, hedge funds, or starting a business. However, banking compensation is generally less volatile than buy-side jobs and certainly less risky than being an entrepreneur. The bottom line is that banking is one of the safer ways to make a lot of money, but not an extraordinary amount of money. Though keep in mind that given the world we live in post–economic crises, nothing is truly safe.

8. Do all roads lead to private equity?

As an analyst at a bulge bracket bank or highly regarded boutique, you have a very good shot at breaking into private equity. Making the transition at the associate level or above is much more difficult.

9. Do the skills that make a good junior banker make a good senior banker?

This is one of the perverse things about investment banking. Being able to build a model has almost nothing to do with being good at pitching a client. Analysts need to have a great attitude, strong analytical skills, and the ability to put their heads down and do the work. Successful MDs are persuasive and relentless salespeople who are also good at playing politics. The skillsets are nearly complete opposites.

10. Is investment banking good for society?

Does the world need investment bankers? Yes. For companies to grow they need money, and investment bankers help raise money. Do we need so many investment bankers chasing the same deals and the same clients? No. Should companies really be making acquisitions left and right? Probably not. Should our best and brightest students be investment bankers? Certainly not. Like all areas of finance over the past two decades, investment banking grew too big and compensation grew too high. Now both are shrinking and will likely continue to shrink. But the industry will never go away.

So, let me answer the question another way. Are you saving the world by being an investment banker? No, obviously not. Investment banking is a job. It is like most other jobs, except that it demands more of you and pays better. And like most other jobs, you're doing your tiny little part to make the world go 'round and to put food, albeit of the gourmet variety, on the table.

11. Is investment banking worth the sacrifices?

Ah, this is the $64,000 question, isn't it? That's why I saved it for last. The answer is, of course, that it depends. And what it depends on, of course, is you. Most of the folks interested in investment banking can be divided into three categories:

- Recruiting for an analyst position as a stepping stone to the buy side.
- Recruiting for an associate position as a stepping stone to the buy-side or some other career.
- Considering investment banking as a long-term career.

Let us discuss the pros and cons of investment banking for each group.

Recruiting for an analyst position as a stepping stone to the buy side

The surest way into private equity and well-regarded hedge funds is to have been an investment banking analyst. In fact, there are very few other routes in. So, if you are looking for a career in private equity or hedge funds, if you want to be the next Henry Kravis or George Soros, then recruiting for an investment banking analyst program out of an undergraduate institution is close to what we call a no-brainer.

Your life for two years will be hard. But you are young, you have lots of energy, and you probably do not have a family yet. Hence, the sacrifices you will make are a little bit easier to swallow than they are for others. Plus, given that most analysts only stay for two years before moving on, there is a light at the end of the tunnel. Two years goes by pretty quickly, even while working 100-hour weeks. Moreover, the skills and experiences that you will receive as an analyst will be valuable for anything you wind up doing professionally later in your career. This includes not just the finance skillset, but the work ethic, attention to detail, and ability to deal with difficult people.

Whether a long-term career in private equity or hedge funds is worth it is a separate question altogether. While we will not discuss it directly, most of the factors you should take into account when considering a long-term career in banking (see the following section) are similarly relevant.

Recruiting for an associate position as a stepping stone to another career

Each year, lots of MBA students recruit for investment banking associate jobs. Some of them are interested in having a career as an investment banker. Others view banking as a bridge to another career, just as do prospective analysts. Then there are those that pursue banking because they do not know what else to do, or they get caught up in the prestige, or because it just seems like a cool thing to do. If you fit into the second or third groups, you need to really think about whether banking is worth it.

Similar to being an analyst, you will learn very valuable finance and life skills as an associate. You should also make pretty good money, which is especially helpful for the majority of associates who have graduated business school with large student loans. But, you need to understand that the exit opportunities as an associate are much more limited than those of an analyst, especially to the buy side. Please don't expect to work two years as an associate and then go and do mega-buyouts at KKR. The odds of that happening are slim indeed.

Furthermore, unlike the analyst program, which is typically two years in length, there is no obvious exit ramp as an associate. The minute you decide that you want out of banking, your performance will suffer, and you will have difficulties mustering the energy to do the work and put up with the hours, lifestyle, and difficult people. It will be hard to hide your lack of motivation from peers and superiors alike. This can impact not only your compensation but also your ability to get a new job.

Lastly, keep in mind that the longer that you stay in banking, the harder it is to leave it. Not only do the exit opportunities diminish over time, but you also get accustomed to the level of compensation, and the lifestyle and ego that the compensation affords. Few other jobs will be able to match this.

Considering investment banking as a long-term career

Now, let's talk about those of you who are considering being an investment banker as a career. You need to decide what is important to you. Long-term, the primary reason to be an investment banker is for the money. As mentioned multiple times in this chapter, there are few careers that pay as well as investment banking. But you need to be willing to make many sacrifices.

Will you be able to take vacations, flying first class and staying at the Four Seasons? Probably. Will you be able to relax by the pool uninterrupted by conference calls? Probably not. Will you be able to send your children to the finest private schools? Probably. Will you be around to attend most of their soccer games and ballet recitals? Probably not. You get the idea.

Money is not the only consideration if you are thinking about a career as an investment banker. You also need to like the work, the culture, and the people. Merely being able to tolerate these things is not enough. Finally, the most successful bankers are often what we call deal junkies. They get satisfaction and an ego boost out of closing a deal—and then they move on to the next deal, the next client.

As for us, let's move on to all of the knowledge and skills you will need to be an investment banker. That is what the rest of this book is about.

CHAPTER 2

Accounting Overview

It is often said that accounting is the "language" of business. To be truthful, one does not really need to be fluent in the language of accounting in order to start or even successfully operate a business. However, to analyze the financial performance of a business is a different story. And analyzing the financial performance of businesses is something that junior investment bankers spend more time doing than perhaps any other task.

Without a basic understanding of accounting principles, the job of an investment banker would be exceedingly difficult. Stated differently, an investment banker without fundamental accounting knowledge will likely not be an investment banker for very long. Nor is it likely that a prospective investment banker without basic accounting knowledge will perform very well in the interview process.

This chapter is meant to provide you with an introduction to the principles of accounting and, as such, serves as a prerequisite for most of the remainder of this book and for many of the technical questions that you are likely to encounter in the investment banking interview process. However, as with the rest of this book, I have not assumed any prior experience. Even if you have never taken an accounting course before, you should be able to follow along and learn the essential basics of accounting by reading this chapter.

Of course, this chapter is not meant to be as comprehensive as a semester-long accounting class or an accounting textbook. You will not pass a CPA exam or be ready to be an auditor after reading this chapter. But that's okay. Investment bankers do not need to be accounting experts. While possessing more accounting knowledge is certainly helpful, one can be a very successful banker knowing (and truly understanding) the basics.

This chapter is laid out as follows. We will start with a brief overview of the different types of accounting and some important general accounting principles. Then we will move on to a discussion of the three financial statements: the income statement, the balance sheet, and the statement of cash flows. For each of the three statements, we will discuss the most important line items and principles relevant to an investment banker. The final section of this chapter discusses how the three financial statements are integrated and includes a number of numerical examples to help demonstrate these interactions.

Of course, if you already have a strong accounting background, you may want to skim or even skip most of this chapter. However, regardless of the strength of your accounting background, I encourage you to read through the final section of this chapter. This section, and especially the examples, serve as a good test of whether you really understand accounting principles and are also helpful preparation for technical interviews. I have found through my own experience that even students with strong accounting backgrounds often struggle with these types of questions, especially under the pressure of an interview.

INTRODUCTION TO ACCOUNTING

You may have heard the statement that companies keep three sets of "books": one for outside investors and lenders, one for the tax authorities, and one to help management run the business. These three books, or sets of financial statements, correspond to the three main types of accounting, which are:

- Financial accounting.
- Tax accounting.
- Managerial accounting.

Financial Accounting

Financial accounting is used to record and classify a business's financial information for use in analyzing the business's performance by outsiders of the company. These outsiders include investors, lenders, and anyone else who needs to analyze or inspect the company's financial performance. For publicly traded companies, financial accounting is used to put together the financial statements that are contained in quarterly and annual financial reports. (These financial reports will be one of the topics discussed in Chapter 4.)

Investment bankers are primarily concerned with this type of accounting, and therefore it is financial accounting on which we will almost solely focus.

Tax Accounting

Tax accounting is used to comply with jurisdictional tax regulations and laws, such as local, state, or national tax authorities. Suffice it to say, tax rules are highly complicated and are typically not something with which investment bankers need (or want) to understand or analyze in great detail. However, there are certain circumstances where tax accounting does have an effect on financial accounting. We will discuss some of these instances, as they come up, throughout the book.

Managerial Accounting

Managerial accounting is used within a company by management for the purposes of internal planning and decision making. For example, suppose that one division of a company produces material that is then used as an input to a product produced by another division. Managerial accounting deals with the sometimes complicated issues of how to price this material (known as transfer pricing) so that management can achieve an understanding of each division's standalone profitability. Investment bankers are rarely concerned with managerial accounting, and, as such, we will not cover it any further in this book.

Generally Accepted Accounting Principles (GAAP)

All developed countries have standards of financial accounting, which are known as generally accepted accounting principles, or GAAP. GAAP includes the standards, conventions, and rules that accountants follow when recording and summarizing transactions, and in the preparation of financial statements.

It is important to be aware that these principles, as detailed as they often are, do not always provide accountants with clear rules for every situation. Often there are leeway and ambiguity in the guidelines. This may sometimes lead to controversial accounting decisions and can leave room for the manipulation of financial performance.

In the United States, the organization whose primary purpose is to develop these generally accepted accounting principles is known as the Financial Accounting Standards Board (FASB). Interestingly, the FASB is a private-sector organization and not a government body.

The International Accounting Standards Board (IASB) is an organization that was founded in 2001 with the purpose of developing (and standardizing) worldwide accounting standards. These standards are known as the International Financial Reporting Standards (IFRS). There have been many discussions and negotiations to have U.S. GAAP and IFRS rules converge, but to date this convergence has not fully occurred.

Even though there are some differences between U.S. GAAP and IFRS, the general accounting principles are the same. However, the financial statements themselves can, and do, differ significantly country to country in both structure and order of line items, and in the terminology used to describe certain line items. A competent investment banker should be able to interpret financial statements of a company from any country with developed financial reporting standards once they familiarize themselves with how those statements are structured.

THE INCOME STATEMENT

Before we introduce the income statement, we need to first discuss the method in which companies record their operating performance for the purpose of creating their financial statements. There are two accounting approaches that a firm's accountants can theoretically use to measure operating performance:

1. Cash basis.
2. Accrual basis.

Cash Basis of Accounting

Under the cash basis of accounting, a company "books" or recognizes revenue from selling goods or providing services at the time in which it receives cash from customers. Correspondingly, the firm recognizes expenses at the time in which it pays for (i.e., makes cash expenditures) goods and services such as raw materials, office rent, salaries, taxes, and so forth.

There are two big advantages to cash basis accounting. First, under the cash basis, financial statements are relatively easy to compile. The company, or its accountants, need simply to monitor and record the inflows and outflows of cash. Profitability is also easy to measure, as it is essentially the difference each period between incoming cash and outgoing cash.

For example, suppose a company receives from its customers $100 this month from the sale of its products. Further suppose that the company paid $80 this month to its suppliers for the raw materials that are used to make the company's products. Assuming no other cash transactions, it is easy to calculate that the company's profit that month is $20.

The second advantage of the cash basis of accounting is that, as stated, it measures the inflows and outflows of cash. While an obvious statement, its significance is large. That is because the generation of cash is the ultimate true purpose of for-profit companies, as we will see when we discuss valuation in Chapter 5. The theoretical value of a company is the sum of its (present valued) cash flow stream. In other words, cash is king.

Unfortunately, the cash basis of accounting suffers from some large disadvantages. In fact, these disadvantages almost always outweigh the two benefits that we've already discussed. The first and most significant downside to cash basis accounting is that the costs of generating revenues are not properly "matched" with the benefits. Without such matching, it is very difficult to analyze whether the company's operations are truly profitable, or to measure the extent of that profitability. Moreover, this mismatch of revenues and costs can make it extremely difficult to compare operational performance from one period to the next.

For example, suppose that in Year 1, a company pays for $100 worth of inventory, and then in Year 2 the company sells all of that inventory for $200. Under the cash basis of accounting, and assuming no other transactions either year, the company would report a loss of $100 in Year 1 ($0 of revenue and $100 of costs) and a profit of $200 in Year 2 ($200 of revenue and $0 of costs). As you can probably tell, this form of accounting distorts any reasonable measure of profitability. A more meaningful measure of profitability would have been $100 ($200 of revenue and $100 of costs).

A further disadvantage of the cash basis of accounting is that it is somewhat easier for a company to manipulate its operating performance by timing sales and purchases. That is, an employee of the company might be able to delay payment to a vendor from December to January (thus reducing the company's costs in Year 1) or ask a friendly customer to prepay for an order in December that isn't supposed to ship until January (thus increasing sales in Year 1), either of which would result in higher profits (and perhaps a higher bonus for the employee) in the first year.

Accrual Basis of Accounting

The alternative method of measuring and recording performance is known as the accrual basis of accounting. The accrual basis of accounting is based on an important concept, known as the matching principle. This matching principle dictates that revenue is recognized when a firm sells goods or provides services, not when the money is actually received from a customer.

Even more importantly, the costs of the assets used to produce those goods or provide those services (known as the direct costs) are recognized and recorded at the exact same time. For a manufacturer, these direct costs typically include such things as the raw materials used to make the product, the packaging, and the direct labor involved.

For example, let's assume that a company sells $100 of widgets. At the exact same time of the sale, the company will also recognize an expense for the direct costs that went into producing those widgets (let's say $80). This holds true even if those widgets were actually produced or the raw materials were actually paid for in a previous fiscal period.

Cost of assets used that do not easily match up with particular revenues (referred to as the indirect costs) are recognized when those assets are "used." These indirect costs includes things such as marketing and advertising, rent on the company's headquarters, and management salaries. Since these types of costs cannot be directly matched to the production and sale of widgets, the company will expense them as incurred.

The advantages of accrual accounting over cash-based accounting are significant. Most importantly, operating performance is much easier to compare from one period to another using the accrual method. In addition, there are fewer opportunities for the firm to distort or manipulate earnings due to deliberate timing decisions. Of course, as periodic accounting scandals show us, regardless of accounting systems, there will always be opportunities for devious management to manipulate financial statements and mislead lenders and investors.

For these reasons, nearly all medium-sized to large companies, including all publicly traded companies and even many small companies, use the accrual basis of accounting. In fact, it is unusual for an investment banker to ever encounter a company that does not use the accrual method. As such, in this book we will always assume the use of this method of accounting.

Income Statement Overview

The income statement presents the results of the operating activities of a firm for a specified period of time. By operating activities, we mean the company's revenue, costs and profits. The specific period time could be any period of time, such as one day, three weeks, seven months, and so on. However, most of the time, investment bankers are using and analyzing audited financial statements, which are typically produced using three-month intervals (a fiscal quarter) or 12-month intervals (a fiscal year).

The basic income statement looks as follows:

Revenue

Less: Cost of Goods Sold (COGS)

= Gross Profit

Less: Selling, General and Administrative (SG&A)

= Operating Income (EBIT)

Less: Net Interest Expense

= Earnings Before Taxes (EBT)

Less: Income Tax Expense

= Net Income

Revenue The first line item on an income statement is revenue, which is sometimes also referred to as sales, the top line or, outside the United States, turnover. Revenue represents the value received from customers due to the sale of the company's goods and services. Under accrual accounting, revenue is recognized (i.e., recorded for financial statement purposes) when both of the following two conditions have been met:

1. A firm has performed all or most of the services it expects to provide; and
2. The firm has received cash or another asset (such as a receivable) that can reasonably precisely measure the revenue to be recognized.

Sometimes companies need to make adjustments to revenue. For example, if the company expects not to be able to collect the entire amount owed to it by its customers, it may reduce revenues for this expected amount of uncollectible amounts or bad debts. Similar adjustments might be made for sales discounts, allowances, and returns, or from delayed payments. Under accrual accounting, these adjustments are made at the same time at which the revenue is recognized.

Occasionally, an income statement will list a line item called gross revenues followed by net revenues. In this case, net revenues will typically refer to gross revenue less any of the kinds of adjustments discussed in the previous paragraph.

Cost of Goods Sold (COGS) Costs that can be easily matched to revenues are known as cost of goods sold, or COGS, and are recognized at the same time as the corresponding revenue. These are the direct costs that were introduced in the previous section on the accrual bases accounting method. Costs of goods sold includes, for example, the cost of the raw materials used to produce the goods being sold and the cost of labor directly responsible for making those goods.

Gross Profit The difference between a company's revenues and its cost of goods sold is known as its gross profit.

$$\text{Gross Profit} = \text{Revenue} - \text{COGS}$$

This is a useful metric for gaining insight into the profitability of a company's basic operations. If gross profit is small or negative, it may be a sign that direct costs are too high or sales prices are too low, or perhaps that the company is inefficient at production.

As with many of the financial metrics that will be discussed, different industries often exhibit varying levels of gross profit. For example, software companies tend to have very high gross profit, owing to the fact that once software code is written (typically an indirect expense and therefore not part of COGS), the cost of actually producing and delivering software is very small. On the other hand, retailers tend to have much smaller relative gross profit since what it costs a retailer to purchase the items its sells from wholesalers tends to be a significant percentage of the retail price of those items.

Often it is also useful to calculate gross profit as a percentage of revenue, which is known as gross profit margin or just gross margin. When analyzing income statements, investment bankers very often show gross margin as an additional calculated line item.

Gross Margin = Gross Profit / Revenue

Selling, General and Administrative (SG&A) Expenses Costs that cannot be directly matched to revenue are known as indirect costs and are recognized when those assets are consumed. Most of these indirect costs are lumped into an income statement category called selling, general and administrative (SG&A). SG&A typically includes such expenses such as marketing and advertising, research and development (R&D), management salaries, office expenses, travel and entertainment, and professional services, such as legal and accounting (among others).

On some companies' income statements, certain indirect expenses may be listed as separate line items from SG&A if those types of expenses are particularly large or noteworthy. For example, a consumer products company that spends a lot of money on advertising may break out marketing expense on its income statement as its own line item. Similarly, a pharmaceutical company might list research & development (R&D) expenses separately from SG&A.

Operating Income (EBIT) Gross margin less SG&A is known as operating income, which reflects the profit from a company's normal operations. A very often used synonym for operating income is EBIT, which stands for earnings before income and taxes.

Operating Income = Gross Margin – SG&A

Just as with gross profit margin, investment bankers will often calculate operating profit margin, (or synonymously, operating margin or EBIT margin) as follows:

Operating Margin = Operating Income / Revenue

A strong EBIT margin indicates a profitable business, while a small or negative operating margin indicates that the company's operating costs are high relative to its revenue.

Depreciation and Amortization Expense One of the key implications of using the accrual accounting method is that the full cost of long-term assets, such as buildings or equipment, is not treated as an expense when the assets are purchased, as they would be under the cash basis. Instead, the cost of the building or equipment is depreciated over time. That is, a portion of the cost of the asset is treated as an expense each period over the asset's useful life.

This depreciation expense is accounting's attempt to "match" the future benefit of the asset with the cost of the asset. It is important to note that depreciation is a process of cost allocation, and *not* meant to measure the decline in value of the asset. This is a very common misconception, even among sophisticated investment bankers.

There are various methods of depreciating assets. For example, depreciation may be straight-lined, whereby the same amount of depreciation expense is taken each period. Other methods include accelerated depreciation, whereby higher amounts of depreciation are expensed in early years and lower amounts in later years.

Accounting rules dictate that different types of assets have different useful lives. For example, buildings typically have longer useful lives than vehicles, which in turn have longer useful lives than computers. Land is not typically depreciated, as it is deemed not to have a finite life.

It is up to the accountants, not the investment bankers, to make decisions on the appropriate methods of depreciation and useful lives for each asset owned by a company, though sometimes bankers do need to make certain assumptions for the purpose of modeling or analysis.

Depending on the type of asset being depreciated, the depreciation expense may be considered a direct cost (i.e., within costs of goods sold) or an indirect cost (i.e., within SG&A). For example, consider a manufacturer that produces widgets. The widget manufacturer would treat the depreciation of a widget making machine as being part of COGS. That same widget manufacturer would treat the depreciation of its corporate headquarters building as being part of its SG&A expense.

Just as companies depreciate tangible assets such as buildings and machinery according to each asset's useful life, they amortize intangible assets according to each intangible asset's useful life in the same manner. (We will discuss intangible assets when we introduce the balance sheet in the next section of this chapter.)

One last thing should be noted about both depreciation and amortization (often abbreviated D&A) expense. Both are considered to be non-cash expenses since no cash changes hand when tangible assets are depreciated or intangible assets are amortized. There is a direct impact on cash only when the asset was first purchased or is later sold.

EBITDA A metric called EBITDA is one of the most useful and most utilized metrics in corporate finance. Though it is not technically part of the income statement, it is often calculated by investment bankers and shown on, or below the income statement as additional analysis. EBITDA is an acronym that stands for earnings before interest, taxes, depreciation and amortization. EBITDA is calculated by taking EBIT (or operating income) and adding depreciation and amortization expense, as follows:

$$\text{EBITDA} = \text{EBIT} + \text{D\&A}$$

Whereas EBIT can be taken, or calculated directly from the income statement, depreciation and amortization expense is typically not listed on the income statement. It is, however, always listed on the statement of cash flows, often aggregated and grouped together as one line item. Even if depreciation and/or amortization is listed as its own line item on the income statement, we should still take its value from the statement of cash flows so we are certain of accounting for the entire amount. This is due to the fact that there may be depreciation expense aggregated within both COGS and SG&A, as discussed in the preceding section.

EBITDA is so widely used because it is an approximation (a proxy) for a company's operating cash flow. That is, by taking operating income (or the profits from operations) and adding what is typically the most significant non-cash expense, we calculate an approximation of the amount of cash that the company generates from its operations.

EBITDA is, however, not a perfect estimate of operating cash flow. EBITDA does not take into account non-cash expenses (or income) other than D&A, nor does it incorporate other inflows or outflows of cash, such as capital expenditures or working capital requirements. However, because for many industries it is a good approximation of operating cash flow and because it is so simple to calculate, it is widely used.

Operating versus Nonoperating Items So far, every item on the income statement (revenue, COGS, gross profit, SG&A, and EBIT) reflects the operations of the company. In other words, everything on the income statement from revenues down to EBIT is considered to be an operating item. This includes EBITDA, which, while not technically part of the income statement, is calculated by summing up two other items, EBIT and D&A, both operating. (Remember that D&A is also operating because those expenses are part of COGS and/or SG&A.)

However, from now on, the items that we will discuss from the income statement will be affected by something other than just operations—namely something called capital structure. We will discuss capital structure in greater detail in Chapter 3. For now, it is only important to know that capital structure reflects a company's choice of how to fund its operations, either through debt or through equity.

This distinction between operating items (also known as unlevered or capital structure neutral) and non-operating (or levered or capital structure dependent) is not material if your sole purpose is to analyze a company's income statement. (However, it will be vitally important for our discussion of valuation in Chapter 5. So for now, keep this distinction in the back of your mind and we will return to it later.)

Interest Expense The next line item in a typical income statement following operating income (EBIT) is net interest expense. Interest expense reflects the aggregated amount of interest that a company must pay to its lenders or noteholders for the money (i.e., debt) that the company has borrowed. Interest income reflects the interest the company receives from its cash balances or other cash equivalents that earn interest.

Net interest expense is calculated as the difference between interest expense and interest income.

$$\text{Net Interest Expense} = \text{Interest Expense} - \text{Interest Income}$$

In fact, while most income statements will have just one line item for net interest expense, some companies will list both interest expense and interest income separately.

For nearly all types of companies, such as manufacturers or retailers, interest expense and interest income are not considered part of a company's operating activities. As discussed in the preceding section, the amount of interest a company expenses is a function of the amount of debt it has raised (as well as the interest rates that it pays).

It is important to realize that for financial institutions such as a bank, interest expense and interest income are indeed considered to be operating activities. That is because the basic business of a bank is to lend money (typically at longer time frames) thereby earning interest from such things as mortgages or car loans or corporate loans, and to borrow money (typically at shorter time frames), thereby paying interest to, for example, owners of checking or savings accounts. The difference, or spread, between what the interest the bank earns and the interest the bank pays out *is* the bank's primary operating activity. For exactly this reason, metrics such as EBIT and EBITDA are not typically calculated for financial institutions such as banks, for they are meaningless.

Earnings Before Taxes (EBT) or Pre-Tax Income Earnings before taxes (EBT), also known as pre-tax income, is calculated as operating income less net interest expense.

EBT = Operating Income – Net Interest Expense

Tax Expense Tax expense (sometimes listed as provision for income taxes or a similarly worded phrase) represents the income taxes that the company owes based on its financial accounting basis. This is *not* necessarily the amount of money that is actually paid to the various tax authorities. Calculating actual taxes paid is for what the second type of accounting, tax accounting, is used.

In the United States, the statutory rate for federal corporate income taxes for most companies is 35 percent, but a company's actual tax may vary significantly depending on many factors, including state taxes, foreign taxes, and tax offsets from previous periods. Other countries have varying levels of corporate tax rates. However, many public companies pay far less than 35 percent due especially to foreign operations, something that is not without political controversy.

Losses in previous periods can also help to lower current tax bills. These net operating loss carryforwards, often abbreviated as NOLs, are created when companies experience net income losses and can be used to offset future taxes. The rules regarding the use of NOLs are highly complicated and usually beyond what an investment banker needs to know. In fact, generally speaking, bankers generally make simplistic assumptions when it comes to analyzing and modeling taxes because of all of the complexities and regulations involved.

Net Income Net income, sometimes referred to as net earnings, or the bottom line, is calculated by subtracting taxes from EBT. Net income represents that accounting profit for the company for that time period.

Net Income = EBT – Tax Expense

Just as with gross profit margin and operating profit margin, we often calculate net income margin (also referred to as net margin) as follows:

Net Income Margin = Net Income / Revenue

A high number represents a profitable business, and a low or negative number an unprofitable one. Keep in mind, however, that net income is often affected by non-operating expenses (and sometimes income) and also many non-cash expenses and/or non-cash income. Therefore, net income and net income margin are not always very useful metrics for analyzing operational profitability or for analyzing the amount of cash flow actually generated by the company.

Earnings per Share Following the net income line, public companies show earnings per share (EPS). Earnings per share equals net income divided by the number of common shares outstanding.

EPS = Net Income / Number of Common Shares

In fact, companies typically calculate earnings per share twice, using two different share figures: basic shares and fully diluted shares. Note that in the two different measures of EPS (basic EPS and fully diluted EPS), the numerator (net income) does not change. Only the denominator (the number of shares) changes.

Basic shares represent the number of common shares currently outstanding. Fully diluted shares represent basic shares plus the effect of additional shares being potentially issued in the future due to certain securities such as stock options, warrants, and convertible preferred stock or convertible debt. We will discuss the calculation of fully dilutive shares, using one method (the treasury stock method) in Chapter 5.

When calculating basic and fully diluted EPS, companies always use the weighted average number of shares from the period. For example, for full-year EPS, the company will divide the full-year's net income by the weighted average of the shares outstanding (basic or diluted) over the course of that year.

There is one additional factor related to EPS worth mentioning: EPS is a metric that garners much attention from equity research analysts and public stock investors. A company's quarterly and annual EPS figures are highly anticipated, and whether or not a company exceeds or falls short of the equity research analysts' aggregated estimates (known as consensus estimates) can have a significant impact on a company's near-term stock price performance.

However, often the EPS figures that equity research analysts forecast contain certain adjustments to net income that deviate from standard GAAP rules. In fact, companies themselves will often provide their own estimates of adjusted EPS, or what is known as pro forma EPS. Regular EPS that does not contain any adjustments is often is referred to as GAAP EPS. We will discuss some of these adjustments in Chapter 4 when we cover normalizing financial statements.

Income Statement Example Exhibit 2.1 is an example of the income statement for Apple Inc. taken from its 2011 10-K.

EXHIBIT 2.1 Income Statement Example

Consolidated Statements of Operations

(In millions, except number of shares, which are reflected in thousands and per share amounts)

Three years ended September 24, 2011	2011	2010	2009
Net sales	$ 108,249	$ 65,225	$ 42,905
Cost of sales	64,431	39,541	25,683
Gross margin	43,818	25,684	17,222
Operating expenses:			
Research and development	2,429	1,782	1,333
Selling, general, and administrative	7,599	5,517	4,149
Total operating expenses	10,028	7,299	5,482
Operating income	33,790	18,385	11,740
Other income and expense	415	155	326
Income before provision for income taxes	34,205	18,540	12,066
Provision for income taxes	8,283	4,527	3,831
Net income	$ 25,922	$ 14,013	$ 8,235
Earnings per common share:			
Basic	$ 28.05	$ 15.41	$ 9.22
Diluted	$ 27.68	$ 15.15	$ 9.08
Shares used in computing earnings per share:			
Basic	924,258	909,461	893,016
Diluted	936,645	924,712	907,005

THE BALANCE SHEET

Unlike the income statement, which reflects a company's financial performance over a period of time, the balance sheet represents the company's financial position at a singular moment in time. For this reason, the balance sheet is dated as of a certain date (for example, December 31). Since most of the financial statements that bankers analyze and work with reflect quarterly or annual time periods, the balance sheet dates that we use tend to be as of the close of business on the last day of a company's fiscal quarter or fiscal year.

There are three sections to the balance sheet: assets, liabilities, and shareholders' equity. The basic equation of the balance sheet, probably the most important formula in all of accounting, is:

Assets = Liabilities + Shareholders' Equity

This equation must always hold true. The left side of the equation (assets) must always *balance* with the right side (liabilities plus shareholders' equity).

This equation is a natural result of what is known as double-entry accounting. Each and every financial transaction that occurs (for example, a sale of goods, a purchase of inventory, or an issuance of debt) must have two corresponding entries in the company's financial books (known as journal entries) in order for the balance sheet to balance.

For example, an increase in one asset must be offset by either an identical decrease in a different asset, or an identical increase in a liability or shareholders' equity account. This key principle will be explored in greater detail in the final section of this chapter. First, let's discuss each of the three sections of the balance sheet and their respective key line items.

Assets

Assets represent economic resources that possess the potential to provide future benefits to the company. In other words, assets are things that can be used in the future to generate revenues and/or be turned into cash. Assets are listed on the balance sheet in a particular order. This order reflects the relative liquidity of the asset, or how easy the asset can be converted into cash.

Assets are divided on the balance sheet into two categories: current assets (or short-term assets) and noncurrent assets (or long-term assets). Current assets are those assets that the company expects to turn into cash, sell, or consume within the period of one year. Noncurrent, or long-term assets, are assets that the firm expects to hold or use for longer than one year.

Monetary and near-monetary assets such as cash and accounts receivable generally appear on the balance sheet at their net present value. Non-monetary assets such as inventory, equipment, building, and land are stated at the company's acquisition cost. It is very important to remember that since the book value of most assets equals the original cost of acquisition, the fair market value of those assets may, and often will, be substantially different.

Current Assets Following are some of the types of current assets commonly found on a company's balance sheet.

Cash and Equivalents The first asset listed on a balance sheet is cash and cash equivalents, since cash is, by definition of course, the most liquid and "cash-like" asset. Cash and equivalents include, for example, money held in bank accounts that can easily be used by the company to make purchases or payments. Next listed on the balance sheet are other cash-like instruments such as marketable securities and other temporary investments in financial instruments that can easily be sold and turned into cash. Cash and cash equivalents are stated as the amount of cash on hand or in the bank.

Accounts Receivable (AR) The next significant line item in the current assets section of the balance sheet is accounts receivables, sometimes abbreviated AR. Accounts receivable represents the money that is owed to a company by its customers for goods or services that have typically already been provided. Accounts receivables are recorded on the balance sheet as the amount of cash the firm expects to receive, but this figured is typically undiscounted (i.e., not present valued) since the firm expects to receive payment in a relatively short period of time (e.g., several days to several months).

Inventories After accounts receivables comes inventories. Inventories typically include the value of such things as raw materials, supplies, work-in-progress, and finished goods. Most of the time, all types of inventories will be aggregated on the balance sheet into one inventory line item.

There are several different methods for calculating the value of inventories, the most common being LIFO (last in, first out) and FIFO (first in, first out). LIFO assumes that the last items put into inventory are the first ones to be sold, whereas FIFO assumes that the oldest items are sold first. The choice of inventory method will typically have an effect on not only the balance sheet, but also on the income statement (through COGS) and on the cash flow statement. Although a very basic familiarity of inventory methods is helpful, it is unusual for investment bankers to have to analyze or be concerned with these different methods of accounting for inventory. However, questions on this topic do occasionally arise in investment banking interviews.

Prepaid Expenses Other commonly listed current assets include prepaid operating costs such as prepaid rent or insurance (usually shown on the balance sheet as prepaid expenses). Prepaid expenses reflect money that has already been spent for goods or services not yet received. For example, if a company prepays its office rent for an entire year, it would book the value of the prepayment as an asset. As the company uses the asset throughout the year, the expense is booked as SG&A (in the case of office rent), which flows through the income statement, and the value of the balance sheet asset (prepaid expense) is reduced.

Noncurrent (Long-Term) Assets

As mentioned, noncurrent assets are the assets for which the company expects to use, sell, or turn into cash beyond a one-year period. Examples of noncurrent assets commonly found on the balance sheet include:

- Long-term investments in securities.
- Property, plant, and equipment (PP&E).
- Intangible assets.

Property, Plant, and Equipment (PP&E) Property, plant, and equipment, often abbreviated as PP&E, includes tangible or real assets, such as buildings, land, machinery, computers, vehicles, and furniture and fixtures. PP&E is also commonly referred to as fixed assets.

Often on the balance sheet, PP&E will be broken up into three separate line items: gross PP&E, accumulated depreciation, and net PP&E, such that:

Net PP&E = Gross PP&E – Accumulated Depreciation

The balance sheet will look something like this, showing a different order of terms but mathematically equivalent:

Gross PP&E

Less: Accumulated Depreciation

= Net PP&E

Gross PP&E reflects that amount of money originally spent to purchase the company's tangible assets. Accumulated depreciation represents the sum of all of the prior depreciation expense that has been recorded on those assets. Lastly, net PP&E equals the difference between gross PP&E and the accumulated depreciation. If, as is often the case, only one line item is listed on the balance sheet, then you can be sure it will be the net PP&E figure, even if it is not labeled as such.

It is very important to remember that the value of PP&E on the balance sheet does not necessarily reflect the fair market value of those assets. For example, it is not unusual for an asset that has been fully depreciated (i.e., has no balance sheet value) to still be used in the business and/or have salable value. Similarly, it is sometimes the case that the fair market value of assets (real estate is a common example) actually increases over time, whereas this increase would not be reflected on the balance sheet.

Intangible Assets Assets that have no physical form are known as intangible assets. Examples of such intangible assets include in-process research and development (R&D), patents and trade secrets, trademarks and copyrights, and a special category called goodwill. Intangible assets must be purchased in order for the accounting value of such assets to be listed on the balance sheet, either through a direct purchase (i.e., acquiring a portfolio of patents) or through the acquisition of a firm that holds such patents.

Consider that a company typically develops technology or patents through the process of research and development. However, this R&D expense is, in most cases, expensed as part of SG&A when it is incurred. Similarly, companies develop trademarks and brand value through the process of marketing and advertising. Marketing and advertising is, like most R&D, treated as an expense when incurred and therefore runs through the income statement. The accounting rules dictate that such business activities be expensed because they are deemed too uncertain and too difficult to measure to warrant capitalizing them.

The implication of expensing items such as R&D and marketing and advertising is that companies that develop, as opposed to acquire, valuable assets such as technology and brands will not show the values of these assets on their balance sheets.

One special type of intangible asset is called goodwill. Goodwill, which arises when a company makes an acquisition, represents the excess of the purchase price of the company being acquired over the fair market book value of the equity of that company. Unlike other types of intangible assets, goodwill does not need to be amortized each period, but does need to be tested once per year for a decline in value (what is known as goodwill impairment).

Liabilities

The second main section of the balance sheet is liabilities. Liabilities are third-party claims on the assets of the firm. It is important to understand that not all obligations of the firm are considered to be liabilities on the balance sheet. In order for an obligation to be considered a liability, it must meet several criteria. Among the most important of these, liabilities must have a high probability of occurring (generally thought to be at least an 80 percent chance of occurring) and must have an estimable amount that the company will have to pay and a determinable date for when the company will have to pay in the future.

If certain obligations do not meet these requirements, then they are not included on the balance sheet. For example, suppose that a company is involved in a large litigation. Further, suppose that if the company loses the lawsuit it will have to pay out $1 million. This is what is known as a contingent liability and would not be included on the balance sheet because the likelihood of the company having to pay out the $1 million is too uncertain. However, a public company would have to disclose such a contingent liability in its public financial reports (typically as a footnote to the financial statements) as long as the potential obligation is significant (often also referred to as being material).

Just as with assets, liabilities are divided into two categories: current (or short-term) liabilities and noncurrent (or long-term) liabilities. Current liabilities are obligations that a company expects to pay within one year, and noncurrent liabilities are those obligations that a company expects to pay beyond one year.

Current Liabilities Following are many of the current liability line items frequently listed on the balance sheet.

Notes and Other Short-Term Debt Payable to Banks Notes and other short-term debt reflect money that a company borrows from banks and other lenders or creditors that is either short-term in nature, or is due to be paid back or mature within one year. Examples include a revolving credit facility and a one-year note.

Current Portion of Long-Term Debt Very often companies borrow money that is due to be paid back over a number of years, which is known as long-term debt. However, any portion of long-term debt that is due (or matures) within one year is considered to be a current asset and is referred to as the current portion of long-term debt. For example, suppose that a company takes a five-year loan that must be paid back in five equal annual installments. In the first year that the loan is outstanding, one-fifth of the amount of the loan will be considered current debt and the other four-fifths will be considered long-term debt.

Accounts Payable Accounts payable (often abbreviated AP) reflects money that is owed to the suppliers or vendors of a company for goods and services provided to the company. Typically this money will be paid to suppliers within 30 to 90 days.

Accrued Expenses Accrued expenses (sometimes referred to as accrued liabilities) reflect items such as employee salaries or taxes that have been earned (or owed) by the company but have not yet been paid. For example, investment bankers often receive the bulk of their annual compensation as a bonus at the end of the investment bank's fiscal year. However, since bankers work to "earn" this bonus throughout the year, investment banks must estimate the amount of compensation and accrue it on the balance sheet as an accrued expense. Remember that this is the result of the accrual accounting method, which attempts to match costs to the firm (i.e., banker compensation) with benefits (i.e., the work that bankers provide as employees).

Noncurrent Liabilities Following are many of the key line items listed in the noncurrent liability section of a typical balance sheet.

Long-Term Debt As we've already seen, borrowings that are due to be repaid or mature in more than one year are considered long-term debt. Typical examples of long-term debt include term loans, mortgages, and bonds.

Capitalized Long-Term Leases Capitalized long-term leases are leases on property that, for accounting purposes, are treated as if the company owned the property. We will discuss capitalized leases in further detail later in this chapter. However, for now it is worth noting that bankers typically include capitalized leases when calculating or analyzing long-term debt.

Retirement Obligations Certain retirement obligations, such as pensions or defined benefit plans, are also listed on the balance sheet as liabilities. It is an understatement to say that the rules involving the calculation of retirement obligations (often referred to as pension accounting) are highly complex and highly specialized. It is unusual for bankers to have to analyze such obligations, though it is not unheard of, especially in distressed situations where retirement obligations often play a key role in negotiations.

Shareholders' Equity

Shareholders' equity represents the owners' claim on the assets of the company. By the accounting definition, shareholders' equity must equal the difference between total assets and total liabilities. Shareholders' equity is sometimes also referred to as stockholders' equity and is also frequently known by the term "book value." Always remember that shareholders' equity (book value) does *not* equal the company's market value of equity!

There are a number of important line items that will typically be listed in this section of the balance sheet. These include:

Par Value of Common or Preferred Stock For reasons historical and relatively unimportant to an investment banker, when a company issues stock (common or preferred stock) it must assign a value to each share of stock (technically to each stock certificate). Often this value is $.01, $.10, or perhaps $1 per share. The par value of stock that is listed on the balance sheet is the aggregated amount for all outstanding stock of that type.

Additional Paid-In Capital Note that the par value discussed is a nominal value and does *not* reflect the market value of the company's stock. Consider a company that issues new shares in an initial public offering (IPO) at $10 per share. Assume that the par value of stock is $1. The other $9 of value per share goes into a balance sheet line item called additional paid-in capital (APIC). Additional paid-in capital is the amount received by the company in excess of par value in the issuance of common or preferred stock.

It is very important to remember that neither par value nor APIC is updated for the daily changes to a company's publicly traded stock price. This is one of the reasons why the book value of a company does not equal its market value of equity.

Retained Earnings Retained earnings represents a firm's earnings since its formation less the total dividends paid out to the firm's owners since formation. Retained earnings can sometimes be negative, and often will be negative, especially for relatively early-stage companies that lose money in their first several years of operation.

Treasury Stock Treasury stock, also called treasury shares, represents the cost of shares to the company when it repurchases its own stock (often referred to as share buybacks). Note that treasury stock will appear as a negative number on the balance sheet because it reflects those shares being extinguished or taken out of circulation.

Additional Balance Sheet Topics

There are several additional topics related to the balance sheet that are important for an investment banker to understand. As with many things in this chapter, the accounting rules for some of these (specifically leases and deferred taxes) are highly complex and often best left to the accountants to decipher. However, a practicing banker should have at least a conceptual understanding of these topics.

Net Working Capital Net working capital (often referred to as simply working capital) is not a line item that is listed on the balance sheet but is a very important concept that is derived from the assets and liabilities sections of the balance sheet. Net working capital reflects that difference between a company's current operating assets (such as accounts receivable and inventory) and its current operating liabilities (such as accounts payables and accrued expenses). Working capital is a measure of the company's operational efficiency (the more efficient, the lower the working capital requirements) and is also sometimes used as a measure of a firm's short-term financial health.

Net Working Capital
= Current Operating Assets
– Current Operating Liabilities

where:

Current Operating Assets
= Total Current Assets
– Cash and Equivalents
– Other Nonoperating Current Liabilities

and

Current Operating Liabilities
= Total Current Liabilities – Current Debt
– Other Nonoperating Current Liabilities

Note that cash and equivalents and current debt should be excluded from net working capital. This is due to the fact that cash is considered a nonoperating asset and debt is considered a nonoperating liability. To be technically correct in our calculation, we should only exclude excess cash but the distinction between total cash and excess cash is rarely made in practice.

Note that you will often see the following abbreviated formula for net working capital, even though it is not really as precise.

Net Working Capital
= Current Assets – Current Liabilities

Leases It is very common for companies to rent or lease certain assets (especially real estate) instead of owning them outright. For example, while some retail companies own their own stores, many lease them. Similarly, it may surprise you to learn that most airlines actually lease their airplanes rather than purchase and own them.

There are two methods of accounting for long-term leases: the operating lease method and the capital lease method. As with most things in this chapter, as an investment banker, you do not need to know all of the intricacies of the specific accounting rules involving leases, but you should understand the basic concepts.

Operating Leases In an operating lease, the company renting the property (the lessee) does not take any risk of ownership of the assets. As such, the rent that the company must pay to the owner of the property is treated as an operating expense. This rental expense runs through the income statement directly, but there is no direct impact on the firm's balance sheet. (There is an indirect effect since expenses do impact net income, which, in turn, affects the balance sheet through retained earnings.)

For example, suppose that a company leases some office space for its corporate headquarters from a landlord. Assume that the lease is for five years and the rent is set at a certain amount per month. This is a straightforward operating lease, for which the monthly rent would be considered to be an operating expense.

Capital Leases In a capital lease, the lessee assumes some of the risks of ownership and enjoys some of the benefits. For example, assume that a company leases an entire building for 30 years and has an option clause in the contract to buy the building at the end of 30 years. Let's further assume that the company is contractually responsible for all costs associated with operating the building, such as taxes and electricity payments. This would be considered a capital lease. The accounting rules treat capital leases as if the firm had actually purchased the rented property and had to borrow money to finance this (assumed) purchase.

In a capital lease, the impact on the financial statements is far more complex than for an operating lease. Both an asset and a liability are created on the balance sheet, equal to the present value of the lease expenses. Each period, several things happen that impact the financial statements:

1. The asset (lease) is amortized and the asset value is reduced on the balance sheet,
2. Interest expense is realized on the income statement, and
3. The liability on the balance sheet is reduced.

It is worth noting that while only capital leases will be listed as a long-term liability on the balance sheet, there are sometimes instances where bankers will want to make an adjustment and treat an operating lease as if it were a capital lease. This is often the case when bankers are trying to compare the financial statements of two or more companies in the same industry that have different accounting treatment for leased property. As we will mention several times over the course of this book, it is vitally important when performing such analysis to have an apples-to-apples comparison between companies.

Deferred Tax Assets and Deferred Tax Liabilities In the opening section of this chapter we mentioned that there are three types of accounting: financial accounting, tax accounting, and managerial accounting. We also stated that investment bankers primarily concern themselves with financial accounting. Deferred taxes, however, are an example of a situation where a little bit of tax accounting also comes into play.

For a number of reasons, most of which are not relevant to investment bankers, the amount of tax expense that a company reports on its income statement (book taxes) often differs from the amount of taxes that the company actually pays to tax authorities. Most of the differences are temporary, and occur when book income includes revenues or expenses in one accounting period and taxable income includes them in a different period. However, permanent differences, though less frequent, can also occur.

When a firm recognizes an expense earlier for financial reporting than for tax reporting purposes, a deferred tax asset (DTA) will appear on the company's balance sheet. If that difference is temporary and is expected to reverse itself within one year, then a deferred tax asset will be created in the current asset section of the balance sheet. If the timing difference is expected to reverse itself beyond a one-year period, or if it is permanent, then a noncurrent deferred tax asset appears. An example of a deferred tax asset is a net operating loss carryforward (NOL), which we briefly discussed earlier in this chapter.

A deferred tax liability (DTL) will be created on the balance sheet when a firm recognizes an expense earlier for tax reporting than for financial reporting. Similar to assets, if the DTL is expected to reverse within one year, it will be considered a current liability and otherwise will be considered a noncurrent liability.

Since these timing differences can occur for many different reasons, it is not uncommon for balance sheets to list up to four different categories of deferred taxes (current DTAs, noncurrent DTAs, current DTLs, and noncurrent DTLs).

Deferred taxes are one of the trickiest accounting topics for which investment bankers need to have at least a basic understanding. To help, let us consider one of the most common situations for which a deferred tax will be created.

Recall that during the discussion of depreciation expense, we mentioned that there are different methods for which assets can be depreciated, including straight-line deprecation and accelerated depreciation. The financial accounting and the tax accounting rules actually allow a company to use a different method of depreciation for financial reporting than it does for tax reporting on the same asset.

Why might a company want to depreciate an asset differently for financial reporting than for tax reporting? Consider that a goal of financial reporting, especially for public companies, is to maximize net income and earnings per share (EPS). Lower depreciation expense will result in higher net income and higher EPS, so a method that results in lower depreciation this year will be preferred by company management.

On the other hand, it is also a goal of management to minimize the taxes that the company is obligated to pay to government authorities (or at least to minimize current taxes). In this case, higher depreciation expense will lead to lower pre-tax income, which results in a lower tax bill. So, as is often the case, companies will employ a straight-line method of depreciation (equal amounts of depreciation each year) for financial reporting purposes and an accelerated method (higher depreciation in earlier years, lower depreciation in later years) for tax reporting purposes.

This difference in depreciation methods will result in a deferred tax liability on the company's balance sheet, since the company is realizing a higher expense in earlier years for tax reporting than for financial reporting. In later years, the difference will start to reverse and the DTL on the balance sheet will shrink. At the end of the asset's useful life (the same for either method), the asset will have become fully depreciated and the DTL will no longer exist.

Deferred Tax Example Given the inherent complexities, let's consider a numerical example, shown in Exhibit 2.2. Assume that a company purchases an asset for $120 that has a useful life of three years. Further assume that the company employs the straight line method of depreciation for financial reporting purposes and an accelerated method for tax reporting purposes. To keep the analysis simple, we have kept revenue and non-depreciation expense constant each year, though these figures do not have an impact on the deferred tax. Finally, let's assume a 40% tax rate.

In Year 1, we see that the company has a depreciation expense of $40 and a tax expense of $16 for financial reporting purposes. For tax reporting purposes, however, the depreciation expense is $60 and the tax expense is only $8. The difference in tax amounts leads to a deferred tax liability of $8.

In Year 2, the company again has a $40 depreciation expense and a $16 tax expense for financial reporting purposes. For tax reporting purposes, the company has the same $40 of depreciation expense and $16 of taxes. There

EXHIBIT 2.2 Deferred Tax Example

	Year 1		Year 2		Year 3		Total	
	Financial Reporting	Tax Reporting	Financial Reporting	Tax Reporting	Financial Reporting	Tax Reporting	Financial Reporting	Tax Reporting
Beginning of Year Asset Value	$120	$120	$80	$60	$40	$20		
Depreciation Expense	40	60	40	40	40	20	120	120
End of Year Asset Value	80	60	40	20	0	0		
Revenue	$200	$200	$200	$200	$200	$200	$600	$600
Expenses (excluding Depreciation)	120	120	120	120	120	120	360	360
Depreciation Expense	40	60	40	40	40	20	120	120
EBT	40	20	40	40	40	60	120	120
Taxes (@ 40%)	16	8	16	16	16	24	48	48
Net Income	24	12	24	24	24	36	72	72
Tax Difference	$8		$0		($8)			
Deferred Tax Liability	$8		$8		$0			

is no difference in tax amounts in Year 2. Therefore, the DTL remains at $8 on the company's balance sheet.

Now, let's examine Year 3. Once again, financial reporting depreciation expense is $40 and financial reporting tax expense is $16. For tax reporting purposes, depreciation expense is only $20 and taxes are $24. Taxes are now $8 higher for tax reporting purposes than for financial reporting purposes. The tax difference has now reversed itself and the DTL at the end of the year is $0.

This example should help to demonstrate several key concepts. First notice that regardless of depreciation method, by the end of the asset's useful life, total depreciation expense for the three years has been the same ($120). Also notice that total tax expense for the three years has been the same for each method ($48). Finally, note that the DTL created (or reversed) in any given year is equal to the depreciation difference multiplied by the tax rate.

Consolidation and Noncontrolling Interest There is one last important balance sheet concept worth discussing before moving onto the statement of cash flows: consolidation and noncontrolling interest. It is especially relevant for the discussion of valuation in Chapter 5.

When a company (let's call it the parent company) owns more than 50 percent of another company (the subsidiary), it is assumed that the parent company has effective operational control over the subsidiary. As such, the accounting rules dictate that all of the assets and liabilities of the subsidiary be added to the parent's balance sheet, a process known as consolidation. However, in many circumstances, the parent owns less than 100 percent of the subsidiary—say, for example, only 80 percent. In this case, the parent company's balance sheet is essentially overstated by the 20 percent of the subsidiary's assets for which the parent does not really own and the same 20 percent of the subsidiary's liabilities for which the parent is not really obligated.

In these circumstances the accounting rules dictate that a line item called noncontrolling interest be created on the parent's balance sheet. This line item is equal to the subsidiary's book value multiplied by the percentage of the subsidiary that the parent does *not* own (20 percent in our example). Noncontrolling interest, should it exist, will be found within the shareholders' equity section of the balance sheet.

It is also worth noting that prior to December 2008 (at least in the United States), noncontrolling interest was known by its previous name, minority interest, and could have been listed on the balance sheet as a liability, within shareholder's equity, or, most commonly, in between those two sections.

Balance Sheet Example Exhibit 2.3 shows the balance sheet for Apple Inc. taken from its 2011 10-K.

EXHIBIT 2.3 Apple Inc. Balance Sheet (in millions)

	September 24, 2011	September 25, 2010
ASSETS		
Current assets:		
Cash and cash equivalents	$ 9,815	$11,261
Short-term marketable securities	16,137	14,359
Accounts receivable, less allowances of $53 and $55, respectively	5,369	5,510
Inventories	776	1,051
Deferred tax assets	2,014	1,636
Vendor non-trade receivables	6,348	4,414
Other current assets	4,529	3,447
Total current assets	44,988	41,678
Long-term marketable securities	55,618	25,391
Property, plant, and equipment, net	7,777	4,768
Goodwill	896	741
Acquired intangible assets, net	3,536	342
Other assets	3,556	2,263
Total assets	$116,371	$75,183
LIABILITIES AND SHAREHOLDERS' EQUITY		
Current liabilities:		
Accounts payable	$ 14,632	$12,015
Accrued expenses	9,247	5,723
Deferred revenue	4,091	2,984
Total current liabilities	27,970	20,722
Deferred revenue—non-current	1,686	1,139

EXHIBIT 2.3 (*Continued*)

	September 24, 2011	September 25, 2010
Other non-current liabilities	10,100	5,531
Total liabilities	39,756	27,392
Commitments and contingencies		
Shareholders' equity:		
Common stock, no par value; 1,800,000 shares authorized; 929,277 and 915,970 shares issued and outstanding, respectively	13,331	10,668
Retained earnings	62,841	37,169
Accumulated other comprehensive income/(loss)	443	(46)
Total shareholders' equity	76,615	47,791
Total liabilities and shareholders' equity	$116,371	$75,183

THE STATEMENT OF CASH FLOWS

The statement of cash flows, also commonly known as the cash flow statement, reports the net cash flows relating to a company's operating, investing, and financing activities for a period of time. This period of time will match that of the company's corresponding income statement. The statement of cash flows is important because (1) understanding and measuring a business's ability to generate cash is important, and (2) the use of the accrual method of accounting means the income statement does not track inflows and outflows of cash. The cash flow statement is often also referred to as the bridge between the income statement and the balance sheet.

There are two methods that can be utilized to construct the cash flow statement: the direct method and the indirect method. The direct method lists the inflows and outflows of cash, with the sum of all cash transactions equaling the change in cash for the fiscal period. While the direct method is slightly easier to interpret, the indirect method is almost exclusively used by companies, so our focus will be on the indirect method.

The cash flow statement is divided into three categories:

1. Cash flow from operating activities.
2. Cash flow from investing activities.
3. Cash flow from financing activities.

The sum of these three sections will equal the total change in cash for the period. This change in cash, when added to the company's beginning cash balance (equivalently, the ending cash balance from the previous fiscal period's balance sheet) must equal the ending cash balance for this fiscal period (as reported on the balance sheet).

Every change on the balance sheet must be reflected somewhere on the cash flow statement. An increase in assets on the balance sheet must correspond to a decrease in cash on the cash flow statement and is thus referred to as a use of cash. A use of cash will be listed as a negative figure on the cash flow statement.

Correspondingly, an increase in liabilities or shareholders' equity on the balance sheet must correspond to an increase in cash on the cash flow statement, considered a source of cash. A source of cash will be recorded as a positive number on the statement of cash flows. Similarly, a decrease in assets (source of cash) will be a positive impact on cash, and a decrease in liabilities (use of cash) will be negative.

Understanding what types of activities will increase cash and what types of activities will decrease cash is very important when it comes to financial modeling, as will be discussed in Chapter 6. Additionally, questions that test this knowledge often arise in investment banking interviews.

Cash Flow from Operating Activities

The first section of the cash flow statement is cash flow from operating activities (equivalently, cash flow from operations). In the indirect method of creating the cash flow statement, this section calculates the result of adjusting net income for non-cash items and for changes in operating assets and liabilities.

The first line in this section is net income, which must equal the reported net income figure from the income statement. Next, depreciation and amortization (D&A) is added, since it is a non-cash expense. After the addition of D&A and any other non-cash expenses (or income), adjustments are made for changes in operating assets and liabilities (i.e., working capital). For example:

- Change in accounts receivable (asset).
- Change in inventories (asset).

- Change in prepaid expenses (asset).
- Change in accounts payable (liability).
- Change in accrued expenses (liability).

These changes are simply the differences between the current period's corresponding balance sheet figure and that of the previous period. As a reminder, when an asset such as accounts receivable or inventories increases, the corresponding cash flow change will be negative (a use of cash), and when a liability such as accounts payable or accrued expenses increases (a source of cash), the cash flow change will be positive.

Cash Flow from Investing Activities

The second section of the cash flow statement is cash flow from investing activities (or, in shorter name, cash flow from investing). This section takes into account the acquisition and sale of investments and long-term assets such as PP&E. For an investment banker, the most important line item in this section (often, though not always, the first line) is capital expenditures. Capital expenditures (commonly abbreviated as capex) may also be referred to on the cash flow statement as something like additions to, or acquisitions of, fixed assets or PP&E.

Capital expenditures represent the money spent to acquire long-term assets such as buildings, equipment, vehicles, computers, and the like. They also include funds spent to maintain such PP&E. As a use of cash, the capital expenditures line item will be listed as a negative number on the cash flow statement. If a company sold some of its PP&E (or other long-term investments), then the cash generated from the sale of such assets would be considered a source of cash and recorded as a positive number.

Cash Flow from Financing Activities

The final section on the cash flow statement is cash flow from financing activities (or just cash flow from financing). This section takes into account the changes to a firm's debt and equity positions. For example:

- Increases or decreases in short-term debt.
- Increases or decreases in long-term debt.
- Payments of common or preferred dividends.
- Issuance of common or preferred stock.
- Repurchase of common or preferred stock (e.g., treasury stock).

An increase in debt or equity is a source of cash and will have a positive impact on the cash flow statement, whereas a dividend payment, stock buyback, or repayment of debt is a use of cash and will have a negative impact on cash flow.

Cash Flow Statement Example

Exhibit 2.4 shows the statement of cash flows for Apple Inc. taken from its 2011 10-K.

EXHIBIT 2.4 Apple Inc. Statement of Cash Flows

Consolidated Statements of Cash Flows
(In millions)

Three years ended September 24, 2011	2011	2010	2009
Cash and cash equivalents, beginning of the year	$11,261	$5,263	$11,875
Operating activities:			
Net income	25,922	14,013	8,235
Adjustments to reconcile net income to cash generated by operating activities:			
Depreciation, amortization, and accretion	1,814	1,027	734
Share-based compensation expense	1,168	879	710
Deferred income tax expense	2,868	1,440	1,040
Changes in operating assets and liabilities:			
Accounts receivable, net	143	(2,142)	(939)
Inventories	275	(596)	54
Vendor non-trade receivables	(1,934)	(2,718)	586
Other current and non-current assets	(1,391)	(1,610)	(713)
Accounts payable	2,515	6,307	92
Deferred revenue	1,654	1,217	521
Other current and non-current liabilities	4,495	778	(161)
Cash generated by operating activities	37,529	18,595	10,159

EXHIBIT 2.4 (*Continued*)

Consolidated Statements of Cash Flows
(In millions)

Three years ended September 24, 2011	2011	2010	2009
Investing activities:			
Purchases of marketable securities	(102,317)	(57,793)	(46,724)
Proceeds from maturities of marketable securities	20,437	24,930	19,790
Proceeds from sales of marketable securities	49,416	21,788	10,888
Payments made in connection with business acquisitions, net of cash acquired	(244)	(638)	0
Payments for acquisition of property, plant and equipment	(4,260)	(2,005)	(1,144)
Payments for acquisition of intangible assets	(3,192)	(116)	(69)
Other	(259)	(20)	(175)
Cash used in investing activities	(40,419)	(13,854)	(17,434)
Financing activities:			
Proceeds from issuance of common stock	831	912	475
Excess tax benefits from equity awards	1,133	751	270
Taxes paid related to net share settlement of equity awards	(520)	(406)	(82)
Cash generated by financing activities	1,444	1,257	663
(Decrease)/increase in cash and cash equivalents	(1,446)	5,998	(6,612)
Cash and cash equivalents, end of the year	$ 9,815	$ 11,261	$ 5,263
Supplemental cash flow disclosure:			
Cash paid for income taxes, net	$ 3,338	$ 2,697	$ 2,997

INTEGRATING THE THREE FINANCIAL STATEMENTS

Being able to read, interpret, and analyze financial statements is one of the most important skills required of an investment banker. Being able to actually create the financial statements, given the myriad generally accepted accounting principles, is not. Generating the financial statements is a task much better left for the CPAs of the world.

However, it is vitally important that a banker (or prospective banker) develop an intuitive understanding of how the three financial statements are integrated. Simply memorizing the definitions and order of the key line items of each statement is not enough. As we will discuss in Chapter 6, this is one of the most important foundations for being able to build financial models, which in turn is one of the most important skills required of junior investment bankers. And because understanding how the statements fit together is so important, this topic is reflected in some of the most frequently asked (and trickiest) technical interview questions generally encountered by prospective investment bankers.

A number of times over the course of this chapter, we have directly stated, or alluded to the fact, that the three financial statements are integrated. In other words, items from one financial statement have a direct effect on another statement. For instance, we have already discussed how the cash flow statement can be thought of as the bridge between the income statement and the balance sheet and how every change in the balance sheet from the previous period to the current period must be reflected somewhere within the statement of cash flows.

Consider the example of net income. Net income is the last line on the income statement but is also the first line of the cash flow statement, and of course these two numbers must be identical. Net income also directly affects the balance sheet through retained earnings in the shareholders' equity section. In reality, every single business transaction will affect multiple financial statements.

How Does [Fill in the Blank] Impact the Three Financial Statements?

We mentioned that certain frequently asked technical interview questions relate directly to the integration of the three financial statements. These questions are designed to test a prospective banker's true understanding of basic accounting principles. The most common variation of this question is: "How would $10 of additional depreciation expense affect the three financial statements?"

To answer this type of question, take the three financial statements one at a time. Always start with the income statement, for it is the shortest and easiest to understand of the three statements. A very common mistake is to forget to tax-affect any change in revenue or costs. Often you will be told to assume a certain tax rate, typically 35 percent or 40 percent. If you are not told what tax rate to use, then make sure to ask your interviewer. Carefully work your way down from revenues and expenses to interest and taxes and ultimately net income.

Remember that the last line of the income statement is always net income, which is also the first line of the cash flow statement. For this reason, always analyze the cash flow statement second. Many students make the mistake of jumping to the balance sheet second, which is much harder if you have not already figured out what happens to cash. If applicable, adjust net income for D&A, changes in working capital, and/or any other relevant changes to sources and uses of cash. The goal is to work your way down the cash flow statement in order to calculate the net change in cash.

Once you think you have correctly calculated the net change in cash, then move onto the balance sheet. The first line of the balance sheet is cash, which you should have just calculated from the cash flow statement. Finally, make any other adjustments that you need to make to applicable assets and liabilities. If there was a change to net income, remember to account for that in retained earnings.

If your balance sheet balances (i.e., Assets = Liabilities + Shareholders' Equity), then chances are you've gotten the right answer. If your balance sheet does not balance, then you have made one or more mistakes somewhere along the way. Start over and try to figure out where you went wrong. The balance sheet serves as the "check" to your answer, which is also always why you should tackle it last.

Exhibit 2.5 shows a simplified income statement, cash flow statement, and balance sheet, with arrows indicating the key relationships among the three statements.

While these types of questions are often challenging and are designed to test your understanding of accounting principles (and to purposely stress you a bit), they are not meant to test your ability to do complex math. Unless you are allowed to use a calculator (or at least a pen and paper), you can usually assume that the math is designed to be relatively simple. If you find yourself with difficult calculations, you've probably made a mistake.

Examples

Following are a number of examples of this sort of interview question. Assume that all information is given in the question ("everything else is equal"). If you are comfortable with the following examples, then you truly

EXHIBIT 2.5 Key Relationships among Simplified Income Statement, Cash Flow Statement, and Balance Sheet

Income Statement	Cash Flow Statement	Balance Sheet
Revenue	*Cash from Operations*	Assets
Less: COGS	Net income	Cash
Gross profit	D&A	Other current assets
Less: SG&A	Change in Operating Assets and Liabilities	PP&E and other long-term assets
Operating income	Total cash from operations	Total Assets
Less: Net interest expense		
EBT	*Cash from Investing*	Liabilities
Less: Taxes	Capex	Current liabilities
Net income	Sale of assets	Debt and other long-term liabilties
	Total cash from investing	Total Liabilities
	Cash from Financing	Shareholders' Equity
	Change in debt	Retained earnings
	Change in equity	Other equity
	Total cash from financing	Total Shareholders' Equity
	Total change in cash	Check (Equals Assets – Liabilities – Shareholders' Equity)

have a good understanding of accounting principles and you are well on your to becoming a successful investment banker!

For each example, assume a tax rate of 40 percent.

Example 1 Assume that a company records an additional $100 of revenue this period due to an increase in pricing (assume no additional costs). How would this additional revenue affect the three financial statements that follow?

Income Statement		Cash Flow Statement		Balance Sheet	
		Cash from Operations			
Revenue	$100			Assets	
Less: COGS	0	Net income	$60	Cash	$60
Gross profit	100	D&A	0	Other current assets	0
Less: SG&A	0	Change in Operating Assets and Liabilities	0	PP&E and other long-term assets	0
Operating income	100	Total Cash from Operations	60		
Less: Net interest expense	0	*Cash from Investing*		Total Assets	60
EBT	100	Capex	0	Liabilities	
Less: Taxes	(40)	Sale of assets	0	Current liabilities	0
Net income	60	Total Cash from Investing	0	Debt and other long-term liabilties	0
				Total liabilities	0
		Cash from Financing		Shareholders' Equity	
		Change in debt	0	Retained earnings	60
		Change in equity	0	Other equity	0
		Total Cash from Financing	0	Total Shareholders' Equity	60
		Total change in cash	60	Check (Assets – Liabilities – Shareholders' Equity)	0

Explanation: Start with the income statement, where revenue increases by $100. Since there is no change to COGS or SG&A or interest expense, pre-tax also increases by $100. At a 40 percent tax rate, taxes are $40, so net income increases by $60. In the cash flow statement, cash from operations increases by $60 due to the increase in net income. There are no other changes to the cash flow statement. On the balance sheet, cash is increased by the same $60, so assets also increase $60. Shareholders' equity also increases by $60 due to the additional net income affecting retained earnings. The left side of the balance sheet (A) increases by $60 as does the right side (L + SE), and thus the balance sheet is balanced.

Example 2 Assume the same increase in revenue of $100 (again, assume no cost increases) but now assume that the company has not yet been paid for the sale and instead has generated a receivable.

Income Statement		Cash Flow Statement		Balance Sheet	
Revenue	$100	*Cash from Operations*		Assets	
Less: COGS	0	Net income	$60	Cash	($40)
Gross profit	100	D&A	0	Other current assets	100
Less: SG&A	0	Change in Operating Assets and Liabilities	(100)	PP&E and other long-term assets	0
Operating income	100	Total Cash from Operations	(40)		
Less: Net interest expense	0	*Cash from Investing*		Total Assets	60
EBT	100	Capex	0	Liabilities	
Less: Taxes	(40)	Sale of assets	0	Current liabilities	0
Net income	60	Total Cash from Investing	0	Debt and other long-term liabilties	0
				Total liabilities	0
		Cash from Financing		Shareholders' Equity	
		Change in debt	0	Retained earnings	60
		Change in equity	0	Other equity	0
		Total Cash from Financing	0	Total Shareholders' Equity	60
		Total change in cash	(40)	Check (Assets – Liabilities – Shareholders' Equity)	0

Explanation: As with Example 1, revenue increases by $100 and net income increases by $60, so the income statement is exactly the same. In the cash flow statement, cash from operations increases by $60 due to the increase in net income but now also decreases by $100 due to the increase in accounts receivable. (Remember that increasing an asset is a use of cash.) There are no other changes to the cash flow statement, so the net effect is a decrease in cash of $40. In the balance sheet, cash decreases $40 but accounts receivable increases $100, so total assets increases by $60. The only change to the right side of the balance sheet is the increase in retained earnings (SE) of $60, and so the balance sheet is balanced.

Example 3 Assume in increase in $100 of SG&A expense.

Income Statement		**Cash Flow Statement**		**Balance Sheet**	
Revenue	$0	*Cash from Operations*		Assets	
Less: COGS	0	Net income	($60)	Cash	($60)
Gross profit	0	D&A	0	Other current assets	0
Less: SG&A	(100)	Change in Operating Assets and Liabilities	0	PP&E and other long-term assets	0
Operating income	(100)	Total Cash from Operations	(60)		
Less: Net interest expense	0	*Cash from Investing*		Total Assets	(60)
EBT	(100)	Capex	0	Liabilities	
Less: Taxes	40	Sale of assets	0	Current liabilities	0
Net income	(60)	Total Cash from Investing	0	Debt and other long-term liabilties	0
				Total liabilities	0
		Cash from Financing		Shareholders' Equity	
		Change in debt	0	Retained earnings	(60)
		Change in equity	0	Other equity	0
		Total Cash from Financing	0	Total Shareholders' Equity	(60)
		Total change in cash	(60)	Check (Assets – Liabilities – Shareholders' Equity)	0

Explanation: This example is very similar to Example 1 except instead of an increase in revenues, we've got an increase in costs. Operating income decreases by $100 due to the additional SG&A expense. Taxes decrease by $40 and therefore net income decreases by $60. In the cash flow statement, the only change is a decrease in cash due of $60 stemming from net income. In the balance sheet, cash is decreased by $40 (A) as is retained earnings (SE), so we are balanced.

Example 4 Just like Example 3, assume an increase of $100 of SG&A expense, but now assume that the company hasn't paid the bill yet for this expense (i.e., there will be a payable created).

Income Statement		Cash Flow Statement		Balance Sheet	
Revenue	$0	*Cash from Operations*		Assets	
Less: COGS	0	Net income	($60)	Cash	$40
Gross profit	0	D&A	0	Other current assets	0
Less: SG&A	(100)	Change in Operating Assets and Liabilities	100	PP&E and other long-term assets	0
Operating income	(100)	Total Cash from Operations	40		
Less: Net interest expense	0	*Cash from Investing*		Total Assets	40
EBT	(100)	Capex	0	Liabilities	
Less: Taxes	40	Sale of assets	0	Current liabilities	100
Net income	(60)	Total Cash from Investing	0	Debt and other long-term liabilties	0
				Total liabilities	100
		Cash from Financing		Shareholders' Equity	
		Change in debt	0	Retained earnings	(60)
		Change in equity	0	Other equity	0
		Total Cash from Financing	0	Total Shareholders' Equity	(60)
		Total change in cash	40	Check (Assets – Liabilities – Shareholders' Equity)	0

Explanation: As with Example 3, net income decreases by $60. However, in the cash flow statement, cash flow also increases, due to the $100 increase in accounts payable. (Remember that increasing a liability is a source of cash). The net effect is a $40 increase in cash. On the left side of the balance sheet, cash (A) is increased by $40. On the right side, accounts payable increases by $100 (L) and retained earnings (SE) decreases by $60, for a net increase of $40.

Example 5 Assume an increase of $100 of depreciation expense. Note that this example is identical (except for the different amount) to the most commonly asked variation of this question ("Assume $10 of depreciation expense.").

Income Statement		Cash Flow Statement		Balance Sheet	
Revenue	$0	*Cash from Operations*		Assets	
Less: COGS	0	Net income	($60)	Cash	$40
Gross profit	0	D&A	100	Other current assets	0
Less: SG&A	(100)	Change in Operating Assets and Liabilities	0	PP&E and other long-term assets	(100)
Operating income	(100)	Total Cash from Operations	40		
Less: Net interest expense	0	*Cash from Investing*		Total Assets	(60)
EBT	(100)	Capex	0	Liabilities	
Less: Taxes	40	Sale of assets	0	Current liabilities	0
Net income	(60)	Total Cash from Investing	0	Debt and other long-term liabilties	0
				Total liabilities	0
		Cash from Financing		Shareholders' Equity	
		Change in debt	0	Retained earnings	(60)
		Change in equity	0	Other equity	0
		Total Cash from Financing	0	Total Shareholders' Equity	(60)
		Total change in cash	40	Check (Assets – Liabilities – Shareholders' Equity)	0

Explanation: There is no change to revenue, but expense is up $100. (We've put categorized the depreciation expense within SG&A, but it could have also been in COGS, as it makes no difference here). After-tax net income decreases by $60. On the cash flow statement, net income decreases by $60, but D&A increases by $100, so the net effect on cash is an increase of $40. On the balance sheet, cash increases by $40 but PP&E decreases by $100 (due to the depreciation expense), so assets decrease by a total of $60. On the right side of the balance sheet, the only change is retained earnings decreasing by $60, and so we are balanced.

When asked this question in an interview, you may also get the follow-up question: "If depreciation is a non-cash expense, explain how this transaction caused cash to increase $40." The answer is that because of the depreciation expense, the company had to pay the government $40 less in taxes, so it increased its cash position by $40 from what it would have been without the depreciation expense.

Example 6 Assume $100 increase in revenue (the company has received payment) due to additional units sold from inventory. Assume a gross margin of 40 percent.

Income Statement		Cash Flow Statement		Balance Sheet	
Revenue	$100	*Cash from Operations*		Assets	
Less: COGS	(60)	Net income	$24	Cash	$84
Gross profit	40	D&A	0	Other current assets	(60)
Less: SG&A	0	Change in Operating Assets and Liabilities	60	PP&E and other long-term assets	0
Operating income	40	Total Cash from Operations	84		
Less: Net interest expense	0	*Cash from Investing*		Total Assets	24
EBT	40	Capex	0	Liabilities	
Less: Taxes	(16)	Sale of assets	0	Current liabilities	0
Net income	24	Total Cash from Investing	0	Debt and other long-term liabilties	0
				Total liabilities	0
		Cash from Financing		Shareholders' Equity	
		Change in debt	0	Retained earnings	24
		Change in equity	0	Other equity	0
		Total Cash from Financing	0	Total Shareholders' Equity	24
		Total change in cash	84	Check (Assets – Liabilities – Shareholders' Equity)	0

Explanation: This one is a little tricky, especially because of the way in which it is worded. First, we must recognize that along with $100 in new revenues, there will also be $60 in new COGS, because we are told that the company's gross margin is 40 percent. So the income statement will show an increase in $40 of operating income, and with $16 of taxes at 40 percent, net income will increase by $24. On the cash flow statement, net income increases by $24 but inventory decreases by $60. Since a decrease in an asset such as inventory is a source of cash, the net effect on cash is an $84 increase. On the balance sheet, cash (A) increases by $84 and inventory decreases by $60, so the total impact on assets is an increase of $24. The balance sheet is balanced due to the increase in retained earnings (SE) of $24.

Example 7 Assume a company purchase $100 worth of equipment and finances this purchase by issuing $100 of debt. (Assume no interest and no depreciation.)

Income Statement		Cash Flow Statement		Balance Sheet	
Revenue	$0	*Cash from Operations*		Assets	
Less: COGS	0	Net income	$0	Cash	$0
Gross profit	0	D&A	0	Other current assets	0
Less: SG&A	0	Change in Operating Assets and Liabilities	0	PP&E and other long-term assets	100
Operating income	0	Total Cash from Operations	0		
Less: Net interest expense	0	*Cash from Investing*		Total Assets	100
EBT	0	Capex	(100)	Liabilities	
Less: Taxes	0	Sale of assets	0	Current liabilities	0
Net income	0	Total Cash from Investing	(100)	Debt and other long-term liabilties	100
				Total liabilities	100
		Cash from Financing		Shareholders' Equity	
		Change in debt	100	Retained earnings	0
		Change in equity	0	Other equity	0
		Total Cash from Financing	100	Total Shareholders' Equity	0
		Total change in cash	0	Check (Assets – Liabilities – Shareholders' Equity)	0

Explanation: In this example, there is no impact to the income statement. On the cash flow statement, cash from investing shows a use of cash of $100 due to the purchase of equipment, but cash from financing shows an increase of $100 due to the offsetting issuance of debt. Thus, there is no change to cash. On the balance sheet, PP&E (A) increases by $100 and debt (L) increases by $100, so there is a balance.

Example 8 As with Example 7, assume $100 purchase of equipment and $100 debt issuance. Now, also assume that the company must pay interest expense at a 5 percent annual interest rate, and assume that the company will depreciate the asset using a straight line method and assume a useful life for the asset of five years.

Income Statement		Cash Flow Statement		Balance Sheet	
Revenue	$0	*Cash from Operations*		Assets	
Less: COGS	0	Net income	($15)	Cash	$5
Gross profit	0	D&A	20	Other current assets	0
Less: SG&A	(20)	Change in Operating Assets and Liabilities	0	PP&E and other long-term assets	80
Operating income	(20)	Total Cash from Operations	5		
Less: Net interest expense	(5)	*Cash from Investing*		Total Assets	85
EBT	(25)	Capex	(100)	Liabilities	
Less: Taxes	10	Sale of assets	0	Current liabilities	0
Net income	(15)	Total Cash from Investing	(100)	Debt and other long-term liabilties	100
				Total liabilities	100
		Cash from Financing		Shareholders' Equity	
		Change in debt	100	Retained earnings	(15)
		Change in equity	0	Other equity	0
		Total Cash from Financing	100	Total Shareholders' Equity	(15)
		Total change in cash	5	Check (Assets – Liabilities – Shareholders' Equity)	0

Explanation: There are a lot of things going on in this example, so take it slowly. On the income statement, depreciation expense increases by $20 ($100 divided by 5 years) (shown in the SG&A line), and interest expense increases by $5 ($100 of debt multiplied by a 5 percent interest rate). EBT decreases by $25 at a 40 percent tax rate, and net income decreases by $15. On the cash flow statement, net income decreases by $15, D&A increases by $20, so cash from operations increases by $5. As with Example 7, cash from investing (–$100) exactly offsets cash from financing (+$100), so the net effect on cash is an increase of $5. On the right side of the balance sheet, cash is increased by $5. Gross PP&E is increased by $100 but then reduced by $20 due to the depreciation expense, so net PP&E increases by $80. Total assets increases by $85. On the right side of the balance sheet, debt increases by $100 and retained earnings decreases by the amount of net income ($15), so liabilities plus shareholders' equity increases by $85 and is balanced with assets.

END-OF-CHAPTER QUESTIONS

1. What is an income statement and why is it important?
2. What is a balance sheet and why is it important?
3. What is a cash flow statement and why is it important?
4. What are the differences between accrual accounting and cash-based accounting?
5. What are the advantages of accrual accounting versus cash-based accounting?
6. How is EBITDA calculated?
7. Why is EBITDA a frequently used metric in corporate finance?
8. Why does EBITDA not equal operating cash flow?
9. In a period of inflation (rising prices), which method of inventory (LIFO or FIFO) would likely result in a higher level of inventories on the balance sheet?
10. What is the difference between an operating lease and a capital lease?
11. What is a deferred tax asset or liability?
12. Give an example of a transaction that would result in a deferred tax asset or liability.
13. Why do we depreciate fixed assets?
14. What are intangible assets?
15. What is goodwill?
16. Explain how the three financial statements are integrated.
17. If a company incurs $10 (pretax) of depreciation expense, how does that affect the three financial statements?

Answers can be found at www.wiley.com/go/gutmann (password: investment).

CHAPTER 3

Finance Overview

It is for good reason that investment bankers are classified as corporate finance professionals. Corporate finance lies at the heart of just about everything that a banker does. And finance, of course, lies at the heart of corporate finance. Just as you cannot be an investment banker without possessing basic accounting knowledge, you also need to have an understanding of the fundamental principles of finance. In order to have a true grasp of these principles, you also need to understand the role of the financial system.

While it is imperative for bankers to have a broad understanding of the finance world and financial securities, the job of an investment banker is mostly to work with corporations. To be an effective adviser, you need to understand how and why companies make the kind of decisions and execute the kinds of transactions for which they employ investment bankers. Plainly said, you cannot value a company, pitch an acquisition, or execute an IPO without understanding basic corporate finance principles.

More than any other, this chapter is a mix of both theory and practice. While much of the work of a junior banker requires plugging formulas into Microsoft Excel, you really should have an understanding of the theory behind what you are doing. Plus, as is the case with just about all of the content of this book, many of the concepts we will discuss in this chapter frequently become interview questions.

In this chapter, we will start with an explanation of the basic principles of finance: time value of money, risk and reward, and discount rate. We will then move onto corporate finance, where we will discuss how companies decide what to invest in and how to finance the investment. Finally we will wrap up with a discussion of how to value financial instruments including bonds, stocks, and options.

THE FINANCIAL SYSTEM

The financial system plays a vital role in the global economy. Without a financial system, the economy cannot function, as we nearly witnessed in 2008. The purpose of the financial system is to efficiently and optimally allocate savings to investments. In other words, to distribute money to those who need money. It is that allocation of savings to investment that is what the study of finance is all about. But before we can talk about the general principles for how money gets allocated through the financial system, let us first introduce the various types of entities involved.

Essentially we can divide the financial world into three groups: those who have extra money to invest (savers), those who need money for some purpose (borrowers), and the financial institutions that bring them together.

Savers

If you've ever taken an introductory macroeconomics class, you may remember that economists often divide the economy into three groups: individuals, companies, and governments. By far, individuals as a group make up the majority of savings, either directly or indirectly, through retirement accounts and insurance policies. Companies tend not to be savers, as they generally prefer to spend excess capital on growth or to distribute excess capital to individuals (by dividends or share buybacks). In today's world, governments nearly always run deficits and are almost never net savers.

Individuals earn money through wages and, to a lesser extent, from investment income and government transfer payments. Let's take me, for example. With the vast sums I will earn from the royalties for sales of this book, I can do two things:[1] I can spend it (what economists call consumption) or I can save it. If I decide to save the money, then I also have two choices: I can keep the cash under my mattress, or I can invest it. Either way, my savings represents money that I can spend later in life, or possibly pass on to my heirs.

Let's assume that I want to invest it, so perhaps I deposit the money into a bank account. Or maybe I use it to buy a government bond. Or if I am feeling extra lucky, I put the money into the stock market. Regardless of how I invest my money, I do have two expectations. The first is that someday I will be able to get my money back. The second is, that over time, I will earn some additional funds (called a return) on the money that I have invested.

[1]A joke, of course. Few people become rich writing finance books.

Borrowers

Sometimes individuals want to make large purchases that require them to spend more money than they earn or more money than they have saved. For example, let's suppose I want to buy a house or a new car, or pay my child's college tuition. In these instances, I will need to borrow money from some source, likely a bank or similar type of institution. Over time, I (hopefully) will earn enough money so that I can pay back what I have borrowed.

Companies also frequently need access to additional funding. Companies sometimes require money to finance their working capital, to build new factories, to enter new markets, or to make acquisitions. Unlike individuals, companies have a vast number of different methods by which they can raise capital. They can borrow from banks and specialty finance companies. They can also borrow through the credit markets by issuing various types of credit instruments. Or they may be able to raise money by issuing stock.

Governments spend money on things like defense and education and healthcare. Governments at the local, state, and federal level tend to require more money than they take in from taxation and other revenue sources. In turn, they typically borrow money through the credit markets by issuing various types of bonds.

The Financial Institutions

We have already hinted at some of the ways in which money flows from savers to borrowers. Next we will discuss the various financial institutions that exist to make this process both possible and efficient. Before we do that, let us consider a world without these financial institutions.

Suppose again that I earn some money for which I have no good use today. In a world without banks and without financial markets, I would have only two choices: either stuff it in the mattress or find someone who needs money. Wanting to put my money to work, I go around and ask all my neighbors if they want to borrow my money. After a time-consuming search, I find that one neighbor does indeed need money to purchase a new car. Of course, before I am comfortable lending this neighbor my money, I need to somehow decide if he or she is creditworthy. This is another time-consuming process and one with which I likely have limited experience and expertise.

Now, let's assume that I do judge my neighbor to be creditworthy, so I lend the money. What would happen if, a year down the road, a tree falls on the new car? Or what would happen if my neighbor gets sick and is unable to work and earn money? Was I wise to lend all my money to one borrower, even if he or she seemed highly trustworthy?

Or consider an alternative scenario. Assume my neighbor is healthy, but I am the one who gets sick and I require money for medical expenses. Likely, I have no way of getting my money back from my neighbor for years.

We have already said that financial institutions exist to efficiently match up savers and borrowers. Now we can be more explicit about the three major services that the financial system provides:

1. Information gathering and distribution.
2. Risk sharing.
3. Liquidity.

The first role of financial institutions is one of gathering and disseminating information about both borrowers and savers. For example, in a properly working system, institutions such as banks are experts at performing due diligence on the creditworthiness of prospective borrowers. Moreover, for public markets, information about both the creditworthiness of borrowers and the risk tolerance of investors is both gathered and distributed through the pricing of securities.

The second key service provided by financial institutions is to share and distribute risk. The financial system allows savers to easily diversify their investments. Savers can put money to work using many types of investment products in order to spread one's risk over different assets, diverse geographic areas, and varying time frames.

The financial system also serves the economy by providing liquidity to investors. Liquidity refers to the ease by which investors can turn their assets into cash. Of course, certain financial assets can be converted into cash much quicker than others. Public financial markets, such as the stock market, are especially good at providing investors with liquidity.

Now that we have discussed the importance of financial institutions as a whole, let us turn our attention to the main types of financial institutions that help keep our economy running. Keep in mind that some of these institutions represent actual companies, while others reflect the more nebulous entities that we call pubic markets.

Banks and Specialty Finance Companies A number of types of financial institutions act directly as intermediaries between savers and borrowers by taking deposits from customers and making loans with those funds. These include retail and commercial banks, savings institutions such as savings and loan associations, and credit unions. For our purposes, we will keeps things simple and refer to them all as banks.

The basic business of a bank is to borrow money from savers at lower interests and lend money to borrowers at higher interests. The difference between the interest rates is called the spread and represents profit to the bank. Banks offer the easiest way for individuals to save and invest money through such products as checking accounts, savings accounts, and certificate of deposits (CDs). Banks then use this borrowed money to make loans to individuals for such things as houses, home improvements, and cars; for credit cards; and to businesses. Most large banks also offer many other services to both individuals (in the case of retail banks) and businesses (in the case of commercial banks).

Specialty finance companies provide asset-based loans to businesses, as well as things like mortgages, car loans, and credit cards to individuals. Historically, they did not take deposits directly like banks but financed their operations through the issuance of short-term securities such as commercial paper. However, this has changed since the financial crises of 2008, as many such companies have opted to become classified (and regulated) as banks.

Financial Markets A second type of entity that helps match savers with borrowers is the financial markets. The financial markets exist to allow companies and governments to raise money, and for the trading of various types of financial instruments amongst investors. Examples of some of the most important financial markets include:

- Stock markets.
- Bond markets.
- Money markets (for the trading of short-term debt securities).
- Foreign exchange markets.
- Commodity markets.
- Futures markets.
- Options markets.

As an investment banker, the most important of these markets are the stock and bond markets, and we will talk more about stocks and especially bonds later in this chapter. However, keep in mind that most of the trading that occurs on the stock and bond markets takes place on what are known as secondary markets, rather than primary markets.

Primary markets refer to when newly issued securities are sold to investors by the companies or governments that are raising funding. Secondary markets refer to trading of existing shares that occur between investors. While secondary trading does not provide any new capital to entities in need of funds, it does significantly help provide those valuable services to the financial system that we mentioned earlier (namely information exchange, risk sharing, and especially liquidity).

Insurance Companies and Pension Funds Insurance companies and pension funds represent two very important players in the financial system because of the enormous pools of money they have to invest. Insurance companies and pension funds, along with the endowments of universities and other nonprofit organizations, are often grouped together under the umbrella term "institutional investors." As large a role that they play in the financial system overall, they are even a larger player in alternative investment strategies such as hedge funds, private equity, and venture capital.

Insurance companies are a type of financial institution that writes contracts (insurance policies) to policyholders. These policies promise to pay out an amount of money in the future if a certain event or loss occurs. In return for the insurance policy and for the financial protection that the policy provides, a policyholder pays money (a premium) to the insurance company. Insurance companies invest these premiums in many different types of financial securities with the hope of not only having enough to cover any future payouts (claims) owed to the insured policyholder but also to attempt to earn an investing profit.

Pension funds are pools of money that are run on behalf of companies or governments for the purpose of providing income to their employees when they retire. Pension funds receive funds annually from employers and sometimes also the employees and then invest that money. There are two types of pension funds: defined contribution plans and defined benefit plans.

Defined contribution plans fix the amount of money contributed each year for each employee. The value an employee receives in retirement depends on the investment returns of the funds that have been contributed. On the other hand, defined benefit plans promise to pay retirees a specified amount of money annually once they retire. It is up to the company to ensure that the pension is fully funded and that its investment returns are sufficient to pay out its future obligations.

Most private companies have switched away from offering new employees defined benefit plans in recent years. However, these types of pensions do represent the vast majority of retirement plans for unionized and government workers. Given that many defined benefit plans have been underfunded and because investment returns have been much lower than anticipated, these plans represent an enormous liability for most governments and many large companies.

Asset Managers Asset managers play a significant role in the financial system by pooling money from many individual and/or institutional investors and investing that money in any number of financial instruments. Investors often employ asset managers to make investments on their behalf because of the asset manager's expertise and because of the economies of scale that asset managers provide. Without the benefits of using an asset manager, many investors would not want to or even be able to invest in certain asset classes, because they do have enough money to have access to those markets or do not have enough money to sufficiently diversify within or between asset classes.

Perhaps the most common type of asset management firms is those that offer their clients the ability to invest in mutual funds. Mutual funds are pools of money that are invested in different types of publicly traded securities. Examples include stock funds, bond funds, and money market funds. Some mutual funds invest in multiple asset classes in an attempt to create well-balanced and diversified portfolios. Mutual funds typically charge annual fees based on the amount of money invested, and some mutual funds also charge fees to purchase and/or sell the funds.

Another subset of asset management is often referred to as alternative investments. We mentioned these previously when we spoke of insurance companies and pension funds. There are a number of types of alternative investment funds, including hedge funds, which invest in all sorts of securities, often employing leverage to amplify returns. Other examples include private equity firms, which make control investments in mature companies, and venture capital firms, which make control investments in early-stage and growth companies. Other types of alternative asset managers specialize in investing in such financial assets as real estate, infrastructure, and natural resources. Most of these firms charge annual fees based on the amount of assets an investor has invested under firm management plus a percentage of the investment profits.

Investment Banks In Chapter 1, we discussed many of the different functions of large investment banks. However, in terms of the financial system, investment banks play three important roles. First, and probably most importantly, investment banks act as direct intermediaries between savers and borrowers by advising companies and governments that require capital, and helping them raise funds by underwriting new securities, such as stocks and bonds. Investment banks, through their sales and trading divisions, also act as intermediaries between investors trading various securities on the secondary markets. Finally, many of the large investment banks have asset management divisions that advise and manage money for individual and institutional investors.

PRINCIPLES OF FINANCE

Now that we have introduced the financial system, let's talk about the key finance principles that underlie the financial decisions made by both savers and borrowers. Without a doubt, the most important concepts in all of finance are time value of money, the relationship between risk and reward, and the discount rate. Based upon an understanding of these concepts, we will learn some key formulas that are useful for valuing and analyzing all sorts of financial securities and investments.

Time Value of Money

Most everyone is familiar with the saying that money today is worth more than money tomorrow, and money tomorrow is worth more than money next week or next year. At first glance it probably seems obvious and intuitive. But why is it really true?

The basic principle we refer to as "time value of money" has three primary explanations. The first relates to the issue of certainty. Let's presume I owe you $100. If I give it to you today, then you have it and can use it to buy something. You may not want to spend it, but at least you have the option to, if you so desire.

Now suppose that I am not going to give you the $100 until next year. What if I lose my job and I cannot pay you? What if I'm not alive in a year to pay you? What if I just decide I don't feel like paying you? What if the world ends? In any of those cases you never had the chance to use the money. These may all be unlikely scenarios, but you cannot rule any of them out completely, either.

The longer you go without having the money, the more things that can go wrong and the more uncertainty you have about receiving it. That is, the probability of actually receiving the $100 goes down. Hence, the value you place on receiving $100 a year from now should decline. And it should decline even more if you expect to receive the money in two years instead of one. Conversely, the sooner you receive the money, the less uncertainty there is and the higher the value you should place on the to-be-paid $100.

The second explanation for money being worth more today than tomorrow is inflation. Inflation makes money worth less over time, as measured by the goods and services that can be bought with it. To use the technical term, money's purchasing power declines over time in an inflationary environment. Hence, the sooner that I receive money and have the option to spend it, the more valuable it is. The longer I have to wait, the less it will buy, and the less valuable it is.

Of course, in a deflationary environment, the exact opposite is true. However, for generations now, the governments and central banks of the world, and the economists who help set policy, have preferred to have perpetual moderate inflation. It is interesting to note that this was not always the case. Throughout most of recorded history, the more natural state of things was deflation at least in times of peace. Only in wartimes and following discoveries of new sources of precious metals was inflation the norm. Whether current inflationary policies are for better or worse is certainly beyond the scope of our discussion and is of little consequence to aspiring investment bankers.[2]

The third rationale for time value of money is probably the most important. Let's now suppose that you are generous enough to lend me $100 today and are willing to accept that same $100 back next year. Since we are assuming that you do not believe in the time value of money, it is perfectly reasonable for you to be indifferent to having $100 today or $100 next year.

You have just given me an incredibly easy way to make money. I will take your $100 and invest it for one year in some ultra-safe place such as an insured savings account or government bond (i.e. 1-year Treasury bill). Since I do believe in the time value of money, I, unlike you, will demand some payment (interest) for allowing a bank or government to use the money. A year from you I will get the $100 back and return it to you, but I will keep the interest. Thanks a lot!

Of course, such a situation should not exist. I should not be able to get something (interest) for nothing (taking no risk and doing no work). This third explanation for time value of money is what academics call the equivalence principle. An amount of money today plus the return that I would receive for investing that money for a specified time period must be exactly equivalent to its value at that future time period.

Do not worry if this is confusing. We will see this concept in action when we learn how to calculate present and future values shortly.

Risk and Reward

So far we have explained why money today is worth more than money tomorrow. But what we haven't yet discussed is how much more is it worth. A little more? A lot more? The answer depends on several factors that are not surprisingly related to the three rationales we gave for explaining time value of money, the most important of which is risk and reward.

Suppose again that you lend me $100. I promise to pay you back in one year's time. Given you now believe in time value of money, you understand that $100 today is worth a little bit less to you next year. Therefore you require me to pay some additional money to make up for the loss of value. In a loan, we call this additional payment interest. We can also think of interest payments as the fee that I pay you for the ability to use your money.

---

[2]They are for worse. Sorry, I couldn't help myself.

How much interest you will charge will depend, most importantly, on how likely you are to get your money back. How trustworthy am I? How creditworthy am I? The more certain you are that you will receive it, the higher the value you will place on it today or, equivalently, the less additional compensation (i.e., interest) you will require me to pay you. The more risky a borrower that I am, the less value you will place on the money today and the more interest you will require. In other words, the riskier the investment, the higher the reward that you require.

This basic concept of risk and reward applies not just to loans but to any type of investment, including investing in a publicly traded stock or a privately held company. Instead of interest being our sole reward, we use the term return. So, the riskier the investment, the more return that I require on that investment. The less risky the investment, the lower return that I require.

Discount Rate and the Opportunity Cost of Capital

Given that uncertainty and risk increase over time, it should not be surprising to learn that the longer the time period for which I invest my money, the higher total return I require. However, to make it easier to analyze and compare investments with different time horizons, we usually measure the investment return required for discrete time periods, such as a year. This figure is called the discount rate. For a simple loan, the annual discount rate is equal to the annual interest rate.

A synonym for the discount rate is an investor's opportunity cost of capital. The opportunity cost of capital reflects the return that an investor forgoes on other investments of similar risk. Given a certain level of risk, investors will always flock to the investments that promise that highest returns. Equivalently, given a certain level of return, investors will prefer the investments with the lowest risk. The market helps ensure that investments with the same set of risks have the same discount rate or opportunity cost.

Another name for the discount rate is the cost of capital. By definition, the return required by investors for putting money into a project or company must equal the cost of money to the project or company. In Chapter 5, we will discuss how investment bankers estimate the cost of capital for an entire company. However, in this section let us discuss how investors typically estimate a discount rate for a particular investment.

Estimating the Discount Rate The discount rate for a particular security or investment is implicitly made up of three components, the real risk-free interest rate, the expected inflation rate and the investment specific risk premium.

$$\text{Discount Rate} = \text{Real Risk-Free Rate} + \text{Expected Inflation Rate} + \text{Risk Premium}$$

Real Risk-Free Rate The real risk-free interest rate represents the return that investors would require on an investment with no risk and in a world without inflation. In theory, this rate should reflect the supply of savings and the demand for investments. In reality, this rate is heavily influenced by the central banks of the world.

We often talk about government securities such as U.S. treasury bills or longer term U.S. treasury bonds representing risk-free instruments. In fact, in many types of analysis that investment bankers perform, we often use the implied interest rates in such government securities as proxies for a risk-free rate. It is important to always remember that even the safest of government securities are not truly risk-free. There is always some risk of default.

Expected Inflation Rate The second component of the discount rate is the expected inflation rate. As we mentioned when we were discussing the various rationales for the time value of money, inflation lowers purchasing power. Investors expect to be compensated for that loss of true value. Since nobody knows what inflation is going to be in the future, discount rates must take into account the market's expected inflation rate.

We said that we frequently use a government debt instrument as a proxy for the risk-free rate. For nearly all such securities, observed rates (the rate we can easily look up) reflect what are known as nominal rates. They include inflationary expectations embedded in them. The real rates, except for special inflation-indexed securities, such as Treasury Inflation-Protected Securities (TIPS), can only be interpolated and approximated.

Risk Premium The risk premium represents the additional risk of a project or investment above and beyond the nominal risk-free rate. Risk premiums are often talked about and quoted as a certain spread over the risk-free rate. For example, safer investments might have a risk premium of only a few percentage points over the risk-free rate, while riskier investments might have a spread of 10 percentage points or more.

We will see an example of how we calculate the risk premium for stocks using something called the Capital Asset Pricing Model (CAPM) formula in Chapter 5, and also later in this chapter when we talk about bonds and credit ratings.

Present and Future Value of Cash Flows

Now that we have covered the basic concepts of time value of money, risk and reward, and discount rate, we can discuss how to apply them. Specifically, we will learn a few of the most important and most utilized formulas used for calculating both the present and future value of cash flows. In turn, these formulas can be used for valuing and analyzing all sorts of financial securities and investments.

Present Value The first formula that we will learn tells us how to calculate the value today of money that we will receive at some specified time period in the future, and based on a specified discount rate.

This basic present value formula has many applications throughout finance. Later in this chapter we will learn how companies use it to help them decide whether or not to make certain investments. We will also use it later in the chapter when we learn how to value bonds, and in Chapter 5 when we cover the discounted cash flow (DCF) method of valuation.

To calculate present value, we take the future cash flow in time period t and divide it by 1 plus the discount rate raised to the power of t.

$$\text{Present Value (PV)} = \frac{CF_t}{(1+r)^t}$$

r = discount rate

t = time until maturity

For example, suppose that you own an investment that pays you exactly \$100 one year from now. Further assume that your opportunity cost (the discount rate) is 10 percent. How much is this investment worth to you today? In other words, what is its present value?

$$\text{Present Value (PV)} = \frac{\$100}{(1+0.1)^1} = \$90.9$$

Given these assumptions and using the present value formula, we see that the value of this investment is \$90.9.

Present Value of a Perpetuity The basic present value formula calculates the value today of a cash flow paid at a single point of time in the future. There are two variations to this formula that often come in handy. The first is what is known as the present value of a perpetuity.

To calculate the present value of a perpetuity, we simply divide the cash flow that we will receive each period by the discount rate, as follows:

$$\text{Present Value (PV)} = \frac{CF}{r}$$

As an example, suppose you own an investment that promises to give you $100 each year forever. Assuming a 10 percent discount rate, what is the present value of that investment?

$$\text{Present Value (PV)} = \frac{\$100}{0.1} = \$1{,}000$$

At a 10 percent discount rate, we see that the value of receiving $100 each year forever is $1,000.

Present Value of a Perpetuity with Growth The previous formula, that of the present value of a perpetuity, assumes that we receive a fixed amount of money every year forever. Let's consider what happens if we own an investment that pays us cash flow each year that grows at a constant annual rate. (We will see this concept again in Chapter 5 when we cover estimating the terminal value when performing a DCF analysis.)

To calculate the present value of a perpetuity with growth, we divide the cash flow that we will receive in the first period by the discount rate less the growth rate. Note that in order for this formula to gives us a sensible answer, the growth rate must be less than the discount rate.

$$\text{Present Value (PV)} = \frac{CF_1}{r - g}$$

For an example, consider that you have a security that promises to pay you $100 in the first year but grows 5 percent each year thereafter. If we assume the appropriate discount rate is 10 percent, what is the present value of this security?

$$\text{Present Value (PV)} = \frac{\$100}{(0.1 - 0.05)} = \$2{,}000$$

At a 10 percent discount rate, we see that the value of receiving a payment of $100 each year that grows 5 percent per year forever is $2,000.

Future Value The final formula that we will discuss is future value. In the previous three examples, we calculated the value today of a certain cash flow or stream of cash flows that we will receive in the future. The future value formula allows us to do the opposite—that is, to calculate what the value of an investment will be in the future, given its value today and a specified discount rate.

To calculate future value, we simply multiply the present value of the investment times one plus the discount rate raised to the number of periods in the future (n), as follows:

$$\text{Future Value (FV)} = PV \times (1 + r)^n$$

r = discount rate

n = number of periods

Let us suppose that you have $100 today. How much will that money be worth one year later at a 10 percent discount rate? Or equivalently, if I invested $100 at a 10 percent annual interest rate, how much money would I have after one year?

$$\text{Future Value (FV)} = \$100 \times (1 + 0.1)^1 = \$110$$

After one year at a 10 percent discount rate, the future value of $100 today is $110. Equivalently, $100 invested today at a 10 percent interest rate will turn into $110 in one year.

INTRODUCTION TO CORPORATE FINANCE

We mentioned earlier in this chapter that the savers and borrowers that make up the economy are often segregated into three groups: individuals, companies, and governments. Correspondingly, the study of finance is also divided into three categories: personal finance, corporate finance, and public finance. Since investment bankers primarily advise companies, we will naturally focus our attention on corporate finance.

The study of corporate finance focuses on how companies make two types of key decisions. The first of these decisions is whether or not to invest in a project. Assuming a company decides to invest in a particular project, the second decision facing the firm is how to best fund the project. Before we can discuss the kind of analysis that companies use to make these decisions, we need to ask ourselves what goal company management has in mind when making these two kinds of decisions.

Nearly all the time we can assume that management's goal is to maximize the value of the company's equity value (i.e., stock price). This goal is consistent with the fact that, in most circumstances (bankruptcy being an exception), a company's management and board of directors have a legal and fiduciary duty to look out for the best interests of shareholders. Maximizing share price is certainly in shareholder's best interests.

Of course, in the real world, management teams also look out for their own interests. Maximizing equity value is usually consistent with this goal as well, since management compensation tends to be correlated with stock performance. Moreover, management teams are frequently rewarded with stock grants and stock options so as to align their incentives with shareholders.

Decision 1: To Invest or Not to Invest

Before we discuss how a company should decide whether or not to invest in a project, let us first talk about what exactly we mean when we use the term "project." Simply put, a project is any kind of investment. Examples of the types of projects in which companies sometimes invest include:

- Building a new factory or expanding an existing one.
- Creating a new product line or extending an existing one.
- Entering a new geographic market.
- Purchasing new equipment or replacing existing equipment.
- Acquiring another company.
- Starting a brand new company.

Companies should invest in good projects that increase the value of the company (or the value of its shares) and avoid bad projects that destroy value. Sounds good, right? But how exactly do companies decide what projects are considered good and what projects are bad? In other words, how can a company predict whether a project will create or destroy value?

There are two criteria that we can use to analyze this kind of decision. The two criteria for a "good" project are:

1. Projects with an expected internal rate of return (IRR) greater than the applicable cost of capital.
2. Projects with a net present value (NPV) greater than 0.

As we will observe shortly, these two different analyses will almost always give us the same answer, since they are mathematically related. We will also see that both of these criteria are based on the basic present value formulas that we covered in the previous section.

Forecasting Cash Flows Both the IRR analysis and the NPV analysis require us to have a set of cash flow forecasts for the project. These forecasts need to include all of the cash flows that directly relate to the project, including the initial investment as well as ongoing costs and capital expenditures, working capital requirements, and revenues and profits.

There are also certain items that we should *not* include in the cash flow forecasts. We should not include costs that have already been spent, which we refer to as sunk costs. For example, suppose that today we are deciding whether or not to build a new factory on land that we previously purchased. The prior purchase of the land represents a sunk cost that we would not include in this analysis.

We should also not include in our cash flow forecasts any allocation of expenses that would have to be spent regardless of whether we invest in this project. Consider again the possibility of building a new factory. While our cash flows should take into account the salaries of the workers who will be operating the factory, we should not include a portion of our CEO's salary. Our CEO would receive his or her compensation regardless of whether we build the factory.

We will discuss how we can forecast operating performance in detail in Chapter 6. For now, however, let us assume that the cash flow forecasts necessary for our analysis of IRR and NPV are given to us.

Internal Rate of Return (IRR) Analysis Recall that an investment will be considered good and be accretive to value if its internal rate of return (IRR) is greater than the project's cost of capital. The IRR is the annualized compounded percentage return rate based on the time-weighted cash flows. IRR is calculated by solving for the cost of capital (r) in the following equation:

$$0=\frac{CF_1}{(1+r)^1}+\frac{CF_2}{(1+r)^2}+\frac{CF_3}{(1+r)^3}+\frac{CF_4}{(1+r)^4}+\cdots+\frac{CF_t}{(1+r)^t}$$

While there is no easy way to manually solve this equation with a pen and paper, Microsoft Excel can easily make the calculation using its built-in IRR or XIRR functions.[3]

The cost of capital (equivalently, the discount rate, hurdle rate, or opportunity cost) represents the minimum rate of return that is required on a project of this risk level. As should be obvious from our discussion earlier in this chapter on risk and reward, the higher the project's risk, the higher the cost of capital or hurdle rate. It is very important to keep in mind that when performing an IRR

[3]Excel's IRR function assumes all cash flows are exactly one period apart, while the XIRR function allows us to specify the timing of cash flows. (We will return to these functions again when we cover leveraged buyouts in Chapter 8.)

analysis, you should use the cost of capital for the particular project and not the company's overall rate. This is still the case even if the company could raise the necessary funds at a lower cost than the project's hurdle rate.

The company should consider accepting the project if the investment's IRR is greater than the project's cost of capital. There are, however, a few things to note when performing an IRR analysis. The IRR formula implicitly assumes that all cash flows can be reinvested and will earn a return exactly equal to the IRR. It may be unrealistic to assume that other projects can be found that have returns as high, especially for projects forecasting a very high IRR. Second, it is worth noting that on rare occasions, depending on the cash flow forecasts, the IRR formula can result in two possible answers. Third, note that it is not always obvious what the appropriate cost of capital to use is. Finally, keep in mind that the IRR analysis is based on a set of projections and, like all forecasts, may not prove to be accurate or reliable.

Example of an IRR Analysis Exhibit 3.1 shows an example of an IRR analysis based on a set of forecasts built in Microsoft Excel and using Excel's IRR function. In this example, we are analyzing the returns to building a new factory. We are assuming the factory requires $1,000 to build in the first year and then operates for nine additional years, at which point it is obsolete and worthless. For each of those nine years, we have forecasted after-tax operating income, depreciation and amortization, ongoing capital expenditures (for maintenance), and the investment in working capital.

Based on these cash flows, we calculate an internal rate of return (IRR) of 12.4 percent. If our hurdle rate for this project is less than 12.4 percent, then we would conclude that this is a good project that will create value. On the other hand, if the project's cost of capital is greater than 12.4 percent, then we should label this a bad project, one that will destroy value. If, in the unlikely circumstance that the project's opportunity cost of capital is exactly 12.4 percent, then this project will neither create nor destroy value. We are indifferent.

Net Present Value (NPV) Analysis The second criterion that we use to analyze a project is net present value (NPV). Recall that a project with a positive NPV (greater than 0) is considered good and will add value, while an investment with a negative NPV (less than 0) will destroy value.

Net present value represents the sum of all cash flows for a project, discounted at the appropriate cost of capital or hurdle rate (r). NPV is calculated by summing the following equation:

$$NPV = \frac{CF_1}{(1+r)^1} + \frac{CF_2}{(1+r)^2} + \frac{CF_3}{(1+r)^3} + \frac{CF_4}{(1+r)^4} + \cdots + \frac{CF_t}{(1+r)^t}$$

EXHIBIT 3.1 IRR Analysis

	Year 1	Year 2	Year 3	Year 4	Year 5	Year 6	Year 7	Year 8	Year 9	Year 10
Operating Income after Taxes	$ 0.0	$100.0	$110.0	$120.0	$130.0	$140.0	$150.0	$160.0	$170.0	$180.0
Plus: Depreciation and Amortization	0.0	105.0	110.0	115.0	120.0	125.0	130.0	135.0	140.0	145.0
Less: Capital Expenditures	(1,000.0)	(50.0)	(50.0)	(50.0)	(50.0)	(50.0)	(50.0)	(50.0)	(50.0)	(50.0)
Less: Change in Net Working Capital	0.0	(50.0)	(5.0)	(5.0)	(5.0)	(5.0)	(5.0)	(5.0)	(5.0)	(5.0)
Net Cashflow	($1,000.0)	$105.0	$165.0	$180.0	$195.0	$210.0	$225.0	$240.0	$255.0	$270.0
Internal Rate of Return (IRR)	12.4%									

Unlike IRR, NPV can be easily solved manually or by using Excel's NPV function. You may note the similarities between the formula used for IRR and the formula used for NPV. As alluded to earlier, IRR and NPV are very much related. Specifically, when a project's IRR is exactly equal to its cost of capital, then the project's NPV should exactly equal 0.

As we said earlier, the company should consider accepting a project if the project's NPV is greater than 0. Just as with the IRR analysis, keep in mind that the NPV analysis is only as reliable as its forecasts for cash flow and that the appropriate cost of capital is not always obvious.

Example of an NPV Analysis Exhibit 3.2 shows an example of an NPV analysis performed using Microsoft Excel. For this example, we are using the exact same cash flow forecasts we utilized for the IRR example earlier.

Based on the cash flows, we have calculated three different NPV values using three varying cost of capitals. At a 10.0 percent hurdle rate, we find that the NPV is positive. If the project's cost of capital is indeed 10 percent, then this should be considered a good project. At a 12.4 percent discount rate, NPV is exactly 0, and we should be indifferent about the project. This helps illustrate the relationship between NPV and IRR. Recall that we calculated an IRR of 12.4 percent based on the exact same cash flows. Finally, at a cost of capital of 15.0 percent, the NPV is negative and should be thought of as a valuing destroying investment.

Do Companies Really Rely on IRR and NPV Analysis? We mentioned in the introduction to this chapter that more than any other, this chapter contains a mix of both theoretical and practical concepts. It is fair to say that the management of companies does make decisions with the goal of maximizing value. And as we have discussed, the theoretically correct way to measure whether an investment will indeed create value is to use the IRR and NPV analyses. But do companies really rely on these methods in practice?

I think the best answer is some combination of yes and no. Most medium-sized to large companies do perform this kind of analysis when contemplating significant investments and new projects. In fact, many companies will develop very detailed forecasts for these purposes. Moreover, companies with sophisticated corporate finance professionals typically have a good sense of a project's appropriate cost of capital.

However, most management teams are also aware that forecasts tend to be very optimistic and unreliable, especially when they are put together by a team promoting their particular project. This fact alone plays a role in undermining the effectiveness of IRR and NPV analyses. Moreover, in a typical company, many factors come into play other than pure economic analysis when management teams consider whether or not to make a significant investment. (We will

EXHIBIT 3.2 NPV Analysis

	Year 1	Year 2	Year 3	Year 4	Year 5	Year 6	Year 7	Year 8	Year 9	Year 10
Operating Income after Taxes	$0.0	$100.0	$110.0	$120.0	$130.0	$140.0	$150.0	$160.0	$170.0	$180.0
Plus: Depreciation and Amortization	0.0	105.0	110.0	115.0	120.0	125.0	130.0	135.0	140.0	145.0
Less: Capital Expenditures	(1,000.0)	(50.0)	(50.0)	(50.0)	(50.0)	(50.0)	(50.0)	(50.0)	(50.0)	(50.0)
Less: Change in Net Working Capital	0.0	(50.0)	(5.0)	(5.0)	(5.0)	(5.0)	(5.0)	(5.0)	(5.0)	(5.0)
Net Cashflow	**($1,000.0)**	**$105.0**	**$165.0**	**$180.0**	**$195.0**	**$210.0**	**$225.0**	**$240.0**	**$255.0**	**$270.0**
Present Value at 10.0%	(909.1)	86.8	124.0	122.9	121.1	118.5	115.5	112.0	108.1	104.1
Net Present Value (NPV)	**$103.9**									
Present Value at 12.4%	(889.3)	83.0	116.1	112.6	108.5	103.9	99.0	93.9	88.7	83.6
Net Present Value (NPV)	**$0.0**									
Present Value at 15.0%	(869.6)	79.4	108.5	102.9	96.9	90.8	84.6	78.5	72.5	66.7
Net Present Value (NPV)	**($88.8)**									

talk about many of these kinds of factors in Chapter 7 when we discuss some of the non-economic reasons why companies make acquisitions.)

Decision 2: How to Fund the Investment

If the first key decision of corporate finance is whether or not to invest in a project, the second important question is how best to finance that investment. Keep in mind that most significant projects will require money to be spent up-front before the project generates enough cash flow to pay for itself. If it is a small project relative to the size of the company, or if the company has a lot of cash, then the company is likely to finance the investment with excess cash. Let's assume that the project is large enough such that the company needs to raise outside money.

Companies should choose a mix of financing in order to minimize their cost of capital (the blended discount rate) but also to match the project's timing and risk profile. Shorter term financing sources should be used for short-term projects, and longer-term funds should be used for longer-term projects. If a company uses shorter-term financing for a longer-term project, then it faces refinancing risk. In other words, the company may not be able to obtain additional funds to complete the project when the shorter-term funds mature, or the new funds may be more expensive, possibly making the project unprofitable. If it uses longer-term funds, then it may be paying money (i.e., interest) for funds it no longer needs. Moreover, riskier projects should have investors that are more risk-tolerant and less risky projects should have less risk-tolerant investors.

Sources of Funds Companies can use many different kinds of funds to finance a project but can generally be segregated into two main types: debt and equity. Furthermore, there are two kinds of equity securities that we will discuss: common stock and preferred stock.

Debt Debt represents money that is borrowed from one or more investors. When a company borrows money it almost always agrees to pay back the amount borrowed (the principal amount) by a certain date or on a certain date (the maturity date). The company also typically agrees to pay some amount of periodic interest to compensate the investor for the use of the investor's money.

In order for a company to raise debt, it typically needs to own valuable and tangible assets and have the ability to generate sufficient cash flows in order to meets its interest obligations. If a company is unable to pay interest or to pay back the principal amount when due, then the company may have to file bankruptcy and possibly even liquidate.

Advantages of Debt There are both advantages and disadvantages to issuing debt, both of which a company must consider. The biggest advantage is that debt is a less expensive form of capital to the company than is equity. Said equivalently, an investor's required return for investing in a company's debt will always be lower than the required return for investing in the same company's equity. This is true for a few important reasons.

First, debt has a higher, or more senior, position in the company's capital structure. What that means is that in the event of a bankruptcy, the company's debt investors or lenders will receive the amount they are owed before the equity investors receive any money at all. This fact makes debt a less-risky asset to the investor and therefore a cheaper form of capital to the company.

In addition, debt has an advantage over equity due to our tax system. The interest expense that a company pays on its debt is tax deductible just like other operating expenses. In other words, interest expense reduces that amount of taxes that a company must pay to the government. Dividends paid to equity holders are generally not tax deductible.

A third reason why debt is less expensive than equity is that the cash flows that the investors receive are much more certain because they are contractual. In other words, a lender typically knows how much money it will receive from interest and principal repayments, and when it will receive that money. An equity investor does not have this same foresight. Since more certainty means less risk, debt is naturally a cheaper form of capital.

In addition to debt having a lower cost of capital, there are some other advantages as well. The transaction costs for raising or issuing debt are typically lower than for equity. Also, many forms of debt, especially secured debt (which we will discuss shortly), can be raised privately (for example, from a bank or group of banks, known as a syndicate). Because the debt is private, there are no public SEC filing requirements like there are for public securities like common stock.

Disadvantages of Debt The most significant disadvantage to using debt is that it raises a company's risk of bankruptcy. Bankruptcy can lead to the company being liquidated. However, even in a successful restructuring transaction through the bankruptcy process, an enormous amount of value is lost. Fees paid to bankruptcy advisers are significant; key employees, customers, and vendors often depart; and shareholders typically see the value of their equity wiped out.

In addition to raising the likelihood of bankruptcy, debt also constrains the company's flexibility in at least three ways. Since companies are typically obligated to make cash interest payments, cash that might have otherwise been used for working capital or capital expenditures, or any other purpose, might not be available. Second, investors typically insist on certain rules with which companies must abide. These rules, known as covenants and contained in a credit agreement (in the case of bank loans) or indenture (in the case of a bond), may restrict a company's ability to raise additional debt or make additional investments. Covenants also often require companies to be in compliance with certain financial ratios. Finally, raising debt can limit how much additional debt a company can take on even if companies are not contractually constrained through covenants. A company may find that there is simply no more appetite from the credit markets for additional borrowing.

Secured Debt A company can raise or issue a vast number of different types of debt. However, we can bifurcate most types into one of the two following groups: secured debt and unsecured debt.

Secured debt is debt that is secured by the assets of a firm. That is, the lender has collateral in case the borrower cannot pay back the debt, in which case the lender can claim the collateral. Examples of types of secured debt include various bank debt such as revolving credit facilities and term loans, as well as capital lease obligations. For an individual, an example of a secured loan is a mortgage. If I can't pay or don't pay my mortgage payments, the banks that own the mortgage can take back my house.

Because of the collateral, secured debt is considered the least risky type of debt. If the company were to file bankruptcy, the secured debtholders would be the first lenders to receive payment. Hence, secured debt will have the lowest interest rate and therefore has the lowest cost of capital to the company of any type of debt or equity. Correspondingly, secured debtholders, such as banks, represent the most conservative investor base. Secured debt also tends to have the most restrictive financial covenants.

Another advantage of secured debt is that there is a lot of flexibility with both maturities and the amount of money borrowed. Companies also typically raise secured debt privately, meaning there are no public filing requirements.

Sometimes the same assets can be used as collateral for multiple loans. In this instance, one lender (or groups of lenders) will have a first lien on the asset and another lender will have the second lien. Sometimes there is even a third lender with a third lien. In a bankruptcy situation, the debtholder with the first lien gets paid in full before the lender with the second lien, and so on. Assets encumbered by liens typically cannot be sold unless the corresponding debt is repaid.

Unsecured Debt Unsecured debt is any kind of debt that is not secured by specific assets. Examples of unsecured debt include bonds such as senior notes, senior subordinated notes, and convertible debentures.

In a bankruptcy situation, unsecured creditors receive payment for their claims only after secured lenders have been paid in full. Therefore, unsecured debtholders require a higher return than do secured debtholders, and companies have a higher cost of capital for issuing unsecured debt, usually in the form of higher interest expense.

An advantage of unsecured debt over secured debt is that it does not encumber the company's assets. In other words, a company would not have contractual restrictions on selling certain assets or on raising secured debt in the future. Moreso than secured debt, unsecured debt can have features that provide additional flexibility to the company. Some types of unsecured debt allow the company to pay interest by issuing more debt (effectively accruing the interest) rather than by paying cash. This is known as payment-in-kind (PIK) interest. Other types of unsecured debt allow the holder to convert its debt into common stock under certain circumstances.

Unsecured debt also has certain disadvantages to the issuer. Many types of unsecured bonds are publicly traded. While this provides liquidity to the holder, which does reduce the cost of capital, it does require the issuer to publicly file financial statements, even if the company is privately held. Additionally, in the case of publicly traded bonds, there is a minimum amount of debt that is practical to raise. This puts many types of unsecured debt out of the reach of smaller companies.

Finally, recall that for secured debt, the lender's required rate of return is typically equal to the interest rate that the borrower pays. This is not always the case for unsecured debt. Sometimes, because of the riskiness of unsecured debt, the return that investors require is higher than the interest expense the company wants to, or can afford to, pay. In these instances, the company must offer the investor some way of receiving additional return, usually in the form of warrants, which represent the right to purchase shares of common stock. (We will discuss warrants later in this chapter.)

Common Stock Common stock, also called common equity, represents the residual claims on a company's assets after all debts and other liabilities have been paid. We can also think of common stockholders as the true owners of the company. Common stock typically (though not always) allows investors to have some limited control over the company through the right to vote for the company's board of directors and certain other matters, such as a sale of the company.

Common stock represents the costliest type of funding to companies and the riskiest to investors. Should a company be forced to file bankruptcy, common stockholders do not receive anything until all other creditors and investors have been paid in full. In fact, as mentioned earlier in this chapter, in most instances, common stock will be worthless once a company is in bankruptcy. Most companies have only one class of common stock, though some companies have multiple classes, typically with each class having differing voting rights.

Advantages of Common Stock As a source of funding, one advantage of common stock is that a company has no obligation to pay dividends. Though it may choose to pay dividends, it can increase, decrease, or even eliminate the dividend at any time. Another advantage is that common stockholders represent the least-risk-adverse investor class. Furthermore, issuing common stock maintains or even increases a company's ability to incur debt, thus affording the company greater financial flexibility.

Common stock also provides a currency that can potentially be used for acquisitions as well as to reward and provide incentive to employees. Finally, issuing common stock and being a public company often provide an ego boost and measure of prestige for the management team, not to mention often higher levels of compensation.

Disadvantages of Common Stock There are also some important disadvantages to common stock. Not only is it the highest cost of capital to the company, as highlighted previously, but issuing common stock has the highest transactions costs (though this is good for investment bankers!). Another important downside is that dividends, unlike interest payments, are not tax deductible to the company. Moreover, issuing additional common stock is naturally dilutive to existing shareholders.

Another disadvantage to publicly traded common stock is that being a public company requires significant financial disclosure and expenses. Lastly, having publicly traded common stock opens up management to the risk that an investor, such as an activist hedge fund, will want to influence or even change management and/or the company's strategy.

Preferred Stock Preferred stock is technically a type of equity. However, it has features of both debt and common equity, and is therefore considered to be a hybrid security. Compared with debt and common stock, preferred stock is a much less frequently chosen method of financing for nearly all companies except for venture capital–backed, early-stage companies.

In terms of the priority of payout in a bankruptcy situation, preferred stock sits in between debt and common equity. This makes it more risky than debt but less risky than common equity. Hence, the return required by investors in preferred stock should be in between that of debtholders and common stockholders. Correspondingly, preferred stock's cost of capital should be in between that of debt and that of common equity.

Preferred stock has a fixed dividend, similar to the interest on a bond. However, there are a number of ways in which preferred stock differs from debt. Most importantly, the dividend is not tax deductible to the company, though certain holders of preferred stock are able to deduct 70 percent of the dividend income, reducing an investor's own tax bill. Moreover, unlike interest expense, which usually requires mandatory payment by the company, preferred dividends can be deferred and accrued at the company's option. Also unlike most types of debt, preferred stock usually has no set maturity date.

There are lots of different kinds of preferred stock, just as there are many different types of bonds. Some types of preferred stock have a feature that allows the securities to be converted into common stock. We call these securities convertible preferred stock. Finally, it is worth mentioning that preferred stock tends to have a much less liquid trading market than does common stock or corporate bonds. This is one of the reasons why companies are much less likely to issue preferred stock.

Capital Structure

Before we move on from our discussion of how companies finance investment projects, there is one additional topic worth exploring, which is capital structure. The term "capital structure" reflects a company's mix of funding for the entire company, rather than for a specific project.

Just like for individual projects, companies can finance their entire operations through raising various types of debt, preferred stock, and common equity. In fact, a typical capital structure for a large company has a blend of many different types of capital.

The Theoretical World of Modigliani-Miller There is a famous idea in corporate finance known as the Modigliani-Miller theorem (sometimes called the M&M theorem) that states that in a perfect world two companies with identical operations should have the exact same value regardless of their capital structures. In other words, the choice of capital structure should not matter at all to a firm, and therefore trying to minimize a company's cost of capital is a waste of time and effort.

The essential rationale for this statement is that investors in a company should be able to borrow and lend their own money in a way that allows them to be entitled to the same cash flows from the company regardless of the way in which the company is financed. Therefore, since investors should be indifferent to the company's capital structure, it follows that the value of the company should also be neutral. Mathematically proving this theorem is the kind of thing you do in school but is certainly not something that a client will ever ask an investment banker to do.

Capital Structure and the Cost of Capital in the Real World Of course even academics understand that we do not live in the perfect world of Modigliani-Miller. This is true for a number of reasons, the most important of which are taxes, bankruptcy costs, and agency costs.

Taxes throw a large monkey wrench into the basic M&M theory for the simple reason that the interest on debt is tax deductible, while stock dividends are not. This tax shield for interest expense contributes to a company's cost of debt being significantly lower than its cost of equity. The second key imperfection of the real world is bankruptcy costs. As we noted early in this chapter, bankruptcy usually results in an enormous amount of lost value to the company.

The final important reason is what is known as agency cost. For a number of reasons, including the fact that management typically owns shares in the company, management tends to have shareholders' best interests in mind rather than lenders'. For instance, facing the possibility of bankruptcy, management may decide to make a very risky investment (i.e., doubling down or shooting for the moon) in the hope of avoiding bankruptcy. This decision can make sense from shareholders' standpoint, because equity might have been worthless anyway, had management not taken the risk. However, if the move fails, lenders might wind up being worse off than they would otherwise have been.

Based on these real-world implications, a company's choice of capital structure is assumed to have an impact on a company's capital structure and value. Specifically, a company's cost of capital is assumed to be U-shaped, as in Exhibit 3.3, although the U shape is not necessarily symmetric as it is in Exhibit 3.3. The U also tends not to be very steep, for reasons that we will discuss shortly.

It probably is obvious to you why the curve slopes up when you move closer to 100 percent equity. After all, equity is always a more expensive form of capital than debt. However, if equity is more expensive, you might be tempted to think that the optimal capital structure should be 100 percent debt. As you can see in Exhibit 3.3, this is not the case. The curve slopes up to the left side as a company's capital structure moves toward all-debt financing.

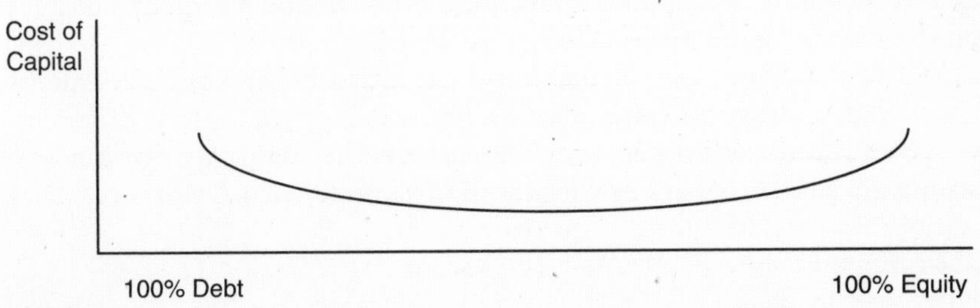

EXHIBIT 3.3 Cost of Capital

Because of the costs of bankruptcy and the related agency costs, increasing the amount of debt raises the cost of capital for all forms of financing, including the equity. So, as a company is more and more levered, the bankruptcy risk rises and its cost of capital actually increases. Moreover, recall that one of the main reasons that debt is cheaper than equity is due to the tax shield on interest. If a company has so much debt that its interest expense exceeds its operating income, then it loses (or delays) the benefit of the tax shield.

The bottom line is that in the real world, capital structure is thought to matter and should influence the value of a company. Therefore, companies should try to choose a mix of funding that does minimize its cost of capital. However, always remember that the U-shaped curve is shallow, so the impact of capital structure on a company's cost of capital and its value is likely very small.

A reasonable question to ask is whether companies in fact do indeed optimize their capital structures, as theory would teach. Here, the evidence is decidedly mixed. On the one hand, the aggregate capital structures of certain industries do differ, as they should. Regulated utilities with high and steady cash flows and a large asset base do tend to have much higher levels of debt than do consumer product companies with less-steady cash flows and a lower asset base. And consumer product companies tend to have more debt than do biotechnology companies that have very risky cash flows and very few tangible assets.

On the other hand, many very successful companies that do generate high and steady levels of cash flow have very little or even no debt. This is especially true in the technology sector and does provide some evidence that the choice of capital structure does not matter very much.

What if There Are No Good Investments?

So far, our study of corporate finance has taught us how to think about two questions. The first is how to decide whether a project is worth investing in. The second is how to best finance the project. But what if a company decides that there are no good projects in which to invest?

If a company has excess cash but does not anticipate any investments that will be accretive to value, then theory says it should return money to investors so that investors can seek out better, higher-returning investments. A company has three ways in which to return money to investors:

1. Paying off debt.
2. Issuing dividends.
3. Repurchasing (buying back) stock.

In returning money to investors, the company should try to maintain an optimal capital structure with the lowest possible cost of capital. To some extent, optimizing its capital structure will influence management's decision of how to return capital to lenders and investors. However, there are some additional considerations as well.

A company may decide it does not want to pay off debt if the debt has prepayment penalties or if the interest rates on existing debt are very low. Of course, the opposite is true, too. The company may prefer to retire debt that is at high interest rates compared with the current environment. It also may favor paying off debt if the company's credit rating (which we will discuss in the next section) will increase. This is especially true if retiring debt will raise the company from a non-investment-grade rating to investment grade.

Assuming a company desires to return money to shareholders rather than lenders, it has two choices: It can issue dividends or repurchase stock. The decision to issue dividends or repurchase stock depends on several factors, including the relative tax treatment of each and the makeup of the company's investor base.

Some investors prefer to receive dividends (for example, investors such as retirees who buy the stock for the annual income; these investors are often referred to as widows and orphans) and pension funds. On the other hand, dividends are taxed when investors receive them, and therefore taxable investors may not be so enthralled with receiving dividends. Additionally, it is much easier for a company to raise a dividend than it is to cut the dividend later. Cutting a dividend sends a negative signal to the market and is often taken as a sign of possible distress. Therefore, companies are sometimes reluctant to raise their dividends as a way of distributing excess cash. An alternative is for the company to issue a one-time special dividend to shareholders.

The other way that companies can return money to shareholders is by repurchasing the company's own stock. A large advantage of repurchasing stock is that while all investors benefit by owning a proportionally greater percentage of the company, only the investors that sell their stock to the company face a tax bill. Moreover, the investment profits (also called capital gains) are typically taxed at a much lower rate than are dividends. Finally, the company has more discretion to change its stock buyback policy in the future since cutting or even eliminating stock repurchases does not typically send the same negative market signal as does cutting dividends.

There are two things that a company should *not* do with its excess cash. First, companies should not pursue investments solely for growth purposes that are likely to decrease value. Second, companies should not make investments or acquisitions purely for diversification purposes. Instead, companies should return money to shareholders, let shareholders seek out better-returning investments, and let shareholders diversify.

Just like we asked ourselves whether companies in practice actually pursue optimal capital structures, let us end this section by asking whether companies really return excess money to shareholders, as theory would dictate. Here, the evidence is even more mixed. Certainly some companies do use excess cash to retire debt, and they do pay dividends and repurchase shares.

However, very often returning money to investors is taken by the public markets as a sign that the company is out of growth prospects, or that the management team is weak and is unable to recognize or find such growth prospects. For this reason, many companies keep large amounts of cash on their balance sheets for long periods of time, earning very low returns on that money. And since stock investors tend to overemphasize the importance of growth, companies often make investments and pursue acquisitions that they should not.

VALUING SECURITIES

Even though the job of an investment banker is not to trade stocks, bonds, and other securities, bankers (and prospective bankers) do need to have a basic understanding of how to value such financial instruments. In this section, we will talk about how to value three of the most common and important types of securities: bonds, stocks, and options/warrants. As you will see, in order to value these securities, we will apply the finance theories and basic formulas that we learned earlier in this chapter.

Bonds

To review what we have already covered, a bond is a type of long-term debt. A typical bond requires the borrower (also known as the issuer) to pay periodic interest to the lender (also referred to as the bondholder) and pay the principal amount (also referred to as the par value or face value) at a certain date in the future (the maturity date). A bond indenture is the legal agreement that dictates the terms of the bond, including any covenants, and governs the relationship between the issuer and the bondholder. Bonds may be secured or unsecured debt.

For most publicly traded bonds, interest (also known as the coupon) is paid semiannually and the interest rate (or coupon rate) is fixed throughout the life of the bond. Some bonds do, however, have variable coupon rates known as floating rates. Most corporate bonds are issued at par, which means at the time of issuance, the bond's coupon rate should approximate the current market yield and that the bond's par value (typically $1,000) represents the amount of money lent to the company by the purchaser of each bond.

Valuing a Bond To compute the value of a bond, we use the net present value (NPV) formula that we learned earlier in this chapter:

$$NPV = \frac{CF_1}{(1+r)^1} + \frac{CF_2}{(1+r)^2} + \frac{CF_3}{(1+r)^3} + \frac{CF_4}{(1+r)^4} + \cdots + \frac{CF_t}{(1+r)^t}$$

In the numerator for each cash flow, we substitute each coupon payment up until the maturity plus the par value to be paid at maturity. The discount rate (r) reflects the market interest rate for a bond of comparable risk and maturity. The NPV is equal to the fair market value or price of the bond, as follows:

$$\text{Bond price} = \frac{\text{Coupon}}{(1+r)^1} + \frac{\text{Coupon}}{(1+r)^2} + \frac{\text{Coupon}}{(1+r)^3} + \cdots + \frac{\text{Coupon}}{(1+r)^t} + \frac{\text{Par value}}{(1+r)^t}$$

r = market interest rate

t = time until maturity

One thing to note is that most bonds pay coupons twice a year. So when using this formula, you need to adjust the interest rate accordingly, since most interest rates are published on an annualized basis (often referred to as APR). Furthermore, the time until maturity (t) becomes the number of periods until maturity. So, for a bond with semiannual coupons and a 10-year maturity, the interest rate should be halved and the time until maturity should be 20 periods (20 half-years).

Example 1 As an example, consider a five-year bond (most bonds are longer, but we will keep the math easier) with a par value of $1,000 and a 6 percent coupon. Further, let's assume that the current market rate of interest for a bond of similar risk is also 6 percent. Finally, in the interest of simplicity, let's assume that the coupon is paid only once a year. How much is this bond worth?

$$\frac{\$60}{(1.06)^1} + \frac{\$60}{(1.06)^2} + \frac{\$60}{(1.06)^3} + \frac{\$60}{(1.06)^4} + \frac{\$60}{(1.06)^5} + \frac{\$1000}{(1.06)^5} = \$1,000$$

Using our NPV formula, we find that the value of the bond is exactly equal to $1,000, which means that the bond is trading exactly at par value. This makes sense since the coupon rate is exactly equal to the market discount rate.

Example 2 Now let's assume that day after this bond is issued, the market discount rate falls to 4 percent. Remember that the coupon is fixed, so it will not change. Now, what should be the price of the bond?

$$\frac{\$60}{(1.04)^1}+\frac{\$60}{(1.04)^2}+\frac{\$60}{(1.04)^3}+\frac{\$60}{(1.04)^4}+\frac{\$60}{(1.04)^5}+\frac{\$1000}{(1.04)^5}=\$1,089$$

Now we see that the value of the bond is approximately $1,089, which is greater than the par value of $1,000. The bond will now trade at a premium to par value since the coupon rate (6 percent) is higher than the market discount rate.

Example 3 In our third example, let's analyze the same bond but assume that the market discount rate rises to 8 percent instead of falling. What should the new price be?

$$\frac{\$60}{(1.08)^1}+\frac{\$60}{(1.08)^2}+\frac{\$60}{(1.08)^3}+\frac{\$60}{(1.08)^4}+\frac{\$60}{(1.08)^5}+\frac{\$1000}{(1.08)^5}=\$920$$

The bond's value has now decreased to $920 and is trading at a discount to the par value of $1,000.

The Relationship between Bond Prices and Interest Rates These three examples have taught us a very important lesson, one that is repeated in the financial press in nearly every single article about bonds and interest rates. The price of a bond moves in an opposite direction to market interest rates. That is, when interest rates fall, bond prices rise. When interest rates rise, bond prices fall.

Zero Coupon Bonds Before moving on, there is one particular type of bond that is worth discussing: a zero coupon bond. A zero coupon bond (sometimes abbreviated as a "zero") is a special type of bond that has no coupon payments. The only payment that the lender receives is the principal payment at the time when the bond matures.

You may be wondering why a lender would lend money and not receive interest. Does that not violate everything we learned about the time value of money? The answer is no. In lieu of receiving coupon payments, an investor of a zero coupon bond will purchase the bond at a significant discount to the par value. The difference between the investor's purchase price and par value represents the value of the interest payments that the lender is forgoing. In other words, the interest payments are embedded in the discount. A zero coupon bond is classified as a type of discount bond because it is issued at a discount to par value.

Just like valuing regular bonds, we can use the NPV formula to value a zero coupon bond:

$$\text{Bond price} = \frac{\text{Par value}}{(1+r)^t}$$

r = market interest rate

t = time until maturity

Does this formula look familiar? It should. It is our basic present value formula.

Let us do an example. Suppose a company issues a zero coupon bond with a 30-year maturity and that the market discount rate is 6 percent. How much should the bond be worth when it is issued?

$$\frac{\$1{,}000}{(1.06)^{30}} = \$174$$

We see that the zero coupon bond is worth only about $174 at issue. Now, let's ask ourselves: How much will the bond be worth one year from now, assuming market rates have not changed?

$$\frac{\$1{,}000}{(1.06)^{29}} = \$185$$

After one year, the bond's value increases to $185. That is because there is less time until the holder of the bond receives the $1,000 par value. In fact, as Exhibit 3.4 shows, assuming interest rates are steady, the value of the zero

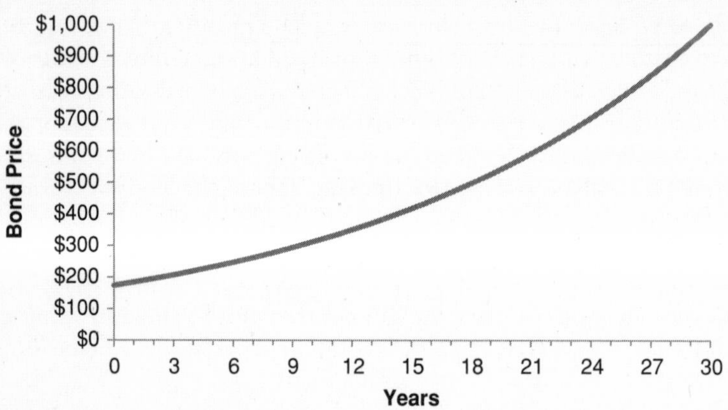

EXHIBIT 3.4 The Value of a Zero Coupon Bond over Time

coupon bond will increase exponentially each year until maturity. At maturity, the bond will be exactly equal to the par value of $1,000.

Interest Rates In the previous section, we learned how to calculate the value of a bond given its par value, coupon rate, and maturity, and the market interest rate. The first three of those variables are negotiated between borrowers and lenders, and are specified in the bond's indenture. However, the interest rate used to value the bond must be estimated.

The two main factors that affect a bond's interest rate are the general level of interest rates for all bonds of that maturity and the default risk for the specific issuer. As a proxy for the general level of interest rates, we often look to the rates on U.S. government bonds as our baseline since they are considered the closest thing to a risk-free rate and they are highly liquid.

The Term Structure of Interest Rates You may recall that when we learned how to value a bond, we discounted all of the coupon payments as well the par value by the same interest rate. Implicitly we were assuming that there is one prevailing interest rate for a bond of a given maturity. In reality, this is not the case. For a number of reasons, investors may require a different return for the first year than they do for the second or third or fourth year, and therefore to be more accurate, we may want to use a different rate to discount each period. For example, the interest rate in the second year is known as a forward rate and can be interpolated using the current rate from a one-year bond and a two-year bond.

That today's interest rates will differ for varying time periods is referred to as the term structure of interest rates. When we plot these rates (known as spot rates) on a graph, it is often called the yield curve. Most of the time (though not always) interest rates for longer maturities are higher than those for shorter maturities and therefore the yield curve has an upward slope. Exhibit 3.5 shows the U.S. Treasury yield curve as of November 30, 2012.

There are a number of theories why long-term rates tend to be higher than short-term rates. One such theory is that more investors simply prefer to lend for a shorter period of time, so longer-term bonds must offer what is known as a liquidity premium. Another idea is that longer-term bonds have a higher risk of default. A third theory says that there is more uncertainty about expected inflation the further into the future you try to predict.

Default Risk and Credit Ratings The second factor that affects a bond's interest rate is the riskiness of the borrower and the bond's risk of default. Obviously, the riskier the borrower, the higher the risk of default and the higher the interest rate that investors will require.

To estimate the return that an investor will require on a particular bond due to default risk, we can look to its credit rating. A credit rating is assigned to most publicly traded bonds by one or more of the major rating agencies. The rating agency analyzes the credit risk of the issuer and determines the appropriate rating. The higher the rating, the lower the likelihood of default.

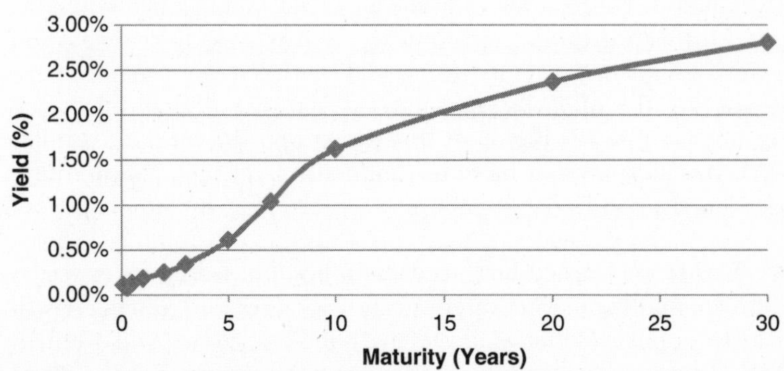

EXHIBIT 3.5 U.S. Treasury Yield Curve

EXHIBIT 3.6 Credit Rating Scale for the Major Rating Agencies

Moody's	S&P	Fitch	Explanation	Type
Aaa	AAA	AAA	Highest rating; minimal credit risk	Investment Grade
Aa1	AA+	AA+	Very high credit quality; very low credit risk	
Aa2	AA	AA		
Aa3	AA-	AA-		
A1	A+	A+	High credit quality; low credit risk	
A2	A	A		
A3	A-	A-		
Baa1	BBB+	BBB+	Moderate credit risk; may be subject to adverse economic conditions.	
Baa2	BBB	BBB		
Baa3	BBB-	BBB-		
Ba1	BB+	BB+	Speculative; significant credit risk	Non-Investment Grade (High Yield)
Ba2	BB	BB		
Ba3	BB-	BB-		
B1	B+	B+	Highly speculative; high credit risk	
B2	B	B		
B3	B-	B-		
Caa1	CCC+	CCC+	Very high credit risk	
Caa2	CCC	CCC		
Caa3	CCC-	CCC-		
Ca	CC	CC	Highly speculative, in or very near default	
C	C	C		
-	D	D	Highly speculative, in or very near default with likely recoveries limited	

Exhibit 3.6 shows a table of credit ratings by the three major rating agencies. Note that bonds rated at or above Baa on the Moody's scale and BBB on the S&P and Fitch scale are considered investment grade, while bonds below that rating are referred to as non-investment grade, high-yield, or junk bonds.

If a bond does not yet have a credit rating, we can perform our own credit analysis on the issuer using the types of credit statistics that we will discuss in Chapter 4. We can then estimate what the credit rating would be. Once we find (or estimate) the credit rating, we can look up the yields on publicly traded bonds of the same rating and maturity to estimate the required interest rate. It is often also useful to calculate the difference between the market interest rate for bonds of this rating and the rate of a similar maturity U.S. treasury or other baseline (quasi-risk free) rate. We can think of this spread as the bond's risk premium.

Bond Yields Earlier we learned how to value a bond based on its expected cash flow stream and the market interest rate. However, very often, we will want to do the opposite—that is, given the bond's price, we will want to infer the rate of return that the investor is expected to receive over the life of the bond. This is known as the bond's yield. There are actually a number of variations of this calculation, but the most commonly used is what is known as yield to maturity. The other types that will cover are the yield to call, yield to worst, and current yield.

Yield to Maturity The yield to maturity (often abbreviated as YTM) represents an investor's average return earned on a bond that is held to maturity. To calculate the yield to maturity we rely on the IRR formula that we covered earlier, shown here:

$$0 = \frac{CF_1}{(1+r)^1} + \frac{CF_2}{(1+r)^2} + \frac{CF_3}{(1+r)^3} + \frac{CF_4}{(1+r)^4} + \cdots + \frac{CF_t}{(1+r)^t}$$

To calculate the YTM, we set this formula equal to the current bond price instead of 0. Like we did for calculating bond values, in the cash flow numerators, we substitute each coupon payment up until maturity and the par value that we will receive at maturity. We then solve (using Microsoft Excel's IRR or XIRR function) for the interest rate (r), which represents the bond's yield to maturity. You should note that this is the exact same formula we used for valuing a bond, except here, we know the bold price and are solving for r rather than the other way around.

Remember that given that most bonds have semiannual coupons, the YTM that will be calculated will be a half-year rate. You will need to double it to estimate the annual percentage rate (APR). Note that the effective annual yield will be slightly higher due to the interest compounding.

$$\text{Bond price} = \frac{\text{Coupon}}{(1+r)^1} + \frac{\text{Coupon}}{(1+r)^2} + \frac{\text{Coupon}}{(1+r)^3} + \cdots + \frac{\text{Coupon}}{(1+r)^t} + \frac{\text{Par value}}{(1+r)^t}$$

r = yield to maturity (YTM)

t = time until maturity

While YTM is the standard way of measuring a bond's return, it does have several disadvantages. Most importantly, the YTM calculation uses the same interest rate to discount each time period, thereby assuming that investors' required returns are constant for all periods until maturity. In reality, an investor may require different rates of return for different time periods, as we discussed when we spoke of the term structure of interest rates. Hence, YTM is considered to be just a proxy for the investor's average required return.

Second, just like with IRR, the YTM analysis implicitly assumes that coupons can be reinvested at the yield to maturity. If this is not the case, then the YTM will not be accurate.

Yield to Call A second type of yield that is sometimes calculated for a bond is known as the yield to call. Many bonds contain a provision that allows the issuer to buy back bonds from investors at a certain price prior to the maturity date. This is known as a call provision, and these types of bonds are known as callable bonds.

The yield to call is calculated the same way as the yield to maturity except that the time until the call is used instead of the maturity date and the call price is used instead of par value. Since the calculation assumes that the bond will be called as soon as it is callable, the yield to call is sometimes also referred to as the yield to first call.

Yield to Worst The yield to worst represents the lowest possible yield that can be received from owning a bond. If there is only one call date, the yield to worst is calculated as the lesser of the yield to call and the yield to maturity. If there are multiple call dates, it is calculated as the lesser of the lowest yield to call rate (given each call date) and the yield to maturity.

Current Yield One final type of yield that is less useful than the others but very easy to calculate is the current yield. Unlike the more useful yield to maturity, the current yield is not reflective of an investor's total return until maturity. The current yield is simply the bond's annual coupon payment divided by the bond price, as follows:

$$\text{Current yield} = \frac{\text{Annual coupon}}{\text{Bond price}}$$

When a bond is selling at a discount to par value, the yield to maturity will be higher than the current yield. When a bond is selling at discount, the yield to maturity will be lower than the current yield. Finally, when a bond is valued exactly at par value, the two yields will be equal.

Duration Before we leave the subject of bonds and move onto discussing stocks, there is one final topic worth exploring: duration. Duration reflects the average maturity of a bond or, equivalently, the average amount of time to each cash flow (the coupon payments and the principal payment).

Duration is an important statistic because it helps us measure how sensitive a bond is to interest rate changes. The longer a bond's duration, the more sensitive it is to interest rate changes. Duration is especially useful for institutions such as pension funds and insurance companies that need to ensure that their investment income will match their expected liabilities (payouts).

For a bond with annualized coupons, duration is calculated as follows:

$$\text{Duration} = \frac{1\times\frac{\text{Coupon}}{(1+r)^1}}{\text{Bond price}} + \frac{2\times\frac{\text{Coupon}}{(1+r)^2}}{\text{Bond price}} + \frac{3\times\frac{\text{Coupon}}{(1+r)^3}}{\text{Bond price}} + \cdots + \frac{t\times\frac{\text{Coupon}}{(1+r)^t}}{\text{Bond price}} + \frac{t\times\frac{\text{Coupon}}{(1+r)^t}}{\text{Bond price}}$$

r = yield to maturity (YTM)

t = time until maturity

In case it is not apparent already, it is worth noting that the duration of a zero coupon bond will always equal its time until maturity. This must be true because a zero coupon bond has only one payment at maturity and no interim coupon payments.

Stocks

We have just spent a fair amount of time (and number of pages) discussing how to value and analyze bonds. We are now going to spend a much shorter amount of time talking about valuing stocks. This is not because valuing stocks is less important than valuing bonds to an investment banker. (In fact, the opposite is true.) Instead it is because we will cover the practical methods of valuation in detail in Chapter 5. The methods discussed here are much more theoretical and much less useful. However, they are still worth mentioning since the theories do underpin some of what we will cover later in the book.

The return that an investor receives for owning a stock is made up of two components: dividend payments and capital gains. Recall that capital gains refers to the difference between the price the investor receives for selling the stock and the price the investor paid to purchase the stock. Therefore in theory, the intrinsic value of a stock reflects the present value of its expected dividend payments plus the present value of the price for which the stock could be sold. We can show this as follows:

$$\text{Stock Value} = \frac{\text{Dividend}_1}{(1+k)^1} + \frac{\text{Dividend}_2}{(1+k)^2} + \frac{\text{Dividend}_3}{(1+k)^3} + \cdots + \frac{\text{Dividend}_t}{(1+k)^t} + \frac{\text{Sale price}}{(1+k)^t}$$

k = market rate of return

t = time until the stock is sold

You may recognize this formula as the same as our basic formula for valuing a bond, except that dividends have replaced coupons, the sale price has replaced par value, and the market rate of return (k) has replaced the market interest rate (r). Note that we will discuss how to estimate the market rate of return for a stock in Chapter 5.

Unfortunately, this formula is much less useful for valuing stocks than it is for valuing bonds. That is because unlike coupon payments, future dividends are unknown. Unlike par value, the future sales price is unknown. Finally, unlike the maturity date, the timing for selling the stock is also unknown.

Dividend Discount Model The dividend discount model (DDM) is an alternative theoretical method to value a stock and represents a variation on the formula we just discussed. Rather than assuming that the stock is sold at some point in the future, the dividend discount model represents the value of a stock as the present value of an infinite series of dividends. Even if the stock does not currently pay dividends, the DDM assumes that at some point in the future the company must pay out cash to investors. The DDM formula can be written as follows:

$$\text{Stock Value} = \frac{\text{Dividend}_1}{(1+k)^1} + \frac{\text{Dividend}_2}{(1+k)^2} + \frac{\text{Dividend}_3}{(1+k)^3} + \cdots$$

k = market rate of return

Just like before, it is easy to see the practical limitations with the DDM. To forecast dividends forever is impossible.

Dividend Discount Model with Constant Growth To make the dividend discount model slightly more useful we will simplify it by assuming that dividends grow forever at some constant growth rate. This is known as the DDM with constant growth, for which the formula can be specified as:

$$\text{Stock value} = \frac{\text{Next year's dividend}}{k-g}$$

k = market rate of return

g = growth rate of dividends

You may recall that this formula is the same as the formula we introduced earlier in this chapter to calculate the present value of a perpetuity with growth. Note that the perpetuity growth formula is also sometimes referred to as the Gordon growth model. Just as we discussed then, a limitation of the constant growth DDM is that the growth rate must be less than the market rate of return. (We will see this formula again in Chapter 5 when we talk about valuing a company using the discounted cash flow method.)

For now, that's enough theory on stock valuation. Let's move on to the last important category of financial security that we will cover, options and warrants.

Options and Warrants

Options and warrants are both types of derivative securities. A derivative is a financial instrument that derives its price from the price of other securities. Options and warrants are very similar and are valued using the same methodologies. We will discuss the differences between them at the end of this section.

There are several reasons why it is important for investment bankers to be familiar with options and warrants. First, as referenced earlier in this chapter, warrants are sometimes issued as part of other securities such as bonds or preferred stock. Investment bankers need to be able to value such warrants in order to properly analyze the expected rate of return to such bondholders or preferred stockholders. In addition, as we revealed in Chapter 2, companies often issue stock options to employees. When we value companies (as we will learn in Chapter 5), we will need to take these stock options into account when calculating fully diluted shares outstanding.

Valuing Call Options A call option gives the option's owner the right to buy stock at a certain price on (in the case of a European option) or before (in the case of an American option) a certain date (the expiration date), whereas a put option gives the holder the right to sell stock. The price for which the option's owner can buy or sell stock is known as either the strike price or the exercise price. The option contract expires after the expiration date.

If the exercise price of a call option is less than the current stock price then the option is known as being "in the money." If, on the other hand, the exercise price is greater than the stock price, it is "out of the money." If the exercise price and stock are equal then the option is "at the money."

On the exercise date it is easy to figure out what a call option is worth. If the option is in the money, its value is simply equal to the difference between the stock price and the exercise price. If the option is out of the money, then the option is worth exactly zero at expiration. Of course, valuing an option prior to expiration is much more difficult. As long as the stock price has positive value, the call option has some value. But how much value?

Let's assume that the current value of a share of stock is $50. Further suppose that exactly one year from now, there are only two possibilities for the stock's value: Either the stock will rise to $80 or it will fall to $30. Assume that we can purchase an option to buy a share of that stock one year from now with an exercise price of $60.

Based on these assumptions, we can easily see that there are two outcomes for the payout of the option. If the stock price rises to $80 a year from now, then the option will be worth $20 at expiration (the difference between the $80 stock price and the $60 exercise price). On the flip side, if the stock price falls to $30 then our option will be worth $0, since the $30 stock price will be less than the exercise price.

The key to valuing the option is to replicate these same exact two outcomes (either $20 or $0) by assuming we own some fraction of a share of stock and by borrowing some amount. First let's figure what percentage of a share of stock that we need to own.

In order to figure out the percentage of stock we need to own, we divide the difference between the two outcomes of the option by the difference between the two outcomes of the stock. This is known as the option delta:

$$\text{Delta} = \frac{\text{Option value}_{\text{high}} - \text{Option value}_{\text{low}}}{\text{Stock value}_{\text{high}} - \text{Stock value}_{\text{low}}}$$

In our example the delta would be 0.4, as follows. In order to replicate the two possible outcomes of the option, we will need to own 0.4 shares of stock.

$$\text{Delta} = \frac{\$20 - \$0}{\$80 - \$30} = 0.4$$

Next, we need to figure out how much money we need to borrow in order to finish replicating the option's two outcomes. In the upside scenario, we need to make up a difference between the profit on the option of $20 and the value of 0.4 shares, which will be worth $32 (0.4 multiplied by $80 share price). Therefore we will need to have an additional $12. In the downside scenario, we also need to have an additional $12 (the difference between the $0 profit for the option and the value of 0.4 shares at $30). The additional money required will always be the same for both of the two scenarios.

For our final assumption, assume that we can borrow at in interest rate of 5 percent. If we need $12 a year from now then we need to borrow approximately $11.43 now ($12 divided by 1.05).

Now we can finally figure out the fair value of the call option. The value of the call option is exactly equal to the value of 0.4 shares of stock at today's price of $50 less the amount we need to borrow today, which is $11.43. Therefore the value of the call option is approximately $8.57.

$$\text{Value of Call Option} = (0.4 \times 50) - \$11.43 = \$8.57$$

The Black-Scholes Formula Yes, valuing options is confusing. In reality, we have just scratched the surfaced. We haven't talked about valuing puts, and we haven't considered other complicating variables such as dividends or implications of the differences between American and European options.

The good news is that as investment bankers, anytime we need to value an option, we will likely use a model that someone else has built for us in Excel. This model will be based on what is known as the Black-Scholes formula. The Black-Scholes formula relies on the same logic that we just discussed in our example of valuing a call option. However, instead of analyzing only two binary choices for a stock's movement, the formula assumes an infinite number of small stock movements until the expiration date.

Chances are, you will never need to know the actual formula used in the Black-Scholes model. If you do, you can look it up in a finance textbook or online. But what you do need to know, and what can sometimes be the subject of an interview question, are the key assumptions on which the Black-Scholes relies. There are five crucial assumptions:

1. Risk-Free Interest Rate The first key assumption used in the Black-Scholes formula is the risk-free interest rate. You should use a maturity for this rate that matches the time until the expiration date of the option. For a call option, the higher the interest rate, the higher the value of the option. This is because we are not paying the exercise price until a later date and, therefore, the holder of the option can invest that money and earn a higher return in the interim period. For put options, the higher the interest rate, the lower the put value.

2. Current Stock Price The next assumption is the current stock price. Since option prices are derived from stock prices, it logically follows that the higher the stock price, the higher the value of a call option that gives you the right to purchase the stock. Since a put option gives a holder the right to sell, the opposite is true for puts.

3. Exercise Price An increase in the exercise price lowers the value of a call option. This is true because, other things being equal, the difference between the stock price and the exercise price will be smaller, and therefore there will be less profit made when the option is exercised. For puts, the higher the exercise price, the higher the put option value.

4. Volatility of the Stock The fourth assumption is the volatility of the stock. This is typically calculated based on the standard deviation of the annualized, continuously compounded rate of return, based on historic stock values. The higher the volatility of the stock, the higher the value of call and put options. This is because the more volatile a stock, the more likely is to move above (in the case of a call) or below (in the case of a put) the exercise price.

5. Time until Expiration The last key assumption is the amount of time until the option's expiration date. The further out the expiration date, the higher the value of both call and put options. Since the stock has more time to move up or down, it has a greater chance of being above or below the exercise price.

Warrants Warrants are essentially call options issued by the same company that has issued the underlying shares. When an investor exercises a call option, in exchange for paying the exercise price, the investor receives already-existing shares from the third party that wrote the call option. The total number of shares outstanding for the company does not change. On the other hand, when an investor exercises a warrant, the investor receives brand new shares issued by the company and therefore, the number of shares outstanding increases.

Options and warrants are valued the same way: using the Black-Scholes formula. The key difference is that issuing warrants is potentially dilutive to existing shareholders. This dilutive effect combined with the fact that the company, rather than a third party, receives the cash associated with the exercise price has some implications on the Black Scholes model. Because of these differences, warrants and call options with otherwise identical terms will have a slightly different value.

END-OF-CHAPTER QUESTIONS

1. What is the primary role of the financial system?
2. Who are some of the key players in the financial system?
3. What is the primary role of financial institutions?
4. What are some examples of institutional investors?
5. What are some examples of alternative investments?
6. Why is money today worth more than money tomorrow?
7. What is a discount rate?
8. Conceptually, how do you estimate a discount rate?
9. What is the basic present value formula?
10. How do you value a perpetuity?
11. How do you value a perpetuity with constant growth?
12. How do you calculate the future value of an amount of money?
13. How should companies decide whether or not to invest in a project?
14. How do you calculate net present value?
15. How do you calculate the internal rate of return?
16. What kinds of things should companies include in cash flow when analyzing NPV or IRR?
17. What kinds of things should companies not include in cash flow when analyzing NPV or IRR?
18. Under what circumstances will the net present value equal zero?
19. What is capital structure?
20. Which is more expensive, debt or equity, and why?
21. Why does adding more debt to the capital structure raise the cost of debt?
22. Why does adding more debt to the capital structure raise the cost of equity?
23. Why is the cost of capital U-shaped?
24. What are some advantages and disadvantages to issuing debt?
25. What are some advantages and disadvantages to issuing stock?
26. What is the difference between secured debt and unsecured debt?
27. What has a higher cost: secured debt or unsecured debt? Why?
28. What is preferred stock?
29. What are some different ways in which a company can return money to investors?
30. What are the pros and cons of dividends versus stock buybacks?
31. How do you value a bond?
32. What is yield to maturity, and how do you calculate it?
33. What is yield to call, and how do you calculate it?
34. What is yield to worst, and how do you calculate it?

35. What is a bond's current yield, and how do you calculate it?
36. If interest rates rise, what will happen to the price of a bond?
37. What is duration and why is it important?
38. What are the key assumptions of the Black-Scholes formula for pricing options?
39. What are the differences between an option and a warrant?
40. How would a change in the level of the risk-free interest rate affect the value of a call? A put?
41. How would a change in the underlying stock price affect the value of a call? A put?
42. How would a change in the exercise price affect the value of a call? A put?
43. How would a change in a stock's expected volatility affect the value of a call? A put?
44. How would a change in the time until expiration affect the value of a call? A put?

Answers can be found at www.wiley.com/go/gutmann (password: investment).

CHAPTER 4

Financial Statement Analysis

In Chapter 2, we introduced the basic accounting knowledge that all investment bankers, and aspiring investment bankers, should possess. However, being able to define the various line items on the financial statements and knowing how the financial statements are integrated are not enough. A banker must also understand how to analyze and interpret the financial statements. It is for good reason that the title of a junior investment banker (and many other professional positions within the finance industry) is "analyst."

In this chapter we will discuss how we interpret, analyze, and compare a company's financial statements. Is a company growing? Is it growing faster or slower than its competitors? How profitable is a company? Is it more profitable than it was last year? Might a company be heading toward financial distress? These are the types of questions for which financial statement analysis helps us answer. Moreover, financial statement analysis also serves as a foundation for much of the valuation analysis that we will cover in Chapter 5.

One of the fundamental principles when using financial statement analysis for comparison purposes is to have consistency across the companies or time periods being evaluated, something bankers often refer to as apples-to-apples comparisons. It is not very meaningful to compare a company's performance over a three-month period with its performance over a 12-month period. Nor is it often helpful to compare financial results of companies in different industries. Keep this in mind as you read this chapter.

Before we start learning how to calculate the various metrics that are used to interpret financial results, we need to discuss how investment bankers obtain the financial statements and other information they use to perform this kind of analysis. Where does this information come from? Is it freely available, or must we pay for it? How do we know if it is reliable?

This chapter will start with a discussion of the sources of information for which investment bankers use to analyze companies and their financial statements. We will focus primarily on SEC documents, from where much of this information can be found. Next, we will discuss the two most important types of SEC documents: the 10-K and the 10-Q. We will then introduce some of the key metrics that investment bankers frequently calculate in order to analyze financial statements, namely growth statistics, profitability ratios, return ratios, activity ratios, and credit ratios. We will also discuss several different types of time periods that are commonly used in financial statement analysis. We will conclude this chapter with a discussion of the adjustments that bankers often make to financial statements, a process known as "normalizing" the financials.

SOURCES OF FINANCIAL INFORMATION

As we mentioned in the introduction to this chapter, before an investment banker can begin to analyze a company's financial statements, he or she first needs to obtain those financial statements. Once the financial statements are gathered, the information needs to be entered into Microsoft Excel so that it can be analyzed. The process of entering financial information into Excel is known as spreading the financial statements.

Sometimes investment bankers will be able to obtain the financial information directly from the management of the company being analyzed. This is usually the case only if that company has hired the investment bank to help execute a transaction (i.e., the company is a client of the investment bank). Most of the time, however, the banker needs to gather the financial statements, as well as additional information, from one or more publicly available data sources.

In fact, when a deal team is assigned to a new project (either a pitch or a live transaction), the first task typically given to the most junior investment banker assigned to the team (usually the analyst but sometimes an intern) is to put together a book containing relevant financial and business information about the company being pitched or advised. It is also the junior member's job to arrange for copies of this book to be distributed to each member of the deal team. This book is often referred to as a public information book (PIB) and typically contains several types of SEC documents, such as a 10-K and 10-Q (discussed in the next section), one or more equity research reports, and other information that the junior banker deems to be relevant.

Introduction to SEC Filings

In the United States, publicly traded companies are required by a government agency, the Securities and Exchange Commission (SEC), to release their financial statements to the public four times per year. Once a year, companies release a 10-K, or annual report, that must be audited by an accounting firm. For each of the three other fiscal quarters, companies release an unaudited 10-Q, or quarterly report.

Other countries have similar rules regarding financial reporting requirements (though some countries have semi-annual reporting, rather than quarterly). In fact, all developed countries have their own securities commissions that oversee their financial exchanges. Foreign companies that trade as American Depository Receipts (ADRs) on U.S. exchanges have many of the same filing requirements as U.S. companies.

Substantially all medium-sized to large private companies, and many small, private businesses, also prepare annual and quarterly financial statements. Often these statements are required by the company's lenders or investors. However, these statements are not made available to the public unless the company has publicly traded securities such as outstanding bonds. Because of this, in the United States, there is no significant source of publicly available financial information for most private companies. However, in certain other countries, even privately held companies with no publicly traded securities must make public and file their financial statements.

In the United States, public financial statements are available for all companies with public equity or debt securities, and they can be downloaded for free from a variety of sources, including:

- The SEC's web site (www.sec.gov).
- Various free financial web sites such as Yahoo Finance (finance.yahoo.com) and Google Finance (finance.google.com).
- The company's own web site (typically in the investor relations section).

SEC filings are considered to be the most reliable source of historical financial information for public companies and are the primary source for much of the analysis performed by investment bankers. There are however some additional data sources commonly used by bankers, which we will briefly discuss later in this chapter.

Types of SEC Filings

All SEC filings have short codes designating the type of filing. While not an exhaustive list of all of the documents that may be filed with the SEC, following are the types of filings most frequently used by investment bankers and other corporate finance professionals.

10-K—Annual Report The 10-K, or annual report, provides a comprehensive overview of the company's business, operations, and financial performance over a 12-month period. The 10-K, which must be audited by the company's accounting firm, must be filed within 60,75, or 90 days after the end of the company's fiscal year (we will discuss fiscal years later in this chapter), depending on the size of the company's market capitalization:

- 60 days for companies with market caps greater than $700 million (large accelerated filer).
- 75 days for companies with market caps between $75 and $700 million (accelerated filer).
- 90 days for companies with market caps less than $75 million (non-accelerated filer).

We will discuss the 10-K in more detail later in this chapter.

10-Q—Quarterly Report The 10-Q provides an overview of the company's financial performance over a three-month (or quarterly) period. The 10-Q is not audited. However, investment bankers typically consider the information to be just as reliable as that contained in a 10-K. The 10-Q must be filed three times per year, within 40 or 45 days from close of the company's first, second, and third fiscal quarters as follows:

- 40 days for large accelerated and accelerated filers.
- 45 days for non-accelerated filers.

We will also discuss the 10-Q in greater detail later in this chapter.

8-K—Current Report An 8-K, or current report, is filed by a company anytime it needs to report important news or events for which investors should be aware. Examples of such events include:

- Changes to the management team or to the company's board of directors.
- Announcement of an acquisition or merger.
- Signing of a new bank financing agreement.
- Win or loss of major customer contract.
- Announcement of quarterly or annual earnings.

8-Ks generally must be filed within four business days after the event, and there are rules and guidelines regarding what events are considered to be material.

14A—Proxy Statement The Schedule 14-A or Definitive Proxy Statement (often abbreviated as "Proxy Statement") is issued to shareholders and filed with the SEC in order to provide information on matters subject to vote at the company's annual shareholder meeting. Some of the important information contained in the Proxy Statement includes:

- A list of board members up for election.
- A list of beneficial owners of the company (such as management that owns shares in the company).
- Board and executive compensation.

S-1 The Form S-1, or Basic Registration Statement, is filed in connection with the offering of public securities. The S-1 is typically a lengthy document that contains a variety of business, financial, and legal information about a company. It includes, for example, a detailed business description, historical financial information, and a list of risk factors. It is designed to help prospective investors make an informed decision on whether to invest in the securities being offered.

The S-1 is also the early version of what is known as the prospectus and must be approved by the SEC. The S-1 typically goes through several rounds of amendments to address comments provided by the SEC. The S-1 is a valuable source of information since it is typically the first publicly available detailed source of financial information for a private company that is going to issue public securities, for example in an initial public offering (IPO).

S-4 The S-4 is filed when a company is going to issue public securities due to a business combination (merger or acquisition) or an exchange offer. The S-4 contains similar information to that found in an S-1.

13-D A Schedule 13-D is filed by investors of a company, rather than by the company itself. Specifically, a 13-D must be filed within 10 days by any person or group of persons who acquires 5 percent or more of a class of registered equity securities and intends to be an active shareholder. It also must also be filed to disclose a subsequent change in holdings. The 13-D requires the investor to disclose his or her "intentions" for owning shares in the company (for example, if the investor is seeking a board seat or intends to effectuate a takeover bid).

13-G A Schedule 13-G is similar to a 13-D but is used for passive investors, such as a mutual funds. As with the 13-D, a 13-G must be filed when an investor acquires 5 percent ownership of a company. The 13-G requires significantly less disclosure than the 13-D since the investor is deemed to be a passive, not an active, investor.

20-F The 20-F is an annual report similar to the 10-K but filed by foreign companies that have stock listed in the United States.

6-K—Current Report A 6-K is used for other interim filings by a foreign company. Similar to the 8-Ks filed by U.S. companies, 6-Ks are used to report material or important information but also may include quarterly or semi-annual financial performance.

"A"—Amendment (e.g., 8-KA) An "A" at the end of any of the types of SEC filings indicates that a document has been amended. The document may be amended or completely restated, and there may be multiple amendments filed for any given filing. Generally, investment bankers are advised to use the most recently amended document (the one with the latest date) since it contains the most currently available information. Amendments may contain very useful information that was not disclosed in the original filing. This is especially true for 8-Ks that contain information about an announced M&A transaction.

10-K Overview

As we briefly discussed earlier in this chapter, 10-Ks are filed once a year, within 60–90 days after the close of the company's fiscal year period, and are audited by the company's accounting firm. 10-Ks are often also referred to as "Annual Reports," though they do differ (mostly in presentation) from the typically glossy annual reports that are frequently mailed out to investors of the company's stock.

10-Ks are relatively standardized documents and generally range from 50 to 150 pages or more, excluding the exhibits often attached to the end of the document. Investment bankers almost never need to read a 10-K from cover to cover. However, it is very important that bankers are familiar with these documents so that they can quickly retrieve the relevant information that is needed for analysis.

Following is a discussion of some of the key sections and important information found in a typical 10-K.

Cover of the 10-K The cover of the 10-K contains some useful information about the company. However, keep in mind that while the cover is technically only one page in length, it often extends onto a second page when the document is converted to electronic format (such as a PDF). Key information included on the cover includes:

- Full legal name of the company.
- State of incorporation.

- Fiscal year end date.
- Stock exchange(s) for which common stock is registered.
- Most recent number of common shares outstanding.

General Business Overview Toward the beginning of the 10-K is an often lengthy section known as the general business overview. Reading this section is very useful for quickly achieving a basic understanding of the company's business model, its operations, and its industry. In addition, parts of this section are often paraphrased by investment bankers for use in presentations when writing company overview sections.

Following is a list of some of the useful information contained in the general business overview. Note that some of these sections may not apply to all companies and may not be found in all 10-Ks.

- Overview of the business.
- Business segments.
- Recent acquisitions.
- Operations.
- Properties owned or leased.
- Supply chain, including a list of significant suppliers.
- Types of customers, including a list of significant customers.
- Competition.
- Research and development.
- Intellectual property.
- Risk factors.
- Ongoing litigation.

Management's Discussion and Analysis (MD&A) Another section of the 10-K that is valuable to investment bankers is the section known as management's discussion and analysis (MD&A). Essentially, this section is management's "commentary" on its financial condition and results of operations. It provides some brief level of detail about the company's performance and how that performance compared with previous periods.

In the 10-K, the MD&A section will compare the results from the most recent year and the previous year, as well as compare the results from the previous year with two years ago. This section can be very helpful in interpreting the financial statements. For example, suppose that we notice from the income statement that revenues declined 20 percent this year from last year. The MD&A section may help tell us what caused that decline and thereby help us to put our analysis in its proper context.

For instance, if management discloses that revenue declined 20 percent because the company lost a key customer, then this is likely to be considered bad news and may portend lower revenues in future years as well. On the other hand, suppose that the company tells us that revenues declined due to an obsolete product but that a new, replacement product is being introduced this year. This news may not be interpreted as negative and may not lead to lower forecasted revenues.

There is also a section contained within the MD&A, often referred to as liquidity and capital resources (or similar wording), that discusses the company's current cash and liquidity position. This section is often extremely valuable for interpreting whether a company might be experiencing signs of financial distress. The MD&A section also sometimes contains management's outlook for certain key items (e.g., how much it expects to spend in future years on capital expenditures). This kind of information can be very helpful when making forecasts, as we will discuss in detail in Chapter 6.

Finally, it is worth noting that the MD&A section is very important for discovering certain non-recurring items, something we will discuss in more detail later in this chapter.

The Financial Statements The balance sheet, income statement, and statement of cash flows are considered by most investment bankers to be the most important three pages contained in the 10-K. These three statements are usually, but not always found in that order. A typical 10-K contains a balance sheet with two years of data, an income statement with three years of data, and a cash flow statement with three years of data.

Footnotes to the Financial Statements Following the three financial statements in the 10-K are a number of footnotes to the financial statements. These footnotes provide more information about the financial statements, including some of the assumptions used, explanations, and additional detail about the financial statements. While a number of the footnotes can be useful, two of the footnotes that are most frequently used by investment bankers include:

1. Debt footnote, which provides a breakdown of short and long-term debt and includes schedule of maturities.
2. Shareholders' equity footnote, which includes stock option information useful for calculating fully diluted shares.

List of Exhibits At the end of most 10-Ks is a page or two that contains a list of documents that were attached to previous SEC filings for that company. This list of exhibits can be very useful. Rather than potentially having to search through years' worth of filings to locate a key document, we can quickly locate it using the list of exhibits. A footnote for each exhibit will tell us to what original document the exhibit was originally attached and therefore where to find each document.

Examples of some of the useful types of documents that are often filed as attachments and can be found in this list of exhibits include:

- Merger agreements.
- Bank credit agreements and amendments.
- Debt indentures.
- Shareholder agreements.
- Management employee agreements.

10-Q Overview

As we mentioned earlier in this chapter, 10-Qs (or quarterly reports) are filed three times per year, within 40 or 45 days after the close of the company's fiscal quarter. These documents are usually significantly shorter than 10-Ks, as they contain less information, often ranging from 15 to 50 or more pages, excluding exhibits. Like the 10-K, 10-Qs are relatively standardized documents. Unlike the 10-K, however, the financial information contained in the 10-Q is not audited by the company's accountants. However, as we've already stated, bankers rely on this unaudited information for analysis equivalently to the audited information contained in a 10-K.

Following is a discussion of some of the key sections and important information found in a typical 10-Q. Keep in mind that many of these sections are similar to what is contained in the 10-K, though with less detail.

Cover of the 10-Q The cover of the 10-Q contains the same useful information as the cover of the 10-K. As with the 10-K cover, the 10-Q cover will also sometimes extend to the second page of a formatted PDF document. Helpful information from the cover includes:

- Full legal name of the company.
- State of incorporation.
- Fiscal year end date.
- Stock exchange(s) for which common stock is registered.
- Most recent number of common shares outstanding.

The Financial Statements Like in the 10-K, the 10-Q also contains the three essential financial statements: the income statement, balance sheet, and cash flow statement. However, whereas in the 10-K the statements are buried somewhere in the middle of the document, in the 10-Q they are conveniently located at the beginning.

The balance sheet will contain two or three columns of data. It always contains the balance sheet as of the latest quarter end and the balance sheet as of the last fiscal year end. It sometimes contains a third column: the balance sheet as of the previous year's equivalent quarter end.

The income statement always contains financial results for the current fiscal quarter, the equivalent fiscal quarter last year, the current year-to-date (YTD) period, and last year's equivalent YTD period. The YTD period reflects the financial results since the beginning of the fiscal year. If the 10-Q represents a first-quarter filing, the income statement will have only two columns of data since the first quarter's figures are equivalent to the YTD figures. If the income statement reflects a second- or third-quarter filing, then it will have four columns of data. Note, however, that there is no consistentcy about the order of these columns, so always be careful when analyzing or spreading 10-Q data that you are looking at the correct columns.

The cash flow statement will typically have only two sets of data, including the YTD period for the current year (either three, six, or nine months) and the equivalent YTD period for the previous year (also three, six, or nine months).

Footnotes to the Financial Statements The 10-Q will include footnotes to the financial statements that contain assumptions, explanations, and further detail about the financial statements. However, these footnotes will be fewer in number and less detailed than those found in the 10-K.

Management's Discussion and Analysis (MD&A) Also as with the 10-K, the 10-Q includes an MD&A section with management's factually based "color commentary" on its financial condition and results of operations. And like in the 10-K, this section is a crucial section for finding non-recurring items and also contains a section on the company's liquidity and capital resources.

List of Exhibits Just as in the 10-K, the 10-Q will contain a list of exhibits disclosing where to look to find previously filed documents.

Other Data Sources

While the SEC documents, especially the 10-K and 10-Q, are considered the most important resources for analyzing a company's financial performance, they are not the only sources of information used by investment bankers. In this section we will point out some of these other data sources.

Subscription-Based Data Sources Bankers will sometimes download the financial statements from a subscription-based data source to save time rather than "spread" them manually from the 10-Ks and 10-Qs. Such paid data sources typically contain all of the numerical data (including the financial statements, the footnotes, and other numerical exhibits) found in the SEC documents in an easy-to-download format.

These data sources also contain additional useful information such as databases of current and historical stock prices, stock ownership information, M&A transactions, etc. These data sources cost anywhere from hundreds to several thousands of dollars per month per user. However, if you are a student, you may also have access to one or more of these resources through your school library system. Examples of data sources commonly used by investment bankers include:

- FactSet.
- ThomsonOne from Thomson Reuters.
- Capital IQ.
- Bloomberg.

Whether the junior banker spreads the financial information from the source SEC documents or downloads it from a data source often depends on a number of factors, including the importance of the analysis (the more important, the more likely to go to source documents) and the investment bank involved (some investment banks and individual groups within banks have rules about when information can be downloaded and when information must be entered from source documents).

Keep in mind that while the quality of these data sources is very high, there are occasionally errors in the data. Additionally, the data providers sometimes reclassify certain line items and/or make adjustments to financial statements (for example, stripping out non-recurring items, which we will come to later in this chapter). For these reasons, when downloading data, it is extremely important that a banker check the figures carefully and make sure that he or she understands and agrees with any adjustments.

Equity Research Reports Another source of data that is heavily used by investment bankers are equity research reports, sometimes referred to as analyst reports. These documents are published by equity research analysts who cover and write about publicly traded companies. These reports often contain a lot of very helpful information and analysis, including business and industry overviews, and assessment of recent earnings. Often the quickest way for a banker to "get up to speed" on a company or an industry is to read relevant equity research reports. This is especially true of "initiating coverage" reports, an often-lengthy document produced when an equity research analyst first starts covering a company.

Equity research reports also typically contain a set of financial projections for a company forecasted by the research analyst. In fact, while SEC documents are considered the primary source for historical financial information, equity research reports are the most widely used source for projected financial information. We will see how these projections can be very useful when we discuss valuation in Chapter 5 and financial modeling in Chapter 6.

However, unlike SEC documents, which can be downloaded for free from a variety of sources, there is no free source for equity research reports. Banks typically pay for subscription-based services to databases of equity research reports. Sometimes these services even allow you to download the Excel model created by the equity research analyst that underlies the report. If you do not have access to a subscription-based service, some brokerage firms and some services will allow you to pay for individual reports. In addition, you may be able to get access to reports from a particular brokerage firm if you have a trading account with that firm.

Additional Sources In addition to SEC documents, subscription-based financial data providers and equity research reports, there are several other information sources worth mentioning. When working on a live transaction for a client, investment bankers often rely heavily on information provided by company's management. Various industry and market research reports are sometimes (expensively) purchased especially when bankers need information for industry trends and industry data. Bankers also often use databases of news articles such as Factiva or LexisNexis and databases of companies (including private companies) such as Hoovers.

Lastly, even free resources such as Yahoo! Finance or Google Finance can be useful, especially for "quick-and-dirty" analysis. However, always be aware of one of the unspoken rules of investment banking: While information contained in a presentation must always be footnoted with a source, you should never cite an unpaid resource such as Yahoo! or Google in a footnote.

FINANCIAL STATEMENT ANALYSIS

As we mentioned in the introduction to this chapter, the goals of financial statement analysis are to analyze, understand, compare, and forecast a company's financial performance and financial position. Specifically, financial statement analysis is useful for:

- Understanding a company's financial performance and financial health.
- Comparing the performance of one time period with another time period (e.g., this year vs. last year).

- Comparing the performance of one company with that of another company or with that of an industry average or industry index.
- Projecting a company's future financial performance (which we will discuss when we cover financial modeling in Chapter 6).

The financial statements contain a lot of information about the performance and health of a company. Revenues and profits, assets and liabilities, sources and uses of cash are all important facts to have when evaluating a company's financial performance. However, without proper context, these financial metrics have limited value and, without additional analysis, it is difficult to truly understand a company's financial performance.

For example, suppose a company records $1 billion of revenue this year. Does that represent good financial performance? Or does it reflect poor performance? If the previous year's revenue figure was $800 million, then perhaps we should conclude that the company had a great year. On the other hand, if last year's revenue was $1.2 billion, we might instead be highly disappointed in the current year's results.

Similarly, assume that along with revenue of $1 billion, the company reported $100 million of profits. Should we be impressed or unimpressed? Perhaps a competitor also had $1 billion of revenue but generated only $50 million of earnings. In this case, our company's performance was pretty good in comparison. But if the competitor instead had $200 million of profits on $1 billion of revenue, we might want to suggest a new management team for our company.

For investment bankers, it is also often important to understand the reasons behind a company's particular financial performance. For example, why did revenue increase last year? Why are one company's profits higher than another's? We have already discussed earlier in this chapter how the MD&A sections of the 10-K and 10-Q give us some insight (based on management's views) into a company's financial results. The tools of financial statement analysis will help provide further insights.

Overview of Ratio Analysis

In order to help analyze financial performance, bankers often calculate various statistics and ratios, a process often referred to as ratio analysis. Calculating such metrics help us to interpret, compare, and analyze a company's financial performance. Determining these metrics for additional companies in the same industry also helps us to benchmark financial results against a peer group and allows us to identify over- and underperforming companies.

There are several categories of statistics and ratios that are commonly calculated by investment bankers. In addition to the types of ratios and statistics to be discussed, there are also industry specific metrics that are used when analyzing companies in a particular industry. However, the following categories tend to be useful for companies in most industries:

- Growth statistics.
- Profitability ratios (margins).
- Return ratios.
- Credit ratios.
- Activity ratios.

There is one other important set of ratios (valuation ratios, also called valuation multiples or trading multiples), which we will discuss in detail when we cover valuation in Chapter 5.

Growth Statistics

Of all of the types of statistics calculated to analyze a company's financial performance, perhaps the most useful one to a banker is a calculation of how fast a company is growing or shrinking. In fact, the calculation of historical growth is especially useful for forecasting and financial modeling purposes, something we will cover in Chapter 6.

Growth can be measured using any number of operating metrics. We might want to analyze growth in the number of employees or the number of subscribers or the number of retail stores. Or we might want to measure growth using a metric from the financial statements such as profit growth or asset growth or the growth of money spent on capital expenditures. In fact, bankers often calculate a number of growth metrics when performing financial statement analysis. However, the most commonly used metric to calculate a company's growth is its revenue.

One-Period Growth Rate Very often it is useful to calculate the growth of a key financial or operating metric, such as revenue, over two consecutive time periods. Each of these time periods could be any such period, such as a day, a month, or a fiscal quarter. Most frequently, though, we tend to use a fiscal year. The following equation is used to calculate the single period growth rate:

$$\text{Growth}\,\% = \frac{\text{This Period}}{\text{Previous Period}} - 1$$

Compound Annual Growth Rate (CAGR) In addition to measuring growth over one period, it is also often valuable to measure growth over a longer period of time and over multiple periods. To do this, we calculate what we call the Compound Annual Growth Rate (CAGR). The CAGR, as its name implies, measures the average, compounded growth over multiple periods. As with the single-period growth rate, we might want to calculate the growth of any number of financial metrics, though calculating revenue growth is again, most common.

$$\text{CAGR \%} = \left(\left(\frac{\text{Last Period}}{\text{First Period}} \right)^{\frac{1}{\#\ \text{periods} - 1}} \right) - 1$$

It is important to remember that the exponent in the CAGR equation is always one less than the number of periods of data. For example, suppose you wish to calculate the compounded annual growth rate of revenues from 2007 to 2012. This reflects six years of data (2007, 2008, 2009, 2010, 2011, 2012) but the exponent used in the formula should be 5. Also keep in mind that we only need data from the first and last year. We do not need the middle years to calculate CAGR.

Profitability Ratios (Margins)

Another extremely important set of statistics used in financial statement analysis is the measurement of a company's profitability as a percentage of revenue. We frequently call these statistics margins. Recall that we have already introduced gross margin, EBIT margin, and net income margin in Chapter 2 when we discussed the income statement. With all of the ratios discussed here, the higher the number, the better.

Gross Profit Margin Gross profit margin (or simply gross margin) is a measure of how much gross profit that company generates for each dollar of revenue. Companies with a large amount of cost of goods sold (COGS) naturally have lower gross margins since gross profit equals revenue less COGS. We calculate gross profit margin as follows:

$$\text{Gross Profit Margin} = \frac{\text{Gross Profit}}{\text{Revenue}}$$

Why might a company's gross profit increase from one year to the next? Perhaps this year the company was able to raise prices while being able to keep its costs steady. Or perhaps, prices were relatively steady but the company was able to lower its cost of goods sold because of lower raw material prices.

EBIT Margin (or Operating Income Margin) EBIT margin (synonymously operating income margin) is a metric used to calculate how much operating income a company generates for each dollar of revenue. By definition, companies with large COGS and/or SG&A relative to revenue will have lower EBIT margins. EBIT margin is calculated as follows:

$$\text{EBIT Margin} = \frac{\text{EBIT}}{\text{Revenue}}$$

Let us consider why one company could have a higher EBIT margin than other company in this same industry. First, if its gross profit margin is higher, then its EBIT margin is also likely to be higher. Or perhaps the company has a lower overhead structure or spends less money on marketing and advertising, or less on research and development. Given that EBIT equals gross profit less SG&A, anything that affects SG&A will have an impact on EBIT margin.

EBITDA Margin Recall from Chapter 2 that EBITDA is often used a proxy for operating cash flow. Calculating the EBITDA margin helps us to measure how much operating cash flow a company generates per each dollar of revenue. The calculation of EBITDA margin is:

$$\text{EBITDA Margin} = \frac{\text{EBITDA}}{\text{Revenue}}$$

Since EBITDA is equal to EBIT plus depreciation and amortization, the same operating activities that affect the EBIT margin will affect the EBITDA margin. In addition, higher depreciation and/or amortization will, by definition, result in a higher EBITDA margin.

Net Income Margin The net income margin reflects how much net income a company generates per each dollar of revenue. Net income margin is calculated as follows:

$$\text{Net Income Margin} = \frac{\text{Net Income}}{\text{Revenue}}$$

Anything that impacts EBIT margin will also impact net income margin. However, the net income margin will also be affected by any nonoperating income or expenses as well as higher or lower interest expense, interest income, and taxes. For example, consider two companies that have the same operating income (EBIT). If one of the companies has more debt in its capital structure and therefore has more interest expense, it will show a lower net income margin. Similarly, if one company has a lower tax rate than another due to its ability to utilize net operating loss carryforwards (NOLs), it would, correspondingly, have a higher net income margin.

Other Metrics as a Percentage of Revenue While technically not a profitability ratio or margin, bankers also often calculate other operating metrics as a percentage of revenue. Just about any expense item or cash expenditure can be analyzed as a percentage of revenue.

For example, it might be useful to analyze how much a company spends on SG&A or research and development as a percentage of revenues compared with other firms in its industry. Higher SG&A might indicate a bloated overhead or an overpaid CEO. On the other hand, we might interpret higher R&D spending as investment that might lead to faster growth and higher revenues in the future.

Similarly, we might want to analyze how much the business is spending on capital expenditures as a percentage of revenues compared with how much it has spent in the past. A sharp increase in capital expenditures might suggest that the company needs to spend more to maintain aging equipment. Alternatively, it might be a sign of the company investing in a new factory or new product line.

Return Ratios

Return ratios measure a company's efficiency of generating, or returning, net income or operating cash flow from its assets or capital. The three most commonly used return ratios are return on assets (ROA), return on equity (ROE), and return on invested capital (ROIC). For each of these metrics, the higher the ratio, the more money a firm earns from each dollar of asset or capital.

Note that with all of these return ratios, you may come across alternative calculations. The most important thing is to use a consistent formula when comparing across companies or time periods.

In each of these ratios, the numerator reflects income over a period of time, typically one year. The denominator should be the average balance of assets, equity, or invested capital over that same period. Therefore, we typically calculate the denominator as the average of the value at the beginning of the period and the value at the end of the period.

Return on Assets (ROA) Return on assets (ROA) reflects how much net income a company generates per each dollar of assets. We need to be careful comparing ROA ratios for similar companies if the companies carry their assets at very different values. ROA is a more useful metric for financial institutions such as banks because their assets are generally carried at fair market value. ROA is calculated as:

$$\text{Return on Assets (ROA)} = \frac{\text{Net Income}}{\text{Total Assets}}$$

Return on Equity (ROE) Return on Equity (ROE) measures how much net income a company generates for its shareholders, based on the company's book value of equity. Keep in mind that ROE will be significantly affected by a company's choice of capital structure. Generally, increasing leverage will increase a company's ROE as long as the interest rate paid on the new debt is not higher than the company's total return on capital (ROIC). Return on equity can be calculated using the following formula:

$$\text{Return on Equity (ROE)} = \frac{\text{Net Income}}{\text{Shareholders' Equity}}$$

Return on Invested Capital (ROIC) For an investment banker, return on invested capital (ROIC) is the most useful and meaningful metric of the three types of return ratios. Note that return on invested capital is sometimes referred to as return on capital (ROC) or return on net assets (RONA). ROIC measures a company's after-tax operating income as a percentage of its invested capital. Return on invested capital is not affected by a company's capital structure and therefore represents a purely operating metric, which makes it more useful when comparing different companies.

There are different ways to calculate ROIC, but most formulas will use after-tax operating income in the numerator, sometimes also referred to as net operating profit after tax (NOPAT). It can be calculated as EBIT multiplied by one minus the company's effective tax rate. Occasionally you will see ROIC calculated with pre-tax operating income (EBIT).

There are also a number of different ways in which to calculate the denominator. The denominator should reflect only a company's invested capital, which should exclude cash. One way to calculate the denominator is to start with total assets, subtract cash and current liabilities, and add back current debt, as we do in the following formula. In essence we are taking into account fixed assets plus net working capital, where net working capital excludes cash and current debt, as we learned in Chapter 2.

$$\text{Return on Invested Capital (ROIC)} = \frac{\text{EBIT} \times (1 - \text{Tax Rate})}{\text{Total Assets} - \text{Cash} - \text{Current Liabilities} + \text{Current Debt}}$$

Credit Ratios

Credit ratios such as the leverage ratio, interest coverage ratio, debt to equity ratio, and debt to capitalization ratio are useful metrics for understanding the magnitude of debt in a company's capital structure. These ratios are especially useful for credit analysis, including analyzing or estimating credit ratings, as well as modeling leveraged buyout (LBO) transactions. They are also very important when analyzing distressed or potentially distressed companies.

In fact, these ratios are commonly found in credit agreements, the contracts that exist between a company and its bank lender. Often these agreements stipulate that a company must maintain certain leverage and interest coverage ratios in order to remain in "good standing." As we learned in Chapter 3, these rules are known as covenants. Should the company's leverage or interest coverage ratio fall (in the case of the interest coverage ratio) or rise (in the case of the leverage ratio) outside of the allowed range, the company may be deemed to be in default. Note that the calculations of leverage and interest coverage ratios contained in the covenant section of credit agreements are often more detailed than the formulas in this section, but the principles are the same.

Remember that companies in less risky industries with steadier cash flows and high asset bases can operate with more leverage (more debt) than companies in riskier industries with more volatile cash flows and lower asset bases. For instance a regulated utility will almost always have more debt on its balance sheet than will a consumer products manufacturer, and a consumer products manufacturer will likely have more debt than a biotechnology company. The same assumption exists for companies within the same industry. Companies with riskier cash flows should theoretically have lower levels of debt.

Leverage Ratios The leverage ratio measures the amount of a company's borrowings as a multiple of its annual operating cash flow. Another way to interpret the leverage ratio is that it measures how many years it would take for the company to generate enough cash flow to pay back all of its debt. The higher the leverage ratio, the more debt it has relative to cash flow and the riskier the company.

Since EBITDA is used as a proxy for operating cash flow, it is typically used in the denominator of the leverage ratio. However, variations of this formula may use other measures of cash flow in the denominator such as EBITDA less capital expenditures or EBITDA less capital expenditures less the change in net working capital. Also, sometimes the leverage ratio is calculated with net debt in the numerator as opposed to total debt. Recall that net debt equals total debt less cash. Following are two variations of the leverage ratio formula:

$$\text{Leverage Ratio} = \frac{\text{Total Debt}}{\text{EBITDA}}$$

$$\text{Leverage Ratio} = \frac{\text{Net Debt}}{\text{EBITDA}}$$

Interest Coverage Ratios The interest coverage ratio measures a company's operating cash flow as a multiple of its interest expense. In other words, it measures the amount of "cushion" a company has to pay the amount of annual interest expense it owes on its debt. For the interest coverage ratio, the higher the ratio, the lower the risk (opposite from the leverage ratio). If the interest coverage ratio falls close to 1 or even below 1, it may indicate that the company might not have enough cash flow to cover its interest expense and might be on the road to distress.

As with the leverage ratio, there are a number of variations of the interest coverage ratio, two of which are shown here. The first formula shows EBITDA divided by interest expense. Other metrics can be substituted for operating cash flow (such as EBITDA less capital expenditures). In addition, cash interest expense or net interest expense is sometimes used in the denominator.

$$\text{Interest Coverage Ratio} = \frac{\text{EBITDA}}{\text{Interest Expense}}$$

$$\text{Interest Coverage Ratio} = \frac{\text{EBITDA}}{\text{Cash Interest Expense}}$$

Debt to Equity Ratio The debt to equity ratio is another statistic that provides an indication of the amount of leverage employed by a company, relative to the market value of the company's equity. The debt to equity (D/E) ratio can be calculated as:

$$\text{Debt to Equity Ratio} = \frac{\text{Total Debt}}{\text{Market Value of Equity}}$$

Debt to Capitalization Ratio The debt to capitalization ratio, also referred to as the debt to capital ratio or the debt to cap ratio, is a variation of the debt to equity ratio. It measures the percentage that debt makes up in a company's capital structure. Investment bankers calculate the debt to capitalization ratio as follows:

$$\text{Debt to Capitalization Ratio} = \frac{\text{Total Debt}}{\text{Total Debt} + \text{Market Value of Equity}}$$

Note that if a company has preferred stock in its capital structure as well, then the value of the preferred stock should also be included in the denominator.

Activity Ratios

Activity ratios are a measure of a company's efficiency of managing working capital. The metrics that we will cover in this section take into account what are typically the three most important components of working capital: inventory, accounts receivable, and accounts payable. These metrics are also useful for forecasting the balance sheet, which we will cover in our discussion of financial modeling in Chapter 6.

Note that in the latter of the three formulas to be covered (days sales of inventory, accounts receivable days, and accounts payable days), 360 is used to approximate the number of days in a year. It is also perfectly reasonable to use the exact number of days in a year (365). Many investment bankers prefer to use 360 because when creating quarterly or monthly models, 360 is evenly divided by 90 days per quarter and 30 days per month.

In each of the activity ratio formulas, the income statement metric, either revenue or cost of goods sold (COGS) should reflect an annual figure. The balance sheet metric, either inventory, accounts receivable, or accounts payable, can reflect either the ending balance sheet figure or an average of the beginning and the ending balance sheet figure. The latter (average of the beginning and ending figures) is preferable though both are commonly performed.

Inventory Turnover Inventory turnover measures the number of times per year a company replaces its inventory. The higher the number, the less inventory the company keeps relative to cost of goods sold (revenue is also sometimes used in the numerator). Since purchasing inventory requires funds, the higher the inventory turnover, the less money the company needs, other things being equal. Companies that utilize so called just-in-time inventory practices will often have very high inventory turnover ratios. Inventory turnover is calculated as follows:

$$\text{Inventory Turnover} = \frac{\text{Cost of Goods Sold (COGS)}}{\text{Inventory}}$$

Days Sales of Inventory Days sales of inventory, also referred to as days of inventory, measures how many days it takes, on average, to convert inventory into sales. Essentially, this ratio is the inverse of inventory turnover and tells us the same information. Here, the lower the number, the less money is tied up in inventory. However, if the number gets too low, it might indicate some riskiness of the business. For example, if inventory is too low, an unexpected problem at a supplier or a sudden shipping problem might result in the production line having to be shut down for lack of sufficient raw materials or supplies, which in turn could affect revenue. We calculate days sales of inventory as:

$$\text{Days Sales of Inventory} = \frac{\text{Inventory}}{\text{COGS}} \times 360$$

Accounts Receivable Days Accounts receivable days, also referred to as AR days, measures how many days it takes, on average, for a company to collect money due from its customers. The lower this number, the faster customers are paying, which is a good thing because the company can use that money for other purposes. Typically payment terms for a company might be between 30 and 60 days. For most companies, receivables outstanding more than 90 days are considered delinquent and the likelihood of getting paid diminishes. Retailers for example tend to have lower AR days since customers typically pay for merchandise via credit cards or cash. Accounts receivable days is calculated as follows:

$$\text{Accounts Receivable Days} = \frac{\text{Accounts Receivables}}{\text{Revenue}} \times 360$$

Accounts Payable Days Accounts payable days, also called AP days, measures how many days it takes, on average, for a company to pay its vendors. The higher the number, the less money is tied up in working capital. Essentially vendors are helping to finance the business. However, if companies take too long to pay their vendors, vendors may become annoyed and stop shipping or demand faster payment terms or even cash in advance. Very high or escalating levels of AP days is often an early sign of financial distress, as it can indicate that a company does not have sufficient funds to pays its suppliers in a timely manner. Accounts payable days can be calculated as:

$$\text{Accounts Payable Days} = \frac{\text{Accounts Payable}}{\text{COGS}} \times 360$$

ANALYZING DIFFERENT TIME PERIODS

We know from our discussion of 10-Ks and 10-Qs that most of the time (at least for U.S. companies), financial performance is reported in either quarterly (three-month) or annual (12-month) increments. Correspondingly, we tend to analyze data in increments of three or 12 months, although these increments need not correspond to a company's fiscal quarter or fiscal year, as we will describe.

Fiscal Year

A company's fiscal year (often abbreviated FY) reflects 12 consecutive months of financial performance, ending when the company closes its books. For many companies, the fiscal year runs equivalent to a calendar year, beginning January 1st and ending December 31st. However, companies are free to choose the date for which their fiscal year ends, and not all companies choose a calendar year. For example, retailers often have fiscal years that end in February or March, rather than on December 31st, so that they do not have to close their books during the busy holiday selling season and can account for the significant amount of returned holiday merchandise.

Investment bankers will often use the company's fiscal year period to analyze a full year of financial results and to compare those results to previous and/or projected fiscal years.

Fiscal Quarter

A company's fiscal year is divided into four fiscal quarters (often designated as Q1, Q2, Q3, and Q4). For purposes of analysis, it is not often very useful to compare consecutive fiscal quarters (for example, Q4 versus Q3). This is because most businesses experience some seasonality whereby different times of the year tend to be more or less active. For example, in the United States many companies have much higher revenues in the fourth quarter (assuming the company's fourth quarter corresponds to October through December), given the holiday selling season. It is usually much more informative to compare like quarters—for example, to compare Q4 of this year with Q4 of the prior year.

Year-to-Date (YTD)

The year-to-date (YTD) period reflects the time from the start of the fiscal year to the latest financial report. At the end of the first fiscal quarter, the YTD period reflects only the first three months of the fiscal year. At the end of the second fiscal quarter, the YTD period reflects the six months from the beginning of the fiscal year. After the third fiscal quarter, nine months of data is reflected in the YTD period. If the most recent financial report is a 10-K, then YTD is the entire year and is equal to the figures in the 10-K.

Last Twelve Months (LTM)

While comparing individual fiscal quarters is sometimes worthwhile, most of the time it is more effective to compare a full year's worth of financial performance. Not surprisingly, a company's fiscal year is a natural period of time for which to analyze, and, indeed, bankers do often use the fiscal year for purposes of analysis. However, there is often a significant disadvantage to using a company's fiscal year as the primary time period for analysis.

Consider a company with a calendar based fiscal year (i.e., January 1st–December 31st). Suppose that today's date is December 1st and that we wish to analyze a full 12 months of the company's financial results. If we were to use data from the company's most recent completed fiscal year (from the latest 10-K), we would be using information from January through December of the previous year. That data is 11 months stale!

Therefore, instead of relying primarily on old data, we typically calculate financial results for the time period known as the last twelve months (LTM) period, sometimes also referred to as the trailing twelve months (TTM) period. The LTM period represents a summation of the four most recent fiscal quarters for which information is available.

We can calculate LTM results using the most recently filed 10-Q and the most recently available 10-K. To calculate LTM revenue, for example, we take the most recent full fiscal year of revenue (from the 10-K), add revenue from the most recent year-to-date (YTD) period (from the 10-Q), and subtract revenue from the previous year's YTD period. Recall that the 10-Q shows us both YTD periods (this year and last year), so we only need the latest 10-Q filing along with the most recent 10-K. Exhibit 4.1 shows a

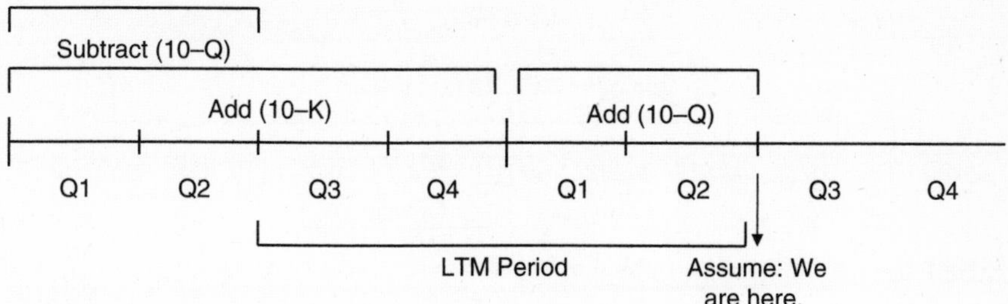

EXHIBIT 4.1 Calculating the Last Twelve Months (LTM) Period

graphical representation of this calculation, assuming that the most recent financial report is for a company's second fiscal quarter.

Keep in mind that the YTD period may be three months, six months, or nine months, depending on which quarter has most recently ended. On occasions when the most recent filing is a company's 10-K (i.e., the company's fiscal year has recently ended), LTM revenue is simply equal to the full year's revenue.

Bankers will often calculate LTM values for each line item of the income statement and for key line items on the cash flow statement, such as depreciation and amortization and capital expenditures. No adjustments need to be made to the balance sheet since the balance sheet reflects data at a point in time as opposed to over a period of time. Hence, there is really no such thing as an LTM balance sheet. For purposes of analysis, the balance sheet from the most recent filing should be used along with the calculated LTM income statement and cash flow statement figures.

Calendarization

In a perfect world, all companies would have the same fiscal year ends. Unfortunately for investment bankers, in the real world this is not the case. Assume that we want to compare the latest fiscal year's results for two companies in the same industry but suppose that the two companies have different fiscal year ends. Let's say Company A has a 2013 fiscal year ending December 31st and Company B has a 2013 fiscal year ending June 30th. As shown in Exhibit 4.2, only six months of data overlap for the two companies (January through June).

This date mismatch makes our analysis less consistent and therefore less valuable. For example, suppose that the economy was in a recession for July through December of the previous year. The macroeconomic effects would show up in Company B's fiscal year performance but not in Company A's. Similarly, suppose that the economy was booming during the second half of

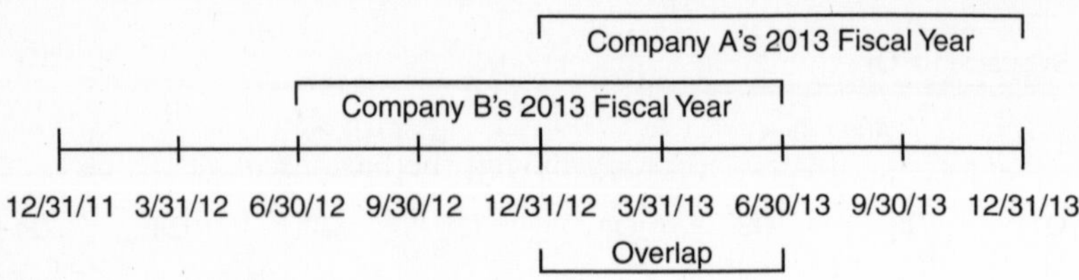

EXHIBIT 4.2 Comparison of Fiscal Years

the current year. Now, this boom would be reflected in Company A's performance but not in Company's B. (See Exhibit 4.3.) Comparing revenues (or any other metric) for the fiscal year is not very meaningful if one set of figures includes six months of poor economic conditions and the other set of figures includes six months of strong economic conditions.

One way to counteract the problem of different fiscal year ends is to rely on LTM figures when comparing performance rather than fiscal years. Since we have the most recent 12 months for each company, we can be assured that we are approximately using the same time period. (At the very most, we are off by no more than three months.) Indeed, bankers rely heavily on LTM figures for analysis.

However, for a variety of different analysis, especially valuation, as we will discuss in Chapter 5, bankers also want to use projected financial information. Unfortunately, financial results taken from equity research are frequently forecasted only annually and not quarterly. Therefore, we again have the problem of forecasts representing different calendar time periods when companies have different fiscal year ends. The solution is a process called calendarization, whereby we adjust all companies in our analysis to approximate having the same fiscal year end.

To perform calendarization, first we need to select a base fiscal year for which to adjust each company's results. We multiply the financial results

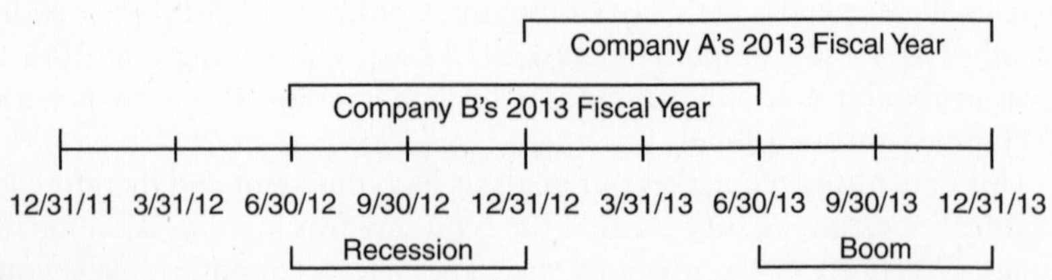

EXHIBIT 4.3 Comparison of Fiscal Years Showing Strong and Weak Economic Conditions

(i.e., revenue) for Year 1 by the percentage of the year that overlaps with the base fiscal year. We then multiply the results for Year 2 by the percentage of that year that overlaps with the base fiscal year. Adding to the two figures together approximates a company having the base fiscal year. Just as with the LTM calculation, we typically will calendarize the full income statement and key cash flow statement items.

For example, consider again two companies with different fiscal years. This time Company A has a fiscal year that ends December 31, 2013, and Company B has fiscal years that end September 30, 2013. Let's adjust (or calendarize) Company B's projected financial results to approximate it having the same fiscal year as Company A (ending December 31, 2013). To do this, we:

- Multiply Company B's 2013 (reflecting 10/1/12—9/30/13) full year figures by 0.75.
- Multiply Company B's 2014 (reflecting 10/1/13—9/30/14) full year figures by 0.25.
- Add the two figures together to approximate a full year ending December 31, 2013.

Exhibit 4.4 shows this calculation.

If we have happen to have access to quarterly projections, we can be even more precise. Using quarterly projections in this example, we can approximate a fiscal year end of December 31st by adding together 2013Q2 + 2013Q3 + 2013Q4 + 2014Q1.

Note that calendarization is only an approximation and is less accurate for very seasonal businesses or businesses that are growing or shrinking rapidly. This calculation can also get fairly complicated, especially when having to adjust multiple companies, all with different fiscal year ends. For this reason, many of the templates used by investment banks automate the calendarization calculation using built in formulas.

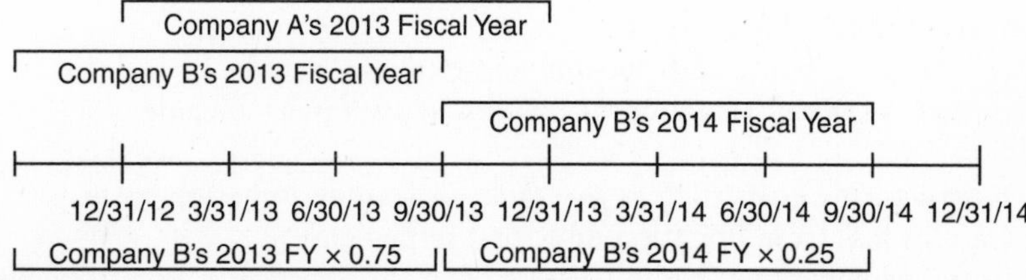

EXHIBIT 4.4 Calendarization Example

"NORMALIZING" THE FINANCIALS

In the previous section, we discussed the problem of comparing companies that have different fiscal year ends and we learned how to make adjustments to the financial statements in order to remedy this issue. There is another important set of adjustments that investment bankers make to financial statements, a process known as "normalizing" the financials or adjusting for non-recurring items.

Normalizing the financials refers to the process of adjusting a company's income statement to remove unusual or non-recurring (one-time) items. The goal of these adjustments is to estimate intrinsic or ongoing operational and financial performance so as to be able to make apples-to-apples comparisons with the metrics of other similar companies and to make apples-to-apples comparisons with future time periods.

For example, suppose that a company experienced a fire in a key manufacturing facility and that a significant expense was incurred in order to repair the damage. This expense would naturally have a negative impact on the year's profits. Further assume that the goal of our analysis is to predict next year's profitability for that company. Typically we would use the previous year's profitability as a baseline for our forecast. However, it would not make much sense to base next year's profitability on the previous year's if the previous year was impacted by an event (in this case, the fire) that we do not expect to happen again. Instead we should base our forecasted probability on last year's level only after we adjust out the negative impact of the fire.

Non-Recurring Items

Normalizing the financials is one of the hardest and most time-consuming things to do when analyzing companies. This is true for a number of reasons. Non-recurring items can be hard to find and they can be hard to adjust out. Moreover, a company might have a number of one-time items that need adjusting for any given time period. Finally, it is not always clear whether something should be considered non-recurring. Considerable judgment is often required for this analysis.

A variety of items, both income and expense, may be considered one-time or non-recurring. Common examples of such items include:

- Restructuring costs such as severance or lease termination costs.
- Gain or loss from litigation or a legal settlement.
- Costs stemming from natural disasters (e.g., fire, hurricane, or earthquake).
- Costs resulting from man-made disasters (e.g., fraud or sabotage).

- Gains or losses from the sale of assets.
- Asset write-down or impairment costs.

However, even these common examples require judgment to be used. For example, if a company closed a division, which resulted in significant severance charges, we would typically categorize the severance as a non-recurring item. On the other hand, suppose that a retailer records severance expense stemming from closing a dozen stores. If each year the retailer opens and closes about a dozen stores, we should not categorize the severance as non-recurring since we can expect a similar charge each year. In fact, some poorly managed companies seem to restructure their operations each year, resulting in charges. In this circumstance, even a large restructuring expense might not be considered a one-time item.

Similarly, the gain or loss from a lawsuit is often considered a non-recurring item. However, there are certain types of companies (tobacco or pharmaceutical companies, for example), for which such lawsuits might be considered part of their ordinary course of business.

Sources for Finding Adjustments

The first step in the process of normalizing the financial statements is to identify possible non-recurring items. There are a number of sources for finding non-recurring items, and in fact all of them should be consulted. This is one of the reasons why normalizing the financials, done correctly, is both time-consuming and challenging.

One source for finding and identifying non-recurring items is a company's 10-K or 10-Q. However, there are a number of places within these two documents where non-recurring items may be found. One such place is the income statement. If an item such as a restructuring expense is very significant then often a company will include the expense as its own line item on the income statement. The company will typically disclose additional detail in a footnote to its financial statements.

More commonly, non-recurring items can be found by reading through the management's discussion and analysis (MD&A) section of a 10-K or 10-Q, specifically in the paragraph that discusses SG&A. Recall that the MD&A section provides management's commentary on recent financial performance. You will often find statements that indicate that SG&A increased or operating profit or net income decreased this year because of some one-item or unusual expense.

Another very important source for discovering non-recurring items is the press release that is issued in connection with a company's quarterly earnings release. Often there is information about non-recurring items that is not found in the 10-Q or 10-K. For example, sometimes companies will disclose a pro forma EPS metric, as we discussed in Chapter 2. Often, many of the differences between pro forma EPS and GAAP EPS relate to one-item expenses and/or income.

Always keep in mind that one of the company's goals in calculating pro forma EPS is to make EPS appear to be strong by adding back what the company deems to be non-recurring expenses. You should do your own assessment, as you may not agree with the company's classification of what is non-recurring.

Finally, given the challenges involved with identifying and adjusting for non-recurring items, it is always wise to compare your adjustments with those of equity research analysts. It can also be helpful to compare adjustments with the analysis available in some of the subscription-based data sources, if you have such access.

Adjusting the Income Statement

Once you have identified the non-recurring items, the next step is to remove their impact from the company's financial results. Before you do this, you need to ask yourself three questions about each item:

1. Was the non-recurring item an expense or was it income?
2. Should the non-recurring item be considered an operating expense/income or a non-operating expense/income?
3. Was the non-recurring item disclosed on a pre-tax or post-tax basis?

Was the Non-Recurring Item an Expense or Income? If the non-recurring item reflected an expense, such as a restructuring charge or a loss on litigation, then you need to add back the item to the income statement. If on the other hand, the item reflected income such as a one-time gain due to an asset sale then you need to subtract it from the income statement. As we mentioned before, the majority of non-recurring items tend to be expenses so you are more likely to be adding them back. Either way, make sure you are adjusting the correct time period.

Should the Non-Recurring Item Be Considered Operating or Nonoperating? Most non-recurring expenses are classified as operating expenses and therefore affect a company's SG&A line. To adjust them out, we need to add them back to SG&A so that they increase EBIT and EBITDA. Similarly, non-recurring income that is considered operating income needs to be subtracted from EBIT and EBITDA. Conversely, non-operating items should only added back to or subtracted from net income and not from EBIT and EBITDA.

Examples of non-recurring items that would be considered non-operating include gains or losses on the sale of marketable securities or unrelated assets.

Was the Non-Recurring Item Disclosed on a Pre-Tax or Post-Tax Basis? The final question that needs to be considered is whether the company disclosed the non-recurring item on a pre-tax or post-tax basis. If the item was disclosed on a pre-tax basis, you can directly adjust it to EBIT and EBITDA, by adding it back (for an expense) or subtracting it (for income). However, in order to also adjust net income, you need to remember to tax-affect it by multiplying the non-recurring amount by one minus the tax rate. If the item was disclosed on a post-tax basis, then you can directly adjust it to net income but you need to reverse tax-affect it in order to adjust EBIT and EBITDA by dividing it by one minus the tax rate.

END-OF-CHAPTER QUESTIONS

1. What are some common SEC documents used by investment bankers?
2. What is some of the key information found in a 10-K?
3. What are some of the differences between a 10-K and a 10-Q?
4. What are some key ratios that we use to analyze financial statements?
5. How would you calculate revenue growth from this year compared to last year?
6. How would you calculate average revenue growth over the past five years?
7. Why might one company have higher gross margin than another?
8. Why might one company have higher EBIT margin than another?
9. Why might one company have higher net income margin than another?
10. What are some of the different return ratios used by bankers?
11. Which return ratio is best to use when comparing companies that have different capital structures?
12. What are some important examples of credit ratios?
13. Would a company prefer to have a high leverage ratio or a high interest coverage ratio?
14. How do you calculate days sales of inventory?
15. Which is better for a company, higher days sales of inventory or lower, and why?
16. How do you calculate accounts receivable days?
17. Which is better for a company, higher accounts receivable days or lower, and why?
18. How do you calculate accounts payable days?

19. Which is better for a company, higher accounts payable days or lower, and why?
20. What are different time periods that we might want to use to analyze financial statements?
21. How do you calculate LTM?
22. How do you calendarize financials? Why is this important?
23. What are some indications that a company might be financially distressed?
24. Why might we make adjustments to a company's financial statements?
25. What are some of the sources for finding non-recurring items?
26. What are some examples of non-recurring items?
27. What key questions do you need to ask yourself when adjusting for non-recurring items?

Answers can be found at www.wiley.com/go/gutmann (password: investment).

CHAPTER 5

Valuation

What is something worth? What is its value? How much should I pay? How much might I receive if I sold? These are the questions that form the basis of many, if not most areas of finance. That is, the question of valuation. And these questions are often the most important ones asked and answered by investment bankers and other corporate finance professionals. In fact, valuation is generally considered to be one of the two core technical skills required by junior investment bankers. (The other is financial modeling, to be discussed in the next chapter.)

Recall that in Chapter 2, we talked about valuing certain types of financial securities, namely bonds, stocks, and options. While the theoretical methods we learned then are fine for bonds and options, they do not work in practice for stocks. We also have not yet learned how to value entire companies. That is the subject of this chapter. In fact, of all of the technical chapters of this book, this one is probably the most important, partly because of the subject matter's relevance to investment banking and partly because what we will learn here differs so much from what is usually taught in school. But there is a third reason as well: The vast majority of the technical questions that are frequently asked during investment banking interviews relate to the topic of valuation.

This chapter will begin with an introduction to valuation, including a discussion of the crucial concept of enterprise value. Then we will cover in detail the three primary valuation methodologies used by all investment bankers to value companies. These are the comparable company analysis, the precedent transaction analysis, and the discounted cash flow analysis. We will end the chapter by talking about how we conclude the appropriate valuation range for a company or its stock based on the three methodologies, and a brief discussion of several additional valuation methodologies that are sometimes employed.

INTRODUCTION TO VALUATION

At the end of the day, value is what someone is willing to pay. But the job of an investment banker is to estimate what that value will be, or should be. To be more precise, the type of value that we are after is what is known as fair market value, defined as the price for which a motivated but not desperate buyer will pay for the assets from a motivated but not desperate seller in a competitive sales process.

Nearly all of the various types of transactions executed by investment bankers require the bankers involved to perform a valuation. For example, when an investment bank is retained by a company that wants to sell itself, or sell a division or set of assets (a sell-side M&A transaction), one of the first things that the deal team will do is to value the company or assets being marketed. Very early in the process (generally even before a bank is formerly retained), the company for sale will want to have an idea of what the sales price will likely be. Later in the process, the banker's valuation will provide a benchmark and help to evaluate the bids that come in from prospective buyers.

The importance of valuation is even more obvious on a buy-side M&A transaction, in which an investment bank is advising the company or entity that wants to make an acquisition. The banker's valuation analysis will help the prospective acquirer decide how much to bid (or whether to bid at all) for the company or assets being sold and to help provide insight into how much other competing buyers might bid.

When working on an equity raise transaction, such as an initial public offering (IPO), it is up to the investment bankers to set an appropriate price for the to be issued new stock. A price that is set too high or too low indicates that the bankers overvalued or undervalued the stock, and will result in a less-than-successful IPO and a tainted reputation for the bankers.

Since this book is geared toward those interested in investment banking, we will naturally focus on the valuation techniques used in the day-to-day work of investment bankers. However, it is worth noting that other corporate finance professionals perform very similar valuation exercises using these exact same methodologies. Valuation is essential in equity research, asset management, hedge funds, private equity, and corporate development. In these areas, valuation analysis helps to answer questions such as:

- Is a company or its stock overvalued, undervalued, or fairly valued?
- How much should we (or our client) pay for shares of stock?
- How much should we (or our client) pay for an entire company?

- How much do we think we would get if we sold our company, and is that better than other alternatives?
- How much would we get if we sold a division, and is that worth more to us than keeping it?

Although the methodologies and analyses used for valuation are very similar, if not identical, in investment banking and other areas of corporate finance, there is one key difference. This difference affects the mindset of the person performing the valuation. For investment bankers, how you get to the answer is generally more important than the answer itself. That is, you will be judged and evaluated on whether you can justify your assumptions, and whether your work is accurate and well formatted rather than on the "correct" value. To be accurate in your analysis means not making data entry, arithmetic, or Excel mistakes, and using the correct formulas and methodologies.

In private equity, at a hedge fund or asset manager, or generally anything on the buy side, the opposite usually holds true. Getting to the right answer is more important than how you get there. This is true because you or your firm is actually making investment decisions based on your analysis. In other words, what is important is not the work itself, but whether your analysis leads to a profitable investment (or avoids an unprofitable one). We will discuss these differences in more detail toward the end of this chapter.

In addition, it is worth noting that most of the time when bankers start out performing a valuation exercise, they have at least an idea of what is the right answer before they even begin any analysis. Either the client or the senior banker has a sense for valuation, or if the banker is valuing a public company, then there is a value based on traded stock prices. Very often the goal as a banker is to create the valuation analysis that will justify this preconceived answer.

There is one last thing to keep in mind before we move on to discussing the various valuation methodologies. The exercise of performing a valuation as an investment banker is to *estimate* fair market value. There is no correct answer. For this reason, it is often quipped that valuation is an art and not a science. For all of the work and all of the analysis and all of the formulas that go into it, to be truly comfortable and competent performing valuations requires both judgment and experience.

The Primary Valuation Methodologies

For an investment banker, the purpose of performing a valuation exercise is to estimate the value of company. We can use the exact same methodologies whether the company is publicly traded or private, or to value a division or part of a company. Once we have an estimate for the company's value we can easily use that to also determine the value of equity (or stock price) if we need to.

Given the complexities of valuation, it may be a surprise to learn that the methods used to value companies are highly standardized. In fact, virtually all investment banks worldwide use the same three primary valuation methodologies to estimate the value of a company, though they are sometimes referred to using slightly different names. These primary methodologies are:

- Comparable public company analysis.
- Precedent transactions analysis.
- Discounted cash flow (DCF) analysis.

There are also a few other valuation methodologies that investment bankers sometimes employ depending on circumstances. Examples of these additional methodologies include a leveraged buyout (LBO) analysis, replacement value analysis, or liquidation value analysis. We will conclude this chapter with a brief discussion of these additional methodologies, but we will focus most of our attention on the main three.

Enterprise Value

Before we can begin to discuss how investment bankers value a company, we need to first define what exactly it is that we are trying to value. We have already met one definition of a company's value in Chapter 2. That is book value or shareholders' equity, which represents the balance sheet difference between total assets and total liabilities. While book value is an important concept, estimating book value is not our goal when performing a valuation exercise.

Another type of value that you might be familiar with is equity value. In fact, when we read about a company's value in a newspaper or business magazine or hear it on a TV program, most of the time they are referring to the company's equity value (sometimes referred to as market capitalization or market cap). In this book, we will usually refer to equity value as market value of equity, or MVE. MVE represents the value of a company that is attributed to the company's common shareholders, and for a public company can be calculated by multiplying the company's current share price by the number of its shares that are outstanding.

While it is a very important concept, the market value of equity does not represent the entire value of a company. It ignores the value attributed to other stakeholders such as debt holders (lenders) and preferred stockholders.

If the goal is to value the entire company, a typical goal for an investment banker, then we need to estimate a value metric called total enterprise value (TEV). In fact, even if our task as a banker is to estimate the fair market value of a company's equity or of its common shares, we will still typically start by estimating total enterprise value and then inferring the value of the company's MVE or its stock price. (We will discuss how to do this later in the chapter).

TEV, like many of the financial concepts in this book, has various synonyms. In fact, we will often abbreviate it as just enterprise value, or EV. You may also see it referred to as firm value (FV) or occasionally as total invested capital (TIC). So what is enterprise value? Let's start with its conceptual definition before we move on to discuss how it is calculated.

Enterprise value represents the value of the *operations* of a firm attributed to *all* providers of capital. Let's break this sentence into two parts, the first of which is "the value of the *operations* of a firm." This means that we are only placing a value on what we consider to be operating assets. We will exclude non-operating assets. The second part of the sentence, "attributed to *all* providers of capital," means that unlike equity value, which is value attributed to only common shareholders, enterprise value represents the value attributed to common shareholders and debt holders and any other providers of funding (such as preferred stockholders).

For an investment banker, enterprise value is one of the most important topics to understand. It is equally important to understand enterprise value being a prospective investment banker, as many of the most common technical interview questions refer to it. However, it is also a concept that tends to be tricky for students and new bankers to truly grasp. To help us, let's consider the analogy of buying a home.

An Enterprise Value Analogy: Buying a Home Suppose that you are a newly minted investment banking associate and you decide that you want to purchase a one-bedroom apartment (close to your office so that your daily commute home at 3:00 AM is short). To keep the math easy, let's further assume that the price of the apartment is $1 million (not an unreasonable assumption in a major financial market such as New York City).

In a typical real estate transaction such as this, you are not likely to write a personal check for $1 million to pay for your new home. Instead you will probably contribute a much smaller amount of your hard-earned savings in what is known as a down payment. Let's assume a typical down payment of $100,000, or 10 percent of the cost of the apartment. Where does the rest of that money ($900,000) come from? You borrow that amount from a bank, of course, in what is known as a mortgage. So what does our very simple transaction look like right now?

House value	=	$1,000,000
Down payment	=	$100,000
Mortgage	=	$900,000

Now, let's move the clock forward a year and make the assumption that after working really hard as a first-year associate, you receive a $300,000 after-tax cash bonus (certainly high given current market conditions, but one can dream). You decide that you want to use all of that money to pay down your mortgage. Lastly, we will assume that house prices have been unchanged since last year. Now what does the financial situation look like?

House value	=	$1,000,000
Equity	=	$400,000
Mortgage	=	$600,000

The house value of your home has not changed because, as we stated, we are assuming that the housing market was flat. Your equity has increased from the initial down payment of $100,000 to $400,000. (Notice that we've changed the middle term from down payment to equity since the definition of a down payment is the initial equity contribution. Therefore it no longer makes sense to call it a down payment.) Finally, the amount that you still owe the bank has been reduced from $900,000 to $600,000.

If a friend of yours asked you how much your apartment is worth, what would you say? You would say that it is worth about $1 million. It would not make much sense to say the home is worth $400,000 just because that is how much of your own money you have put in. Nor would it have made sense to say it was worth only $100,000 a year ago because that was the size of your down payment.

If you haven't already guessed, the key point we are trying to make is that the fair market value of the apartment is an estimate of what someone would pay for it, not how much money you've contributed or how much you've borrowed. Since the purchase price was $1 million and since, by our assumption, housing prices have not changed, our estimate of its value must still be $1 million. Over time, the home's value might be affected by changes in interest rates, employment growth, or the quality of the local school system, but it is not affected by your choice of funding.

Investment bankers do not typically value homes (real estate agents or brokers or appraisers usually do that), but investment bankers do value companies. So let us translate our housing analogy into one more helpful to an investment banker.

When valuing a company, the equivalent of the house value is its enterprise value. The down payment or equity is the company's market value of equity (MVE). The equivalent of the mortgage is the company's total amount of debt. And just like with the housing analogy, the percentage of debt and equity, which we call the company's capital structure, does not, at least in a theoretical world, have an impact on its enterprise value (this was the Modigliani-Miller theorem that we spoke of Chapter 3). Even in the imperfect world in which we live, the impact is minimal.

The Enterprise Value Formula Even though the exercise of valuation is to estimate enterprise value using the three primary methodologies, for reasons that should become clear through the chapter, it is also very important to be able to calculate enterprise value. Also, it is worth pointing out that one of the most commonly asked technical interview questions is "What is the formula used to calculate enterprise value?" For a public company, enterprise value can be calculated as follows:

$$EV = MVE + Debt + Preferred\ Stock - Cash + Noncontrolling\ Interest$$

You may sometimes see a shorter version of this formulas as:

$$EV = MVE + Debt - Cash$$

or

$$EV = MVE + Net\ Debt$$

These second two formulas are equivalent since the definition of net debt is total debt – cash, as we learned in Chapter 4. These shorter formulas ignore preferred stock and noncontrolling interest, since many companies do not have preferred stock and noncontrolling interest on their balance sheets. However, both in practice and when responding to an interview question, it is preferable to use the longer and more complete version of the enterprise value formula.

Recall that the conceptual definition of enterprise value is the value of the operations of the firm attributed to *all* providers of capital. This is why we aggregate the value of common equity (MVE), the value of debt, and the value of preferred stock when calculating EV. As we learned in Chapter 3, these three types of funding in aggregate represent all of a company's outside sources of capital.

Next we will discuss how we calculate the values for MVE, debt, and preferred stock, and explain the rationale for subtracting cash. We will return to the issue of noncontrolling interest a little later after we introduce the concept of valuation multiples.

Market Value of Equity (MVE) A public company's market value of equity is equal to the company's current share price multiplied by the number of common shares outstanding. We can easily get the current share price from any number of free web sites, such as Yahoo! Finance or Google Finance, or a paid data source such as a Bloomberg terminal. For the share count, we need to remember to use the number of fully diluted shares outstanding rather than the number of basic shares.

Recall from Chapter 2 that the fully diluted share count equals the basic number of shares outstanding plus the potentially dilutive effect of certain securities such as employee stock options. As we mentioned in Chapter 4, we can find the basic share count from the cover of the company's most recent 10-Q or 10-K. We will learn how to calculate the dilutive component later in this chapter using what is known as the treasury stock method.

For a private company, we have no way to directly calculate its MVE because it is not publicly traded and therefore has no observable share price. However, we can estimate a private company's equity value using the valuation techniques we will learn in this chapter.

Debt The debt component of the enterprise value formula should include all interest-bearing liabilities and capitalized leases. Note that we do not include all of the company's liabilities, such as accounts payable or accrued expenses. To be technically correct, we should use the market value of the company's debt rather than the book value of debt. However, investment bankers usually make the assumption that the market value of debt is equal to the book value. Therefore we typically use the values found on the company's most recent balance sheet. If we do use the market values, we will need access to a data source that provides debt prices such as a Bloomberg terminal. Note though that not all types of debt are publicly traded, and therefore you may not be able to get market values.

In circumstances where we have reason to believe that the market value and book value of debt are very different, then we should always use the debt's market value. For example, the debt of distressed companies often trades well below its book or par value. Furthermore, when analyzing distressed companies where debt does trade below par value, we also usually assign $0 value to equity even if the company's stock price has some positive value.

Preferred Stock There are two possibilities for ascribing value to preferred stock in the enterprise value formula (assuming a company has preferred stock in its capital structure). If the preferred stock trades publicly and we have access to preferred stock prices from a data source such as a Bloomberg terminal, then the value will be equal to the preferred stock's per-share price times the number of shares outstanding. In the more frequent case, where the preferred does not trade publicly or we do not have access to pricing information, then we can use the preferred stock's liquidation value (not the par value) found on the latest balance sheet. The liquidation value represents the amount of money that preferred stockholders are due to receive upon a liquidation event such as a sale of the company.

Cash Remember that enterprise value reflects the value of the operations of the firm attributed to all providers of capital. So far we have talked about how to calculate each of the types of capital, namely equity, debt, and preferred stock. But we also need to subtract cash from our enterprise value formula. First let's discuss why we subtract cash, and then we can talk about how we calculate it.

There are two reasons for why cash is subtracted in the enterprise value formula:

1. Cash is not considered to be an operating asset.
2. Cash is already implicitly accounted for in the market value of equity since cash represents value to stockholders.

Before we move on, you should be aware of a very common misconception about why we subtract cash. Many investment bankers believe that the reason cash is subtracted is that the company could use the cash to pay down debt. In essence this is the concept of net debt. However, this is both conceptually incorrect and potentially wrong mathematically. Not all debt can be retired prior to maturity. Moreover, even debt that can be retired immediately will typically include prepayment penalty provisions. Therefore cash cannot necessarily be netted against debt.

Now that we have explained why cash is subtracted we can talk about what cash number to use in the enterprise value formula. We typically start with cash from the latest balance sheet. Most of the time, we also include any short-term investments and marketable securities found on the balance sheet, as we consider them to be cash equivalents. We do this unless there is reason not to (for example, if the cash is restricted).

To be technically correct, we should be subtracting a company's excess cash and not all of its cash. Excess cash reflects that amount of the cash that a company does not need to operate its business. Take, for instance, a retailer such as Walmart. Walmart has lots of stores, and each store has many cash registers, and each cash register has cash. Officially, this cash should be considered part of working capital and not excess cash. More broadly, even most non-retailers cannot operate their business without any cash for use in operations. However, for the vast majority of companies, this kind of operational cash is small compared with total cash. Hence, investment bankers rarely make the distinction between total cash and excess cash, and almost always subtract the full amount of cash and equivalents when calculating enterprise value.

Enterprise Value Example #1 Before we move away from the calculation of enterprise value, let us do two examples. Suppose that a company has 100 million common shares outstanding and its shares trade at \$20 per share. Further assume that the company has \$1 billion of debt outstanding, \$500 million of cash (all of it excess), and no preferred stock or noncontrolling interest on its balance sheet. What is the company's enterprise value?

Recall that:

$$\text{EV} = \text{MVE} + \text{Debt} + \text{Preferred Stock} - \text{Cash} + \text{Noncontrolling Interest}$$

First, let's calculate the market value of equity:

$$\text{MVE} = 100 \text{ million shares} \times \$20 \text{ per share} = \$2 \text{ billion}$$

So:

$$\text{EV} = \$2 \text{ billion} + \$1 \text{ billion} + \$0 - \$500 \text{ million} + \$0 = \$2.5 \text{ billion}$$

Enterprise Value Example #2 Example #1 required only knowing the enterprise value formula and some very basic math. This type of calculation is actually a fairly common interview question. Now let's try a second example that actually tests your understanding of the concept of enterprise value. Consider the following.

As investment bankers, we estimate that the fair market value of a company is \$1 billion. The company also has \$200 million cash on its balance sheet and no debt, preferred stock, or noncontrolling interest. Our client wants to purchase the company for its fair market value. How much will our client pay to purchase 100 percent of the company?

If this was a multiple choice test, we'd probably see the following three possible answers:

(a) \$800 million
(b) \$1.0 billion
(c) \$1.2 billion

Which is correct? To acquire 100 percent of the company, our client only needs to purchase the equity. Our client, like any buyer, will receive the cash just as it will assume all other assets and liabilities. Remember that equity value always includes cash but enterprise value does not.

Therefore, the correct answer is \$1.2 billion. Our client will pay \$1 billion for the operations of the company since that is what we assumed it was worth and it will pay \$200 million for \$200 million of cash.

Again remember that:

EV = MVE + Debt + Preferred Stock – Cash + Noncontrolling Interest

Hence, using basic algebra:

MVE = EV – Debt – Preferred Stock + Cash – Noncontrolling Interest

Therefore:

MVE = \$1.0 billion – \$0 – \$0 + \$200 million – \$0 = \$1.2 billion

Valuation Multiples and Relative Value

So far in this chapter we have learned about the concept of enterprise value. We have also explained how to calculate it, with the one exception of noncontrolling interest, to which we will return shortly. The next crucial topic that must be understood before we can dive into each valuation methodology is the concept of relative value and valuation multiples.

Recall that there are three main valuation methodologies:

1. Comparable public company analysis.
2. Precedent transactions analysis.
3. Discounted cash flow (DCF) analysis.

The first two valuation methodologies, comparable company analysis and precedent transaction analysis, are based on what is known as relative value. With these methodologies, we will value a company by comparing it with another company or set of companies. That is, one company will be valued relative to another.

The third method, the discounted cash flow, is considered an intrinsic valuation methodology. Here we estimate the value of a company based solely on metrics and analysis specific (or intrinsic) to that company. In reality, this is a small white lie, because in practice, the DCF analysis actually uses both intrinsic and relative information. Therefore the DCF is really a hybrid methodology.

A Valuation Multiple Analogy: Selling and Valuing a Home Now allow us to return to our housing example. Let's assume we are interested in selling our apartment. The first thing we would probably want to know is how much it is worth. So we would probably hire a real estate agent to give us an assessment of our home's value. How in turn would the real estate agent do this? Likely, they would use the sales prices of similar homes to ours that have recently sold to estimate the approximate price for which our apartment will sell.

The easiest thing to do would be to find an identical apartment that has recently been sold. Let's assume that the apartment next door to us has the exact same layout, size, and views; is in the same condition as ours; and recently sold for $1 million. In that case ours is probably worth about $1 million, too.

Of course, the odds of finding an identical home are pretty small indeed. More likely, an appraiser would look for recent sales of *similar* apartments. By similar, we mean that the homes should be in our building or in our neighborhood, and of similar size and condition. It would make no sense to compare our one-bedroom apartment in New York City with a three-bedroom house in the suburbs. Nor would it make sense to compare our apartment with a similar-sized apartment in San Francisco, London, or Hong Kong.

Let us suppose that a similar one-bedroom apartment in our building recently sold but that it was a little bit bigger than ours. Rather than compare the absolute price of a home (i.e., $1 million), we could calculate a metric such as price per square foot (or price per square meter) and use that metric for comparison purposes. By using such a metric, we can account for (and compare) the size differences between similar apartments.

A metric such as price per square foot is known as a valuation multiple. A valuation multiple, also sometimes called a trading multiple, is a ratio between a metric of value in the numerator, and an operating or balance sheet metric in the denominator. Using the example of real estate, the value in the numerator is the home price and the operating metric in the denominator is the size of the home measured in square footage.

The Two Types of Valuation Multiples: Operating and Equity In the first two valuation methodologies, comparable companies and precedent transactions, we are going to estimate the value of a company by comparing it to other, similar companies using valuation multiples. While there are many different multiples that we can use, we can separate valuation multiples into two types: operating and equity.

Operating Multiples Operating multiples reflect ratios that use metrics affected by operations only and not by a firm's choice of capital structure.

For this reason, they are also sometimes called debt-free multiples, unlevered multiples, or capital structure neutral multiples. These ratios use enterprise value in the numerator. Remember that enterprise value is neutral of capital structure because it includes the values of all sources of capital (i.e., debt and equity).

The denominator of the ratio must also be an operating metric not affected by capital structure. Recall our discussion from Chapter 2 regarding operating and nonoperating metrics on the income statement. Operating metrics are those at or above the EBIT line. These include revenue, EBIT, and EBITDA.

The most common valuation multiples of the operating type include:

- EV/revenue.
- EV/EBIT.
- EV/EBITDA.

Equity Multiples An equity valuation multiple represents a ratio that uses metrics that are affected by capital structure. Therefore we also refer to these type of multiples as nonoperating multiples, levered multiples or capital structure dependent multiples. The market value of equity or share price is in the numerator. To be consistent, we need to use a levered or capital structure dependent metric in the denominator. This is anything below the EBIT line from the income statement, starting with interest expense. Book value, another name for shareholders' equity, is also a levered metric.

The most common equity multiples include:

- Price/earnings (P/E).
- Price/book value (P/BV).
- Price/earnings/% growth (PEG Ratio).

Comparing the Types of Multiples When using multiples to help value companies, one of the most important things to remember is that the numerator and denominator must be consistent, or apples-to-apples. If a multiple uses enterprise value in the numerator, then it must contain an unlevered metric in the denominator. If a multiple uses equity value in the numerator then it needs to have a levered metric in the denominator. You should not create apples-to-oranges metrics such as price/EBITDA or EV/earnings.

Investment bankers often use both types of multiples though they tend to rely more heavily on the operating ratios that have enterprise value in the numerator. Finance professionals that are concerned solely with valuing stock prices, such as equity research analysts, tend to rely more on levered multiples such as P/E.

To illustrate the differences between the two types of multiples, let's show an example. Consider two companies with identical operations but very different capital structures. Assume both companies have an enterprise value of $100. This makes sense since finance theory tells us that two companies with the same operations should have (approximately) the same value. Suppose however that one company (Firm A) is financed with 90 percent equity and 10 percent debt, and the other company is financed (Firm B) with 10 percent equity and 90 percent debt.

To keep the example simpler, let's assume that both companies pay an interest rate of 10 percent on debt. In reality, of course, the more highly levered company (Firm B) should pay a higher interest rate. However, the difference will not affect the analysis significantly.

Exhibit 5.1 shows the income statement for both companies. At the bottom, it also shows three implied valuation multiples. The first two, EV/revenue and EV/EBIT are unlevered, and the third, P/E, is levered.

EXHIBIT 5.1 Comparison of Two Companies with the Same Operations and Different Capital Structures

	Firm A	**Firm B**
Enterprise Value	$100.0	$100.0
Equity Value	90.0	10.0
Debt (10% interest)	10.0	90.0
Revenue	100.0	100.0
COGS	50.0	50.0
Gross Profit	50.0	50.0
SG&A	30.0	30.0
EBIT	20.0	20.0
Interest Expense	1.0	9.0
EBT	19.0	11.0
Tax Expense (40%)	7.6	4.4
Net Income	11.4	6.6
EV/Revenue	1.0x	1.0x
EV/EBIT	5.0x	5.0x
P/E	**7.9x**	**1.5x**

We can see that the income statements of both companies are identical through the EBIT line. This makes sense since we assumed that the two companies had the same exact operations. The figures differ as soon as we get to the interest expense line. In fact, Firm A's net income is almost double that of Firm B.

When we calculate the valuation multiples, things get especially interesting. As we should expect, the EV/revenue multiple and the EV/EBIT multiples are the same. However, the price/earnings (P/E) multiples are vastly different. Firm A's P/E multiple of 7.9x (equity value of $90 divided by net income of $11.4) is more than five times greater than Firm B's P/E ratio of 1.5x (equity value of $10 divided by net income of $6.6).

It is not to say that one type of multiple is correct and the other is incorrect. We are just trying to illustrate the difference between operating and equity multiples. Always remember that these differences will be magnified when you compare two companies with very different capital structures.

Noncontrolling Interest We are finally ready to return to the issue of noncontrolling interest in the enterprise value formula, as promised. Recall from Chapter 2 that when a company owns more than 50 percent of another entity the accounting rules state that the two sets of financial statements must be consolidated. That is, the parent company's financial statements must include 100 percent of the operations (sales, EBITDA, net income, etc.) and 100 percent of the assets and liabilities of the subsidiary, even though it may really own less than 100 percent.

The noncontrolling interest line on the parent company's balance sheet represents the percentage of the subsidiary's book value of equity that the parent company does not own. We can find this number on the balance sheet in the shareholders' equity section.

Once again, recall the enterprise value formula:

EV = MVE + Debt + Preferred Stock – Cash + Noncontrolling Interest

The reason that we add noncontrolling interest in the enterprise value formula reflects the fact that we will use enterprise value in the numerator for many of the valuation multiples that we will use to value companies. Consider one such multiple: EV/revenue. The denominator of this ratio will include 100 percent of a subsidiary's revenue even if the parent company owns less than 100 percent. However, the market value of equity (MVE) will account for only the percentage of the subsidiary that the parent owns. In other words, the numerator is correct but the denominator is overstated, so we are left with an apples-to-oranges situation.

In order to fix the mismatch, we add the value of noncontrolling interest to enterprise value. Now both the numerator and denominator are overstated, but since we are calculating a ratio, the valuation multiple will be correct. You may be wondering why we do not subtract revenue from the denominator instead of adding noncontrolling interest to the numerator. In theory this would be better, however in practice we almost never have the information to do so.

COMPARABLE COMPANY METHODOLOGY

The first of our three primary valuation methodologies is the comparable company methodology. Other names for this methodology include comparable companies, compcos, trading comps, market comps, public comps, or just comps. The basic purpose of comparable companies is to value a company by comparing it with other similar publicly traded companies. Specifically, we will use a set of valuation multiples to help us make the comparison.

Bear in mind our real estate example. We said earlier that if we were trying to value an apartment we would first look for similar apartments that recently sold. Then we would calculate a valuation multiple such as price/square foot for each of the similar apartments. If similar homes have sold for $1,000/square foot then we will likely conclude that our apartment is also worth approximately $1,000/square foot. Assuming the size of our home is about 1,000 square feet, then we can say that our home should be worth about $1 million ($1,000/square foot multiplied by 1,000 square feet).

We will do this same exercise for companies. Let's suppose that we are trying to value a manufacturing company and let's suppose that our analysis informs us that similar manufacturing companies have an enterprise value of about eight times their recent year's EBITDA. If the company we are valuing has an EBITDA of $100 million, then we can estimate our company's enterprise value at about $800 million.

There are five steps to performing the comparable companies methodology:

1. Selecting comparable companies (selecting comps).
2. Spreading the comparable companies (spreading comps).
3. Normalizing the comparable companies (normalizing comps).
4. Calculating valuation multiples.
5. Analyzing and applying appropriate multiples to the company being valued.

You are not likely to be asked in an interview what the five steps you go through when performing a comparable company analysis are. Others may categorize or aggregate them into fewer or more steps. However, you should be able to walk an interviewer through the general process.

Step 1: Selecting Comps

The first step in performing the comparable company methodology is to select a number of companies that are similar, or comparable, to the company being valued. The company being valued is often referred to as the subject company. This process is often referred to as picking comps, with "comps" being short for "comparable." The set of comparable companies selected are often referred to as the comp universe.

Before we discuss how to go about selecting comparable companies, we need to mention a few ground rules. Most importantly, the comps must all be publicly traded. This is because we need to be able to calculate enterprise value for each comp. In order to calculate enterprise value, we need the market value of equity (MVE), and in order to calculate MVE we need to know the company's current stock price. Remember that the requirement of our comps being publicly traded does not mean that we cannot value a private company. We can value a private company in exactly the same way we value a public company, assuming we have access to the private company's financial statements.

In additional to being publicly traded, companies used as comps should ideally not be distressed or in bankruptcy unless the entire industry being analyzed is distressed (which does happen from time to time). We also should not use conglomerates where only one business segment is comparable to the subject company. The reason is that we have no way of directly measuring the equity value from only one portion of a publicly traded company.

Criteria for Selecting Comps Now that we have set our ground rules, we are ready to talk about what exactly we mean by "similar" companies and how we go about finding and selecting our comps. Once again, recall our discussion from earlier in this chapter about valuing a home. We said that we should look for apartments of similar size and type, condition, and neighborhood. For selecting comparable companies there are also a number of factors to consider. Ideally, we want to find companies that are similar in the following ways:

- Industry.
- Business model.
- Geography.

- Size.
- Growth and risk characteristics.

Industry Most of the time when looking for comparable companies the first and easiest place to look is for companies in the same industry. This is probably the most obvious criteria. If we are valuing an automobile manufacturer, we should look for other automobile manufacturers. If we are valuing a food retailer we should look for other food retailers. If we are valuing a bank, we should look for, you guessed it, other banks. It would make little sense to compare an automobile manufacturer with a food retailer or a food retailer with a bank.

Business Model However, just because two companies are in the same industry does not necessarily mean they will make good comparables. They may have very different business models. For example, suppose we need to value a company that manufactures clothing. We would not want to use a clothing retailer as a comp even though they are both in the clothing industry. This is because manufacturers and retailers have very different business models. They have different types of customers, different cost structures, different risks, and so forth. Similarly, suppose you are valuing a large pharmaceutical company that has a huge research and development department in order to develop its own novel drugs. We would not want to use as a comp a pharmaceutical company that only manufacturers generic drugs and does no research. The two business models are too diverse.

Geography Another important criterion for selecting comps is geography. Here we mean two things by using the term "geography." The more important criterion is the geographic markets in which a company operates. Companies that do business in the same markets will be subject to similar macroeconomic factors like overall economic growth, labor markets, regulatory environments, and so on. However, also important, though less so, is the country in which a company is based or incorporated, due to the influence of taxes, financial reporting requirements, and the liquidity of a country's financial markets.

For example, suppose we are valuing a Japanese company that only operates in Japan. Ideally we would only use other Japanese companies for our comps. On the other hand, if we are valuing a Japanese company that is truly multinational, then it is more important that we find other companies that operate globally regardless of where they are incorporated or headquartered.

Often it is difficult to find comps that operate in the same geographic market, especially if we are valuing a company that operates in a smaller country or emerging economy. Suppose we need to value a retailer that operates only in Vietnam. Chances are there are not so many other publicly traded Vietnamese retailers. In this instance, we might look for companies that operate in faster-growing emerging markets similar to Vietnam such as China, India, or Thailand. What is paramount is that the characteristics of the markets, especially with regard to growth, are similar. For that reason, comparable companies from more mature markets such as Japan or the United States would be less relevant.

Size Size is another significant factor to consider when picking comps. There are many different measures of a company's size, including financial metrics like enterprise value, market capitalization or revenue, or nonfinancial metrics such as the number of employees or the number of store locations. For the most part within a given industry, these metrics tend to be correlated. Therefore we can use any of them as a proxy for a company's size.

It is unlikely that we will ever find similar companies that are exactly the same size. What we are really looking for are companies that are in the same range. For example, a company with $200 million of annual revenue is in a similar size range to a company with $300 million of sales. Even though one is 50 percent larger than the other, they would both likely be considered small-cap companies. Similarly, we would determine that a $40 billion company is similar to an $80 billion company because they are both large-cap firms.

In practice when performing valuation, it is often difficult to find similar companies of similar size, especially when valuing a very large or very small company. Most publicly traded companies are considered small-caps, with revenues or market caps less than $1 billion. If we are valuing a very large company we will likely have no choice but to include companies substantially smaller. Similarly, if we need to value a small company with revenues of perhaps $25 million then we will likely have to use larger companies as comps. (We will return to the impact that size has on valuation later in the chapter.)

Growth and Risk Characteristics Just because two companies are in the same industry and have the same business model does not necessarily make them perfect comps. Suppose one company is growing rapidly because it is has new technology and another in the same industry is shrinking because of old or obsolete technology. These two companies will have very different growth prospects and therefore would not be considered good comps.

Moreover, companies that have very different risk profiles are also not ideal comparables. For instance, if a company is highly dependent on a single customer or on one geographic market for most of its business, then it will be much riskier than another company with a diversified customer base and market.

As investment bankers, most of the time when we perform this valuation methodology, when companies are in the same industry, have the same business model, and are of a similar size then we will consider them to be comps. But you should be aware of those companies with vastly different growth and risk characteristics and if you do choose to include them, you may want to rely less on them in your analysis.

Sources for Selecting Comps Now that we have an understanding of what we are looking for when we pick our comps, the next issue to address is how to find them. Sometimes the chore of selecting comps is very easy and we can name them off the top of our head. This is especially likely if we work as a banker in an industry coverage group and have good knowledge of the publicly traded companies in that industry. At most, we might have to spend just a few minutes of research to ensure that we do not miss any good comparables or to eliminate the weaker comps if we have too many.

For many valuation exercises, unfortunately, the task of selecting comps is much more difficult and requires more work. There are a number of different data sources that can be helpful to bankers. One such resource is equity research reports. Research analysts perform valuation exercises on the companies they cover frequently using this same methodology. The list of comparable companies used by the research analysts (commonly disclosed in research reports) is a great starting point. Another good resource is the section of a public company's 10-K that discusses competition. Very often publicly traded competitors are good comps. There are also both paid and free resources that provide lists of similar companies. One such high-quality paid data source is Hoovers. Even Google Finance, a free resource, shows such a list. Sometimes a basic Internet search is also helpful, as can be talking to the senior investment bankers with whom you work who may be more familiar with the industry of the company you need to value.

The Number of Comps One thing we have not talked about yet is the question of how many comparable companies we need. In theory, we should use as many comps (or as few comps) as there are similar companies to the company for which we are valuing. In practice, however, there is no correct answer. The average number that bankers use tends to be somewhere between six and 10. You will sometimes see more and occasionally fewer.

The answer also sometimes depends on the specific analyst and associate assigned to the project. It is not uncommon in banking for the associate to require the analyst to use more comps than needed, either because the associate is inexperienced or to make the analyst perform extra work. In fact, spreading extra comps is not an uncommon punishment for an analyst who has not been staying in the office late enough or who has just returned from a vacation. Such is the life of an analyst.

Sometimes bankers will segregate the list of comparable companies into tiers. This is especially true when there are only a handful of good comps. Tier 1 might include the two or three good comps, with tier 2 being comprised of the less-similar companies.

What if There Are No Good Comps? When selecting your comp universe, you are obviously limited to the publicly traded companies that actually exist in the world. We cannot make up companies just to have better comps! So what happens if there are no good comps for the company we need to value? Your first thought might be that we should skip this methodology, but that is rarely what bankers do. As investment bankers, we always need to show that we do a lot of work (after all, we are getting paid a lot of money).

In this instance, we tend to still perform comparable company analysis, but we will need to expand the universe of possible comparables by some or all of the criteria. We can look for comps that are much larger or smaller or that operate in different geographies. If we still cannot find any comps then we can look for companies in different industries that have similar growth and risk characteristics. For example, perhaps we can find a company that makes different products but has similar customers and suppliers. However, you should remember that the less similar the comps, the less valuable the analysis. Therefore, in these situations, we may rely more heavily on the other valuation methodologies to conclude an appropriate value.

There is one exception to the rule of expanding the universe until we find some similar comps. That is if we need to value a very large conglomerate. Here there really are no good comparables. Instead what we can do is use different sets of comps for the various business units. We can then aggregate the value of each business unit to come up with a value for the entire company in what is known as a sum of the parts valuation.

Step 2: Spreading Comps

The term "spreading comps" refers to the data entry task of entering in historical and projected information into a valuation template or model in Microsoft Excel. All investment banks, and many of the industry coverage groups within banks, have their own versions of a valuation template. As we discussed in Chapter 4, sometimes the needed information is downloaded from a data source directly into Excel, and sometimes analysts enter this information manually.

Required Information While valuation templates can differ slightly on the information that must be inputted, most of the data will be the same. For each of the comparable companies, we usually need to gather and spread the following information:

- Current stock price.
- Full income statement for the most recent full fiscal year, the most recent year-to-date (YTD) period, and the previous year's YTD period.
- Key balance sheet items from the most recent fiscal period.
- Key items from cash flow statement for the most recent full fiscal year, most recent YTD, and previous year's YTD, including depreciation and amortization and capital expenditures.
- Most recent basic share count figure and stock option information.
- Breakdown of the company's debt from the most recent period.
- Two years of projected income statement information (the current fiscal year and the next full fiscal year).
- Other industry-specific information.

Historical financial information will come from a 10-K and/or 10-Q for companies traded in the United States or similar public documents for companies traded in other countries. Remember that to be a comparable company, a company must be publicly traded, so we will always have the historical information that we need for our analysis. We will also need to spread this same information for the company being valued. If the subject company is publicly traded, then we can also rely on 10-Ks and 10-Qs. On the other hand, if the subject company is private then we will typically need to obtain this information directly from the company's management.

The projected information that we need typically comes from equity research analysts. Sometimes we will use aggregate estimates for key projected metrics such as revenue, EBIT, EBITDA, net income, and EPS. There are services such as the Institutional Brokers' Estimate System (I/B/E/S) that collect and average the estimates from each of the research analysts that cover a particular company.

More often we will use a specific equity research report for each comp. Ideally we want to use a report authored by the same brokerage firm and analyst for each of the comps to ensure that macroeconomic and industry-wide assumptions are consistent. However, this is not always possible, as analysts may not cover all of our comps. Therefore, we are often forced to use research reports from a number of different analysts. Regardless, we should make sure that the analyst's projections for EPS are similar to that of the consensus (I/B/E/S) estimates. We do not normally want to use outliers.

Just as with the historical information, we also will need a set of projections for the company being valued. Forecasts can come from equity research reports if the subject company is public, from management, or from our own model.

Additional Tips for Spreading Comps There are a number of important things to keep in mind when spreading comps. First of all, always make sure to use the most recently filed documents for historical information and the most recent research reports for projected information. Also make sure to verify that the company has not released a new set of quarterly earnings. Remember that there is always a lag between an earnings release and when the 10-Q or 10-K is filed. You do not want your analysis to be tainted by outdated information.

Make sure that the data from each of the comparable companies is entered in the same units. You may have to make adjustments since the financial statements contained in 10-Ks and 10-Qs are sometimes entered in billions, millions, thousands, or actual dollars. You also may need to make currency adjustments if the subject company or some of the comps are from different countries. You should adjust income statement and cash flow statement data using the average exchange rate over the time period and balance sheet items using the exchange rate as of the balance sheet date. Some valuation templates have these kinds of currency adjustments built in.

Step 3: Normalizing the Financials

Once the information is spread, the next step is to normalize it. Remember from Chapter 4 that normalizing refers to the action of adjusting financial statements for unusual or non-recurring items. As a reminder, common examples of such items include restructuring costs such as severance and lease termination, charges for natural disasters, asset impairment costs, gains or losses from unusual litigation, and gains or losses from the sale of assets.

The goal is to have apples-to-apples comparisons. That comparisons are consistent is one of the most important things about the comparable company methodology, since the focus is to value a company based on comparisons. As we discussed earlier in the book, normalizing the financials for each comp is often difficult and time consuming.

Step 4: Calculating Valuation Multiples

Once both historical and projected information for the comps are entered into Excel and adjusted for non-recurring items, the next step is to calculate the valuation multiples. Remember that there are two types of multiples. Operating or unlevered multiples have enterprise value in the numerator. As we mentioned earlier, the most common operating multiples used to value companies in most industries include EV/revenue, EV/EBIT, and EV/EBITDA. Equity or levered multiples have the market value of equity (MVE) in the numerator. Frequently used equity multiples include P/E, P/BV, and the PEG ratio. As investment bankers, we typically will calculate both types.

In addition, there are other multiples that are frequently used in certain industries. For example: EV/subscribers might be used to help value telecommunications companies, and EV/reserves might be used for oil and gas companies. To value retailers we often use Adjusted EV/EBITDAR, where the R in the denominator indicates that we are adding back a retailer's rental expense.

Regardless of whether the trading multiple uses enterprise value or equity value, the numerator always represents a value at a single point in time, typically the current date. The share price used to calculate MVE will be the current date's price and the number of shares, debt, cash, preferred stock, and noncontrolling interest will reflect the most recent available information from the latest balance sheet.

For most of the metrics used in the denominator, such as revenue, EBIT, EBITDA, and net income, we have a choice of time periods. In fact, we typically will calculate multiples for several time periods using both historical and projected information. Multiples that utilize historical data will reflect time periods such as the last full fiscal year and the last twelve months (LTM). We often call these types of multiples trailing multiples. The multiples calculated with projected information in the denominator will usually reflect the next full fiscal year and the fiscal year following. These types are referred to as forward multiples. Sometimes we will also want to calendarize the historical and especially projected financial information to approximate each comp having the same fiscal year, as we discussed in Chapter 4.

Calculating Total Enterprise Value Just to review what we have already learned, enterprise value is calculated as follows:

$$EV = MVE + Debt + Preferred\ Stock - Cash + Noncontrolling\ Interest$$

Recall that MVE is equal to the current share price multiplied by the number of fully diluted shares outstanding. Debt is typically taken as the value from the latest balance sheet, unless the company is distressed, in which case we will use the market value of debt. If preferred stock is traded, then we multiply the number of preferred shares by the preferred share price. Otherwise, we take the liquidation value from the latest balance sheet. Finally, cash and noncontrolling interest also come from the latest balance sheet.

Calculating Fully Diluted Shares The one thing that we have not yet discussed is how to calculate the number of fully diluted shares. The market value of equity (MVE) must always be calculated using fully diluted shares since the "market" implicitly takes into account potential dilution when valuing the share price of a stock. Recall that fully diluted shares is equal to basic shares plus the potential dilutive effect from certain securities such as employee stock options, convertible preferred stock, and convertible preferred debt.

We will always get the number of basic shares from the cover of the latest 10-K or 10-Q, as it represents the most recent available share count. Before using this figure, verify that there have not been any stock splits since the 10-K or 10-Q was filed. Otherwise, MVE will be significantly wrong, which can have a material impact on the valuation. To estimate the dilutive effect of stock options, bankers most frequently use a technique called the treasury stock method.

The Treasury Stock Method Recall from Chapter 3 that stock options give the holder the right to convert an option into a share of stock at a given price (the strike or exercise price). Also remember that the kind of stock options issued to employees is technically warrants and therefore results in new shares being issued, which is why they have a dilutive effect. For purposes of calculating dilution, we only take into account stock options that are in the money. In other words, the exercise price of the options must be less than the current stock price.

When an employee exercises an option, the employee pays the company the exercise price and, in return, the company gives the employee a share of stock. The treasury stock method assumes that the proceeds a company receives from the exercised option are used to offset the cost to issue a new share of stock. Therefore, the amount of dilution caused by an option is less than one full share.

For example, suppose that the current share price is $50 and that the option's exercise price is $30. When an employee exercises the option, the treasury stock method assumes that the employee gives the company $30 and the company uses that money to issue a new share. The additional amount that the company needs is $20 ($50 share price less $30 exercise price). The dilutive effect is the \$20 needed divided by the \$50 share price, or 0.4 additional shares.

To calculate the total effect of dilution for all options, we then multiply the dilutive effect per option by the number of options. In summary, the dilutive effect using the treasury stock method can be calculated for all in-the-money options as follows:

$$\text{Diluted Shares} = \text{Exercisable Options} \times \left(\frac{\text{Share Price} - \text{Exercise Price}}{\text{Share Price}} \right)$$

In order to make this calculation we need three pieces of information: the current share price, the number of options, and the exercise price. The current share price is easy to look up. The number of options and the exercise price are typically found in a footnote to the 10-K. The information we need is usually not included in a 10-Q. Therefore, the information can be somewhat stale, but for us, it is the best we can do. Note that the exercise price will be labeled the weighted average exercise price since it usually reflects an average of options granted to employees at different times and at different prices. Sometimes companies will aggregate options into several different groups, by different weighted average prices. Remember to only account for those options that are in the money.

In the 10-K footnote that has the stock option information, there will most often be two sets of figures for the number of options: options exercisable and options outstanding. The options exercisable column represents the number of options that employees are able to exercise as of the date of the 10-K, because those options have vested. The options outstanding column reflects the total of both exercisable (i.e., vested) options and non-exercisable (i.e., not yet vested) options. For computing fully diluted shares for the comparable company methodology, we use only those exercisable options that have vested.

Convertible Preferred Stock and Convertible Debt In addition to accounting for employee stock options, we also need to address the potentially dilutive effect from convertible preferred stock or convertible debt if a company has such securities. In order calculate the dilution from these types of securities we need to find out their conversion features. The conversion features can usually be found in a footnote to the most recent 10-K. If the information is not found in the 10-K, then we will need to consult the original bond indenture or preferred stock offering document, which should have been filed as an attachment to another publicly filed document. Remember that you can use the list of exhibits at the back of any 10-Q or 10-K to help locate old exhibits.

The first decision we need to make is whether to treat the security as if it was converted to common stock or to leave it as is. If we convert it, then it will have a dilutive effect and add to the fully diluted share count. If we leave it, then it will have no dilutive effect. We generally follow the principle that if the conversion features would allow it to be converted today and if the conversion price is such that it would make sense for holders to convert (i.e., it is in the money) then we treat the security on a converted basis as common stock. Otherwise we leave it alone. The most important thing to remember is not to double-count the security. If you convert it and add to the fully diluted share count, you must *not* also add it as debt or preferred in the enterprise value formula.

Calculating Additional Financial Metrics In addition to calculating the appropriate valuation multiples, we also want to calculate some other financial metrics that will be helpful for our analysis and in determining valuation. These are the kinds of statistics that we discussed in Chapter 4 when we covered financial statement analysis. Some of the common and most useful metrics to calculate include:

- Growth of revenue, EBITDA, net income, and EPS.
- EBIT, EBITDA, and net income margins.
- Debt/equity or debt/total capitalization.
- Leverage ratio.
- Capital expenditures/revenue.
- Net working capital/revenue.
- ROA, ROE, and ROIC.

It is usually valuable to calculate both the growth statistics and margins utilizing both historical (i.e., LTM) and projected figures. We also want to make sure to calculate any important industry specific metrics.

Step 5: Analyzing and Applying the Multiples

Once all of the data is spread for the subject company and for each of the comparable companies, and we have calculated the appropriate valuation multiples and other key metrics, then we are ready to finally determine valuation. However, before we can discuss how to select the appropriate multiples based on the comparable companies and apply them in order to value our subject company, we need to talk about what factors actually determine how companies are valued.

Key Drivers of Valuation Multiples Let's start with an EV/revenue multiple. What does it mean, for example, for the market to value a company's enterprise value at one times revenue? An EV/revenue of 1.0x implies that each dollar of revenue is worth one dollar of enterprise value. Now let's suppose that a competitor is valued at two times revenue or in other words, each dollar of the competitor's revenue is worth two dollars of enterprise value. Why might one company trade at a higher revenue multiple than another relatively similar company?

Growth Probably the most important factor that influences a company's revenue multiple is the company's growth prospects. Other things equal, a company that is growing faster will garner a higher revenue multiple than a more slowly growing company. Let's suppose that two companies in the same industry both had $1 billion of revenue this past year. Further assume that the first company's revenue is expected to grow 5 percent going forward but the second company is predicted to grow 15 percent. Which company would you rather own? The market is naturally going to value the second company's enterprise value at a higher rate relative to current revenue.

Since understanding a company's growth prospects plays a key role in determining valuation, this is why we calculate growth metrics for the comparable companies. Finally, keep in mind that growth is not just an important factor when analyzing an EV/revenue multiple but is also typically the most crucial determinant of other multiples such as EV/EBITDA and P/E.

Profitability Another very important factor that influences a company's EV/revenue multiple is profitability. Let's return to our example of two companies that both have $1 billion revenue this year. This time, instead of assuming different growth prospects, let's assume that the first company has EBITDA margins of 20 percent but the second company has EBITDA margins of only 10 percent. In other words, the first company generates twice the cash flow (remember that EBITDA is a proxy for cash flow) from each dollar of revenue, as does the second company. Other things equal, the market will place a significantly higher valuation multiple on the first company's revenue.

Again, this is another example of why we need to calculate additional metrics when analyzing the comps and the subject company. In this case, the key statistics are EBITDA, EBIT, and net income margins. One very important thing to note is that while profitability is very important for the EV/revenue multiple, it should not play a factor in the EV/EBITDA or P/E multiples. In fact, this is very commonly misunderstood among investment bankers.

For example, take two companies with the same amount of revenue but one has EBITDA of $100 million and the other has EBITDA of $200 million. Suppose the appropriate EV/EBITDA multiple to use is 8.0x. The company with double the EBITDA will also have twice the enterprise value ($800 million vs. $1.6 billion). The higher profitability is already factored into the enterprise value when you apply the multiple, so the multiple itself is not impacted.

Risk A third factor that will influence nearly all types of valuation multiples including EV/revenue, EV/EBITDA, and P/E is risk. Other things equal, since all investors are risk-adverse, a company with more risk will have a lower valuation multiple. However, risk is much harder to quantify than is growth or profitability. One way to quantify a company's level of risk is to examine the volatility of its historical and projected revenues, cash flows, and profits. The more steady these metrics, the lower the likely risk, and the higher the valuation.

Many other factors also affect the riskiness of a company, for which simple metrics are less helpful. For instance, we would typically consider a company to be more risky than its peers if it is overly dependent on a small number of key customers, vendors, products, or geographic markets. Also, a company's valuation should be negatively impacted if it is highly associated with or reliant on one key executive (key man risk) or if there is political instability in its core markets.

Capital Expenditures, Working Capital, and Other Items that Impact Cash Flow While valuation multiples tend to be influenced most by growth, profitability, and risk, there are myriad other factors that will also have some impact. These include important uses of cash for companies such as capital expenditures and working capital.

Most of the time, higher capital expenditures are associated with higher growth prospects. However, consider two companies with the same growth prospects and identical revenue and profits. Suppose that one company has older equipment in its factory and the other company has brand-new equipment. Which company would you rather own? The company with older equipment will likely have to spend more money on capital expenditure in the future to maintain or upgrade its equipment. Since capital expenditures have a negative impact on cash flow, other things equal, that company will trade at lower multiples.

Similarly, companies that more efficiently manage working capital should have higher valuation multiples than companies that have more money tied up financing working capital. Of course, we have to be careful not to take this example too far. Companies that run inventory too lean might have a higher risk of production stoppages. Whether the positive impact on valuation because of lower working capital offsets the operational risk is up to the market (or the investment banker performing the valuation) to decide.

Leverage As we witnessed earlier in this chapter when we discussed the differences between operating and equity multiples, leverage and capital structure can have a very large impact on a P/E ratio. However, the impact on unlevered multiples such as EV/Revenue and EV/EBITDA should be much smaller, if there is any impact at all. The exception is for highly levered or distressed companies, which often trade at significant discounts to healthy companies. This is due to the risk of bankruptcy and the enormous loss of value that typically occurs in bankruptcy, as we discussed in Chapter 3.

However, we do need to be very careful when analyzing distressed companies. While multiples should in theory show discounts to healthy companies, they often do not. This is because frequently the EBITDA and earnings of distressed companies are abnormally low, making the multiples appear to be very large. This is one of the primary reasons why we try to exclude using distressed companies as comps for this methodology.

Size Larger companies have higher valuations than smaller companies, other things being equal, due to a number of factors. For example, the stocks of small companies often have much less trading volume and therefore have less liquidity. Small companies also tend to have less diversification in their businesses and are perceived to have lower-quality management teams. Moreover, small companies usually have fewer, if any, equity research analysts covering them. Therefore, information is not disseminated to the public as quickly or efficiently, making the stock more risky. We will turn to the issue of size again when we discuss calculating a company's weighted average cost of capital later in this chapter.

Management, Investors, and Corporate Governance Issues Nearly all the time, a company's valuation multiples will be positively impacted by having a well-regarded management team. This makes sense since good management will more likely result in strong growth, high levels of profitability and lower risk. However, other things equal, the worse the management team, the higher the valuation multiple. The key to understanding this statement are the words "other things equal." Given two companies with identical growth prospects, profitability, risk, and other operational factors, the one with the weaker management has more upside to do better in the future, or for the management to be replaced by a stronger team. The company with the better management is already performing well, and therefore has less upside.

Along similar lines, companies with poor corporate governance or strong takeover defenses should trade at lower multiples. Being less investor-friendly means less of a chance of a takeover at a high premium and also means weak CEOs and boards of directors have less of a chance to be replaced by stronger individuals. Finally, a company that is rumored to be a takeover candidate or one that is already "in play" will likely trade at a higher multiple on anticipation of a deal being consummated.

Applying the Multiples and Valuing the Subject Company Now that we have an understanding of the key factors that influence a company's valuation multiples, we are finally ready to turn to the crucial matter of how we apply the valuation multiples calculated for the comparable companies to our subject company in order to determine an appropriate and justifiable valuation.

In a typical analysis, we will have a set of different types of multiples, such as EV/Revenue, EV/EBITDA, P/E, and others. For each type, we also will usually have multiples based on different time periods, such as the previous fiscal year, LTM, and the projected next fiscal year. However, it is critical to determine the most important multiples, for which you need a good understanding of drivers of valuation in that industry. For many industries, this will be EV/LTM EBITDA, but not always.

Let's assume that we know that EV/LTM EBITDA is the key multiple to use. We will have already calculated the EV/EBITDA multiple for each of our comparable companies. If all of the comps are very similar to the subject company and if the range of values for the multiples is tight, then we can use the average or median multiple of the comps to value the subject company. If there are one or two outliers, we may exclude them from the average. For instance, suppose that all of the comparable companies reflect very good (i.e., similar) comps and have EV/EBITDA multiples between 7 and 8. Thus, we will probably conclude that the subject company's enterprise value should be valued between 7 and 8 times LTM EBITDA. If the company's EBITDA was $1 billion, then we can conclude that the company's EV should be between $7 billion and $8 billion.

In practice, it is unusual for all of the comps to be equally similar to the company being valued. Most of the time, some of the companies will be more comparable than others. In that case, we can rely more heavily, or even exclusively, on the range of values for the better comps. Say, for instance, that all of the comps fall in a range of 7 to 10 times EBITDA but the most comparable companies are clustered between 9 and 10 times EBITDA. In that case, we are likely to conclude a value at the higher end of the range.

Unfortunately, it is not uncommon for the multiples of the comparable companies to be in a wide range and for it to be difficult to determine the most relevant companies. This is a circumstance when valuation becomes much more of an art than a science. In order to have confidence in our valuation, we will need to rely on many of the other financial statistics that we have calculated in addition to our knowledge of the industry, the subject company, and the comparable companies.

Suppose that we expect the subject company to grow at 10 percent annually over the next few years. Is this higher or lower than the average for the comparable companies? If expected growth is above the industry average, then we will likely conclude that the subject company should trade at a multiple that is correspondingly above average. If expected growth is lower than for most of the comps, then we will likely value the company at a lower multiple.

We can perform the same exercise for the other key drivers of valuation such as profitability, risk, size, and so on. This is known as benchmarking the subject company to the comparable companies. Benchmarking also helps us determine which of the comps are most comparable from the perspective of these statistical factors as well as why some of the comparable companies trade at higher or lower multiples than do others.

We will repeat this exercise for each of the other types of multiples (e.g., EV/revenue, P/E, etc.) and for each time period of each multiple (e.g., last fiscal year, LTM, next fiscal year, etc.). Once we have done this for the one or two most important metrics (i.e., EV/EBITDA), then it is usually relatively easy to pick the remaining values.

The final step is to conclude a valuation range for the subject company based on the comparable company methodology. If all of the different types of multiples reflect a similar range of value then we might use an average or median of all of the multiples. Otherwise, we will probably conclude a valuation range based on what we determine to be the most appropriate multiples to use for this particular industry.

PRECEDENT TRANSACTION METHODOLOGY

Just like the comparable company methodology, our second primary valuation methodology, precedent transactions, also relies on relative value. In fact, as we will see, the two methodologies are very similar. Other names for the precedent transaction methodology include precedent deals, deal comps, acquisition comps, transaction comps, comparable deals, comparable acquisitions, and compaqs.

The goal of this methodology is to value a company by comparing it not to publicly traded companies but to similar companies that have been acquired in an M&A transaction. As we did in the comparable company method, we will calculate valuation multiples to help us make the comparison.

There are the same five steps to performing the precedent transaction methodology:

1. Selecting comparable acquisitions.
2. Spreading the acquisition comps.
3. Normalizing the acquisition comps.
4. Calculating valuation multiples.
5. Analyzing and applying appropriate multiples to the company you are valuing.

Because these five steps are very similar to what we just covered in the section on comparable companies, we will move quickly through them, highlighting the important differences between the two methodologies.

Step 1: Selecting Acquisition Comps

The first step in performing the precedent transaction analysis is to pick the comparable acquisitions. Here, we are seeking companies that are similar to the company being valued that have been acquired in recent years. This makes our task more challenging. Whereas there are many sources for discovering similar publicly traded companies, there are fewer resources for finding the targets of M&A transactions, and most of them are paid data sources.

Sources for Acquisition Comps The most common sources are databases of M&A transactions such as those provided by SDC Platinum (a product of Thomson Financial), Mergerstat, or Capital IQ. These databases allow us to query deals by industry, transaction date, transaction size, and other criteria. If you do not have access to such a data source, there are some possible alternatives. You can look for equity research reports that cover companies within the industry of the valuation's subject company. Sometimes research analysts, when performing their own valuations, will list comparable transactions. Other possible sources include press releases, news articles, and industry research. It can also be useful to read through the 10-Ks for the various comparable companies used in the first methodology. The 10-Ks will disclose recent acquisitions and, often, such acquisitions executed by comparable companies will represent good transaction comps.

Criteria for Selecting Acquisition Comps When we search for comparable acquisitions, we typically look back about five years, though sometimes we will include even older deals. The average number of transactions we utilize will vary significantly based on the level of M&A activity in that particular industry. Generally, the higher number of recent deals, the shorter the time frame we need to use. Note that some investment banks or bankers will only consider pending or completed transactions, while others will use all announced deals—even those deals that never closed.

One of the most important things to remember when performing this methodology is that for purposes of finding acquisition comps, it only matters that the company acquired (the target) is similar to the subject company. The buyer need not be from the same industry or similar at all. In fact, frequently the buyer will be a financial buyer (i.e., a private equity firm) rather than a strategic buyer.

Just like with the first methodology, we look for acquired companies from the same industry, with the same basic business model, operating in the same geographies, of similar size, and with similar growth and risk characteristics. Again, we want to exclude the acquisitions of distressed or bankrupt companies unless there is a good reason to include the transaction or if the entire industry is distressed. We also want to exclude the acquisition of a conglomerate where only one business segment was comparable.

There is, however, one very important difference between selecting comps for this methodology versus the comparable companies. In our first valuation method, we required that our comps be publicly traded so that we could calculate the company's market value of equity and enterprise value. With precedent transactions, the acquired company need not have been publicly traded prior to the acquisition, provided that we have enough information to perform our analysis.

Steps 2 and 3: Spreading and Normalizing Acquisition Comps

Just as with the comparable company methodology, the second step is to enter into Excel the financial information that we need for our analysis. In order to calculate valuation multiples, we need historical financial information for the target as well as the details of the transaction. Specifically, for each of the acquisition comps, we usually need to obtain and spread the following information:

- Terms of the transaction, including purchase price and the type of consideration paid (cash, stock, or both).
- Stock prices for both the target and acquirer, if publicly traded, immediately prior to the announcement of the transaction as well as several days or weeks prior to the announcement.

- The target's full income statement for the most recent full fiscal year, the most recent year-to-date (YTD) period, and the previous year's YTD period prior to the announcement of the transaction.
- Key balance sheet items from the target's most recent fiscal period prior to the announcement of the transaction.
- Key items from the target's cash flow statement for the most recent full fiscal year, the most recent YTD, and the previous year's YTD prior to the announcement of the transaction, including depreciation and amortization and capital expenditures.
- Most recent basic share count figure and stock option information prior to the announcement of the transaction for the target.
- Other industry-specific information about the target.

One of the main challenges of this methodology is that the information required to calculate valuation multiples may or may not be available, depending on the transaction. If the target company was publicly traded prior to the acquisition, then we can be sure that the information we need will be available in public filings. If, on the other hand, the target was a privately held company, then the information may or may not be available.

Generally, if the transaction consisted of a public company purchasing a private company and if the deal was large in size or considered "material" to the acquirer, then we should be able to find information about the transaction and its purchase price, likely in an 8-K filed by the acquirer. The acquirer also may disclose some historical financial information (at least revenue, for example) about the target in the 8-K. However, for a nonmaterial deal or in transactions where a private company acquired another private company, we will likely not have access to the information we need. Sometimes we will still include the deal in our list of transactions but will not be able to calculate any valuation metrics.

As with the comparable company methodology, the historical financial information for public companies will come from historical 10-Ks and 10-Qs. It is crucial that you only use information that was public and available to the buyer at the time the acquisition was announced. For private targets, you may be able to obtain some or all of the information from the buyer's public filings (e.g., 8-K) if the buyer was a public company. Occasionally in deals where the target was private, we can find a little bit of information about the transaction and the target's approximate annual revenue in a news article or industry publication. Such news articles and industry publications, as well as press releases issued by both buyer and target, can also be extremely valuable for understanding the circumstances and dynamics of the transaction.

When we spread the target's financial information, we typically only take into account historical time periods such as the last full fiscal year and

LTM prior to the transaction, whereas with the comparable company methodology, where we look at forward projections, it is much more difficult to find forecasts for the target that existed prior to the acquisition. We may have access to old equity research reports, but more often than not we rely only on historical data rather than projected data. Just like with the comparable company methodology, the historical financials of the target should be adjusted for non-recurring items (step 3). However, truth be told, while this is theoretically just as important a step as in the comparable company methodology, bankers usually spend much less time normalizing the financials for the precedent transactions methodology.

Step 4: Calculating Valuation Multiples

The next step is to calculate the appropriate multiples, both unlevered multiples, such as EV/Revenue and EV/EBITDA, and levered multiples, such as P/E. As we discussed in the previous section, more often than not we can only calculate these multiples using historical information, so we will only have trailing multiples and not forward multiples.

For the unlevered multiples, we will need to calculate enterprise value using our standard formula:

$$\text{EV} = \text{MVE} + \text{Debt} + \text{Preferred Stock} - \text{Cash} + \text{Noncontrolling Interest}$$

The values for debt, preferred stock, cash, and noncontrolling interest will all usually come from the target's most recent balance sheet prior to the announcement of the acquisition. However, the market value of equity will need to be calculated based on the transaction's purchase price. We will also use the purchase price as the numerator for levered multiples such as P/E.

Calculating the Purchase Price The purchase price reflects the value of the equity of the target based on the price paid by the acquirer for the target's equity. In most situations where the buyer acquires 100 percent of the target's existing shares, the purchase price will be equal to the aggregate amount paid by the acquirer to buy out the target's shareholders. Information for calculating the purchase price for a public transaction will usually come from 8-K filings. For a private transaction, you may find this information in press releases, news articles, or industry publications, or you may not find it at all.

Consideration There are a number of different forms of payment that a buyer can use to acquire the shares of the target. In an M&A transaction, the form of payment is known as the purchase consideration. The most common ways in which a buyer can acquire shares are by paying cash, stock, or a combination of cash and stock. In smaller, usually private transactions, other forms of consideration including contingent payments such as earnouts are possible. However, these are rare in the kinds of transactions analyzed by investment bankers, so we will not cover them.

Calculating the Purchase Price of an All-Cash Transaction If the buyer uses only cash to acquire the target's shares, then calculating the purchase price of the transaction is easy. We simply multiply the cash price per share by the number of fully diluted shares outstanding. For example, if the buyer pays $20 per share and there is 1 billion fully diluted shares outstanding, then the purchase price, and hence the market value of equity (MVE), will be equal to $20 billion.

Just like we did for the comparable company methodology, we will need to calculate fully diluted shares by adding the basic number of shares to the dilutive effect of stock options and convertible securities. For a public company, we can get the basic share count from the cover of the most recent SEC filing (10-Q or 10-K) prior to the transaction. We can calculate the dilutive effect of stock options using the treasury stock method just as we did before. The difference is that now we need to use all of the options outstanding and not only the exercisable options since all employee stock options will vest upon the transaction. Remember to only account for stock options that are in the money based on the purchase price. Out of the money options will be extinguished. Also do not forget to account for (but not double-count) the dilutive effect of any convertible debt or convertible preferred stock that will convert upon the transaction.

Calculating the Purchase Price of a Stock Transaction In an all-stock or partial-stock transaction, the buyer will issue new shares of its own stock and use that stock as payment for the target's existing shares. In order to calculate the purchase price for a stock deal, we need to know the value of the acquirer's stock. We also need to know the number of shares that will be exchanged for each share of the target, referred to as the exchange ratio.

Let's assume that a transaction calls for the buyer to issue the target's shareholders two shares of stock for every existing share of the target. Therefore the exchange ratio is equal to 2. Further assume that the buyer's shares traded for $30 immediately prior to the announcement of the transaction. Therefore we can determine that the purchase price per share is equal to $60 ($30 per buyer's share times the exchange ratio of 2). The total purchase price is then equal to $60 multiplied by the number of target's fully diluted shares.

More broadly, we can calculate the aggregate purchase price of an all-stock or partial-stock deal as follows:

Purchase Price (MVE) = (Cash Paid per Share + (Buyer's Share Price × Exchange Ratio)) × Target's Fully Diluted Shares Outstanding

One very important thing to note is when we calculate the purchase price of a stock transaction, we use the buyer's share price as of the announcement of the transaction, not the price when the deal closed, which is typically many months later. The reason for this is that we want to determine the value that the buyer expected to pay. Between the announcement date and the closing date, the stock prices of both the buyer and target can fluctuate for many different reasons, resulting in the final purchase price being very different from the purchase price on the announcement date.

For purposes of valuation, investment bankers only care about the price on the announcement date. However, both the buyer's shareholders and the seller's shareholders do care about the final purchase price. Shareholders of the target want to know how much value they will actually receive, and shareholders of the acquirer desire to understand by how much they will be diluted by the new shares being issued.

For this reason, many stock deals are negotiated with exchange ratios with various features (referred to as caps, floors, and collars) that limit how much the actual purchase price can vary. Other stock deals are based on a floating exchange rate rather than a fixed exchange rate. In a transaction with a floating exchange rate, the value of the transaction is fixed and the number of shares actually exchanged is determined by the relative share prices of the two companies at the closing date.

Control Premium In addition to calculating various valuation multiples for each transaction comp, bankers also calculate what is known as the control premium for each deal. As its name implies, the control premium reflects the premium that a buyer must pay in order to control and manage a company, rather than to be a minority shareholder with little or no control. The control premium is also sometimes referred to as the acquisition premium.

The premium that a buyer must pay over the current trading price of a public company's stock varies with the industry and with market conditions. Most of the time, transaction premiums range from 20 percent to 40 percent. However, the premium can be larger if there are multiple buyers bidding up the purchase price, or lower if there is only one buyer for the company and/or the company is distressed or facing challenges. Often transactions billed as merger of equals, in which two similar sized companies merge, see little to no premiums. Because most transactions do contain control premiums, the precedent transaction methodology will usually exhibit higher valuation multiples than the comparable company methodology, something we will discuss further later in the chapter.

To calculate the premium, we simply take the difference between the per share purchase price and the target's share price and divide by the target's share price prior to the announcement, as follows:

$$\text{Control Premium} = \frac{\text{Per Share Purchase Price}}{\text{Target's Share Price}} - 1$$

Just like we did for calculating the purchase price, when we calculate the control premium, we use the target's share price just prior to the deal's announcement date and not on the date the deal actually closes. We often also calculate the control premium based on the target's share price several days or even several weeks prior to the announcement. This is because sometimes details of the transaction leak to the public prior to the announcement and the seller's stock increases in anticipation of the deal. Often, an indication of such a leak is if there is unusually high trading volume in the days or weeks prior to the transaction's public disclosure.

Step 5: Analyzing and Applying the Multiples

The final step of the precedent transactions analysis is to analyze the valuation multiples that have been calculated for each comparable acquisition and apply the appropriate multiples in order to place a value on the subject company. Just as with the comparable company methodology, this is the stage where valuation requires a lot of judgment.

If all of the targets of the acquisitions are similar to the company being valued and if the range of multiples is reasonably small, then we might be able to get away with using the median or mean of the multiples. Or perhaps we can use the mean of the multiples excluding the outliers or use the mean of a fewer number of transactions that are more comparable to the company being valued. As a simple example, if we determine again that the most appropriate multiple to use is EV/LTM EBITDA and the most relevant deals had purchase prices that implied enterprise values of 8.0 to 10.0 times EBITDA, then we can use that range to value the subject company.

Most of the time, however, the range of multiples will be large, and we will have to do more analysis and use more prudence. Exactly as we did when analyzing comparable companies, we need to try to benchmark the subject company with the transactions in order to identify those deals that are most relevant and/or to be able to make a determination of value based on the what we know about each transaction.

Many of the criteria used for determining the most relevant transaction comps are similar to what we discussed in the section on comparable companies. For example, we should look for the transactions where the target had growth prospects, profit margins, size, and risk similar to that of the subject company. However, there are a number of additional factors that can affect purchase price that need to be taken into account in this methodology that were not relevant before. As you will see, in order to analyze these factors, you need to have a strong understanding of the circumstances of each transaction.

Market Conditions Remember that the list of precedent transactions will often include deals that happened several years in the past. Sometimes it is the case that the more recent the transactions are the more relevant ones. But this is only true if market conditions have not changed. The market conditions that existed at the time of a transaction can have an enormous impact on valuation multiples. Other things equal, deals completed in robust economies with strong credit and stock markets will have higher multiples than transactions that occurred during weaker conditions. You might want to favor those acquisitions that were announced when market conditions were analogous to the current market conditions or, likewise, discount the weight you place on those deals announced when economic conditions were very different.

Transaction Rationale Another factor that can have a significant impact on a transaction's purchase price is the rationale of the buyer. If a buyer was desperate to make the acquisition for some reason or expected very high synergies, then the purchase price, and therefore the valuation multiple, might have been abnormally high. Or as we mentioned previously, the purchase price paid in a "merger of equals" might be abnormally low due to the absence of an acquisition premium. Also, whether the buyer is a financial buyer (i.e., private equity firm) or strategic buyer can also have a big impact on valuation (in either direction, depending on market conditions).

Deal Dynamics One additional important factor that has bearing on the purchase price is what we call deal dynamics. For example, was the company being sold in an auction and if so, were there many interested buyers? Was there a bidding war that pushed up the valuation? Was this a negotiated deal where the buyer was friendly, or was it an unsolicited deal where the buyer was hostile? Was it known that the company was for sale for a long time? Were there potential regulatory or antitrust issues that might have scared some buyers away? All of these types of deal dynamics can have a large effect on valuation and should be taken into account when selecting the appropriate range of valuation multiples for the precedent transaction methodology.

DISCOUNTED CASH FLOW (DCF) ANALYSIS

The third and final of our primary valuation methodologies is the discounted cash flow (DCF). The DCF analysis represents a company's intrinsic value. It is different from the first two methodologies, which reflect relative value. As we remarked earlier in this chapter, the DCF is really a hybrid method for reasons which should soon become clear.

If you take an introductory corporate finance class as an undergraduate or MBA student, you will likely be taught that the DCF is the theoretically correct way to value a company. Your professor would not be wrong; the DCF is indeed the theoretically correct way to value a company. In practice, however, the DCF has limited value in helping us estimate a company's value, for reasons we will discuss. Having said that, the discounted cash flow analysis is one of the three primary methodologies, and investment bankers nearly always create a DCF when performing a valuation exercise. Finally, in limited circumstances the DCF can be the best (or only) way to estimate a company's value.

The basic goal of the discounted cash flow analysis is to project a company's operating cash flows into the future and then to discount those cash flows back to today's value at the appropriate cost of capital. The sum of the discounted cash flows is equal to the company's enterprise value.

Performing a DCF analysis requires five steps:

1. Forecasting free cash flow.
2. Forecasting the terminal value.
3. Estimating the weighted average cost of capital (WACC).
4. Discounting the projected cash flows and terminal value.
5. Running sensitivity analysis.

Once again, memorizing the five steps exactly as written is not important. However, "Walk me through a DCF analysis" is probably the single most-often-asked technical question in investment banking interviews. Therefore, it is crucial that you understand and are able to articulate the general methodology of a discounted cash flow analysis.

Step 1: Forecasting Free Cash Flow

The first step when creating a discounted cash flow analysis is to forecast free cash flow for a number of years into the future. A typical DCF analysis forecasts five years of cash flow, but the forecast period can be longer. Ideally it is not shorter, though in unusual circumstances it can be. The figures used for the forecasts of cash flow can come from a variety of sources, including equity research, company management, or your own projection models. In this chapter we will assume that forecasts come from one of the third-party sources such as equity research or management. (In Chapter 6 we will discuss making our own forecasts when we cover financial modeling.)

Unlevered Free Cash Flow The answer that we want the DCF analysis to provide is an estimate of a company's enterprise value. Therefore we will use what is known as unlevered free cash flow or debt-free cash flow. These cash flow forecasts exclude any impact from interest expense. Unlevered free cash flow represents the after-tax cash flow available to all providers of capital. For this reason, the discounted cash flow that we will perform is also referred to as an unlevered DCF. As we will learn later in this chapter, once we estimate enterprise value, we can easily derive equity value or a per share price.

It is possible to perform a DCF analysis that directly provides equity value, which is known as a levered DCF. This is much less frequently done, but to do so, you would need to forecast levered cash flows, which include the impact of interest expense. You would also discount the cash flows at the cost of equity rather than the weighted average cost of capital.

Unlevered free cash flow can be calculated as follows:

EBIT
Less: Taxes
Plus: Depreciation and amortization
Less: Capital expenditures
Less: Change in net working capital

EBIT Recall that EBIT is another name for operating income. EBIT reflects a firm's revenue less its cost of goods sold and SG&A. Of course, EBIT comes before the interest line in the income statement.

Taxes To estimate taxes we multiply EBIT by the company's effective tax rate. Remember that we can calculate the company's historical effective tax rate by taking a previous period's income tax expense and dividing it by the same period's pre-tax income. When performing a DCF analysis for U.S. companies, we often just use the federal statutory rate of 35 percent, or an approximation of combined federal, state, and all other taxes of 40 percent.

Depreciation and Amortization Free cash flow, as its name implies, must reflect the actual cash available to the company. Since depreciation and amortization are non-cash expenses we add back the projected figures for D&A.

Capital Expenditures We subtract forecasted capital expenditures since companies must invest in order to maintain operations and to grow.

Change in Net Working Capital Finally, we also subtract the expected change in net working capital for each forecasted period. It is very important that this line reflects the *change* from one period to the next and *not* the amount of net working capital. In fact, if a DCF analysis contains a mistake, it is most frequently found in this line. Always also remember that an increase in net working capital reflects a use of cash and therefore must reduce free cash flow.

Step 2: Forecasting the Terminal Value

Let's assume that we have forecasted unlevered free cash flow for five years. What happens after the five years? Presumably the company does not go away and there is still substantial value after the five-year projection period. What we call the terminal value reflects the value of the company beyond the projection period.

There are two generally accepted methods for calculating the terminal value. The first method is the perpetuity growth methodology, which is also sometimes referred to as the Gordon growth methodology. The second method is the terminal multiple methodology, also called the exit multiple methodology. Frequently, only the first method is taught in school. However, the second technique, the terminal multiple methodology, is the one more frequently used in investment banking. Often as bankers we will actually perform both methods and use the perpetuity growth method as a "sanity check" for the terminal multiple method.

Perpetuity Growth Methodology The perpetuity growth method provides an estimate of terminal value by assuming that cash flows grow forever at some constant growth rate. Typically, investment bankers use an estimate of expected long-term GDP growth or long-term inflation expectations as a proxy for the long-term growth rate. If GDP growth is used, the GDP estimate should be reflective of the company's country of operations (or worldwide GDP growth for multinational companies). If expected inflation is used, the rate should be representative of expected inflation of the same currency used to make the cash flow forecasts.

Truth be told, bankers do not usually do any work to justify the long-term growth rate used for the perpetuity growth method. As long as the growth rate is a relatively small number, nobody will have an issue with it. For example, in today's world (2012) most bankers probably use a long-term estimated growth rate of between 2 and 2.5 percent when valuing

U.S. companies. Back in the boom years of 2005–2007, the numbers were higher, perhaps 3.5–4 percent. If you are valuing a company in a faster-growing economy, such as a Chinese company, then you can probably use a higher rate. But it cannot be too high. Even China cannot perpetually grow 8 percent.

One other thing to keep in mind when using the perpetuity growth method is that the forecasted cash flows of the company must have reached steady-state growth before you can consider the terminal multiple. For instance, suppose we have five years of forecasts and in the fifth year the company is still growing 20 percent. In this case, we need to extend our forecasts further until the company reaches a growth rate much closer to the long-term growth rate.

Using the perpetuity growth methodology, the terminal value can be estimated by multiplying the final year's projected free cash flow by one plus the growth rate. This gives us one additional year of cash flow. We then divide the cash flow by the discount rate less the growth rate. The discount rate will correspond to the weighted average cost of capital, which we will turn to shortly. You may actually recognize the following formula from Chapter 3. It is the same formula we learned when we covered calculating the present value of a perpetuity with growth.

$$\text{Terminal Value} = \frac{CF_t \times (1+g)}{r-g}$$

g = growth rate

r = discount rate

t = last year of the projection period

Terminal Multiple Methodology The second technique for estimating the terminal value, and the one more commonly used in investment banking, is the terminal or exit multiple method. This method is even simpler to calculate than the perpetuity growth method. Here, we take an operating metric such as EBITDA from the last forecast period (e.g., year 5) and multiply it by the appropriate corresponding valuation multiple to estimate what the market will likely value the company at the end of five years.

$$\text{Terminal Value} = \text{EBITDA}_t \times \text{Exit Multiple}_t$$

t = last year of the projection period

For most industries, we use EBITDA as the operating metric, though occasionally we might use revenue, EBIT, or some other industry-appropriate metric. For the appropriate exit multiple, we use the concluded LTM EBITDA multiple (or other matching valuation multiple) from our first valuation methodology, comparable companies. The rationale for using today's multiple is that we can justify it with all of the work we have done, and because we typically have no basis for assuming valuation multiples will be higher or lower several years in the future than they are today. This is one of the several reasons why the DCF, in practice rather than theory, is really a hybrid intrinsic and relative value methodology.

If the industry is cyclical and we believe that we are at a peak or trough of the cycle, or if we have justifiable reason to believe that we are in an abnormal macroeconomic period of time (i.e., an economic bubble or recession), then we may adjust the exit multiple. What we might do is to average historical valuation multiples (e.g., EV/EBITDA) over a period of time (for example, over a full economic cycle). However, in practice, bankers rarely do this. Nearly all the time, we simply use the concluded LTM EBITDA multiple (or other appropriate multiple) from the comparable company methodology.

Step 3: Estimating the Weighted Average Cost of Capital (WACC)

The next and most complicated step in creating a discounted cash flow analysis is to estimate the rate that we will use to discount the projected cash flows and terminal value to today's value. This rate is called the weighted average cost of capital or, for short, the WACC.

As we covered in Chapter 3, a company's cost of capital, which is also sometimes referred to as the discount rate or hurdle rate, is equal to an investor's required rate of return (or opportunity cost) for investing in a company with this particular risk profile. Equivalently, the cost of capital is the company's blended or weighted cost of funds from all such funding sources. Remember the following:

- The riskier the company, the higher the investor's required return and the higher the company's cost of capital.
- Debt is always cheaper than equity, but increasing debt raises both the cost of debt and the cost of equity.
- A company's cost of capital is assumed to be U-shaped.

The weighted average cost of capital (WACC) represents the required rate of return for *all* sources of capital weighted by the percentages of each type of capital. The two main sources of capital are common equity and debt, though some companies also have preferred stock. Assuming no preferred stock, we can estimate a company's WACC as follows:

$$\text{WACC} = \left(\text{Ke} \times \frac{\text{E}}{\text{E}+\text{D}}\right) + \left(\text{Kd} \times \frac{\text{D}}{\text{E}+\text{D}} \times (1-\text{T})\right)$$

Ke = cost of equity

Kd = cost of debt

E = market value of equity (MVE)

D = market value of debt

T = tax rate

As you can see, there are a number of variables in the WACC formula. Specifically, we will need to estimate four key inputs:

1. Cost of equity (Ke).
2. Cost of debt (Kd).
3. Capital structure (or the relative percentages of debt and equity).
4. Tax rate.

We will cover the first three of these inputs (the cost of equity, the cost of debt, and the appropriate capital structure) in detail. Estimating the tax rate is relatively easy, at least compared with the other inputs. We will discuss the tax rate in the context of the other three inputs.

Cost of Equity The company's cost of equity is calculated using a rather famous formula called the Capital Asset Pricing Model, often referred to by its acronym, the CAPM. As we will see, the key input in the CAPM is something called beta, which we will estimate using the comparable companies we analyzed in the first methodology.

Capital Asset Pricing Model (CAPM) You may recall from Chapter 3 that we can estimate any discount rate as the prevailing nominal risk-free rate (which takes into account inflationary expectations) plus some spread reflecting the riskiness of the investment. This is exactly how the CAPM is derived. The CAPM estimates a company's cost of equity by taking the risk-free rate and adding a premium based on the riskiness of that company's equity.

However, rather than simply estimating the risk premium for the company's equity, the CAPM starts with the risk premium for all stocks (i.e., the overall market). The CAPM then adjusts the market's risk premium based on the specific risk associated with the company's equity.

Two equivalent variations of the CAPM formula are listed as follows:

$$Ke = Rf + (\beta \times ERP) \text{ or}$$

$$Ke = Rf + (\beta \times (Rm - Rf))$$

Ke = cost of equity

ERP = equity risk premium

Rf = risk-free rate

Rm = market return

In the first variation, the cost of equity (Ke) is equal to the risk-free rate (Rf) plus the product of the overall market's risk premium (ERP) and the company-specific risk metric called beta (β). The second formula shows the same formula except that the market's equity risk premium is equal to the expected return of the stock market (Rm) less the risk-free rate (Rf). Now we will discuss each of the components of the CAPM in turn.

Risk-Free Rate As we pointed out in Chapter 3, the risk-free rate reflects the required rate of return on a hypothetical investment that has no default risk. In reality, there is no such thing as a truly risk-free investment. As a proxy for a risk-free rate, both financial professionals and academics use the government borrowing rate in countries such as the United States where the government's creditworthiness is viewed to be extremely high.

There is some academic controversy over the correct maturity to use in the CAPM formula. However, the consensus among nearly all professionals and many academics is to use a longer-term maturity, such as a 10-year or 20-year rate. It is thought that a 20-year bond best matches the duration of the cash flows (including the terminal value) of a discounted cash flow analysis. However, 10-year bonds are more liquid, and most professionals choose to use the 10-year government yield in the CAPM formula.

Equity Risk Premium (ERP or Rm-Rf) The equity risk premium is the rate that investors expect all stocks (i.e., the "market") to return over the very long-term in excess of the risk-free rate. In reality, nobody knows what the overall stock market will return over the long term or the short term. And in fact, there is no consensus as to what is the correct premium to use.

Academics who study the equity risk premium try to measure the figure by analyzing how the stock market has actually performed over a very long period of time.

Currently, most investment banks use a rate somewhere between 3 and 6 percent. Some investment banks prefer to use the equity risk premium calculated by a data source such as Ibbotson Associates so that they have some justification for the assumption. The final thing to note is that in the current environment of extraordinarily low interest rates due to the activities of central banks worldwide, it is especially difficult to estimate the current market premium.

Beta The last piece of the CAPM puzzle is what we call beta. Beta is a measure of the volatility, or systematic risk, of a security compared to the market as a whole. When we use the term "market" we mean the entire market of all stocks. However, we can think of the S&P 500 or a similar broad index as a proxy for the entire market. Technically, beta is calculated as the covariance of a stock with the market divided by the variance of the market.

By definition, the market has a beta exactly equal to 1.0. A stock with a beta of less than 1 is considered to be less risky than the overall market and is expected to have lower returns. A stock with a beta of greater than 1 is considered to be riskier than the market and has higher expected returns. Betas can also theoretically be negative. A stock with a negative beta is expected to move in the opposite direction of the market. A security that shorts the market should have a beta of approximately –1.

Outside of a classroom, it is unlikely that you will ever need to know the exact statistical definition of beta for a particular stock, nor will you likely ever need to calculate beta yourself based on the historical volatility of a stock. Instead, as a banker, you will use one of several resources that calculate beta for all publicly traded stocks. The two most common sources of beta are Bloomberg and Barra.

Estimating a Company's Beta Now that we have talked about the CAPM formula, we are ready to discuss how we use the formula to estimate the cost of equity of the company we are valuing. We can easily look up the current 10-year treasury rate from any number of sources, and we can choose a reasonable estimate of the equity risk premium. Estimating beta, on the other hand, is more challenging.

For a private company there is obviously no way to directly calculate beta since there is no tradable stock prices that we can compare to a market index. If we are valuing a public company, we could use a data source such as Bloomberg or Barra that calculates beta for us. However, this is not what we do, for two important reasons. The purpose of our valuation exercise is to form our own opinion of value. Using the subject company's historical stock price to estimate beta and therefore its cost of capital means we are not valuing the company independent of the market. Second, as we will see very shortly, beta is dependent on a company's capital structure. To properly perform our valuation we need to make our own assessment of the company's capital structure, and we need to make our own estimation of the company's beta.

Instead, we will use the beta of our comparable companies to estimate the subject company's beta. Before we can do this, we need to "unlever" the beta for each comp.

Unlevering Beta As we have discussed, adding debt to a company's capital structure makes the company's equity more risky. Therefore we would expect that, other things equal, the stock of companies with more debt would be riskier and therefore have a higher beta. The beta that we can calculate from a company's actual stock movements includes the impact of the company's debt. Therefore this beta is known as a "levered" beta.

In order to make an apples-to-apples comparison of our comparable companies' betas, we need to strip out the impact of debt on each company's levered beta. This is process is referred to as unlevering beta. The formula to unlever a company's beta is:

$$\beta_U = \frac{\beta_L}{1+\left(\frac{D}{E}\times(1-T)\right)}$$

β_U = unlevered beta

β_L = levered beta

E = market value of equity (MVE)

D = market value of debt

T = tax rate

This formula actually is derived from the Modigliani-Miller theorem that states that the value of the firm is independent of its capital structure. The best way to understand the formula is think of unlevered beta (β_U) as the beta for enterprise value.

Consider a firm that is 100 percent equity financed. If enterprise value increases 10 percent, then equity value also must increase 10 percent. As you can see, unlevered beta will be equal to levered beta when there is no debt.

Now, consider a firm that is 50 percent financed with debt and 50 percent with equity. Suppose that enterprise value is equal to $1,000. Therefore debt is $500 and equity is $500. Now suppose that enterprise value increases 10 percent to $1,100. Assuming debt stays the same, equity value must have increased to $600 ($1,100 enterprise value less $500 debt), or 20 percent. You can see that equity value (i.e., levered beta) is twice as volatile as enterprise value (i.e., unlevered beta). Hence as long as there is debt, unlevered beta must always be less than levered beta. Taxes complicate the matter slightly but the basic principle is the same.

To actually calculate unlevered beta for each comparable company, we use the company's actual debt/equity and its effective tax rate.

Relevering Beta Once we have unlevered the betas for each comp, we can select an appropriate unlevered beta to use for the subject company. If all of the comparable companies are very similar to the subject company, then we can use the mean or median unlevered beta. Otherwise, we can use judgment to select the appropriate beta given the range of the comps.

Next, the unlevered beta that we've selected needs to be "relevered" with the subject company's capital structure, since the CAPM formula requires a levered beta. The formula used to relever beta is:

$$\beta_L = \beta_U \times \left(1 + \left(\frac{D}{E} \times (1 - T)\right)\right)$$

β_L = levered beta

β_U = unlevered beta

E = market value of equity (MVE)

D = market value of debt

T = tax rate

In the formula for levering beta, we can use the effective tax rate for the subject company. However, we do not want to use the company's current capital structure. We will want to use the optimal capital structure, which we will discuss shortly.

Cost of Debt Now that we have finished discussing the cost of equity we can move on to the cost of debt. Once again, we will use the comparable companies to help us determine the appropriate cost of debt for the subject company. There are several methods that can be used to calculate the cost of debt for each comp. The first method is the longest but also the most accurate.

Method 1: Calculating the Weighted Average Cost of Debt The first method is to calculate the cost of debt for each of the comparable companies based on a weighted average of each company's various pieces of debt. We should include both long-term and short-term debt as well as capital leases. We can get the breakdown of debt from the footnotes to each company's 10-K. Typically the 10-Q does not have enough detail, so our information will be stale; therefore we do need to make sure that the amount of debt and its components has not changed materially since the 10-K was filed. Rarely will we be able to account for 100 percent of a company's debt since many companies have small loans or credit facilities that are not disclosed. However, we should be able to account for the vast majority of the total amount of debt.

Once we have the breakdown, we need the interest rate or yield to maturity for each type. Most short-term debt will have a rate as some spread over LIBOR (LIBOR is an acronym for London Interbank Offered Rate and is the base interest rate for which nearly all company's bank debt, and many other types of debt, is set worldwide) and we can use the current rate of LIBOR. For long-term debt such as bonds, we need to look up the bond's yield to maturity from a data source such as a Bloomberg terminal. After we have all of the interest rates and yields, we can calculate each comparable company's weighted average pre-tax cost of debt. To estimate the subject company's cost of debt, we can take the mean or median cost of debt for the comps or use appropriate judgment.

Method 2: Using Credit Ratings Rather than calculating the weighted average cost of debt for each comp, which is a time-consuming process, some investment bankers use a shorter method for estimating the cost of debt for each comp. This alternative method uses credit ratings of the comparable companies to estimate the subject company's cost of debt.

With this method, we need to look up the credit rating on long-term debt for each comparable company using a data source such as a Bloomberg terminal. To approximate the appropriate credit rating for the subject company we can then take the average or median of the comparable companies' credit ratings or use appropriate judgment. For example, let's assume the average credit rating for the comps is BBB. We can then look up the current yield to maturity on an index of BBB-rated bonds, which we can then use as the subject company's pre-tax cost of debt. One disadvantage of this method is that it ignores short-term debt, so most of the time the cost of debt will be overstated by a small amount.

Method 3: Using Interest Rates The final method of estimating the cost of debt for the company being valued is even easier than the first two, but it is not really recommended because it can be inaccurate. However, it can be used to give a quick estimate of cost of debt in circumstances where time is short, or if you have no access to credit ratings and corresponding yields.

Using this technique, you estimate the cost of debt for each comp by taking the annual interest expense from the income statement and dividing by the average of the company's beginning of the year and end of the year debt figure from its balance sheets. This estimate will be wrong if current yields on debt are very different from when the company issued its debt. The figure will also be imprecise if debt was refinanced in the middle of the year at different rates. Once you have a "quick and dirty" estimate for each comparable company's pre-tax cost of debt, you can choose the appropriate cost of debt for the subject company.

Cost of Preferred When we showed the WACC formula earlier in this chapter we ignored the impact of preferred stock. However, if a company does have preferred stock in its capital structure, or if you believe that the subject company should have preferred stock in its capital structure, then the formula for WACC needs to be modified as follows:

$$\text{WACC} = \left(\text{Ke} \times \frac{\text{E}}{\text{E}+\text{P}+\text{D}}\right) + \left(\text{Kp} \times \frac{\text{P}}{\text{E}+\text{P}+\text{D}}\right) + \left(\text{Kd} \times \frac{\text{D}}{\text{E}+\text{P}+\text{D}} \times (1-\text{T})\right)$$

Ke = cost of equity

Kp = cost of preferred

Kd = cost of debt

E = market value of equity (MVE)

P = market value of preferred

D = market value of debt

T = tax rate

The cost of preferred can be calculated several different ways, depending on what information is available to you. Just like with the cost of debt, we need to first calculate the cost of preferred for each of the comparable companies that has issued preferred stock. If the preferred stock is publicly traded, then we can calculate the cost of preferred as the preferred dividend divided by the preferred share price. If the preferred stock is not publicly traded or if you do not have access to its price, then the cost of preferred is calculated as the preferred dividend divided by the preferred stock's liquidation value.

Once we have calculated the cost of preferred for each applicable comp, then we can use the mean, median or "eyeball it" based on judgment for the subject company. However, we typically do not account for preferred stock in the subject company's capital structure unless most of the comps have preferred stock in their own capital structures.

Assuming a Capital Structure The third and final key input needed to estimate the weighted average cost of capital is an assumption for the subject company's capital structure. If you recall, we also need this assumption in order to relever beta before we can use the CAPM formula to calculate the subject company's cost of equity.

The appropriate capital structure to use is the subject company's optimal capital structure. The optimal capital structure is the one that minimizes the company's cost of capital. To estimate the company's optimal percentage of debt and equity, investment bankers once again rely on the comparable companies. The assumption we make is that while some comps may not have the best capital structure, the comps in aggregate should have the right mix of debt and equity for the particular industry. So, we will assume that the subject company's optimal amount of debt and equity approximates the average of the comps.

Of course, if we have reason to think that the average debt and equity for the comps is not the optimal structure, then, as long as we can justify it, we can adjust it. Keep in mind, though, that if you choose a capital structure with a higher amount of debt then the company's cost of debt should also be higher. Similarly, if you decide on more equity than the aggregate comps, then the cost of debt should be lower. Remember that there is no need to manually adjust the cost of equity because it already takes into account the capital structure when beta is relevered.

Before we move on, it is worth pointing out two widely held misconceptions about the appropriate capital structure to use in the WACC formula. You should not use the subject company's current capital structure, nor should you use the company's expected post-transaction capital structure if you are valuing a company in the context of an M&A or LBO transaction.

Additional Considerations for Calculating WACC As complicated as calculating the weighted average cost of capital is, there are still a couple of additional modifications that can be made to it that are worth mentioning.

Adjusting the Cost of Equity for a Company-Specific Risk Premium One such adjustment is to add a company-specific risk premium to the cost of equity. If we believe that there is some risk specific to the company (and not the entire industry) that is not reflected in the projections, then we can make the cost of equity a little bit higher. Examples of such risk include key-man risk or risk due to a dependence on one large customer or supplier.

Adjust Beta for Size An additional adjustment that some investment bankers make is to adjust beta for a company's size. Large companies are considered less risky and have lower observed betas than smaller companies. We talked about the reasons for this when we discussed the key drivers of valuation multiples in the comparable company methodology section.

Just as we unlever the betas of the comparable companies to remove the effect of debt, we can do a similar adjustment to remove the effect of size. Then we add a size adjustment for the subject company, similar to the way in which we relever its beta. We will not go into the detail, but note that certain data sources such as Ibbotson Associates (the same source many banks use for equity risk premiums) publish size adjustments for stocks by deciles. Adjusting for size can be especially helpful when the company we are valuing is significantly larger or smaller than most of the comps.

Step 4: Discounting the Cash Flows and Terminal Value

So far we have discussed how to calculate free cash flow, how to estimate terminal value, and how to assess a company's cost of capital. The next step is to discount all of the forecasted cash flows and the terminal value back to today's value using the weighted average cost of capital as the discount rate.

Recall from Chapter 3 the basic formula used for present value (PV) cash flows:

$$PV = \frac{CF_t}{(1+r)^t}$$

r = discount rate

t = time period

While we use this basic formula for present value cash flows, there are two important adjustments that we often will need to make.

Stub Period If the first year of cash flows does not represent a full fiscal year, then we will have what we call a stub period. This situation occurs very often since statistically most of the time you are performing a valuation exercise, the calendar date will not be at the very beginning of a company's fiscal year. For instance, suppose that a company's fiscal year runs January through December but that today's date (the valuation date) is July 1st. The six months remaining in the year represent the stub period.

Having a stub period requires us to make two adjustments to our analysis. First, we need to reduce the first year's free cash flow by the amount of time that remains in the year. Continuing with our example, if there are six months remaining in the year, we typically multiply the first forecasted year's cash flows by one half (six months out of 12). Of course, this assumes that the first year's forecasted cash flow did indeed represent a full year. Naively multiplying the full year by the stub percentage may not give us precise answers for seasonal businesses or for companies that are growing or shrinking rapidly; however, it is the method that is most frequently used. If you happen to have quarterly forecasts then you can be even more accurate. Keep in mind that there is no need to adjust subsequent years, as they will always represent a full year of cash flows.

The second adjustment that we need to make due to a stub period is to the discount period. The discount period is the name given for the time period t in the present value formula. When we learn about present value in school, we are ordinarily taught to use whole numbers as the discount period. In other words, you discount the first year's cash flow by one full period, the second year's cash flow by two full periods, and so forth. However, if we have a stub period, then we need to make a modification to each discount period.

Suppose again that there are six months remaining in the year so we have a stub period of 0.5. We should discount the first half of year not by one period but by 0.5 periods. The second year should be discounted by 1.5, the third year by 2.5, and so on. More broadly, the discount period should be equal to the stub period in the first year. Every subsequent year is discounted by one additional year.

Mid-Year Discounting The second adjustment that investment bankers almost always make to the DCF is to discount cash flows in the middle of the year rather than at the end of the year. This is known as mid-year discounting. We do this because a company generates cash flows throughout the year, not just on the very last day of the year. Discounting in the middle of the year is therefore more accurate because it approximates the company generating cash flows throughout the year.

Ignoring for the moment a stub period, rather than use a discount period of one for the first year, two for the second year and so on, as we learn in school, we should discount the first year's cash flow by 0.5, the second year's by 1.5, and so forth. One important wrinkle regards the proper discount factor to use for the terminal value. If you are using the perpetuity growth method, you should discount that cash flow in the middle of the year (the same discount period used for the last year of projected cash flow). Alternatively, if you are using the terminal multiple method, then you should discount the terminal value at the end of the year (half a year greater than the discount period used for the final year's cash flow).

Combining a Stub Period and Mid-Year Discounting Most of the time bankers find themselves in the situation of having a stub period and wanting to use mid-year discounting. Let's assume again today's date is July 1st and the company has a calendar fiscal year. Therefore we have a stub period of 0.5. Using mid-year discounting, we would want to discount the first year's cash flows on about October 1st, or halfway until the end of the year. This corresponds to a discount period of 0.25. Next year we want to discount in the middle of the year, which is July 1st. July 1st is exactly one year from now, so we would use a discount period of 1.0. We can then add one to the discount period for each subsequent year.

More generally, using mid-year discounting, the discount period for the first year should be equal to the stub percentage divided by two. The next year's discount period will be equal to the stub year plus 0.5. The following year will be equal to the stub year plus 1.5, and so on.

The Discount Factor Once we have figured out the appropriate discount period to use for each year (or partial year) of cash flow, we can calculate the discount factor. The discount factor is simply the standard present value formula with a 1 in the numerator instead of the cash flow. Notice that we have now relabeled r as the WACC and t as the discount period.

$$\text{Discount Factor} = \frac{1}{(1+r)^t}$$

r = WACC

t = discount period

Discounting the Cash Flows and Summing Them to Estimate Enterprise Value Once we have calculated both the discount period and the discount factor, the final step in the process of discounting the cash flows is to multiply each cash flow by the discount factor.

$$\text{PV of FCF}_t = \text{FCF}_t \times \frac{1}{(1+r)^t}$$

FCF = free cash flow

r = WACC

t = discount period

Once we have discounted each cash flow as well as the terminal value, we sum them. This total equals our estimate of the enterprise value of the company based on the discounted cash flow analysis.

Step 5: Running Sensitivity Analysis

One of the disadvantages of the discounted cash flow analysis is that it is very sensitive to its various inputs. For this reason, investment bankers always run sensitivity analysis on the DCF. This sensitivity analysis also helps bankers define a range of values for the subject company rather than a single point of value. The standard method in which bankers sensitize the DCF is to rerun the analysis with varying inputs for both the WACC and either the terminal multiple (if using the terminal multiple method to calculate terminal value) or the long-term growth rate (if using the perpetuity growth methodology).

Suppose, for instance, we have concluded that the company's cost of capital should be 8.0 percent and the appropriate terminal EBITDA multiple is 7.0x. To perform the sensitivity analysis, we would run the DCF again using a WACC of perhaps 7.0, 7.5, 8.0, 8.5, and 9.0 percent, and a terminal multiple of, let's say, 6.0x, 6.5x, 7.0x, 7.5x, and 8.0x. Typically the middle value being sensitized is equal to our concluded estimate (the base-case).

As you may have calculated, if you sensitize the DCF with five different values for WACC and five different values for the terminal multiple, then you will have to rerun the DCF analysis 25 times. This would be a time-consuming and error-prone process. Luckily, Microsoft Excel has a built-in feature, referred to as a "Data Table," that performs this sensitivity analysis for us.

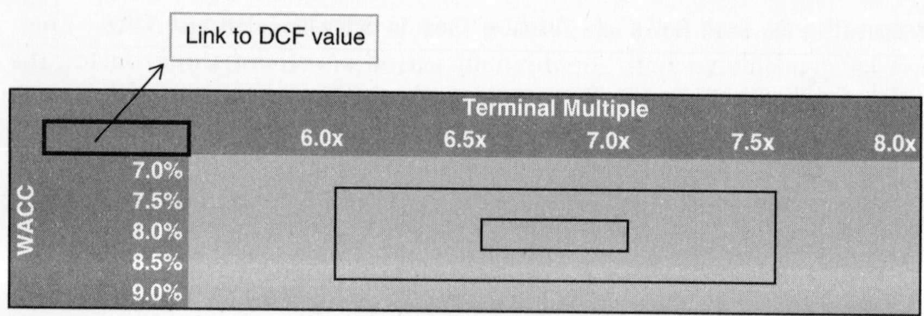

EXHIBIT 5.2 DCF Setting Up the Sensitivity Table

To use this Data Table feature, we first need to set up the sensitivity table as per Exhibit 5.2. As you can see, we have listed the five values we wish to sensitize for WACC going down the first column and the five values for the terminal value going across the top row. We also link the upper left cell of the table to the concluded enterprise value from the DCF analysis.

Next, we need to highlight the entire table using the mouse or keyboard and then select Excel's Data Table feature as follows:

- In Excel 2003: Select the Data menu and then select Table.
- In Excel 2007 and 2010: Select the Data menu on the ribbon, then Select What-If Analysis and then Select Data Table.

You should now see a box that looks like Exhibit 5.3.

This popup box prompts you for two inputs: the row input cell and the column cell. The way we have set up our data table, the row input cell corresponds to the cell in our DCF analysis that contains our estimate of terminal value, and the column cell contains our assumption of WACC.

Data Table
Row input cell:
Column input cell:
OK Cancel

EXHIBIT 5.3 Data Table Input Box

We input these two cells and then click OK. Excel should now populate the sensitivity table with 25 values. Make sure that you test a few of the values in the table to ensure that the table was populated correctly. Finally, we can base our concluded range of values for the DCF based on the range of values in this sensitivity table.

DCF Conclusions

As we alluded to in the introduction to this section on discounted cash flow, and in the previous section on sensitizing the analysis, the DCF is generally not very useful as a valuation technique. The primary reason is because it is so sensitive to its various inputs. In other words, the DCF suffers from "GIGO" syndrome: garbage in, garbage out.

The DCF is not only sensitive to the WACC and the terminal multiple (or long-term growth rate) but also to all of the inputs that drive the free cash flow forecasts. Moreover, the WACC itself is sensitive to many variables that can be massaged, including beta, equity risk premium, the company-specific risk premium, the cost of debt, and the optimal debt to equity ratio.

On the flip side, there is an inherent advantage to a valuation methodology whose output is very sensitive to its inputs. It is relatively easy to come out with a wide range of values. This makes the DCF very useful when we, as bankers, need our valuation analysis to justify a predetermined value.

As difficult as it is to rely on the value attributed to a discounted cash flow analysis, there are certain circumstances where the DCF is considered useful. Typically these are instances where we cannot rely on the first two methodologies (comparable companies and precedent transactions). This is most often the case when valuing early-stage or pre-revenue companies where we cannot use multiples based on revenue or cash flow. We might be able to use a ratio such as EV/employees or EV/patents or EV/web site visits, but more likely we will have no choice but to rely on a DCF. The DCF is also more valuable for companies with very predictable and steady cash flows, such as regulated utilities.

Probability Weighted DCF There is one final variation of the DCF worth mentioning: a probability-weighted DCF. Suppose we need to value a biotechnology company that has only one drug in its pipeline, and the one drug is currently in clinical trials. Let's assume that there only two equally likely scenarios: Either the drug fails its trials, in which the company's value is worth $0, or the drug succeeds and becomes a blockbuster. We can make a forecast for the blockbuster scenario and then run a DCF analysis based on that forecast, which let's assume results in a value of $1 billion. We can therefore conclude that the value of this company is worth (very roughly given the uncertainties) $500 million (a 50 percent chance of $0 value and a 50 percent chance of $1 billion value). We are not limited, of course, to only two scenarios. We could create as many forecasts as there are scenarios, perform a DCF on each, and then probability weight them, and aggregate them all to come up with an approximate value.

VALUATION CONCLUSIONS

We have completed our three valuation methodologies: We have picked and spread comps, we have found and analyzed M&A transactions, and we have forecasted cash flows and estimated WACC. For each of the three methodologies we have concluded an appropriate value or, better yet, range of values. As investment bankers, we typically summarize our analysis graphically in an exhibit known as a football field. The football field is a graph that shows a different bar for each methodology representing a range of values. We can then indicate graphically our concluded range for all three methodologies. Exhibit 5.4 shows an example of such a football field valuation summary.

The one question that remains is how we estimate the appropriate value of the company based on the three sets of answers.

The correct interview answer is to state that you triangulate value based on the three methodologies. Use the word "triangulate" and you almost guarantee yourself an offer from Goldman Sachs. Of course, nobody except the engineers who build GPS systems understands what triangulate really means.

The real answer is less straightforward. As we discussed at the beginning of this chapter, most of the time as investment bankers we have a good idea of value before we start doing any of the valuation work. In these instances, we try to pick valuation ranges for each methodology that conform to the value we want. Usually there is a large enough range of values from aggregating all three methods to conclude the appropriate value. But we also hope that the different techniques give us a similar range. We do not want them to be too far apart. Sometimes once we see where each method falls out, we will have to go back and adjust some of our inputs.

If we do not have a preconceived sense of value, then we have to use a little bit more judgment. If all of the methodologies imply a similar range of value then it is usually easy. We can take an average of the three methodologies and call it a day. Or we can use the methodologies with the highest and lowest values to come up with a concluded range. If, however, the values

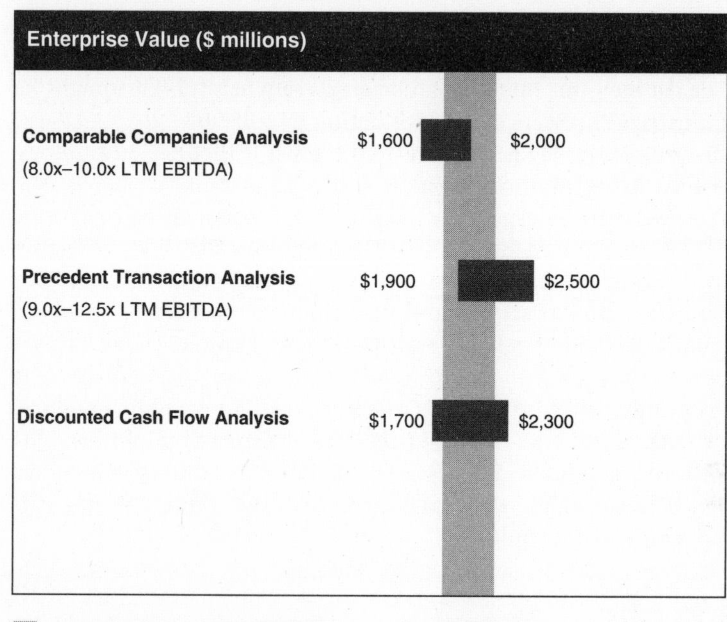

EXHIBIT 5.4 Example of a Football Field Valuation Summary

based on three techniques differ, then we need to determine which one or two methods are more reliable.

Most often this will be the comparable company methodology. This method uses current market information and requires the fewest assumptions. Valuation is easiest to justify based on publicly traded comparables. In reality, it is the way the market values most companies. However, if the comparable companies are not so comparable, then it is less suitable. Also, if the company we are valuing has very low or no EBITDA or earnings, is distressed, or is pre-revenue, then we may not be able to use the method at all, or at least may not have a high degree of confidence in it.

The precedent transaction method is often harder to rely on because the range of values of the comparable deals tends to be quite large. Also this method suffers from the disadvantage that valuations are dependent on market conditions at the time of the deal. It is much harder to compare a deal completed in a robust economy with one executed in a recession.

You also need to be aware of specific deal dynamics that may make certain transactions much less relevant. However, if there are a lot of very recent, very similar deals, then this method can be extremely helpful. This might be the case in industries experiencing consolidation or roll-ups.

As we discussed, the DCF is typically the most difficult methodology on which to rely. More than anything, it serves as a sanity check for the other two. You need to be especially careful if management's projections were used to forecast free cash flow, since management tends to be highly optimistic. But in instances where cash flows are very predictable, where there are few or no similar comps and no similar transactions, or where for other reasons we cannot rely on multiples, then it can be the most useful method.

Always remember that valuation is much more of an art than a science. For all of the data and the analysis and the Nobel Prize–winning formulas that are baked into a valuation analysis, to be good at valuing companies takes experience and a high level of familiarity with the company being valued and the dynamics of its industry.

Estimating Equity Value

So far, for each valuation methodology, our goal has been to estimate a company's enterprise value. Very often, though, bankers want to also calculate the implied aggregate equity value of the company or a per share equity value. There are a number of ways we could do this. As we discussed in the discounted cash flow section of the chapter, we could perform a levered DCF instead of an unlevered DCF, but we rarely do this. We also could estimate equity value directly from the comparable company methodology or precedent transaction methodology using equity multiples such as price/earnings (P/E).

Generally, however, bankers prefer to calculate equity value based on the concluded enterprise value. This way we can base equity value on any and all of the valuation methodologies. Recall the formula for calculating enterprise value:

$$\text{EV} = \text{MVE} + \text{Debt} + \text{Preferred Stock} - \text{Cash} + \text{Noncontrolling Interest}$$

With some simple algebra, we can calculate equity value as follows:

$$\text{MVE} = \text{EV} - \text{Debt} - \text{Preferred Stock} + \text{Cash} - \text{Noncontrolling Interest}$$

To calculate our estimate of the market value of equity, we start with enterprise value and then subtract the company's value of debt, preferred stock, and non-controlling interest, and add the amount of cash. We typically get these figures from the company's most recent balance sheet.

Per Share Price If we want to calculate equity value per share, then we just need to divide the total market value of equity by the number of fully diluted shares as follows:

$$\text{Per Share Value} = \frac{\text{Market Value of Equity}}{\text{Fully Diluted Number of Shares Outstanding}}$$

For a public traded company, we can easily compare our estimated per share valuation to the current share price to help us determine if believe a stock to be overvalued, undervalued, or fairly valued.

Additional Valuation Considerations

Before we end this chapter with a discussion of some alternative valuation methodologies, we need to discuss several additional considerations that investment bankers should keep in mind when valuing companies. Specifically, we will talk about some of the differences between valuing a publicly traded and a privately held company. We will also discuss how the purpose of the valuation can impact the analysis. Finally, we will point out some of the ways in which valuing companies on the buy side differs from the work of an investment banker.

Considerations for Valuing a Public Company versus a Private Company As we have mentioned previously, a publicly traded company and a privately held company can be valued using the same three primary methodologies. There are, however, several things to keep in mind and a few differences worth reviewing.

Valuing Public Companies The value that the stock market places on a company's equity and the implied enterprise value serve as crucial benchmarks anytime we are valuing a publicly traded company. In fact, nearly all of the time we will conclude a range of values based on our own analysis that is at or very close to the value implied by the market. Except for small and illiquid stocks, the market is highly efficient, so we better have a very good rationale if our valuation differs significantly. If we are valuing a public company we also usually have the opportunity to verify our own assumptions with those of equity research analysts. So, if our valuation does differ from that of the market's, we can at the very least understand why.

Valuing Private Companies When valuing privately held companies we have no benchmark. This is both good and bad. We have more leeway with our own analysis, and it is harder for someone to say we are wrong. On the other hand, it is more difficult to feel comfortable with our answer. Private companies also are often much smaller than publicly traded companies. This can make it harder to find suitable comps or at least rely on those comps. And as we spoke of earlier, small companies tend to trade at a discount to larger companies. Especially if your comparable companies are considerably larger, you may need to add what is known as a lack of marketability discount since investors in privately held companies do not have the same liquidity as do investors in larger, publicly traded companies.

Valuation Context One thing that we have not yet talked about is how our valuation analysis is affected by the type of transaction or project for which we are performing the analysis. Suppose, for example, our bank has been hired by a publicly traded company looking to sell itself and we need to value the company to estimate what the purchase price might be. We know from our discussion of the precedent transaction methodology that valuations based on acquisitions tend to be higher than valuations based on comparable companies because buyers typically pay some control premium. Therefore in our valuation in the context of an M&A transaction, we would likely also want to include an appropriate control premium.

You may be thinking that in this circumstance we should rely on the precedent transactions and ignore the comparable company methodology because the latter does not include a control premium. However, this is not the case. Instead what we can do is add an appropriate premium to the comparable company valuation range. Let's say that we conclude the appropriate valuation multiple based on comparable companies is 8.0x EV/EBITDA. Since a buyer will likely have to pay a control premium, we can increase that value by some amount, perhaps 30 percent. The appropriate control premium to use will come out of our precedent transaction analysis.

Similarly if we are valuing a company that is going to do an initial public offering (IPO), we do not want to include a control premium. However, we can still use the precedent transaction analysis to help us determine valuation. Here what we can do is remove an estimate of the control premium from the precedent transaction's concluded value, or to be semantically more accurate, reduce the value for what is known as a minority discount.

Valuation on the Buy Side Some of you reading this are probably considering working for a private equity firm, hedge fund, or other asset manager as an alternative to investment banking. Or you might view investment banking as a feeder to those types of buy-side jobs. Therefore, I think it would be helpful to briefly discuss how valuation on the buy side differs from that of investment banking. Practically speaking, the analysis is the same. You perform the same types of valuation methodologies. However, there are some important differences.

As we discussed in the earlier parts of this chapter, valuation in investment banking is about justifying your work, not necessarily about being "right." Investing, on the other hand, is about being right. Bankers tend to do a lot of work just to show they do a lot of work. On the buy side, it is usually more important to get to a good answer quickly and efficiently, especially at a hedge fund, where investment opportunities are often fleeting. Bankers tend to do all three methodologies regardless of their reliability. On the buy side, you are much less likely to do a valuation methodology if you don't think it will give you helpful results.

There is also more variability to the level of detail that goes into buy-side valuations as opposed to those performed in investment banking. For instance, on the buy side, you may build a very detailed projection model for quarterly or annual earnings, whereas in an investment bank you might just rely on equity research for projections. On the other hand, at a hedge fund you might do a very quick and dirty WACC analysis because you know it will not "move the needle" of your analysis. In contrast, as a banker, you may spend hours on your WACC analysis.

Lastly, you should understand the limits of valuation, especially working at a hedge fund. It is hard enough to identify undervalued or overvalued stocks or other securities, given a highly if not perfectly efficient market. But being right on valuation is only half the battle. You also need to be right on timing. If a stock is undervalued today, why won't it also be undervalued tomorrow? What is the catalyst that is going to force the market to agree with your valuation? An earnings release? An announcement of a new product or new customer? A takeover offer? Hedge funds rarely succeed because of the quality of their valuation analysis. Hedge funds succeed because they possess information that the market does not yet have, or does not yet understand.

Additional Valuation Methodologies

When investment bankers need to value a company, they almost always use the primary three methodologies. In case you have forgotten already, these are the comparable company methodology, the precedent transaction methodology, and discounted cash flow analysis. Sometimes bankers also perform one or more additional valuation techniques, depending on the circumstances. In this final section, we will briefly talk about some of these additional valuation methods.

Leveraged Buyout (LBO) Valuation We are going to cover leveraged buyouts in much more detail in Chapter 8, so we will keep this section short. An LBO analysis is sometimes considered the fourth primary valuation methodology by bankers and is used very often when valuing companies in the context of an M&A transaction. To refresh your memory, a leveraged buyout is when a company is acquired by a private equity firm with the help of a substantial amount of borrowed money.

To perform an LBO valuation, we first need to have a forecast for the company being valued, similar to that of our DCF forecasts but more detailed. By making certain assumptions, including how much debt can be raised for the deal as well as the private equity firm's target rate of return, we can back into today's implied enterprise value and/or equity value and use that for valuation.

Replacement Value Replacement value is not a methodology that investment bankers typically perform but it is worth briefly discussing nonetheless. The concept of replacement value is simple: How much money would it cost today to replicate or re-create the company we are trying to value? Essentially, we would need to go through each line item on the balance sheet and determine, for instance, how much it would cost today to build its factories or purchase its inventory. We also need to make sure to include intangible assets that may or may not be listed on the balance sheet such as brand names, trademarks, and technology. The replacement cost of such intangible assets is much harder to determine. However, there are methods that can be employed. For example, to estimate the replacement cost of a brand name we could determine how much a company would need to spend on marketing and advertising, or to approximate the value of technology we could estimate how much it needs to spend on research and development.

Sum of the Parts Valuation Another alternative valuation methodology is a sum of the parts valuation. As we mentioned earlier, this kind of technique is most useful when valuing companies that have diverse business units, such as conglomerates. In essence we can use any or all of the primary three methodologies to value each business unit as long as we have sufficient financial information on the segments. We can then sum the values of each business unit to estimate the value for the entire company. Sometimes companies also own minority equity stakes in other publicly traded companies, in which case we can value that equity stake using the public share price, perhaps with a moderate liquidity discount if the holding is large.

Liquidation Value The last of the additional valuation methodologies that we will discuss is liquidation value. Liquidation value is most relevant for companies in distressed situations. Fundamentally, the liquidation value tells us how much value would be realized if a company sold off all of its assets in a fire sale or liquidation. As you might expect, this method is likely to give us the lowest value of any valuation technique. In fact, this method does not comply with our definition of fair market value, which requires a willing but not desperate seller. A liquidating company is a perfect example of a desperate seller.

Just like for replacement value, to perform a liquidation analysis, we can walk through the balance sheet and value each asset. Except for cash, most other assets will likely be valued at less than book value. For example, accounts receivables might be worth 80–90 percent of book value, while inventory might be worth only 50 percent. Fixed assets might be valued at only 30 percent or even at zero if there are no likely buyers. The value of an asset can even be negative if there are shutdown costs or environmental remediation costs associated with the asset. In a non-bankruptcy situation, we also need to net our estimate of asset value against a company's liabilities. However, in a bankruptcy certain liabilities can be eliminated through the bankruptcy process.

END-OF-CHAPTER QUESTIONS

1. How do investment bankers value companies?
2. What are the primary valuation methodologies that investment bankers use to value companies?
3. What is total enterprise value?
4. How do you calculate total enterprise value?
5. What is the difference between total enterprise value and equity value?
6. What is noncontrolling interest?
7. Why do you add noncontrolling interest in the enterprise value formula?
8. Why do you subtract cash in the enterprise value formula?
9. How do you calculate the market value of equity?
10. What is the difference between basic and fully diluted shares?
11. How do you calculate fully diluted shares using the treasury stock method?
12. What are some examples of commonly used valuation multiples?
13. What is wrong with using a multiple such as EV/earnings or price/EBITDA?
14. What are some factors to consider when picking comps?
15. Walk me through a DCF.
16. How do you calculate free cash flow?

17. Why do you use unlevered free cash flow?
18. What is the terminal value and how do you calculate it?
19. Why do you present value the cash flows?
20. Conceptually, what does WACC represent?
21. What is the formula for WACC?
22. How do you calculate the cost of equity?
23. What is the CAPM formula?
24. What is beta?
25. Why do you unlever and lever beta?
26. What is the formula for unlevering and levering beta?
27. How do you calculate the cost of debt?
28. How would you value a biotechnology startup with one potential blockbuster drug that is currently in clinical trials?
29. How do you use the three main valuation methodologies to conclude value?
30. Of the three main valuation methodologies, which ones would you expect to give you higher or lower value?
31. What are the advantages and disadvantages of each of the three main valuation methodologies?
32. What are some other valuation methodologies that you might use to value a company?

Answers can be found at www.wiley.com/go/gutmann (password: investment).

CHAPTER 6

Financial Modeling

As we mentioned in the previous chapter, financial modeling is, along with valuation, one of the two core technical skills required of junior investment bankers. But what exactly do we mean when we use the term "financial modeling," and why is it so important of a skill?

To some finance professionals, any analysis done in Excel can be called a model. In fact, the valuation analysis that we covered in the previous chapter is often referred to as a valuation model. However, when we speak of an investment banker having financial modeling skills, what we are really referring to is the ability to make forecasts of a company's financial performance based upon a set of assumptions. We sometimes refer to this kind of model as a projection model.

The key is to build the model in such a way that it is dynamic, rather than static. In other words, the assumptions must drive, or flow through, the model. The output of the model (i.e., the forecasts) must depend on the chosen assumptions. Change the assumptions and the forecasts must reflect those changes.

There are times as a banker where we may just to need to forecast a single operating metric of a company, perhaps revenue, EBITDA, or net income. However, the core modeling skill required of investment bankers is to be able to create a forecast of a company's three financial statements: income statement, balance sheet, and cash flow statement. This type of model is known as an integrated cash flow model and is the subject of this chapter.

Nearly all investment banking activity requires the creation of an integrated cash flow model. Models are built by analysts or associates when advising on buy-side and sell-side M&A transactions, leveraged buyouts (LBOs), issuance of new equity or debt, and restructurings. In addition, financial modeling is a key skill for many other roles within corporate finance, including equity research, private equity, asset management, hedge funds, and corporate development.

The purpose of this chapter is not to make you an expert at financial modeling. It is not an Excel how-to. (There are plenty of good Excel books on the market.) Nor is this chapter intended to be a comprehensive reference guide, describing how to model every possible line item for every company, industry, or situation. Instead, like much of the content contained in this book, the goal of this chapter is to introduce you to basic modeling skills so that you can begin to build your own financial models and are able to intelligently talk about building models in an interview.

In this chapter, we will discuss how to build a basic integrated cash flow model. This chapter begins with a general overview of an integrated cash flow model and a discussion of modeling best practices. Then we will move on to describe the manner in which we forecast the income statement, balance sheet, cash flow statement, and an additional schedule, the debt schedule. Finally, we will wrap up the chapter with a discussion of how to check and analyze your model, and a brief discussion of some of the additional analysis that can be performed with this type of financial model.

OVERVIEW OF AN INTEGRATED CASH FLOW MODEL

An integrated cash flow model is a forecast of a company's income statement, balance sheet, and cash flow statement. For reasons (hopefully) obvious, this kind of model is sometimes also referred to as a three-statement model. We refer to the model as integrated because of all of the different ways in which the financial statements are linked together, which we covered at length in Chapter 2. This is why an intuitive understanding of basic accounting principles is a prerequisite for being a competent modeler.

We also refer to this model as a cash flow model because only with the three financial statements projected can we accurately estimate what will happen to a company's cash and liquidity position based upon our set of assumptions. Once we have built the model, we can use it to answer such questions as:

- Does the company have enough liquidity for working capital?
- Can the company make necessary capital expenditures for anticipated growth?
- Will the company be able to make its required interest payments?
- Will the company be able to pay back or refinance debt when the debt matures?
- Can the company afford to pay dividends?

Modeling Best Practices

Before we begin to discuss how we go about creating an integrated cash flow model, it is worth laying out some guidelines and general modeling recommendations, which we often refer to as modeling best practices. Always keep in mind that these best practices are indeed guidelines and recommendations, but they are not rules. You should make an attempt to follow them, especially as you are first learning how to build financial models. However, they may not apply to every situation, and you may need to deviate from them on occasion.

Simplicity vs. Complexity Conceptually, all integrated cash flow models work the same way. They rely on the same accounting and finance knowledge, and the same basic Excel skills. However, some models are small, perhaps a few hundred rows of Excel. Others are large, containing dozens of worksheets or even dozens of linked workbooks (files), and measuring hundreds of megabytes. Some models can be created from scratch in a few hours. Others can take weeks or even months to build.

Broadly speaking, there are two types of complexities related to building financial models. One type of complexity is simply the sheer amount of detail contained. The more detail, the more links, the more complex is the model. For example, a small model might have a typical income statement containing one projected revenue line, whereas a large model might have one sales line for each of 100,000 different products, summing to equal projected revenue.

The other kind of complexity refers to what we call "bells and whistles." This is special functionality that we can build into our Excel model to make the model more dynamic, flexible, or reusable. Typical bells and whistles include such things as drop-down menus, macros, and switches. They often utilize some of Excel's more advanced functionality, including behind-the-scenes Visual Basic programming. With such functionality, we can do things like analyze multiple scenarios or have the ability to turn on and off certain parts or divisions of a business.

The degree of complexity and detail of our model generally depends on the situation and specifically on three main factors:

1. The amount of information to which we have access.
2. The purpose for building the model.
3. How much time we have to build the model.

The most important of the three factors is generally how much information you possess on the company being modeled. Very often as an investment banker, you will build a model based on public SEC documents such as a 10-K, and without having any access to the company's management. This is most frequently the case when building a model for a pitchbook. Since the financial information contained in a 10-K is limited to the three financial statements, the footnotes, and little more, a model based primarily on this information will naturally have a limited scope and level of detail.

In other instances, bankers build models having access to much more information. If your investment bank has been hired by a company to execute a transaction then you will have the ability to perform due diligence with that company's management. For example, you can ask specific and detailed questions about what key factors determine the level of revenue or cost, capital expenditure, or dividend payment. You may also have access to substantially more information, and in some cases, you may even use the company's own internal projection model as a starting point for your model. It is safe to say that a model based on detailed internal company information will be larger than one based solely on a 10-K and other publicly available information.

The second factor that dictates the complexity and size of a model is its purpose. Often it is enough to build a basic financial model to get a broad or high-level understanding of whether or not a transaction might be feasible or prudent. For instance, suppose we want to have a reasonable idea of whether a company can afford to make a large acquisition. We typically would not need an enormous amount of modeling detail to achieve this sort of understanding.

However, other times the circumstances require a much more detailed model. Suppose our firm has now been hired to advise the buyer on that potential acquisition. Now we may need to build a very detailed model to analyze such things as the best way to finance the acquisition, potential synergies and cost savings, and the likely impact of the acquisition on the company's credit rating.

The third factor that dictates how detailed our model will be is how much time we are given to build it. There are instances as an investment banker where you will have to build a model in a very short period of time, perhaps 48 or even 24 hours. Obviously in this circumstance, you will likely have the time to build only a relatively simple model with limited detail. On the other hand, there may be situations where you have several weeks or even months to perfect a model, in which case you can build more detail, build in more complexities, and spend more time specifying and fine-tuning model assumptions.

Regardless of the situation, there is one best practice to always keep in mind. Do as Albert Einstein is credited with saying: Build your model as simple as you can, but no simpler. If for whatever reason, your analysis requires forecasting more detailed financial results or warrants more detailed assumptions, then by all means, build it that way. But never add unnecessary complexities or unneeded bells and whistles just because you can. A simple model is hard enough to debug and to check. A larger model with more links and more complications simply raises the likelihood of error. Moreover, you should always build your model keeping in mind that someone else might use it at some later date. A simple and useful model will result in your name being praised rather than cursed if ever a fellow banker needs to use it.

Starting from Scratch vs. Using a Template Most investment banks, and even the various groups within an investment bank, have standard templates for projection models, just as they have standard valuation templates. Suppose as a new analyst or associate you are given the task of building a model. Do you start from a blank Excel workbook (starting from scratch) or do you start with a template?

First of all, the decision may not be yours to make. Sometimes you must follow firm or group policy and use the template. Other times your associate or vice president will dictate what you do. However, when you do have the choice of either starting from scratch or using a template, there are a number of factors to consider.

There are certain advantages to using a template. First, the cell formulas and the links between the three financial statements as well as other supporting statements are typically already created. So, you just need to input the historical financial figures and your assumptions and—voila—you've got a working model. In addition, often the output of your model will need to be inserted into a pitchbook or other type of presentation. Typically, templates already have this output analysis already created, standardized, and formatted. To re-create this analysis might be an arduous process. Finally, templates also often contain lots of those bells and whistles that under some circumstances make your life easier.

There are, however, some significant disadvantages to starting from a template. Most importantly, templates can be very difficult to modify, especially if there are macros or Visual Basic code behind the scenes. If, for instance, the financial statements of the company that you are forecasting do not fit the template well, you may need to add or subtract rows from the template, a potentially challenging, a time-consuming, and sometimes a virtually impossible task.

Moreover, using a template with which you are not intimately familiar makes it difficult to truly understand what is going on with your model. This makes it hard to both debug and check your model and to have a high degree of confidence in its output.

The advantage of starting from scratch is that you can make it fit your company and situation perfectly. Of course, you will need to do all the work, including linking, formatting, and creating all of the output pages that you need. But there is a better chance that you will understand what is going on and be able to explain forecasted financial performance to your firm's client or to the other members of your deal team.

The bottom line is that there is no correct answer as to whether to use a template or start from scratch. Like the answer to most of life's important questions, it depends. My personal preference as an investment banker was always to start from scratch if I had sufficient time to do so. I also highly recommend you start from scratch when you are first starting out in investment banking. Modeling is a very important skill, and there is no better way to become proficient then to build models starting with a blank spreadsheet.

One last thing before we move on. There are times when you might be tempted to build your model starting not with an empty template but by trying to modify a completed model that someone else built for a similar company or situation. This seems like an idea that can save you a lot of time and effort. However, this is typically a bad idea.

Not only is it often hard to understand all of the links and formulas of a model already built, but it is very hard to debug someone else's model. (It is hard enough to debug your own!) You also need to be very careful to delete all of the information that you no longer need, without modifying formulas that you do need. Moreover, most models regrettably do contain mistakes (often, but not always minor ones). Remember that if you start with someone else's model, those mistakes become your mistakes.

Setting up the Model Let's assume that you are starting a model from a blank Excel worksheet. You have a number of choices to make about how you set up your model. But one thing is clear: It is always hugely beneficial to set up your model the right way from the beginning than to have to modify it later.

Setting up the financial statements means to enter the names of each line item (e.g., revenue or costs of goods sold) for each statement going down each row, in the correct order and all in the same column. (These row headers should be in one of the first few columns of the worksheet.) The relevant time periods we want to forecast (e.g., quarters or years) should be listed going across columns in one of the first few rows of the worksheet. A typical model containing annual forecasts might have five to seven years of projected data.

Ideally, you should build the three projected financial statements as well as any supporting schedules on the same worksheet or tab (worksheet and tab meaning the same thing), one on top of the other. You want to set up the income statement and below that, the balance sheet, and beneath that, the cash flow statement. Under the cash flow statement should be any additional supporting schedules such as the debt schedule. It is very important that the same Excel column reflect the same time period for each of the three financial statements (and supporting schedules).

Since many of the formulas that you will build will need to link between the different statements, organizing your model in this manner will help minimize linking and formula mistakes. As long as you are linking the same columns together (e.g., Column D of the income statement links to Column D of the balance sheet) you can be certain that you are linking the same time period (e.g., 2013 to 2013). Plus, having all of the financial statements on the same worksheet means that you do not have to switch back and forth between tabs when entering in cell formulas.

There are however, instances, when putting the statements on the same worksheet is not advisable, especially when you are building a very large, detailed model. In such a model, putting the three financial statements and supporting statements together may result in a worksheet that is simply too long (has too many rows) in which to easily work. Generally if a worksheet grows to be more than a few hundred rows, you may want to switch to the alternative method, a multi-worksheet model.

In a multi-worksheet model, the income statement, balance sheet, cash flow statement, and supporting schedules each have their own tab. When setting up a model in this manner, make sure that each column reflects the same time period for each financial statement. For example, Column D of each worksheet should always reflect that same time period (e.g., 2013).

With either method, make sure that the time periods in each column are both consistent and consecutive. For example, if Column D represents 2013, Column E should be 2014, Column F should be 2015, and so forth. Setting up your model like this allows you to very easily and quickly copy and paste formulas across columns. That is, you only need to create the formulas for the first year, and then copy and paste them for the other years.

There are times when you will need a model that has mixed time periods. For example, suppose that you need to model fiscal quarters but you also want to aggregate the fiscal quarters into fiscal years. In this case it is best practice to create a model worksheet that only contains consecutive quarters, and then do the summation into fiscal years on a separate worksheet. Mixing different time periods on the actual model worksheet can easily lead to mistakes since there will need to be different formulas for the columns containing quarters and those containing years.

Another very strong modeling recommendation is that you create a separate worksheet that will contain all of your assumptions. Ideally, the worksheet (or worksheets, in a multi-tab model) that contain your forecasts should have only formulas and no inputted (hardcoded) assumptions.

One final suggestion for setting up your model is that you have a tab that shows both historical and projected financial statements together. (This can be on the model page or on a different worksheet that is linked to from the model page.) On this worksheet, you should calculate key financial ratios and statistics for both the historical and projected time periods. Doing this helps you compare historical with projected results and will help you when you are checking your model to find mistakes or poorly chosen assumptions.

Use the Keyboard, Not the Mouse Most of us who have grown up using computers have gotten pretty used to relying on the computer mouse for navigating around the various software that we use. However, if you want to be efficient at financial modeling, you should start using the keyboard as much as possible in lieu of the mouse. Once you become familiar with using the keyboard for navigating Excel, you will find that you are much quicker, and you will save a substantial amount of time.

I often tell students that as an investment banker, the difference between using the keyboard and using the mouse can be getting home at 2:00 am versus getting home at 3:00 am. To an often-sleep-deprived junior banker, that extra hour of sleep has enormous value! In fact, some investment banks during their summer training programs purposely do not allow new analysts and associates to use a mouse, so they start becoming acclimated to using the keyboard.

Excel has hundreds of default keyboard shortcuts, plus you can even define your own custom shortcuts. While you will never memorize or even use the majority of Excel's keyboard shortcuts, learning even a few of the most helpful ones will save you substantial amounts of time. This is especially true for navigating around and between worksheets. Using the arrow keys, Page Up and Page Down, and other navigation shortcuts is much faster than using the mouse. There are plenty of resources on the Internet where you can download a free list of Excel shortcuts. You can do a Google search for "Excel shortcuts."

Saving Your Model As with every document you work on as an investment banker, you should save your files very often, even as often as every several minutes. As you become more proficient at Excel (and using the keyboard shortcuts), you'll get in the habit of typing "Ctrl-S" to save your files. However, it is not enough to just save your workbook often. You should also save your model with a different filename every so often (for example, "model v1," "model v2," "model v3," etc.). Make sure to save a new version at least every couple of hours and *before* you make any significant changes to the model or to your assumptions.

For reasons that we will discuss in the section of this chapter on circularity, an integrated cash flow model can easily break. When this happens, it is often better to revert to the last saved version of the model than to try to fix your model. Of course, if you haven't saved a new version in a few days, you are in trouble. Save often and save new versions often.

Check Your Model as You Go Don't wait until you think you have finished building your model to check it. Check as you go. For instance, if you expect revenues to grow 10 percent annually but your COGS line is growing at 50 percent, then you probably have a mistake in a formula or a poor assumption. If a line item does not look right, fix the formula or fix the assumption then and there.

However, given the manner in which the model and the financial statements are integrated, there is also a limitation on what line items you can check as you go. Many line items will not reflect an accurate value until your model is substantially or even fully complete. For example, while net income incorporates revenue and operating costs, it also reflects interest expense. Interest expense is a function of the amount of debt on the balance sheet, which we will not forecast until the end of our model. Hence net income cannot be accurate until our model is completed.

That you will not know the answer to key financial metrics before your model is finished sometimes causes issues when dealing with senior bankers. Every now and then your managing director will come over to your desk while you are building a model and ask you how the numbers look. This is a delicate question to answer, since few MDs understand (or remember) the process of model building. On the one hand, you may have no idea how the numbers will look when you are done, and you certainly do not want to give your MD an answer that turns out to be wrong. On the other hand, saying you don't know the answer can open yourself up for criticism that you are not working hard enough or are working too slowly. Usually the best response is non-committal, something to the effect of "looking okay; I will get back to you soon with the final results." Then you hope and pray that your MD leaves you alone long enough to conclude the model.

Keep a List of Your Assumptions and Sources Most of the time when working in investment banking, various output and analysis from your model will be inserted into some type of presentation. In any presentation, you will very likely need to document and footnote the data sources and assumptions you used to build your model. Make sure to keep track of all of your assumptions and sources as you build your model. One good way to do this is to insert comments into the appropriate cells in Excel. You might also want to keep a list of assumptions and data sources on a separate worksheet in the model Excel file or at the very least write them down in a notebook.

Formatting the Model

With just about everything you will do in investment banking, formatting your work is extremely important. Modeling is no different, since, as we just mentioned, the output or analysis from your model will most likely be used in some kind of presentation. That presentation will be given to a client, prospective client, or another party involved in the transaction on which you are working. So naturally, all of the output worksheet and exhibits will need to be formatted properly, perfectly, and prettily. In fact, it is usually easy to tell if a model was created by an investment banker solely by its appearance.

Even the worksheets that will not be inserted into a presentation should be formatted well. A poorly formatted model is harder to use and will reduce the confidence that others have in your forecasts. The last thing you want is for your associate or VP to take a quick look at your model and not trust its output because the model looks like a mess.

When formatting a model, perhaps the most important thing is to be consistent. Cell to cell and worksheet to worksheet, your number styling, fonts, colors, and margins should be uniform. And just as you should check your model as you go, you should also always format your model as you go. The last thing you want is to have to format your worksheets after you have finished creating the model. Anytime you make changes to a cell, you risk making accidental changes to the formula contained in the cell. Moreover, you are less likely to notice that you have changed the formula if you think your model is finished and has already been checked.

Following are some general recommendations and best practices for formatting a model.

Formatting Worksheets The first formatting suggestion is something we already mentioned. Make sure you have consistent columns (i.e., dates and time periods) on every worksheet. In addition, anytime you show both historical and projected information on the same worksheet, you should indicate the difference by separating the columns with a dotted line. It is also recommended that you turn gridlines off on your worksheets. Gridlines are the borders that Excel, by default, puts around each cell. Your model looks cleaner with the gridlines off. In fact, one thing that often differentiates a model built by a banker from a model built by someone outside the industry is whether Excel's gridlines are off.

You should label each worksheet clearly in the upper left with the name of the company you are modeling (or project name) and a brief description of what is on that worksheet (e.g., "Model Assumptions"). You should also label each tab clearly. If your model uses a large number of tabs, you may want to group certain tabs together visually by color coding the little tabs at the bottom of the screen (not the entire worksheet).

Make sure to set Excel's print ranges on each worksheet so that all of the important pages of your model, including your assumptions, the actual model, and all output exhibits, can be printed cleanly. Your model should print out in as few pages as possible as long as the font size remains legible. Ideally, all forecasted time periods (columns) should be on the same printed page, and if possible try not to split up each financial statement on separate pages.

Sometimes your model will contain rows or columns that are important to the model but that you want to hide when the model is printed or inserted into a presentation. A good example of this is the balance sheet check line (which we will discuss later in this chapter in the section on forecasting the balance sheet). We typically want the check line visible when we are working on our model but hidden when we print it. Rather than use Excel's hide and unhide functionality, we are much better off using Excel's grouping functionality. Grouping rows or columns allows us to easily close (hide) and open (unhide) the group using a small toggle that Excel inserts for us on the screen.

Formatting Cells When formatting cells there is actually one guideline that is more of a rule than a recommendation: You should always use blue text in cells that contain what we call inputs or hardcodes. These represent cells that contain numbers that we type in. For example, most of our model assumptions will be hardcoded numbers. Anytime a cell contains a formula, the font color should be black. Differentiating between hardcodes and formulas using blue and black text is a rule to which nearly all investment bankers worldwide adhere.

You can use other colors if they are helpful, but certainly use them sparingly. Some bankers will use green to indicate a formula that links to another cell or another worksheet. You should always make sure to use the same font type (one that is easy to read) and font size throughout your model. Also, try to avoid naming cells. (Excel has a feature that allows you to refer to a cell by a name, rather than its location.) Naming cells can make it exceedingly difficult for others to use and understand your model.

Following are some additional formatting guidelines that will help make your model look professional.

- One decimal point for cells containing currency amounts.
- One decimal point for percentages (except interest rates).

- Two decimal points for interest rates.
- Negative numbers shown with parenthesis and in black (not red).
- Only the first line of a group of numbers has a currency symbol.
- The last line before a total should be underlined.
- Use Excel's custom formatting feature when you need to add text into a cell but still want to be able to make calculations on the cell (e.g., "3.0x" or "4% APR").

Circularity

Before we start learning how to actually create our forecasts, there is one additional aspect of an integrated cash flow model that we need to discuss: the concept of circularity (sometimes also referred to as a model being iterative).

Suppose you want to add a series of numbers in Excel. Let's assume you have three consecutive cells containing numbers, and then in a fourth cell you use Excel's sum function to add them. What would happen if, by accident, you included the fourth cell (the "total" cell) in the sum formula? Since the sum relies on itself, the answer is infinity. And obviously, Excel cannot calculate infinity. Instead, Excel warns you of a circular reference.

Trying to calculate a sum of itself is obviously a mistake. However, when building financial models, we deliberately create circular references in our models. The most common reason for our model being circular relates to interest expense and interest income.

Circularity, the Revolver, and Interest An integrated cash flow model implicitly reflects everything that affects a company's cash position. When the results of the model predict that the company needs more money than the company has, the model needs a way to get those additional funds. If there is no way to acquire those funds, the model would show a negative cash balance on the balance sheet, which is, of course, not possible.

The standard way to build an integrated cash flow model is to include a special type of debt called a revolving credit facility (often abbreviated as the revolver). The revolver is a type of bank loan that allows a company to borrow funds when it needs to and pay back those borrowed funds when money is available.

The revolver in our model serves as a source of funds whenever the model forecasts a need for additional cash. Of course, the revolver, being a type of debt, is not free. Whenever the company borrows (or, synonymously, draws down) from the revolver, the company will owe additional interest expense, which must flow through our model.

If the company owes additional interest expense, then it must borrow a little bit more money from the revolver. Borrowing a little bit more from the revolver once again increases the amount of interest expense, which in turn increases the amount of money to be borrowed, which increases the amount of interest expense, and so on and so on. Hence, the model is what is referred to as being circular or iterative.

The exact same concept of circularity comes into play when the model predicts that the company will earn excess cash. Typically this excess cash is invested and earns some interest income, which in turn means more cash, which means more interest income, which means more cash, and so forth. Again, the model becomes circular.

All properly built integrated cash flow models will be circular in this manner. Without such a mechanism, the three statements are not technically accurate, and the balance sheet will not balance. However, often in academic corporate finance classes this technique is not taught. Instead, students are told to "plug" the balance sheet, whereby an additional line is added to the balance sheet to force the balance sheet to balance. Properly built models should never need such a plug.

The result of our model being circular is that there is no formula that will make our model perfectly accurate. However, the good news is that Excel has built-in functionality to handle this type of circular model. Excel essentially guesses and guesses until it gets very close (within as many decimal points as we tell it) to making the model perfect. We just need to make sure this feature is activated anytime we are building this kind of model.

To turn this feature on in Excel 2007 and 2010, click on Excel's Option menu from the File tab of the ribbon in the 2010 version or the Office button in the 2007 version, and then in the Formulas tab, make sure that "Enable iterative calculation" is checked, as demonstrated in Exhibit 6.1.

#REF! Errors due to Circularity There is, unfortunately, an unavoidable downside to our model being circular: It is also easy to break or blow up the model when it becomes circular. A broken model is indicated by lots of #REF! errors throughout the model. Entering the wrong formula, accidently deleting a row or column, or lots of other mistakes can confuse Excel and cause these dreaded #REF! errors.

Alas, even using the Undo feature will not fix this kind of problem. This is also one of the reasons why you should save new versions of your model often, as we mentioned earlier in this chapter. It is often quicker to go back to a previous saved version assuming you saved it recently than trying to fix it, especially for a large model.

However, if you do want to try to repair your model, you need to find the row in your model that will fix the #REF! errors. Start with the rows

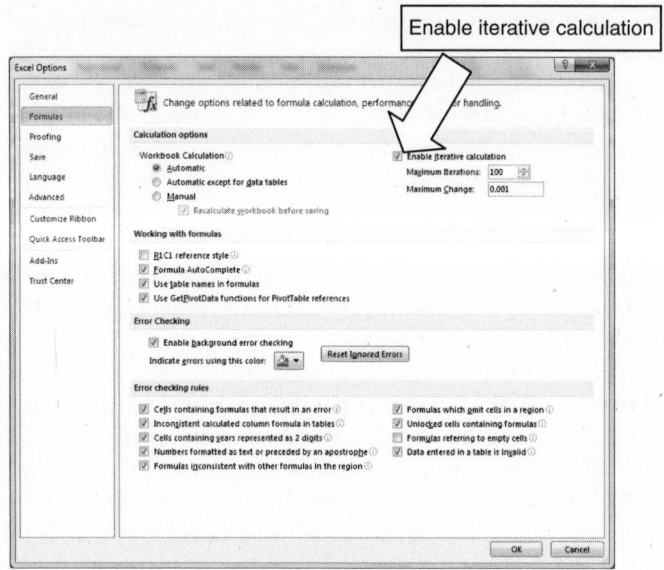

EXHIBIT 6.1 Enabling Excel's Iterative (Circular) Functionality

that are circular, such as interest expense. Input a random number in one of the cells in the interest expense line and see if that fixes all of the #REF! errors in that column. If it does, then you have found the correct line. Put the correct formula back into that cell and make sure the #REF! errors do not return in that column. Repeat the process for the rest of the cells (the other columns) in that row.

If you have trouble finding the row that will fix the model, then go line-by-line through your model until you find the correct row. Sometimes it will not be a circular row such as interest expense but a row that refers to one of the circular rows in its formula.

Some bankers advise building a model with what is known as a circuit breaker. A circuit breaker is a formula (usually an "IF" statement) that allows you to switch on and off the circular reference in a given cell. You can leave the circularity switch off when building your model and then turn it on once your model is completely built. For example, we could build an IF statement in our interest expense line that makes interest equal to zero whenever the circularity switch is off and makes interest correctly link to the interest calculated in the debt schedule whenever the switch is on. If you do build such circuit breakers, make sure not to forget to turn on circularity before printing your model or giving the results to your managing director!

Manual vs. Automatic Calculation One additional thing you can do to mitigate the risk of your model blowing up due to circularity issues is to change a setting in Excel to manual calculation. By default, Excel is set up to automatically recalculate your entire workbook the instant that you lift your finger off of the keyboard or mouse. Excel calls this automatic calculation.

Under manual calculation, Excel will not make any calculations whatsoever until you tell it to. This allows you the opportunity to fix a formula or undo some other mistake before Excel makes any calculations, and thus before you risk breaking the model. Typing the F9 key on your keyboard tells Excel to recalculate the entire model. Just like with the circuit breaker, remember to always recalculate the model before printing or inserting into a presentation. Otherwise your model is not updated.

To set Excel to manual calculation in the 2007 and 2010 versions, you need to click on Excel's Option menu and then in the Formulas tab, make sure that the "Manual" circle under "Workbook Calculation" is filled in, as demonstrated in Exhibit 6.2.

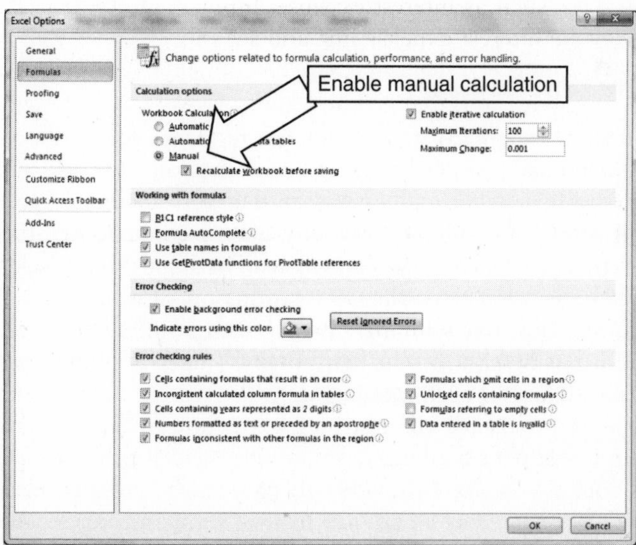

EXHIBIT 6.2 Enabling Manual Calculation in Excel

BUILDING AN INTEGRATED CASH FLOW MODEL

So far in this chapter we've explained what an integrated cash flow model is and talked about some best practices for setting up the model in Excel. Now we are finally ready to discuss the actual process of building a model. There are a number of steps for creating an integrated cash flow model:

1. Understand the company's business model, the industry dynamics and trends, and relevant macroeconomic factors.
2. Spread the historical financials and adjust for non-recurring items.
3. Calculate growth statistics and key financial ratios.
4. Select the model drivers and assumptions.
5. Project the three financial statements and other necessary supporting schedules.
6. Stress-test the model and analyze the financial statements for formula errors and poor assumptions.
7. Create any applicable sensitivity analysis or other output analysis based on the model forecasts.

As you read through the rest of this chapter, keep in mind the following. While it is highly unlikely that you will ever be asked in an interview to name the seven steps involved in creating a model, you should be prepared to walk an interviewer through this general process.

Step 1: Learn about the Company

Before you can (or should) start building a model to forecast a company's financial statements, you need to learn about the company. Specifically, you will want to achieve a thorough understanding of the company's operations, its business model, its industry, and any macroeconomic or other factors that might affect its business going forward. Without this knowledge, your model is likely to suffer from the GIGO affliction, also known as "garbage in, garbage out," just like with a DCF analysis. In other words, if you don't understand a business, how can you possibly make a credible forecast of that business's financial performance?

The best way to learn about a business is talk to the company's management. In investment banking terminology, we call this process due diligence. Of course you are only likely to have such access to management if your bank is retained as an adviser to that company. But if you do have access to management, take full advantage and ask good questions. Make sure that you have an understanding of what goes into and what influences each line item of the company's financial statements. If you have access to a projection model built by the company, make sure that you understand how the model works and what assumptions are used.

Most of the time in investment banking, you unfortunately will not have access to management. More often than not, you will be building models based solely on publicly available information. In these instances, you will likely need to do some reading to get "up to speed." Make sure that you read through the latest 10-K and 10-Q, the latest earnings press release and conference call transcript, and any recent 8-Ks. Another great source of information is equity research reports. Look for recent equity research about the company, its industry, and its competitors. Try to find an initiating-coverage equity research report. These lengthy publications are generally a great source of background information about the company, its industry, and recent trends. Also look for any relevant industry reports, trade publications, or market research.

Step 2: Spread and Normalize the Historical Financial Statements

Once you have done your research and your due diligence, and you are "up to speed" on the company, you are ready to move onto the second step, which is to spread the historical financials. Recall from earlier chapters that spreading refers to the process of entering information into Excel. You may be tempted to download the financial statements in lieu of entering them manually, but I don't recommend this. By spreading the financial statements, you will start to become familiar with the various line items. The more familiar you are with the historical statements, the easier time you will have projecting them, and the fewer mistakes you will likely make.

Generally, it is advisable to spread at least three to five years of historical data. The further you look back, the more information you have, as long as the company's business model has not changed. If the business has changed substantially, then the historical financials are less relevant. For cyclical industries, you should make sure to spread at least a full business cycle.

It is also prudent to enter the entire income statement and the entire balance sheet. Especially for the balance sheet, it is helpful to use the exact same line items found in the 10-K or 10-Q. It is usually not necessary to spread the full cash flow statement but only the line items that you will need to forecast, such as depreciation, amortization, capital expenditures, dividends, and so forth. Remember that many of the line items of the cash flow statement just reflect the changes from the balance sheet, year to year (or period to period).

As we discussed in Chapter 5, it is very important to normalize the historical income statements in order to adjust out any non-recurring items.

Since we will use the historical information to help us select the assumptions we will use to make our forecasts (as we will discuss shortly), we need to make sure that we exclude one-time historical events.

There are other normalizing adjustments that we may need to make as well. For instance, suppose a company recently sold or shut down a major segment of its business. In this case, we should try to adjust the historical financials to strip out that business segment. Similarly, if a company recently made a significant acquisition, we should adjust the historical financials to include the acquired company's financial performance, even in the years prior to the acquisition.

Step 3: Calculating Key Growth Statistics and Financial Ratios

After spreading the historical financial statements and making any necessary adjustments, the next step is to calculate some key financial statistics and ratios based on the historical data.

There are two important reasons why we calculate these figures. The first is that we often use many of them to help us select our model assumptions. We will discuss this further in the next section. The second reason is that, once we have completed our model, they will be useful in helping to verify that our model is built correctly and that our assumptions are reasonable. (We will cover this further toward the end of this chapter.)

In order to know what metrics to calculate, we need to understand what metrics are important to the business and the industry. Assuming we've done a good job of due diligence and learning about the company, the appropriate business and industry specific metrics should be obvious. There are also a number of generic metrics that are sensible to calculate most of the time and for most industries. Many of these metrics will be very familiar to us from our discussion of financial statement analysis in Chapter 4.

Following is a list of some of the key metrics that should be calculated from the historical income statements, balance sheets, and cash flow statements. For each of these metrics it is usually worth calculating both the annual figure for each historical year that has been spread and the average figure over the entire historical period. For example, suppose we have five years of historical income statements. We would want to calculate the gross margin for each year and then also calculate a five-year average of the gross margins.

Make sure to be cognizant of any outliers in the data, which you should investigate. Outliers sometimes indicate data entry mistakes and often hint at possibly non-recurring items that should be adjusted out. Even if you determine that they are correct and should not be adjusted, you may want to exclude outliers from your long-term average figure.

Income Statement Metrics

- Revenue growth rate.
- EBIT growth rate.
- EBITDA growth rate.
- Net income growth rate.
- COGS/revenue.
- Gross margin %.
- SG&A/revenue.
- EBIT margin %.
- EBITDA margin %.
- Other income or expense/revenue.
- Effective tax rate (income tax expense/pre-tax income).

Balance Sheet Metrics

- Accounts receivable days.
- Days sales of inventory.
- Accounts payable days.
- Other operating assets/revenue.
- Other operating liabilities/revenue.
- Other long-term assets/revenue.
- Other long-term liabilities/revenue.

Cash Flow Statement Metrics

- Depreciation/revenue, depreciation/net PP&E, or depreciation/gross PP&E.
- Capital expenditure/revenue.
- Dividends/net income.

Step 4: Selecting Model Assumptions

Financial projection models are always wrong. Always. We don't mean that they always contain formula mistakes (though they often do). What we mean is that they can never accurately predict the future. The future is, of course, unknowable. It is difficult enough to forecast one quarter or one year into the future, let alone five years or more. In fact, nearly all projection models wind up widely optimistic, especially those created by a company's management.

Having said that, our goal as investment bankers is to build a model that is accurate and credible given the available information. By accurate, we don't mean we are accurate in predicting the future; we mean that our model has no mistakes. By credible, we mean that our assumptions that drive the model are reasonable and that we can support them with data.

This is analogous to our goals as investment bankers when performing a valuation, which we discussed in Chapter 5.

We have already mentioned once in this chapter the concept of "garbage in, garbage out." The more you understand the industry and the company being modeled, the more accurate and reliable the model. The converse is true as well. The less you understand about the company, the less reliable your model. While it is relatively easy to learn the mechanics of building financial models, it is much more difficult to build a model with good assumptions. Selecting good assumptions really is the most important step in model building.

When we think about our model assumptions, we need to think about two things: (1) What are the key drivers of the company's business, and (2) What are the appropriate assumptions for those drivers? Hopefully we know the key drivers of the business from learning about the business. With regard to the appropriate assumptions for those drivers, there are three main sources for our model assumptions. We often use a combination of all three in any given model. These are:

1. Company management.
2. Equity research reports.
3. Historical figures and your own knowledge.

Company Management When working on live transactions, you will often base the assumptions of your model on the company's assumptions, or even start with and then modify the company's own internal model. At the very least, if you have the opportunity to do due diligence with company management then you can discuss and confirm the reasonableness of your own assumptions.

Very often when we are given the task of building a model, we will not have such access to management. We will be basing our assumptions on publicly available information such as what is found in 10-Ks and 10-Qs, as we will discuss shortly. However, even in these instances, there may be opportunities to develop certain assumptions based on what we call management's guidance.

Sometimes management will disclose to the public its own expectations about future financial performance, or about certain important sources or uses of cash. If such guidance exists, it may be found in the company's press release or 8-K issued for an earnings release, in the transcript of the conference call held with equity research analysts in connection with the earnings release, or in the MD&A section of a company's 10-K or 10-Q.

Note that for most items, you are much more likely to find near-term guidance (one year or less) than longer-term guidance. Following are some of the key model drivers on which you may occasionally find management's guidance:

- Revenue.
- EPS.
- Capital expenditures.
- Dividends.
- Share repurchases.

In additional to guidance, there are certain future financial transactions for which the company has a contractual obligation and must disclose such an obligation to the public in SEC filings. Whenever we have insight into the future that is contractual, we almost always will reflect this information in our forecasts. Two good examples of this include the maturities on long-term debt and the number of stock options issued to employees; information on both of these can be found in footnotes to a company's 10-K.

Equity Research Reports The second frequently used source of model assumptions is information contained in equity research reports, provided that the company being modeled is publicly traded. Recall from Chapter 5 that we often use the projections contained in equity research reports for performing valuation exercises. These reports often contain the assumptions and output from detailed projection models built by the research analyst. Sometimes data sources even provide access to the analyst's actual Excel model.

Since research analysts often know more about a company and its industry than do the investment bankers, many bankers build models using the assumptions developed by the research analysts. Sometimes bankers will use only a handful of key metrics such as revenue, EBITDA, and EPS. Other times, bankers may take the detailed assumptions for each line item. Just as we spoke about in Chapter 5, if you do rely on equity research for your assumptions, make sure that the particular analyst you use has projected similar figures to other analysts (i.e., is near the consensus) and is not an outlier.

Lastly, even if you do not use equity research as a source of your model assumptions, you can and should use it as a sanity check for your model. The forecasts built by research analysts can help verify that your own model has justifiable assumptions and reasonable output.

Historical Figures and Your Own Knowledge Suppose you do not have access to management or the company's internal model. Let's further presume that you do not want to use or cannot use equity research reports. Then what?

In that case, you will need to base your assumptions on a combination of the company's historical performance, your knowledge of the company and its industry, and your intuition about the future.

In the previous section, we talked about calculating a number of income statement, balance sheet, and cash flow statement metrics based on the company's past financial statements. Now let's discuss how we can use these ratios and statistics as the basis for our model assumptions. Remember that it is important that we have adjusted for any non-recurring items in the historical figures. Otherwise these metrics can mislead us.

When relying on the historical metrics, it is important to identify any trends in the data. If we spot a trend, then we need to decide if we expect the trend to continue. For instance, let's suppose that we are selecting our assumption for cost of goods sold and that the historical values of COGS as a percentage of revenue were as follows, as per Exhibit 6.3.

EXHIBIT 6.3 COGS/Revenue (Example 1)

2008	2009	2010	2011	2012
50.4%	50.1%	50.0%	49.7%	49.5%

You can clearly see from the data in Exhibit 6.3 that over the past five years, the company has improved the ratio of COGS to revenue each year. (Remember that a lower percentage reflects lower costs and a higher gross margin.) Knowing nothing else, we might decide to continue this trend going forward, perhaps by lowering the percentage by 0.2 percent each year. This would certainly be reasonable and justifiable based on the historical data. Alternatively, we might determine that the company has cut costs as far as it can and that there is no more room for improvement. In that instance, we might keep the assumption steady at 49.5 percent for each of the projection years.

Now, consider a different set of historical values for COGS/revenue, as shown in Exhibit 6.4.

EXHIBIT 6.4 COGS/Revenue (Example 2)

2008	2009	2010	2011	2012
50.2%	49.7%	50.0%	50.3%	49.8%

There is no discernible trend to these figures. COGS varies a little bit each year but seems to be centered right around 50 percent. In this instance, and having no further insights into the business, the best and most justifiable assumption would probably be the five-year average of about 50 percent. Suppose, however, that you are aware that in 2013 the company is introducing new products that have higher gross margins than older products. Knowing that, you may decide that the five-year average for COGS/revenue is too high, and that it should decline over the next few years as customers switch to purchasing the higher margin product.

The bottom line is that historical values can be very helpful to us in determining our assumptions, but they should not be used blindly. First of all, as the age-old financial adage goes, past performance is no guarantee of future success. Past performance is useful as a benchmark, as long as the company's business model has not changed, and industry and economic conditions have not changed. But even still, historical metrics should be used in conjunction with your knowledge of and insight into the company's future financial performance.

As a summary of the guidelines for coming up with reasonable and justifiable assumptions based on historical data, consider the following:

- Utilize several years of data, such as a multiyear average.
- Make sure to investigate and possibly exclude any outliers.
- Identify any trends in the data and determine if those trends should continue.
- Use the most recent values if only the most recent time periods are relevant. For example, if the company made a larger acquisition or divested a large part of the business, data prior to that transaction may not be relevant.
- Do not blindly use the historical data if business conditions have changed.
- Compare assumptions with management and/or equity research, if possible.

Inputting Assumptions As a matter of best practice, all of your assumptions should be on a separate worksheet from the one that will contain the projected financial statements. Remember that those assumptions that are hardcodes should be formatted as blue text. If each forecasted year has the same assumption, then you should enter the assumption only once in the first forecast year and then link the other years to the first. This way, if you want to change the assumption you only have to change it one place, rather than for each period.

Bear in mind that the process of coming up with the appropriate assumptions is often iterative. Often the analyst or associate who is actually building the model will take the first crack at producing a figure for each model driver. Once the model is completed and the output reviewed, assumptions are often adjusted. Frequently assumptions are modified so that the forecasts seem more reasonable or better match those of equity research analysts. And sometimes assumptions will be tweaked so that valuation analysis relying on the projections will help support the desired valuation range.

Multiple Scenarios Before we move on from the subject of assumptions, there is one more point worth making. Investment bankers often build models that contain multiple sets of assumptions, or what we call cases or scenarios. Though we will not get into the particulars, it is relatively easy to build a switch (i.e., a drop down menu) into our model that allows us to change back and forth which set of assumptions drive the forecast. For instance, a banker might have three sets of assumptions, representing a conservative or downside case, an aggressive or upside case, and a base case in the middle. Sometimes only the major assumptions will differ, such as revenue, costs, and/or profit margins, while other times most or all of the assumptions will vary between the cases.

Projecting the Financial Statements

Now we are finally ready to begin our discussion of how we actually forecast each significant line item of each of the three financial statements. Note that the line items that we will discuss are not an exhaustive list of every financial statement line item that you will encounter. They are the most common ones. However, if you have an understanding of how we project these items and you have good knowledge of the business you are modeling, you should be able to forecast most any line item that you encounter.

Similarly, we will discuss the commonly used methods to forecast each of these line items. There are often alternative methods for certain line items, some of which we will mention. Always remember that there is no one correct way to forecast each of the financial statement line items. What matters is that the forecast is reasonable and credible.

For the purposes of our discussion we will make several assumptions. First, the company we are modeling is a U.S. company in almost any industry except financial institutions. There is no conceptual difference to modeling non–U.S. companies, but as we mentioned in Chapter 2, the financial statements can be structured differently. Modeling a financial institution such as a bank does have some differences that would take us too far beyond the intended scope of this book.

The second assumption is that we are building our model based solely on publicly available information such as that found in a 10-K. We will assume that we only need to project annual figures. Conceptually, though, we could just as easily build a model that forecasts weekly, monthly, or quarterly statements. Finally, we will assume that the latest SEC filing is a

10-K and not a 10-Q. In other words, we will be projecting financial statements from the beginning of the company's fiscal year, not from the middle of the year. If you are in the middle of the year, you will need to project the remainder of the current year before you can start projecting annual figures.

As we've already mentioned earlier in this chapter, we will build our model with the different periods (i.e., years) going across consecutive columns in Excel. The magic of Excel (or any modern spreadsheet software) is that we only need to provide formulas for the first period. Then we can simply copy and paste the formulas for as many periods (columns) as we need. That saves us enormous amounts of time and allows us to very easily extend our model for as long as we want (or for as many columns as Excel allows). But always keep in mind something: Just because we can, doesn't mean we should. Because it is so easy to extend our forecasts by copying and pasting formulas, we often forget to think about whether the assumptions are still valid and reasonable in the outer periods.

Projecting the Income Statement The following section discusses how we forecast the income statement. For reference, recall a simple income statement as in Exhibit 6.5.

EXHIBIT 6.5 Basic Income Statement

Revenue
Less: COGS
= Gross Margin
Less: SG&A
= Operating Income (EBIT)
Less: Other Expense
Less: Net Interest Expense
= Pre-Tax Income
Less: Taxes
= Net Income
Number of Shares
Earnings Per Share (EPS)

Revenue Revenue is often the most important single line item in the model. As we will see, so many other line items are dependent on the revenue line and include the revenue line in their formulas.

In a relatively simple model, like the one we are contemplating, revenue is typically projected using a growth rate, based on some combination of historical and expected growth. For example, assume revenue averaged 5 percent steady annual growth over the past five years. If there is no reason to expect faster or slower growth going forward, then it would be reasonable to project revenue continuing to grow 5 percent. Hence we would project revenue as follows:

$$\text{Current Period Revenue} = \text{Last Period Revenue} \times (1 + .05)$$

Now consider an alternate scenario. Suppose that the company has a new product coming out this year or has just announced plans to enter a new market. In that case, we would likely want to forecast revenue growth exceeding 5 percent, at least for the next few years. On the other hand, what if the previous five years experienced very strong macroeconomic conditions but we have recently entered into a recession? In this instance we would likely want to forecast growth lower than 5 percent (perhaps even negative growth).

More complex models derive revenue projections by projecting the key drivers of revenue, rather than a simple growth rate. For example, consider a model for a retailer. Here we might want to forecast revenue by first making an assumption for the number of stores (or total store square footage) operated each year and multiply that by the average amount of revenue per store (or revenue per square footage) each year. Forecasting revenue in this manner allows us to have more control in our model of new store openings or closings. An even more detailed model might aggregate sales forecasts by individual store, by region, or even by product.

To model a telecommunications company's revenue, we might want to first project the number of new subscribers each year, the number of subscribers that cancel their contracts ("churn") each year, and the average revenue per subscriber. When modeling an oil and gas company, we would almost certainly have a forecast for oil and gas prices, which would have an enormous influence in our model on revenue. As you can see from these examples, modeling revenue using the important metrics that influence revenue allows us to more finely tune our forecasts.

Cost of Goods Sold (COGS) In a simple model based on information from 10-Ks, we typically project COGS as a percentage of revenue, based on historical ratios. For example, if cost of goods sold averaged a steady 60 percent of revenue (implying a 40 percent gross margin) over the past five years, then it would probably be reasonable to assume that COGS will continue to be about 60 percent of revenue going forward. To forecast COGS each period, we need simply to multiply the current period's revenue by our assumption of 60 percent.

In a more detailed model, we might want to forecast the components of COGS separately. For example, fixed costs might remain constant over the near term while variable costs such as raw materials or labor would vary with revenue.

SG&A Just like with costs of goods sold, in a basic model we will typically project SG&A as a percentage of revenue. For instance, suppose that SG&A has averaged 20 percent of revenue over recent years. Absent other information, we would likely project SG&A to continue to be 20 percent of forecasted revenue. To project SG&A, we multiply the current period's revenue by our 20 percent assumption.

Again, just as with COGS, more complex models will forecast SG&A in a more granular manner. We might want to derive SG&A forecasts using a detailed breakdown of SG&A costs (for example, projecting marketing, advertising, research and development, and overhead) all separately. Or if we have access to the information, we might have aggregate the SG&A budgets for each company division or even of each individual employee's salary and compensation.

Other Income or Expense Items The other income or expense line item found on the income statement typically reflects nonoperating items and often non-recurring items, such as gains or losses on a sale of assets. Therefore it is unusual for there to be an historical pattern to this line item. If there is a steady historical pattern (i.e., either a figure that is relatively constant in absolute terms or as a percentage of revenue), then we can project this line item using the historical pattern. However, most of the time, the best projection for other income or expense is $0.

Interest Expense and Interest Income Unlike COGS and SG&A, we do not forecast interest expense and interest income as a percentage of revenue, nor should we project these line items based on any metric derived from their historical values from the income statement. Instead we will calculate projected interest expense based on the amount of debt outstanding each period. We will forecast interest income based on the excess cash balance each period.

We will make these forecasts in the debt schedule later on and then link those calculations to the appropriate line items on the income statement. In other words, at this point in our model, if we have already set up our debt schedule, we just have the formulas in these cells equal to the appropriate interest line items from the debt schedule. Since they will be linking to blank cells, the value will be $0 for now.

Recall from our discussion of circularity that interest expense and interest income are the primary reasons that our model is circular. However, keep in mind that the model will not be circular until we complete the debt schedule.

Taxes Taxes are typically projected as a percentage of pre-tax income based on the company's average effective tax rate in recent years. For example, if the effective tax rate has averaged 30 percent and we expect it to remain approximately the same, then to forecast taxes we would multiply each period's pre-tax income by 30 percent.

One thing to keep in mind, however, is the impact of net operating losses (NOLs) on the effective tax rate. If the company has NOLs from prior years, the company might be able to use these NOLs to offset its pre-tax income. These rules can be tricky since there may be limits on how much NOLs can be used each year to offset current income. Make sure to read the footnotes to the 10-K and make sure to try to understand the appropriate tax regulations. Similarly, if pre-tax income in any period is negative, then the model should keep track of the accumulating NOL's that can, in turn, be used to offset taxes in future years.

Earnings per Share (EPS) For many of the models that investment bankers frequently build, it is not necessary to forecast earnings per share. It is often enough to only forecast the income statement down to net income. However, sometimes we do need to project EPS, in which case we will need to forecast the number of fully diluted shares outstanding each year, a somewhat tricky task.

To forecast the number of shares outstanding at the end of each period, we start with the number at the beginning of the period (or, equivalently, the end of the last period), and then add the number of shares issued and subtract the number of share repurchased. We will make assumptions for the dollar amount of each of these items in the section on projecting the balance sheet.

Once we have the dollar amount, we need to estimate what the share price will be, in order to forecast the number of shares. Of course, if we really had a good way of forecasting share price, we wouldn't be junior investment bankers; we'd be on our way to becoming hedge fund billionaires! The standard way to do so is to take the current share price and grow it with each year's EPS. That is, if we forecast EPS growing 10 percent next year, then we model the share price as increasing 10 percent. Implicitly by growing share price with EPS, we are keeping the company's P/E ratio constant. This is typically the safest and most conservative assumption (or at least the easiest assumption to justify).

Once we have the shares at the end of each period, we need to take the average from the beginning of the period and end of the period since EPS is always calculated based on the weighted average number of shares over the fiscal period.

Projecting the Balance Sheet There is a very significant difference to projecting the balance sheet than projecting the income statement (or cash flow statement). Since the income statement reflects financial performance over a period of time, when we project the income statement, we are starting each time period at 0 (i.e., $0 revenues, $0 costs, etc.). While the assumptions that we use to project the income statement typically rely heavily on prior period's performance, the income statement itself does not.

The balance sheet is different because it reflects the company's financial position at a moment in time. The balance sheet on the first day of any fiscal period must be exactly equal to the last day on the previous period. Said differently, for each balance sheet line item, each period's beginning balance must equal the last period's ending balance.

The implication of this is that when we project the balance sheet for our first period (i.e., year) we must be starting with the actual balance sheet from the most recent historical period (i.e., the most recent 10-K or 10-Q). If our most recent historical balance sheet is wrong, then our balance sheet will be wrong going forward. This is why it is important to spread the exact line items from the historical balance sheet.

When we project the balance sheet, certain line items will be forecasted with assumptions, some items will be linked to from one of the other financial statements or supporting schedules, and a few items will likely be kept constant.

For reference, Exhibit 6.6 shows an example of many of the key line items found in a basic balance sheet.

Assets Following are some of the key lines items in the asset section of a typical balance sheet. If there are line items that you are not sure about or that have no obvious historical pattern, then the best assumption is often to keep the item constant. This is because keeping a balance sheet item constant implicitly means that it has no impact on cash flow. So in a sense, keeping a balance sheet item constant is a more conservative assumption than forecasting a change.

Cash Like interest expense on the income statement, cash does not get forecasted based on a growth metric or percentage of sales. Instead, the cash balance will be calculated in the forecasted cash flow statement. On the cash line of the balance sheet, we just need to set the formula equal to the ending balance of cash on the cash flow statement.

EXHIBIT 6.6 Example of a Balance Sheet

ASSETS
Current assets
Cash and cash equivalents
Accounts receivable
Inventories
Deferred tax assets
Prepaid expenses and other
Total current assets
Property and equipment, gross
Less: accumulated depreciation
Property and equipment, net
Deferred tax assets
Goodwill
Intangible assets, net
Other assets
Total assets
LIABILITIES AND STOCKHOLDERS' EQUITY
Current liabilities
Accounts payable
Income tax payable
Accrued expenses and other
Short-term debt (revolving credit facility)
Total current liabilities
Long-term debt
Deferred tax liabilities
Other non-current liabilities
Total liabilities
Stockholders' equity
Common stock
Additional paid-in capital
Retained earnings
Treasury stock
Accumulated other comprehensive income
Total stockholders' equity
Total liabilities and stockholders' equity
Check

Keep in mind that once our model is complete, if we have built it correctly, we should never see a negative cash balance, regardless of what assumptions we use. A negative cash balance is usually an indication that our revolving credit facility mechanism is modeled improperly. Sometimes we will want to model in an assumption that cash can never fall below some minimum value, which we will discuss later in this chapter when we get to the section on the revolving credit facility.

Accounts Receivable To forecast accounts receivable, we typically rely on the accounts receivable days formula, based on historical values. Recall that:

$$\text{Accounts Receivable Days} = \frac{\text{Accounts Receivable}}{\text{Revenue}} \times 360$$

For example, if accounts receivable days figure has been steady over the past few years at 45 days, we will likely use that for our assumptions going forward. To forecast each year's accounts receivables, we would multiply the year's revenue by 45 days and divide by 360.

Inventory Inventory is typically projected similar to accounts receivables, using an assumption of days sales of inventory. As we learned in Chapter 4:

$$\text{Days Sales of Inventory} = \frac{\text{Inventory}}{\text{COGS}} \times 360$$

For example, if inventory has been steady at 100 days of sales over recent years, we can forecast each year's inventory by multiplying that year's cost of goods sold by 100 and dividing by 360.

In a more detailed model, we might have separate projections for the components of inventory, such as raw materials, work-in-process, or finished goods.

Other Current Assets Other current assets are frequently forecasted as a percentage of revenue (or sometimes COGS). As with the other working capital assets, we typically rely on the historical data for our assumption. For example, if we determine the other current assets tends to be at 5% of revenue historically, then to project other current assets, we would multiply revenue times 5%.

Property, Plant and Equipment (PP&E) On our balance sheet, it is helpful to separate property, plant and equipment (PP&E) into three components: gross PP&E, accumulated depreciation, and net PP&E. This is true even if the company's actual balance sheet from its 10-K or 10-Q does not do so. Recall that:

$$\text{Net PP\&E} = \text{Gross PP \& E} - \text{Accumulated Depreciation}$$

To forecast gross PP&E for the current period, take last period's gross PP&E and add this period's capital expenditures.

$$\text{This Period Gross PP\&E} = \text{Last Period's Gross PP\&E} + \text{Capex}$$

We will discuss how we forecast capital expenditures when we get to the cash flow statement. However, remember that capital expenditures represent a use of cash, so will be listed as a negative number on the cash flow statement. So to forecast this period's gross PP&E, we actually need to subtract the figure from the cash flow statement (i.e., subtract a negative number, which means we are adding it).

To forecast this period's balance sheet value for accumulated depreciation, add last period's balance sheet value and this period's depreciation expense from the cash flow statement.

$$\begin{matrix}\text{This Period Accumulated} \\ \text{Depreciation}\end{matrix} = \begin{matrix}\text{Last Period's Accumulated} \\ \text{Depreciation}\end{matrix} + \begin{matrix}\text{This Period's} \\ \text{Depreciation}\end{matrix}$$

Finally, to forecast net PP&E, we add subtract this period's accumulated depreciation figure from this period's gross PP&E figure.

Intangible Assets Just as PP&E is depreciated according to its useful life, intangible assets are amortized in a similar manner. So intangible assets value can be forecasted as follows:

$$\begin{matrix}\text{This Period's} \\ \text{Intangible Assets}\end{matrix} = \begin{matrix}\text{Last Period's} \\ \text{Intangible Assets}\end{matrix} - \begin{matrix}\text{This Period's Amortization} \\ \text{Expense}\end{matrix}$$

The amortization expense will come from the cash flow statement, and we will discuss how to forecast it when we reach that section of this chapter. Note that goodwill (if listed separately on the balance sheet) should remain constant since it is not amortized. Moreover, we rarely assume that goodwill will be impaired in the future.

For both intangible assets and goodwill, we typically do not assume any increases unless we assume the company is making acquisitions in the future, an infrequent assumption except for when creating a merger or LBO model. If we do assume new intangible assets or goodwill arising from an acquisition, then we would need to increase the corresponding balance sheet value, just as we increase PP&E for new capital expenditures.

Other Assets If there is an historical pattern to other assets (for example, as a percentage of revenue), then we can forecast it accordingly. However, often there is no discernible pattern so we keep this line item constant (that is, this period's balance sheet figure equals last period's).

Liabilities Following are some of the key liability items of a typical balance sheet. Just like with assets, if you are not sure about a line, or it has no obvious historical pattern, the most reasonable assumption is to keep it constant.

Accounts Payable We most frequently forecast accounts payable using the accounts payable days formula, based on historical values. As we learned in Chapter 2:

$$\text{Accounts Payable Days} = \frac{\text{Accounts Payable}}{\text{COGS}} \times 360$$

For example, if accounts payable days has averaged about 60 days in the past, then we will likely use that to drive our model going forward. To forecast the current year's accounts payable line, multiply the current year's COGS by 60 days and divide by 360.

Accrued Liabilities and Other Current Liabilities Accrued liabilities and other current liability line items are typically forecasted based on the historical pattern (for example, as a percentage of revenue of COGS). So, for instance, if accrued liabilities were historically steady at about 3 percent of revenues, then we could forecast each year's accrued liabilities by multiplying this year's revenues by 3 percent.

Debt Debt is one section of the model where we will likely want to deviate slightly from the company's actual historical balance sheet. Specifically, rather than have just one current debt line item and one long-term debt item, it is helpful to have one line item for each of the different kinds of debt that the company has issued. We especially want to make sure to include a separate line on the balance sheet for the important revolving credit facility (a type of short-term debt).

This means that we will probably have to insert a few rows into our balance sheet. This also means that we will need the breakdown for historical debt for the different kinds, since we need each type of debt's beginning balance (equivalently, the ending balance from the most recent historical period). (We will discuss how we find this information when we get to the section on the debt schedule later in this chapter.)

As with cash, debt will not be forecasted based on some balance sheet assumption. We will forecast debt in the debt schedule below the cash flow statement. In our balance sheet, we just need to link to the ending balance for each type of debt from the debt schedule.

Other Long-Term Liabilities If there is a discernible pattern to other liabilities (for example, as a percentage of revenue), then we can use that pattern to forecast it. If there is no identifiable pattern, as is often the case, then the prudent method is to keep it constant (i.e., this period is equal to last period).

Shareholders' Equity Following are some of the key line items typically found in the shareholders' equity section of the balance sheet. Just like we discussed for assets and for liabilities, if there is no clear rationale for how to project an item, then you are better off keeping it constant.

Retained Earnings Retained earnings for each year is forecasted by adding last year's balance sheet value of retained earnings plus this year's net income from the income statement and subtracting this year's common dividends from the cash flow statement, as follows:

$$\begin{array}{c}\text{This Period's}\\\text{Retained Earnings}\end{array} = \begin{array}{c}\text{Last Period's}\\\text{Retained Earnings}\end{array} + \begin{array}{c}\text{This Period's}\\\text{Net Income}\end{array} - \begin{array}{c}\text{This Period's}\\\text{Common Dividends}\end{array}$$

We will discuss how we estimate common dividends when we get to the section on projecting the cash flow statement. Remember, though, that dividends on the cash flow statement represent a use of cash, so will be recorded as a negative number. Therefore we must add the dividend payments (a negative value) in the retained earnings formula in order to actually subtract it.

Common Stock and APIC There are generally two reasons why a company would issue stock: Either the company needs the money, or when employees exercise stock options. Stock options are typically small and often ignored when modeling. For this reason, common stock and APIC typically remain constant unless significant new stock issuances are anticipated.

Often in investment banking models it is assumed that companies do not increase the number of shares outstanding unless they need to raise a lot of money. An example of this would be if they make a significant acquisition. However, most companies do in fact issue shares in the ordinary course of business because employees exercise stock options. The net effect on cash is typically pretty small, which is why we often ignore it when modeling.

However, sometimes we do want to model the impact of stock issuances due to exercised stock options (or other reasons). This is especially true if we need to estimate earnings per share, in which case we need a reasonably good approximation of share count, as we discussed earlier in this chapter.

We could look to historical values to get a sense for how much the company has issued (in value) each year and use this average going forward. If we really want to get detailed, we could do an analysis of the options that become exercisable each year and estimate how many will be exercised. As an investment banker, this is rarely worth doing.

Treasury Stock Recall that the treasury stock line is a negative number on the balance sheet reflecting the value of shares repurchased by the company. If we are assuming share buybacks then we need to estimate how much the company will spend each period on such buybacks. We can look historically at how much the company has bought back each year. We can also look at the company's guidance on how much it expects to spend to buy back shares.

Keep in mind that buybacks, unlike dividends, are generally fairly discretionary. For this reason, this is a difficult line item to forecast with any accuracy over the long run. One other thing we could assume in our model is that the company will buy back shares if it has excess cash, or that the company will use a certain percentage of its excess cash to buy back shares. We could easily make a formula in our model that sets the treasury stock level each period at some percentage of excess cash flow (cash beyond some minimum) or some set amount as long as the cash flow was greater than some minimum.

The Balance Sheet "Check" Line We are just about finished with the balance sheet. Before we move on to the cash flow statement, there is one more line to add, the "check" line. The check line will tell us if the balance sheet does indeed balance. It can be calculated as:

Check Line = Total Assets − (Total Liabilities + Shareholders Equity)

It is important to keep in mind that the balance sheet will not, and should not balance until the model is complete, given all of the interactions between the three financial statements. Once our model is complete, the check line not only helps us see if we are balanced but also can be helpful in finding mistakes if we are not balanced. We will come back to this issue at the end of this chapter.

Projecting the Cash Flow Statement Once we have built the projected income statement and balance sheet, forecasting the cash flow statement is relatively simple. This is because the majority of the line items contained in the cash flow statement are obtained by linking to the other two statements. Only a few of the cash flow statement line items need to be forecasted.

However, the cash flow statement is probably the easiest of the three statements in which to make modeling or formula mistakes. Never forget that every single change from one period to the next one from the balance sheet *must* be reflected as a source or use of cash in the cash flow statement.

A very common mistake is to forget to account for the changes in one or more line items from the balance sheet. A second mistake that bankers frequently make is to reverse the positive or negative signs when accounting for a change in the balance sheet. That is, to record a use of cash instead of a source of cash or vice versa. If either of these errors is made, the balance sheet will not balance and the model cannot be correct.

Exhibit 6.7 shows an example of a basic cash flow statement.

Net Income The net income line on the cash flow statement is simply linked to (set equal to) the same period's net income line from the bottom of the income statement.

Depreciation There are a number of different methods that can be used to project depreciation expense. In a perfect world, depreciation should be forecasted using what is known as a depreciation schedule. In a depreciation schedule, we depreciate existing PP&E according to its remaining useful life and depreciate new capital expenditures according to their useful life. Different types of assets will have different useful lives. Unfortunately, there is usually not sufficient information to perform this analysis.

Instead, we typically forecast depreciation as a percentage of net PP&E, gross PP&E, or, less commonly, as a percentage of revenue. As we did with many of the forecasted items on the income statement and balance sheet, we will typically look at the average historical values for our depreciation assumption.

As a rule of thumb, keep in mind that for a mature company with little growth, depreciation should approximately equal capital expenditures. This implies that the company is essentially replacing or maintaining fixed assets but not growing them. For a growing company, we would expect that capital expenditures will exceed depreciation expense.

Changes in Operating Assets and Liabilities (Working Capital) The next several lines of our cash flow statement reflect the changes to operating assets and liabilities (i.e., working capital). As a gentle reminder, recall that

EXHIBIT 6.7 Example of a Basic Cash Flow Statement

Cash flows from operating activities

Net income
Adjustments to reconcile net income to net cash:
Depreciation expense
Amortization expense
Changes in operating assets and liabilities:
Accounts receivable
Inventories
Deferred tax assets
Prepaid expenses and other current assets
Other assets
Accounts payable
Income taxes payable
Accrued expenses and other current liabilities
Deferred tax liabilities
Other non-current liabilities
Net cash provided by operating activities

Cash flows from investing activities

Capital expenditures
Other investing activities
Net cash provided by investing activities

Cash flows from financing activities

Change in revolving credit facility
Change in long-term debt
Payments of dividends
Repurchases of common stock
Net cash provided by financing activities

Net increase (decrease) in cash and cash equivalents

Cash and cash equivalents at beginning of period

Cash and cash equivalents at end of period

increasing an asset is a use of cash and will be listed with a negative sign on the cash flow statement. Increasing a liability is a source of cash and will be listed with a positive sign.

When accounting for the change in operating assets such as accounts receivable or inventory, we make the cash flow statement line equal to the negative of this period's balance sheet figure less last period's, for example:

Change in Accounts Receivable = – (This Period's AR – Last Period's AR)

Equivalently, we could have the formula be last period less this period, but having the negative sign and the parentheses makes it easier to distinguish between operating assets and operating liabilities in this section of the cash flow statement.

To calculate the change in an operating liability such as accounts payable, we set the cash flow statement line equal to this period's balance sheet figure less last period's figure. For example, the formula to calculate the change in accounts payable would be:

Change in Accounts Payable = This Period's AP – Last Period's AP

This section is one of the easiest places of the model to make a mistake (just like in the discounted cash flow analysis we discussed in Chapter 5). Take extra care to make sure you get the formulas correct and properly distinguish between assets and liabilities.

Capital Expenditures We typically project capital expenditures as a percentage of revenue, often based on historical values. For example, if historically the company has spent approximately 5 percent of revenue on capital expenditures each year, then we would likely use that figure as our model assumption. To forecast this period's capital expenditures, we simply multiply this period's revenue times 5 percent.

If we have enough information to do so, it is helpful to separately forecast maintenance capital expenditures and growth capital expenditures. However, we rarely have the information to do so if our model is based on public information such as a 10-K.

As with all other items that we forecast, if we have more insight into the future then we should make sure to use that information. For example, if we know that the company is planning to build a new factory next year, then we might want to show higher capital expenditures next year than the historical averages might predict. Also keep in mind that sometimes management will give guidance about expected future capital expenditures spending. This guidance can sometimes be found in the MD&A section of a 10-K or 10-Q, or in the transcript of the company's earnings conference call with equity research analysts.

Sale of Investing Assets In a typical investment banking model, it is unusual to forecast that a company will sell assets, so this line item is frequently $0. If we do project a sale of assets, remember that a corresponding balance sheet item (e.g., PP&E) will have to also be adjusted downward, but only on the amount not yet depreciated. A gain or loss on the sale of those assets may also need to be realized, which would flow through the income statement.

Changes in Debt and Equity (Cash Flow from Financing Activities) Most of the line items in the third section of the cash flow statement, "cash flow from financing activities," represent the change to debt and equity. To calculate these changes on the cash flow statement, we simply need to take this period's balance sheet value and subtract last period's balance sheet value. For example, we would calculate the change in any debt line as follows:

$$\text{Change in Debt} = \text{This Period} - \text{Last Period}$$

Make sure to account for all of the changes in debt and equity accounts on the balance sheet. Otherwise, when our model is done, the balance sheet will not balance.

Total Cash Flow for the Period and Ending Cash Balance Total cash flow for any period is the sum of that period's cash flow from operations, cash flow from investing, and cash flow from financing. We project total cash flow as follows:

$$\text{Total Cash Flow} = \begin{matrix}\text{Cash from}\\\text{Operations}\end{matrix} + \begin{matrix}\text{Cash from}\\\text{Investing}\end{matrix} + \begin{matrix}\text{Cash from}\\\text{Financing}\end{matrix}$$

The cash flow statement's last line, ending cash balance, is forecasted by adding the beginning cash balance and total cash flow for the period, as follows:

$$\text{Ending Cash} = \text{Beginning Cash} + \text{Total Cash Flow}$$

This ending cash balance should be linked to the first line of the balance sheet.

Debt Schedule So far, we have covered how to forecast the major line items of the income statement, balance sheet, and cash flow statement. These are, of course, the three main financial statements. However, we are not yet finished with our model. In this section, we will discuss a supporting financial statement called the debt schedule (sometimes also referred to as the debt and interest schedule). All integrated cash flow models should include such a supporting schedule.

The debt schedule is where we will calculate the changes to different types of debt, including the very important revolving credit facility. We will also calculate how much interest expense and interest income the company is projected to have each period, which will be linked to the income statement.

If we have built our model with the three financial statements on the same worksheet (as recommended for most models), then we should put the debt schedule on the same worksheet, below the other three statements. For each type of debt that the company has (or is forecasted to have), we should create a section of rows that looks something like this:

Beginning Balance
Less: (Paydown)/Drawdown
Ending Balance
Interest Rate
Interest Expense

The different types of debt should be ordered by seniority (for example, list secured bank debt above unsecured bonds). The first section should be the revolving credit facility.

Beginning Balance For each type of debt, the beginning balance always equals last period's ending balance, just like for all other balance sheet items. For the first year, remember that you will have to get the breakdown of debt from footnotes to the 10-K or from a source such as a Bloomberg terminal in order to have the beginning balance for each type of debt.

(Paydown)/Drawdown The (paydown)/drawdown represents the change in that type of debt for the period. If the company is paying back or decreasing debt, we call that a paydown. If the company is increasing debt, we call that a drawdown. Note that we put "paydown" in parenthesis to signify that it should be entered as a negative number, since paying down debt will reduce the amount of debt outstanding. Alternatively, we could call this line item the change in debt.

For a publicly traded company, the maturity schedule for most types of long-term debt should come from 10-Q or 10-K footnotes. If that information is not found in the footnotes, consult the original credit agreement or bond indenture. Remember that the quickest way to find the needed credit agreement or bond indenture is to use the exhibit index included at the end of every 10-K and 10-Q. You may also be able to find the maturity schedule on a data source such as a Bloomberg terminal.

The (paydown)/drawdown for the revolver credit facility is a special case that we will discuss in the next section.

Ending Balance The ending balance simply equals the beginning balance plus that period's (paydown)/drawdown. Remember that paying down debt reduces the balance, and drawing down debt increases the balance.

Interest Rate The interest rate line is where we forecast the amount of interest expense owed on each type of debt. For all existing types of debt, the interest rates can often be found in 10-Q or 10-K footnotes. Just as with the maturity schedule, if it is not found in the footnotes, consult the original credit agreement or bond indenture or a Bloomberg terminal.

For bonds, the interest rate will typically be fixed, so we can just plug in that rate. However, most types of bank debt, including the revolver, will be based on some fixed spread over LIBOR—for example, LIBOR plus 300 basis points (three percent). There are many different types of LIBOR rates, but a three-month term is most common.

For the revolving credit facility interest rate, you can use the interest rate on the company's actual bank credit facility, which most companies will have. If the company does not have one, then look for the interest rate paid on short-term debt by a similarly rated company in the same industry.

If we have debt modeled on LIBOR (and we almost always should, given the revolving credit facility), then in order to model the interest rate for such bank debt, we can either keep LIBOR at the current rate or use the forward yield curve, which can be obtained from a number of sources including a Bloomberg terminal.

Interest Expense Interest expense should equal the average of the beginning balance and ending balance multiplied by the interest rate. Using the average balance is more accurate than using either the beginning or ending balance since we assume that the company pays down or borrows over the course of the year, not on the first day or last day of the year.

Modeling the Revolving Credit Facility ("Revolver") We introduced the importance of the revolving credit facility when we talked about circularity earlier in this chapter. Recall that when the forecasts show that the company needs more cash than it has, then it needs a place to get it. Otherwise, we risk having a negative cash balance. In a model like ours, the revolver is where the company will get these additional funds. In essence, the revolving credit facility is like the keystone to the model.

To be more precise, we will build our model based on the following principles. When the company needs cash, it will borrow whatever amount is needed from the revolver. When the company has excess cash, it will pay back the revolver with all of its excess cash until the revolver balance is equal to zero. Once the revolver has a zero balance, the model will show that the company accumulates cash on its balance sheet.

You may be asking yourself why we are inserting an artificial source of funds into our model. In actuality, most companies do have revolving credit facilities that can be tapped when they need funds, though in most cases they are used primarily to finance working capital. And of course, in the real world, companies cannot borrow infinitely from such facilities, as our model theoretically allows. To make our model more realistic, we can build in higher interest rates if the company exceeds a certain level of borrowing (as the terms of many credit facilities specify) and/or build in some kind of warning to our model.

Cash before Revolver Line Before we can model the change to the revolver, we need to make one additional calculation, which we will refer to as the cash before revolver. The cash before revolver figure reflects whether the company needs funds or has extra funds for each period. It accounts for everything affecting cash flow, except the revolver itself, and can be calculated from various lines on the cash flow statement. It equals the beginning cash balance plus cash flow from operations plus cash flow from investing plus each line item in the cash flow from financing section except the change in revolver balance.

The Revolver Formula To model the (paydown) or drawdown of the revolver we can use the following formula:

Revolver (Paydown)/Drawdown = – MIN (Cash before Revolver, Beginning Revolver Balance)

In this formula, Excel takes the lesser of:

1. The amount of cash the company has this period, or
2. The beginning revolver balance.

If the amount of cash is negative, the company will borrow that amount. If the amount of cash is positive and *less* than the revolver balance, the company will pay back the revolver using all available cash. If the amount of cash is positive and *greater* than the revolver balance, the company will pay back the entire revolver balance, leaving cash left over. Note the negative sign in front of the formula. The sign must be reversed since needing cash increases the revolver (a drawdown) and having excess cash decreases the revolver (a paydown).

Modeling a Minimum Cash Balance Using that formula to calculate the revolver paydown or drawdown will guarantee that the cash can never be negative. However, sometimes we will want to assume that the company requires at least a minimum amount of cash, a more realistic assumption since most companies do indeed require at least some cash for day-to-day business operations.

We can easily modify the revolver formula to include a minimum cash value as follows:

Revolver (Paydown)/ Drawdown = – MIN (Cash before Revolver – Minimum Cash, beginning Revolver Balance)

With this formula, cash can never fall below the minimum level. How might we forecast what the minimum cash level should be? Like countless times before, we will typically look at the historical values and see how much cash a company has on its balance sheet, either as an absolute number or as a percentage of revenue.

Checking the Model and Analyzing the Results

Once you've finished building your model, the first thing you need to do is check it to make sure it works properly. The first check is whether it balances. Nearly all the time when you've finished linking up the model, it won't balance. In fact, it is very common to spend more time debugging the model than you spent building it in the first place.

After getting the model to balance, the second thing to do is to stress-test, which is to put in some extreme assumptions, and make sure that the model is still working properly and is still balanced. Once you are very confident that the model is built properly, you are ready to actually look at the output and make sure that your forecasts and assumptions are reasonable. The final step of modeling is to build any additional exhibits or output that are based on your forecasts.

Balancing the Model Never forget that the model's balance sheet must balance, but just because it balances does *not* necessarily mean that the model is correct. Keep in mind the two most common modeling mistakes. The first such error is to forget to account for one or more changes in the balance sheet that are included as sources or uses of cash in the cash flow statement (or vice versa, including them in the balance sheet but not in the cash flow statement). The second common mistake is to have the positive or negative signs wrong when calculating changes to asset and liabilities in the balance sheet or in the cash flow from operations section. Especially make sure to check the line items that make up working capital.

If the model does not balance, the first thing to do is to examine the check line of the balance sheet. If the check line is a constant figure for each time period, then chances are the problem will be easy to fix. Try going through each line of your model and look for a line item that is exactly that amount of the check line. Also seek items that are exactly half the amount of the check line, since having a positive or negative sign wrong somewhere can result in an error of twice the figure. Sometimes the model will be wrong because of multiple line items, in which case you need to try to identify lines that add up to the check line (or half the check line). Once you have identified the appropriate line or lines, you should be able to fix the formula(s) accordingly.

If the check line is not constant each year, it can be helpful to calculate the change in the check line from year to year as follows:

Change in Check = This Period's Check – Last Period's Check

If the change in the check line is constant then, as we discussed previously, look for one or more items in the model that are equal to, or exactly half of, the change in check line figure. Very often, the difference can be found in the first projected year. If you cannot spot the line or lines that contain the error, you might have no choice but to go line by line and verify your formulas and links.

Stress-Testing the Model Stress-testing your model refers to the process of inserting some extreme assumptions, and making sure that the model still works and still balances. This can help you determine if the model is built properly. Before you change your assumptions to stress-test your model, don't forget to save your model first!

Assuming the model works properly and the balance sheet still balances, you need to ensure that the forecasts make sense based on the mock assumptions. For example, if you use a very high revenue growth assumption to stress-test your model, make sure that revenue, net income, cash flow, and cash on your balance sheet all grow accordingly. Similarly, if you make an assumption that costs increase significantly, then net income, cash flow, and cash should decline. Also, make sure to test your revolver under such a stress-test. If you have modeled your revolver correctly, the model's cash balance should never go negative (or below the minimum cash level, if you have one).

Once you have finished your stress-testing, make sure to go back to the saved version of your model that contained your correct assumptions. You do not want to show your model output to your MD or e-mail it to your client with highly unrealistic assumptions.

Analyzing the Forecasts Once your model is balanced and you have stress-tested it to identify obvious errors, the next step is to analyze the actual forecasts of the model. You need to make sure that the model is linked properly and does not contain formula errors. You also need to verify that your assumptions are reasonable.

Given the number of cells and rows used in even a relatively simple model, it is not realistic to check your model cell by cell. And while Excel does contain some built-in error-checking capabilities, this feature tends to be of limited usefulness. In fact, most bankers turn off this feature.

The best method to check a model is to print the model and spend some time analyzing the output. Ask yourself if the projections make sense. Do the assumptions seem reasonable based on historical data? Do the forecasts also seem realistic? Make sure also to compare calculated statistics such as growth rates and margins with their corresponding historical values. Also look for unusual increases or decreases from one period to the next, especially from the last historical period to the first projected period. Often such a large change indicates a mistake in a formula or a link to the wrong cell.

Also use a calculator to compute and verify key statistics such as growth rates and margins. Make sure that your calculated values equal the values computed in Excel. If something looks wrong, circle it with a red pen. Then you can go back into the Excel model, and verify the formulas and the assumptions. Checking a model is time-consuming and hard. It is especially difficult to check someone else's model. However, the more time you spend checking a model, the more confidence you will have in its output.

Additional Model Analysis and Output The last step in model building is to create any additional output or analysis. If we are also doing a valuation exercise, then we can create a discounted cash flow analysis based on the forecasts from the model. If we need to do a credit analysis, we can calculate various credit statistics for each forecasted time period and analyze how they change over time. The type of model we learned how to build also often serves as the foundation for a full-blown merger model or an LBO analysis, which we will discuss in Chapters 7 and 8, respectively.

Improving Your Modeling Skills The best way to improve your modeling skills is to practice. There are a number of self-study modeling programs available in the marketplace (including one by this author) that provide one or more example templates (with solutions) on which you can practice. However, you can also work on your modeling skills without such a tool.

Pick a random public company with a simple business model and download the company's 10-K. Starting with a blank Excel spreadsheet, spread a few years of historical data from the 10-K and calculate those key historical statistics of which we spoke. Think about reasonable assumptions. Then build a five-year projection model. Once your model is built, make sure it balances, stress-test it, and analyze the output. If you happen to have access to equity research, compare your forecasts with those of one or more research analysts.

Do this a few times and you will get more comfortable with financial modeling. If you can build a model from a 10-K and a blank Excel spreadsheet in, say, four to six hours, then you have good modeling skills.

END-OF-CHAPTER QUESTIONS

1. Why are models circular?
2. What are some best practices for building financial models?
3. How do you calculate the revolver?
4. How might you forecast revenue for a retailer?
5. How might you forecast revenue for a telecommunications company?
6. Why is it important to spread historical financials when building models?
7. Walk me through building a model.
8. What is the best way to check a model?

Answers can be found at www.wiley.com/go/gutmann (password: investment).

CHAPTER 7

Mergers and Acquisitions

When most people think of the kinds of deals that investment bankers execute, often the first thing that comes to mind are mergers and acquisitions (M&A). Thoughts turn to such exciting themes as hostile takeovers and boardroom battles, white knights, and corporate raiders. Even saying you are an M&A banker makes you feel cool—sexy, in fact. And nothing beats waking up in the morning after a couple hours of sleep and seeing the transformational deal you've worked on secretly for weeks or months finally show up on the front page of the *Wall Street Journal* or *Financial Times*.

Of course, M&A isn't really as glamorous as it sounds. Nearly all deals are friendly, not hostile. And like most other types of transactions that investment bankers execute, the vast majority of M&A deals follow a very standardized process. For a junior banker especially, the work is similar to what is performed for any other type of transaction. However, given the prominent role that M&A does play in the industry, aspiring bankers should have a basic understanding of both the rationale for acquisitions and how they are executed.

In this chapter we will introduce you to mergers and acquisitions and discuss the kind of work that investment bankers do when advising on an M&A transaction. We will start this chapter with a discussion of why companies acquire other companies. Then we will talk about the standard M&A process, with a focus on the role of a junior banker. Finally, we will discuss the kind of analysis particular to M&A that bankers perform. Most importantly, we will cover the accretion/dilution analysis, a topic that often comes up in investment banking interviews.

M&A OVERVIEW

In this section, we will provide a short overview of mergers and acquisitions. First we will discuss the various reasons why companies pursue acquisitions.

After that, we will talk about the basic mechanics involved in the execution of a deal. In other words, the section covers, on a high level, the why and the how of M&A.

Acquisition Rationales

Companies pursue acquisitions for many different reasons. However, before we get into the details of the various rationales, we need to make a distinction between two types. Some reasons are what we will call stated motivations. These are the ones that companies use to publicly or privately justify deals in press releases and press conferences, to Wall Street, to customers and vendors, and to a company's own employees and the employees of the target company.

Then, of course, there are the unstated motives. These are the ones that, for obvious reasons, management does not disclose or discuss. There is certainly overlap between the two types, however, as we will see, it is often the unstated reasons that truly drive M&A activity.

As an investment banker you should be aware of both types. You need to be highly familiar with the stated reasons since you will be providing the analysis that will help justify the deal to the market. You also need to understand how these rationales will affect how the market will likely react to the deal announcement.

But always remember that to an investment banker, all deals are good deals. As we talked about in Chapter 1, when a senior banker's bonus depends on bringing in revenue each and every year, you can be assured that a banker is pushing for a client to do a deal. Therefore you need to have an understanding of the true motivations of your client, so you are in a better position to help steer the company into doing a deal and support management through the process.

The Stated Reasons As mentioned, acquisitions are often justified by a company's management with a number of stated reasons. For a public company, the quality of theses motives will have a big impact on whether the public markets react positively or negatively to an announcement of an acquisition. If the company does a good job of justifying the acquisition then the stock will often trade up on the news of the deal. If the market is less convinced that the deal makes sense, which is often the case, then the acquirer's stock will likely decline following the announcement.

Growth Probably the common reason for a company to make an acquisition is to grow. Broadly speaking, there are two ways a company can grow. A company can grow organically or grow through acquisition; as some say, the decision is "build versus buy." Organic growth is hard and takes time. To grow organically, a company has to develop new products or expand to new markets. It has to hire new employees and open new offices. Acquisitions, on the other hand, are much easier and quicker. Hire an investment bank, buy another company, and instantly you are larger.

The public markets have a strong bias for companies that are growing. Companies that are perceived as "growth" companies tend to have valuation premiums and receive much more interest from equity research analysts. Plus CEOs of growth companies tend to be the ones who wind up on the covers of prominent business magazines. Companies that are not growing are perceived as boring and not worthy of attention, and are ignored by research analysts and investors alike. Moreover, companies often make acquisitions as a desperate measure to appease Wall Street because the company's own organic growth has slowed or stalled.

Private companies like growth, too. Managers tend to receive higher compensation for running larger companies. (This is true at publicly traded companies as well.) Moreover, the investors of most private companies require an exit to their investment at some point in the future. Maximizing growth tends to lead to a higher valuation as well as more options for investors to achieve a liquidity event since it is usually easier to sell or IPO a larger company than a smaller one.

Synergies The second most prominent reason that companies use to justify acquisitions is synergies. In simple terms, synergy occurs when two plus two equals five. In other words, we can say an acquisition has synergy if the buyer and target combined are worth more than they would be if they were separate. As a banker working on a buy-side deal, you may spend a lot of time performing analysis around potential synergies.

There are two categories of synergies: cost synergies and revenue synergies. Cost synergies refer to the ability to cut expenses of the combined companies due to the consolidation of operations. Cost synergies can result from such things as closing one of the two corporate headquarters, laying off one set of management, shutting redundant stores or distribution centers, or consolidating marketing and research and development functions.

The other type of synergies is revenue synergies. Revenue synergies refer to the ability to achieve higher sales from the combined company over and above the aggregate revenues that would have been realized had both companies been on their own. For example, these opportunities can come from selling the product of the target company to the acquirer's customers and vice versa, or rebranding one company's products to that of the other company's more recognizable brand. Another possible revenue synergy is to be able to raise prices because of the elimination of what had been a competitor prior to the merger.

In reality, synergies are much easier to discuss and forecast than they are to actually achieve. It is often much more difficult than anticipated to cut costs and consolidate operations. In fact, there are often negative cost synergies due to integration and restructuring costs. As difficult as cost synergies are to achieve, revenue synergies are even harder. Companies often lose customers as a process of integration, and the opportunities for cross-selling and co-branding opportunities tend to be overstated.

Finally on the topic of synergies, keep in mind that there are virtually no synergies for vertical acquisitions or acquisitions of diversified businesses. You tend to see significant synergies in industries with enormous economies of scale and industries where companies have significant competitive advantages due to some kind of barrier to entry. However, these situations are relatively rare, and transactions of this nature are the ones that governments tend to block for anti-trust reasons.

Valuation of the Target Another justification for an acquisition relates to the issue of valuation. Sometimes buyers will acquire companies because they view the target as undervalued and therefore they are getting a "good deal." Alternatively, a company may pursue an acquisition because the target is in a more desirable, faster-growing industry and trades at higher valuation multiples. In these instances, the acquirer is hoping that the market will treat the newly combined company as the market treated the highflying target.

On the flip side of valuation, companies sometimes justify acquisitions as being accretive to earnings, which is often the result of the acquirer trading at a higher valuation multiple than the target. (We will discuss this point in much greater detail later in the chapter.)

Diversification We learned in Chapter 3 that companies should not pursue diversification purely for the sake of diversification, but instead should return excess funds to investors and let investors diversify. Investors can diversify much more cheaply and efficiently than can companies since investors can diversify by buying stock in different kinds of companies. On the other hand, management teams tend to have enough challenges running one type of business, let alone multiple businesses.

Of course, finance theory rarely gets in the way of a management team intent on making an acquisition. And in fact, many acquisitions are justified by the effects of diversification, including such things as a reduction in risk, steadier cash flows, a lower cost of capital, potential tax savings, and less dependence on general economic conditions.

Unstated Reasons So far, we have discussed some of the various reasons that companies use to publicly justify acquisitions. Now let's discuss some of the reasons that are not typically divulged. Both types are important influences, but often it is the unstated reasons that really motivate a CEO to pursue an acquisition.

Competition The competitive dynamics of a company's industry often play an enormous role in driving acquisitions. Take the hypercompetitive airline industry, for instance. The airline industry in the United States has undergone significant consolidation in recent years. In each transaction, the acquirer will justify the merger publicly as a way to expand their networks and to service customers better due to economics of scale. In reality, the primary motive to merge is to eliminate a large competitor in order to raise fares. Of course, companies cannot state this for fear of the negative reaction from the public and from government agencies involved in approving the deal.

Sometimes companies also make acquisitions in order to prevent a competitor from buying the target. Companies may want to prevent a competitor from obtaining a key piece of technology, or becoming too large or powerful with customers or suppliers. This is an example of one type of defensive acquisition. Another type of defensive acquisition is to purchase a company for its patent portfolio to help the acquirer defend itself legally from companies with competing or overlapping technology. This type of acquisition has become common in recent years in the technology sector.

Diversion Now and then a company will pursue an acquisition because its financial results have been subpar and management views an acquisition as a way of diverting attention away from the company's subpar performance. A large acquisition may also give the company some time to work out problems in its core business since the equity research analysts covering the company will be focused more on the integration of the acquisition.

Valuation of the Acquirer We have already discussed how the valuation of the target can be used to justify an acquisition. Sometimes the valuation of the acquirer plays a crucial role as well. If management of a public company feels its own stock is overvalued, it may view its stock as "cheap currency" and pursue acquisitions using its stock as the purchase consideration. I put this rationale in the unstated category because it would be highly unusual for management to publicly state an opinion that its own stock is overvalued.

CEO Ego and Compensation The last acquisition rationale we will discuss is probably the most important of all, especially when explaining large and high-profile deals. Here we refer to the ego and the bank account of the CEO running the company making the acquisition. As we mentioned earlier, the larger the company, the more a CEO tends to earn, especially with stock options and stock grants taken into account. Plus, the larger the company a CEO runs, the higher his or her public profile is likely to be.

Never underestimate the role a CEO plays driving a company toward a large deal. But as an investment banker, also keep in mind that the ego of a CEO can play just as vital a role in quashing a prospective deal. Regardless of the merits of the transaction to the company and its stockholders, if the CEO of the target risks losing his or her job post-acquisition, or will not play a prominent enough role in the combined company, the deal will often be scuttled.

Why Do Most Acquisitions Fail? Finance research tends to show that the vast majority of acquisitions destroy shareholder value to the acquiring firm in the long run. In fact, many acquisitions wind up "undone" some years after the deal with the original target being divested (not a bad thing for a banker, either!). As we mentioned earlier, executing a transaction is easy. Making a successful acquisition is much, much more difficult.

Deals fail for a number of reasons, the most important of which relates to the acquisition premium that a company must pay. Remember from our discussion of the precedent transaction valuation methodology in Chapter 5 that in most cases, a company that wants to acquire a public target will usually have to pay a 20–40 percent premium over the target's current stock price. This acquisition premium represents a very significant difference from what an investor would have to pay to invest in the target by purchasing stock and an enormous hurdle for the acquirer to overcome.

In order to justify the premium, the acquirer had better be able to improve the target's performance significantly and/or achieve large enough synergies. Alas, performance often does not improve and synergies are not often realized (or realized in a much smaller amount than expected). In addition, as we discussed earlier, there are often negative synergies related to the loss of important customers and employees due to integration issues and culture differences between the acquirer and target. Management also often gets distracted from its core job of running the business by the integration process. Furthermore, the direct integration costs, such as severance for terminated employees, lease termination costs, and the cost of integrating complex IT systems, tend to be underestimated.

The consequence of these challenges is that for most deals, the acquirer will never realize anywhere near enough incremental value over time in order to justify the acquisition premium paid. This is especially true when you take into account the impact of present value, as you should. The acquisition premium is paid in current dollars, and most integration and restructuring costs are likewise near term. Therefore in present value terms, the negative impact is large. However, synergies, if they appear at all, tend to be realized over a longer period of time, thus mitigating their value to the company and its shareholders today.

Now let's put our investment banker hat back on. That many deals wind up destroying shareholder value instead of creating it is of utmost importance to management teams, to asset managers, and to hedge fund analysts. But not to investment bankers. We do not talk about this subject when we pitch M&A deals. Always remember that, to a banker, all deals are good deals. So forget what you just learned until you are working on the buy side.

Mechanics of M&A

In this section, we will talk about the mechanics of an M&A transaction. In order words, what are the legal ways in which a company can actually buy another company? This is a topic that is highly specialized and, in a real transaction, best left to the M&A attorneys. However, as a banker, you should have at least a very basic understanding of the mechanics for how an acquisition is effectuated.

We can categorize the ways in which to acquire a company into three types. An acquirer can do a merger, pursue a tender offer, or purchase assets. The first two of these types involve a company buying the equity or shares of the target. Normally the goal is to acquire 100 percent of the outstanding shares. In the third method, the acquirer purchases only assets from the target and not shares. Whether a company buys equity or buys assets has a number of tax consequences, which we will also briefly mention.

Before we continue there is one final clarification worth making. As we have in this book, and as is customary in the industry, we use the term "mergers and acquisitions" (or M&A) to classify any transaction whereby one company mergers with or acquires another. Beyond the legal differences, a few of which we will discuss, there are no practical differences between a merger and an acquisition from the standpoint of an investment banker.

Merger A merger (also known as a single-step or one-step merger) is a type of transaction whereby the acquirer purchases the stock of the target from the target's shareholders. For reasons that should become obvious, a merger is generally used in friendly transactions and not for hostile or unsolicited deals.

In a merger, the buyer and seller will negotiate the terms of the transaction and enter into a merger agreement. Then the board of directors of the seller will approve the agreement and put the transaction up for a shareholder vote. In the United States the threshold required for voter approval is subject to state, not federal law, but is most often a majority of shareholders (i.e., greater than 50 percent). Assuming the vote meets the threshold, and all other regulatory requirements such as anti-trust clearance are met, the transaction will be consummated and the buyer will purchase 100 percent of the outstanding shares of the target for the agreed-upon price and consideration.

Merger of Equals Sometimes M&A transactions are described as mergers of equals, whereby two companies of similar size decide to merge. Note that there is no such legal definition. In fact, a merger of equals can be executed as a merger transaction as described previously or as a tender offer, which we discuss shortly. In a typical merger of equals, the board of directors is often split evenly between members from the two companies, and sometimes the CEO role is even shared.

However, you should be aware that there really is no such thing as a merger of equals, as much as merging companies like to pretend that there is. Ultimately, if not immediately, one CEO will control the company (co-CEOs never work out well or persist), and one group will wind up controlling the board. Whoever winds up with such power is the true acquirer, even if they came from the smaller company. And that company's culture will likely dominate the combined entity and that company's employees will usually fare better through the integration process.

Tender Offer The second way in which a company can make an acquisition is through a tender offer process. In a tender offer, the acquirer makes an acquisition offer directly to the shareholders of the target to buy their shares at a certain price (usually at some premium to the current share price). In a friendly transaction, the price and consideration will have been negotiated between the two companies. In a hostile or unsolicited bid, they will not be.

The board of directors of the target must then make a formal recommendation to the company's shareholders as to the board's opinion on the offer as well as make other disclosures. The shareholders will then have a specified amount of time to decide whether to tender their shares at the offered price. (The minimum amount of time is dictated by federal securities laws in the United States.)

In addition to the offer price, the prospective buyer must also disclose the percentage of shares it desires to purchase. If not enough shares are tendered then the buyer can abandon its effort or raise the offer price. A successful tender offer will usually not result in 100 percent of the target's shares being purchased, as it will in a deal structured as a merger. However, there are two methods available to the buyer that can enable it to purchase the remaining shares in order to own 100 percent of the stock of the target. This process is known as "squeezing out" the minority shareholders.

Generally if the buyer is able to acquire 90 percent of the target's shares then it can implement what is known as a short-form merger without the approval of the target's shareholders. In a short-form merger, the acquirer is allowed to purchase all of the remaining shares at no less than the price paid as part of the tender offer. Alternatively, and assuming a friendly deal, the company can effectuate a merger transaction with the target in order to acquire the remaining shares. Since the buyer will now control the majority of shares of the target, it will obviously be able to get shareholder approval since it will be able to vote its own shares.

Finally, it is worth mentioning that a tender offer will be more likely to be used when there are no regulatory or other delays anticipated. Also, tender offers are frequently utilized when the purchase consideration is only cash, since the transaction can typically be completed faster. All-stock or partial-stock friendly deals are more likely to be structured as a merger, especially given some of the tax consequences that arise in a stock transaction as well as the fact that the deal will take longer to complete due to regulatory and disclosure requirements relating to the issue of new shares of stock by the acquirer.

Asset Purchase As we mentioned, both merger and tender offers represent transactions in which the acquirer purchases the shares of the target from its existing shareholders. Most large deals and deals involving publicly traded companies are structured as stock transactions. The other type of acquisition is an asset purchase. In an asset purchase, an acquirer buys certain assets from the target and then the target typically distributes the proceeds of the asset purchase to its shareholders in the form of a dividend.

Asset purchases are usually used only in small, private transactions or when public companies divest only a portion of their assets (for example, selling one of the company's divisions). They also tend to be used in distressed sales. There are a number of advantages and disadvantages to each the buyer and the seller in a deal structured as an asset purchase.

An advantage to the buyer is that the buyer can pick and choose the assets that it wants. It can also leave behind liabilities that it does not want such as environmental liabilities, as well as any unknown or contingent liabilities. In a stock transaction, on the other hand, the buyer will acquire all of the target's assets and liabilities. However, asset purchases tend to take longer because each asset being acquired needs to be valued and transferred.

The other important difference between asset and stock deals relates to tax treatment. In an asset purchase, the buyer usually can write up the value of the acquired assets allowing the company to realize tax deductions for depreciation and amortization in the future. This can be a substantial advantage to the acquirer. In a stock transaction, there is typically no such step-up of the tax-basis of the acquired assets.

On the other hand, there is often a tax disadvantage to the seller in an asset deal. In such a transaction, gains are double-taxed. First the company must pay taxes on the capital gains of the assets being sold. Then the shareholders of the seller must pay taxes on the distributed cash resulting from the sale. To make matters worse, dividends that the shareholders receive due to the sale are typically taxed as income rather than at lower capital gains rates.

In a stock deal, there is only a single layer of taxes because the buyer is acquiring shares directly from the shareholder. There is no tax consequence to the company, and the shareholders owe only capital gains taxes. Moreover, under certain circumstances, a stock transaction may be able to be structured to have no immediate tax consequences to the selling shareholders if the purchase consideration is made up of the seller's shares rather than cash. These are known as tax-free transactions or tax-free reorganizations.

In summary, in small or private transactions buyers tend to prefer deals structured as asset purchases even though they tend to take longer to complete because of the step-up of the tax basis, and because of the ability to pick and choose assets and leave certain liabilities behind. Sellers, on the other hand, tend to prefer stock deals because of the single layer of taxation and because there are no bad assets or liabilities that remain. In most cases, the way in which the transaction is structured will be negotiated between the two parties and will likely play a role in determining the final purchase price.

THE M&A PROCESS

To an investment banker, M&A is a process. Bankers follow the same procedures and do the same kind of work for most merger and acquisition transactions. In this section we will walk through the standard process for executing a sell-side M&A deal, with an emphasis on the specific tasks that junior bankers perform. Afterward, we will also briefly discuss the role of investment bankers on a buy-side M&A transaction.

Before we start describing the process, it is worth reviewing one key difference between sell-side deals and buy-side deals. Unlike lawyers or accountants or consultants, who typically get paid by the hour or project regardless of the outcome of a transaction, for the most part, investment banks only get paid upon the successful completion of a transaction. This is known as a transaction fee or success fee. Even if the bank negotiates a monthly retainer fee, this amount will tend to be very small compared with the transaction fee. The transaction fee also usually includes a variable component, which rises if the sales price exceeds a certain amount, thus providing incentive for the investment bank to help achieve the highest sales price.

The consequence of this typical fee structure is that investment bankers, and the investment banks for which they work, almost always prefer to be on the selling side of an M&A deal. The vast majority of sell-side transactions are successfully completed, and thus banks representing the seller receive their transaction fee. On the other hand, in a given transaction there might be any number of buyers bidding for the company being sold, each one probably represented by an investment bank. The odds of any one buyer being the winning bidder are therefore small. Correspondingly, so are the odds of the investment bank receiving substantial payment for all of its hard work.

M&A Sell-Side Process

Except in the case of very small transactions, a company almost always hires an investment bank to help it sell itself in its entirety or to sell a division or business segment. The role of the investment bank is to work with the company to help prepare it for a sale, create the necessary marketing materials, contact potential buyers, and then help negotiate the highest possible price. As long as the seller is motivated, most deals will close unless market conditions drastically change.

For an investment banker, the more efficient the sell-side process, the more likely a deal will close and the more likely the sales price will be maximized. It is up to the bankers to minimize the involvement and distractions of management as much as possible since management still needs to run the company during the process. Most of the time, a good process is also one that is confidential as long as possible, to the public markets, to all but key employees, and to customers and suppliers.

A poorly run process can result in leaks of confidentiality, few interested buyers, a disappointing sales price, or even a failure to close the transaction. Such a process reflects very poorly on the investment bank. It is also embarrassing for the company, especially if the fact that the company was for sale had been made public.

Generally, it takes about six to nine months for an average sell-side process. Occasionally, a process can be accelerated and take a shorter amount of time if there is urgency to the transaction. Deals can take longer if there are regulatory issues or other hurdles.

The sell-side process that we describe in this section is what is known as an auction process or two-stage auction process since there are two rounds of bidding. This is the standard process used by bankers when a company is put up for sale and there is more than one possible buyer. Some transactions are negotiated directly between two companies without an auction being run. We will not discuss such a "negotiated sale" since it is both less standardized and less common than an auction process.

Pitch For bankers, the process of a sell-side transaction nearly always starts with a pitch. As we discussed in Chapter 1, bankers have to pitch for nearly all transactions, and M&A deals are no exception. Most of the time when a company decides it wants to sell itself or sell off substantial assets, it will invite a number of investment banks to pitch for the business. Recall that we typically refer to this kind of pitch as a bakeoff or beauty contest.

For junior bankers, sell-side M&A pitches tend to be a lot of work, containing a number of sections. In addition to descriptive sections such as a company, industry, and situation overview, they will also contain valuation analysis, a description of likely buyers, and an overview of the sell-side process and time line. Note that as we discussed in Chapter 1, valuations for a sell-side pitch tend to be aggressive (i.e., high) and time lines tend to be aggressive (i.e., short).

Most of the time the winning investment bank is picked because of its prior relationship with the company or because it has significant experience executing similar deals in the industry. And as we mentioned in Chapter 1, the fees that banks charge are very standardized, so it is unusual for an investment bank to win a deal based on its fee proposal. Especially for large transactions, the investment banks that lose the bakeoff often rush to try to represent one of the likely buyers. Finally, note that in very large transactions, a seller and/or buyers may choose to retain more than one investment bank as an adviser.

Due Diligence and the Beginning of the Process Once an investment bank is hired, the first step is for the deal team working on the transaction to meet with the company's management to discuss the anticipated process and to start due diligence. The goal of the due diligence process is for the bankers working on the deal to learn enough about the company so that they can successfully put together the necessary marketing documents and financial model and so that they can knowledgably speak about the business to prospective buyers and the buyers' advising investment banks. Due diligence also often includes site visits to key facilities.

During this very early stage, the bankers (typically the analyst) will put together the working group list, which, as a reminder, is the list of contact information for all of the individuals from all of the firms involved with the transaction. In addition, responsibilities will be assigned to the bankers, to various members of management, and to other advisers such as the attorneys so that everyone knows who needs to do what and by when.

Once due diligence and the initial meetings are completed, the junior bankers on the deal will start doing the work. They will start building a detailed financial model for the company, perhaps utilizing the company's own internal model. They will also start revising the valuation used in the pitch for new information with which they now have access. In addition, the bankers will begin creation of the various marketing documents, such as the teaser and confidential information memorandum, and populate the data room, all of which we will discuss shortly.

Buyer's List Another early task for which the junior bankers are responsible is to put together an initial buyer's list. The buyer's list contains the companies that may have an interest in pursuing the acquisition and that should therefore be invited to receive the initial marketing material. As we mentioned earlier, the investment bankers will likely have included a preliminary buyer's list in their pitch. However, now the bankers will be able to discuss the appropriateness of each buyer with the company and amend the list to include any additional parties that the company feels should be included.

There is often a degree of tension between the company and the investment bankers over the size of the buyer's list. Companies often prefer to include fewer parties in the auction process in order to raise the likelihood of keeping the sales process confidential, to make the process run faster, and to minimize the amount of time required by management. Bankers, on the other hand, typically prefer as wide an audience as possible to maximize the likely sales price. Often, a process with a small number of prospective buyers is referred to as a targeted auction and a process with a large number of buyers is known as a broad auction.

A typical buyer's list segregates buyers into two types. One type of buyer is private equity firms, usually referred to as financial buyers. The other type is strategic buyers, reflective of companies in the same industry or a related industry that might be interested in making the acquisition for strategic reasons. Just as there is often sensitivity from the company about the total number of buyers who will be invited into the process, there is sometimes also sensitivity about the type of buyer.

Some companies may prefer one type of buyer over another. For instance, companies may wish to exclude key competitors from the process or prefer to exclude buyers likely to lay off many employees (especially senior management), close facilities, or relocate the company. Alternatively, some management teams are generally opposed to selling to private equity firms for any number of reasons.

Teaser The first marketing document that typically is sent to prospective buyers is known as a teaser. The teaser is a small document, often only two or three pages in length, and contains a very basic introduction to the company being shopped, including some summary financial information and a business overview. Sometimes the teaser is written on an anonymous basis, without the name of the company disclosed. As its name implies, the teaser is meant to tease, or to whet the appetite of, possible bidders. The teaser is usually accompanied by a confidentiality agreement.

Once the teaser is sent to each company on the buyer's list, the members of the investment banking deal team usually call and follow up with each possible buyer to confirm receipt and to gauge each buyer's interest level. Sometimes it is pretty easy to determine the likeliest buyers, especially in a targeted auction. If this is the case, the managing director on the deal may even follow up rather than a junior banker.

After a period of a week or two, the bankers determine who is interested and help facilitate the negotiation of the confidentiality agreement between the buyer and the company's lawyers. The next step is to send each interested buyer a copy of what is often referred to as the Confidential Information Memorandum, or CIM.

Confidential Information Memorandum (CIM) The CIM, also referred to as just the Information Memorandum (IM) or Offering Memorandum (OM), is a much longer document than the teaser, often 50 pages or more, and in some ways is similar to a 10-K. Prepared by the junior bankers with the help of the company, it typically contains a detailed business overview including information on each division or business segment and each of the company's key departments, such as sales and marketing, R&D, operations, information technology, human resources, and so forth. The CIM also contains detailed historical financial information as well as projected financial information that is based on the model that the junior bankers have created.

Although the CIM contains mostly factual information like a 10-K, it is considered a marketing document. In other words, it is written in a way that makes the company seem as desirable as possible. Moreover, historical financial results are typically normalized in a way that makes the company's performance appear as strong as possible, within reason.

First-Round Bids Along with, or shortly after, sending the CIM to the prospective interested buyers, the bankers will also send a letter stating when first-round bids are due. Buyers usually have several weeks to review the CIM and submit a bid. For a banker, and the client, receiving first bids is exciting since it is the first indication of what companies might pay for the company or assets that are for sale.

Often first-round bids are presented as a range of values, and also must include the buyer's form of consideration (i.e., cash or stock) and how the company expects to finance the purchase, potential regulatory issues, and additional information. Once all of the bids are received, the bankers discuss the bids with their client and decide which buyers to invite into the second round of the sell-side process.

Management Presentations The second round of the process begins with management presentations. Each prospective buyer will be invited to a presentation prepared by the investment bankers and the company, and given by senior management. These management presentations are usually held at the company's headquarters or at the company's law firm that is working on the transaction. These meetings can take up a very large amount of management's time, which is one of the reasons why management teams tend to want to restrict the number of prospective buyers invited into the second round of bidding.

Like the CIM, the actual PowerPoint presentation used by management will contain information about the different functional areas of the company as well as financial data. Also like the CIM, the presentation will be written and prepared in an optimistic manner that highlights the strengths of the company. Management presentations usually last several hours to a full day, and include time for the prospective buyers and their advisers to ask questions. Sometimes management presentations conclude with a site visit or tour of key facilities.

For a junior banker, a lot of time and effort go into the creation of the management presentation. In addition, senior bankers on the team will work with members of the company's management to rehearse the presentation prior to any meetings with prospective buyers. The entire deal team may attend the first such meeting, but subsequently usually only one member of the deal team is assigned to chaperone these meetings and ensure that management does not stray too far from the presentation and from the key marketing points. Needless to say, it can be awkward for a 22-year-old analyst to have to politely remind a 60-year-old CEO to keep quiet.

Data Room Immediately subsequent to the management presentation, the sell-side bankers will usually open up the data room to each prospective buyer. The data room is an electronic database of documents pertaining to the company that buyers will want to review in order to perform due diligence and make a final bid. These documents often include historical financial statements, marketing materials, minutes from board meetings, employment agreements, patents, all sorts of other contracts, and much more. From almost the time an investment bank was first hired, the junior bankers on the deal will work with the company to procure and organize these documents and to upload them into the data room.

The data room takes its name from the days when data rooms were physical and usually windowless rooms where prospective buyers and their advisers would be invited to read important documents. Modern technology allows bankers to control these virtual data rooms by monitoring which buyers use the data room and which documents are downloaded and/or read. Bankers can also block access of sensitive information to certain buyers.

In a typical process, buyers will have several weeks or more to review the contents of the data room and to request any additional information that they need. At this stage of the deal, the role of the junior bankers is mostly to coordinate information requests and document exchanges between the company for sale and the various investment bankers representing each buyer. Bankers also will help arrange conference calls between the various parties, as well as due diligence trips and site visits for prospective buyers.

Final-Round Bids At some point during the phase of the data room and buyers' due diligence, the sell-side investment bankers will send out a standard letter to each prospective bidder letting them know when final-round bids are due. Unlike first-round bids, final-round bids are typically binding. Similar to first-round bids, final-round bids must include not only the bid price but other information. Each bidder will have to disclose how it will pay (the purchase consideration), any financing contingencies, any likely regulatory issues, the anticipated amount of time it will take the buyer to close the deal, the buyer's internal approval process, any outstanding due diligence issues, and other information.

At this point, the senior members of the sell-side deal team will review the offers with the company and make a decision as to which buyer will win the auction. Often bankers will negotiate with prospective buyers and their advisers to try to encourage them to raise their bids at this point. In some cases, the field is narrowed down to two buyers and both are asked to raise their bids, something buyers clearly do not like, since second-round bids are supposed to be the final round.

Closing the Deal Most of the time, the buyer with the highest bid will win the auction. However, this is not always the case, as a company's board of directors is generally allowed (state law governs a board's duties) to take into account considerations other than solely price, especially the certainty of the deal closing. For example, the highest bidder may not be chosen if their offer is in stock and a second bidder's offer is in cash. Or, the board may choose a buyer with a lower price but one that does not face regulatory hurdles that may slow or even prevent the deal from closing.

Once the winner is chosen, it is mostly up to the attorneys on each side to negotiate the final purchase agreement. The role of the bankers is to make sure this process goes smoothly, to be on important conference calls, and to facilitate any confirmatory due diligence or other issues. The process until close can take anywhere from weeks to months depending on the regulatory approval process or if there are other issues. Finally the deal is closed, and everyone gets invited to an expensive and fancy closing dinner. The junior bankers also typically design a Lucite memento of the deal (sometimes called a deal toy) to be distributed to each person involved in the transaction.

Fairness Opinion The sell-side investment bank may also be asked to provide a fairness opinion for the transaction. A fairness opinion is a very standardized document, based mostly on the banker's valuation conclusions, that states that the transaction is fair to the shareholders from a financial point of view. In a contentious deal (for example, if the highest bid was not accepted), then an outside investment bank may provide the fairness opinion. A fairness opinion is used to help protect the board of directors of the target from lawsuits by any shareholders who are not satisfied with the terms of the deal.

The Role of Investment Bankers on a Buy-Side M&A Deal

Investment bankers play a number of roles when advising a prospective buyer on an acquisition. Just like sell-side deals, buy-side deals typically begin with the investment bank having to pitch for the business. Generally, a buy-side M&A transaction is significantly less work for an investment bank than a sell-side transaction because the buy-side advisers do not have to create the marketing materials like the teaser, CIM, and management presentations, or populate the data room. Moreover, whereas the sell-side investment bank has to deal with multiple buyers and their advisers, the buy-side advisers need only to interact with one counterparty. However, investment banks acting as buy-side advisers still often perform a considerable amount of work and play an important role in the M&A process.

As you might expect, one of the most important tasks of the buy-side investment bank is to advise its client on valuation. Beginning with the pitch, bankers will perform a valuation analysis on the company or assets being sold. As more information becomes available through the CIM, the management presentation, and the data room, bankers will continue to update their valuation in order help their client form an appropriate bidding strategy.

Junior bankers working on a buy-side transaction often also perform a significant amount of modeling. In addition to creating forecasts for valuation purposes (i.e., for the discounted cash flow analysis), bankers sometimes create very detailed models to analyze the impact of the transaction on the buyer, to analyze various acquisition financing alternatives, and to assess potential synergies and restructuring costs. Especially once the data room is opened, bankers will have a lot of information on which to base their models. We will discuss M&A modeling in more detail later in this chapter.

A third role that investment bankers play when representing a prospective buyer is to act as an intermediary between the buyer and the seller's investment banking advisers in order to facilitate due diligence and to request additional information. Bankers also often accompany their clients to the management presentation, and to due diligence trips and site visits. Note that bankers do not actually perform heavy due diligence, which is left to the company and other advisers such as accountants and consultants. The MD working on the transaction will also often become involved in negotiations during the later stages of the transaction, especially if his or her bank's client is the one picked as the winning bid.

The final key role of buy-side advisers on an M&A transaction is to help arrange financing for the acquisition. As a junior banker on a deal from an M&A group or industry coverage group, you will often work with your firm's equity capital markets (ECM) or debt capital markets (DCM) groups and leveraged finance group to analyze various financing structures and put together financing commitments. If it will take some time to arrange the acquisition financing (for example, to issue public bonds), then the buy-side bank may also arrange a bridge loan for its client.

Helping to arrange the acquisition financing can involve such work as putting together credit memorandums and investor presentations. Sometimes the investment bank representing the seller will offer to finance the acquisition for any qualified buyer in what is known as staple financing. The investment bank on the buy side will help its client evaluate the terms offered through the staple financing and compare them with other alternatives.

M&A ANALYSIS

M&A deals, like all other transactions investment bankers execute, require junior bankers to perform various analysis including valuation and financial modeling. However, there are a few types of analysis specific to mergers and acquisitions that are important to know. The most important of these is an accretion/dilution analysis, which is a common subject of technical interview questions, especially for associate candidates.

Accretion/Dilution Analysis

An accretion/dilution analysis, sometimes also referred to as a "quick and dirty" merger model, is used to analyze the impact of an acquisition on the earnings per share (EPS) of the acquiring company. It is used for transactions in which the buyer is a publicly traded company. If EPS of the newly combined company is projected to be higher post-acquisition than it was forecasted to be had the acquirer not executed the transaction, then we refer to the deal as being accretive. If we expect EPS to decrease due to the acquisition, then the transaction is considered dilutive. A deal is considered breakeven if no change to EPS is forecasted.

Recall that we learned in Chapter 3 that finance theory dictates that companies should pursue projects, including acquisitions, that create value and avoid projects that destroy value. Remember that the definition of value creation is when the net present value (NPV) of an investment is greater than zero, or when the internal rate of return (IRR) of an investment exceeds its cost of capital. In order to measure the NPV and IRR for an acquisition we would have to examine the acquisition's impact over a long-term period.

An accretion/dilution analysis measures the impact of an acquisition over a short period, usually only one or two years after the transaction occurs. Even though finance theory teaches us that this is too short a period to measure the true value of an acquisition, investors nevertheless are perceived to care about the near-term impact of an acquisition on a company's EPS. Since it is thought that many public companies trade (in the short-term) based on P/E multiples, any dilution to EPS could result in a subsequent drop in the stock price.

Since the management of many companies care deeply about their near-term stock performance, they, too, pay a great deal of attention to the accretion/dilution analysis when contemplating an acquisition. In fact, some companies will only pursue acquisitions that will be accretive. Of course in the long run, the market should reward a good, value-creating deal regardless of its near-term impact to EPS.

Investment bankers typically perform an accretion/dilution analysis whenever they are representing a publicly traded buyer. In addition, bankers working on the sell side of an M&A transaction may also perform this analysis in order to assess a potential buyer's likelihood of pursuing a bid or to estimate its maximum bid based on an accretive transaction. In essence, accretion/dilution can be used for valuation purposes if we make an assumption that a public buyer will pursue only accretive deals.

There are a number of steps to creating an accretion/dilution model. The reason that this analysis is sometimes called a "quick and dirty" merger model is that especially with the use of a template, this analysis can be completed very quickly.

1. Gather the necessary information.
2. Calculate pro forma net income.
3. Calculate new fully diluted share count.
4. Calculate pro forma EPS and determine accretion or dilution.
5. Run sensitivity analysis and other analysis.

Step 1: Gather the Necessary Information The first step is to gather the necessary information required to perform the accretion/dilution analysis. You will need the basic terms of the transaction, including the purchase price and the purchase consideration (cash, stock, or both). If the acquirer will use cash to finance the purchase, then you will also need to know the source of that cash. You will also need historical and projected net income or EPS for the acquirer and the target as well as the most recent fully diluted share counts for both companies. If the transaction is a stock deal, then you will also need the current share prices for both companies in order to calculate the exchange ratio.

Following is a more detailed list of the information needed for a typical accretion/dilution analysis:

- Fully diluted share count for the acquirer and the target.
- Current share price of acquirer and target (if a stock transaction).
- Last twelve month (LTM) and projected net income and/or EPS for the acquirer and the target.
- Purchase price.
- Purchase consideration (percentage of cash and stock or exchange ratio).
- Financing detail for cash consideration (new debt or cash from balance sheet).

Just like most of the other types of analysis that we have covered in this book, historical net income and current share count figures will typically come from 10-Qs and 10-Ks. Projected net income or EPS can come from a variety of sources, including equity research, company management, or your own forecasts. Information about the transaction including the purchase price and the purchase consideration will have to be estimated (and sensitized) if we are in the early stages of a transaction or performing an accretion/dilution analysis for a pitch.

Step 2: Calculate Pro Forma Net Income Once we have obtained the information we need for our analysis, the next step is to calculate pro forma net income. Recall that EPS is calculated as:

$$\text{EPS} = \frac{\text{Net Income}}{\text{Number of Fully Diluted Shares}}$$

In order to calculate the new EPS, we need to determine what the new net income will be and what the new number of fully diluted shares will be. We typically will calculate pro forma EPS using three time periods, including the LTM period, the next full year projected, and the following projected year. Therefore we need net income for each of those three time periods for both companies.

As a starting point for pro forma net income, we add net income from the acquirer together with net income from the target for each time period. Then we make appropriate adjustments to net income. The basic adjustments are as follows:

- Subtract after-tax interest expense if the acquirer will raise new debt to finance the cash portion of the purchase price.
- Subtract after-tax forgone interest income if the acquirer will use cash from its balance sheet to finance the cash portion of the purchase price.
- Add the impact of any anticipated synergies, tax-affected.
- Subtract the after-tax amortization expense for newly "created" intangible assets.
- Subtract the after-tax depreciation expense for written up tangible assets.

Once we have estimated each type of adjustment, we can calculate pro forma net income for each time period as:

Pro Forma Net Income
= Target's Net Income + Acquirer's Net Income
−After-Tax Interest Expense
−After-Tax Forgone Interest Income
+After-Tax Synergies − After-Tax Amortization
−After-Tax Depreciation

Interest Expense and Interest Income If the buyer is using cash as part or all of the purchase consideration, then we need to know how the buyer will get that cash. If the buyer will be raising new debt to finance the purchase, then we will have to reduce pro forma income of the combined company for the interest expense on the new debt. If, on the other hand, the buyer will use cash that it already has (i.e., from its balance sheet) then we will also have to reduce pro forma net income for the foregone interest income. Either way, net income will be reduced, though it will likely go down more if the buyer raises new debt since the interest rate on debt will likely be higher than the interest rate the company was earning on its excess cash. Also do not forget that we need to tax-affect the new interest expense or lost interest income at the buyer's effective tax rate before we can subtract it from net income.

Synergies Often when creating an accretion/dilution analysis, we will assume that a strategic acquisition will result in some moderate amount of synergies. When working on a live transaction, bankers will often receive significant guidance from their client as to the appropriate amount of synergies to model. Otherwise, we will have to estimate synergies, often as some percentage of revenue or EBITDA. Typically we only include cost synergies and not revenue synergies since revenue synergies tend to be much more speculative. Just as with interest, we need to tax-affect the amount of synergies before adjusting net income higher. Also note that we usually do not take into account expected restructuring costs such as severance payments when performing an accretion/dilution analysis.

Amortization Expense When an acquisition actually occurs, accountants are brought to do what is known as a purchase price allocation. In this analysis, the target's balance sheet will be adjusted so that each asset and liability reflects fair market value. As we discussed in Chapter 2, often intangible assets such as brand names, trademarks, or patents will be created on the balance sheet and then must be amortized according to each asset's useful life. This amortization expense will have a negative impact on the newly combined company's net income and will therefore affect pro forma EPS.

Adjusting pro forma net income for amortization expense is not always done by bankers creating accretion/dilution analyses because it is difficult to estimate the value of the to-be-created intangible assets. However, some bankers do make such an approximation, by assuming that a portion of the difference between the equity purchase price and the tangible book value of the target will be assigned to intangible assets. Note that the tangible book value is equal to book value less the value of intangible assets, including goodwill.

For example, suppose that the purchase price is $1 billion and the tangible book value of the target is $400 million. A banker might assume that, say, 20 percent of the excess purchase price of $600 million will be assigned to identifiable intangible assets, which will then need to be amortized over, perhaps, seven years. Hence, $120 million of intangible assets will be created, resulting in approximately $17 million of annual pre-tax amortization. Note that the assumption for the amount of intangible assets created will vary highly with the industry. Once again, you will need to tax-affect the annual amount of amortization expense before adjusting pro forma net income.

The remaining 80 percent of the excess purchase price will be assigned to goodwill, which does not get amortized and therefore does not affect pro forma EPS. In an actual purchase price allocation, the difference between the equity purchase price and the tangible book value of the target's newly adjusted balance sheet will be assigned to goodwill.

Depreciation Expense Just as intangible assets can be created through the purchase price allocation to reflect their fair market value, the value of tangible assets like PP&E will also be adjusted to fair market value. If the value of assets is increased, then the newly combined company will have an additional depreciation expense. Just like amortization expense, this depreciation expense, on a post-tax basis, will negatively impact pro forma net income. It is very unusual for bankers to account for estimated depreciation expense when doing a simple accretion/dilution analysis, but it is often done when performing a very detailed analysis.

Step 3: Calculate Pro-Forma Shares After we have calculated pro forma net income for each time period, the next step in performing the accretion/dilution analysis is to calculate the pro forma fully diluted share count. In a cash transaction, there is no change to the number of shares, so we can use the acquirer's current number of fully diluted shares or projected shares from equity research.

However, in an all-stock or partial-stock transaction, there will be an increase in the number of the acquirer's shares because it will be issuing new shares to use as a form of payment to be given to the target's shareholders. Before we can calculate the number of shares to be issued, we first need to calculate the exchange ratio, as we learned in Chapter 5 when we discussed the precedent transaction method of valuation.

In an all-stock transaction, we can calculate the exchange ratio as:

$$\text{Exchange Ratio} = \frac{\text{Purchase Price per Share}}{\text{Acquirer's Share Price}}$$

For example, if the purchase price is \$10 per share and the acquirer's share price is currently trading at \$30, then the exchange ratio is equal to one third. In other words, for every three shares owned by the target's shareholders, the acquirer will issue and pay one of its own shares.

In a part-stock, part-cash transaction, we need to multiply the exchange ratio as calculated above by the percentage of purchase consideration to be paid in stock. Let's keep the same assumptions as before, but now assume that the transaction calls for half of the consideration to be paid in stock and half in cash. In this case, the target's shareholders will receive \$5 in cash and one sixth of a share of acquirer stock for each share owned in the target.

More broadly, we can calculate the adjusted exchange ratio for a partial stock deal as:

$$\text{Adjusted Exchange Ratio} = \frac{\text{Purchase Price per Share} \times \text{\% Stock Consideration}}{\text{Acquirer's Share Price}}$$

Once we have calculated the exchange ratio, we can calculate the number of new shares to be issued by multiplying the exchange ratio times the number of the target's fully diluted shares outstanding. Remember that the target's fully diluted shares must take into account the automatic vesting of stock options and other convertible securities that will occur upon a change of control transaction.

$$\text{New Shares Issued} = \text{Exchange Ratio} \times \text{Target's Fully Diluted Shares}$$

Finally, we can calculate the number of pro forma shares that we will use in the denominator of our EPS calculating by adding the current number of acquirer's fully diluted shares and the new shares to be issued.

$$\text{Pro Forma Shares} = \text{Acquirer's Fully Diluted Shares} + \text{New Shares Issued}$$

Step 4: Calculate Pro Forma EPS and Determine Accretion or Dilution Now that we have calculated both pro forma net income and the pro forma number of shares, we can easily calculate pro forma EPS as follows:

$$\text{Pro Forma EPS} = \frac{\text{Pro Forma Net Income}}{\text{Pro Forma Fully Diluted Shares}}$$

Once we have calculated pro forma EPS for each time period, we can compare the pro forma EPS with the acquirer's projected EPS assuming no transaction. If the pro forma EPS figure is higher than it would have been without the acquisition, then the transaction is considered to be accretive. If the pro forma EPS figure is lower than it would have been, then the deal is dilutive. We usually calculate the absolute amount of accretion or dilution (measured in dollars per share) as well as the percentage accretion or dilution.

For instance, suppose that we project that the buyer's next year's EPS would have been $2.00 per share had it not executed the transaction and we calculate next year's pro forma EPS to be $2.10 assuming the transaction. We can then state that we expect the transaction to be $0.10 or 5 percent accretive to next year's EPS.

Finally, note that it is not uncommon for deals to be dilutive using LTM net income but accretive using one or two year forward net income since it often takes a few years for synergies to be fully realized.

Step 5: Run Sensitivity Analysis and Other Analysis In addition to the impact on EPS, we typically perform a number of additional analyses and create a few additional schedules based on the information used to build the accretion/ dilution analysis.

Additional Synergies Required for Breakeven One such analysis that always accompanies accretion/dilution is what is known as additional synergies required for breakeven. If the accretion/dilution analysis indicates a dilutive deal, then bankers will calculate the amount of additional pre-tax synergies that would be required to make the deal neither accretive nor dilutive. This figure can be calculated as follows:

$$\text{Pre-Tax Synergies} = \frac{(\text{Pro Forma EPS} - \text{Acquirer's EPS}) \times \text{Pro Forma Shares}}{1 - \text{Tax rate}}$$

Bankers will typically calculate this figure for each time period for which pro forma EPS was calculated. Bankers often also show this synergy figure as a percentage of pro forma revenue and pro forma EBITDA to help determine the feasibility or likelihood of realizing this amount of synergies.

Pro Forma Ownership Structure Another analysis typically performed is to examine the pro forma ownership structure. In a stock transaction, the acquirer will be issuing new shares to the target's existing shareholders. It is helpful to know what percentage of the newly combined company's shareholders will be the acquirer's shareholders and what percentage will be the target's shareholders. The ownership structure can also have influence on the makeup of the new board of directors. Generally, the acquiring company will want to maintain at least a majority ownership so bankers may run sensitivity analysis to analyze the maximum purchase price or the maximum amount of stock that can be issued to maintain a certain ownership percentage of the combined company.

Sensitivity Analysis When performing an accretion/dilution analysis, junior bankers almost always run a number of sensitivity analyses. Bankers usually analyze the expected accretion/dilution percentage for the various time periods based upon a range of a number of key variables. Usually, sensitivity analysis will be created using Microsoft Excel's Data Table functionality, which we covered when we discussed the discounted cash flow analysis in Chapter 5. Recall that this feature of Excel allows us to analyze a result (in this case, the change to EPS) by varying two inputs at a time. Often we will want to run sensitivity analysis varying different combinations of the following inputs:

- Purchase price or acquisition premium.
- Purchase consideration percentages (stock vs. cash).
- Method by which cash portion of consideration is financed.
- Expected synergies.

The Impact of P/E Ratios on Accretion/Dilution One of the most common technical interview questions relating to M&A focuses on the impact of P/E ratios on an accretion/dilution analysis. In an acquisition, if the acquirer's P/E ratio is higher than the target's P/E ratio and if the acquirer is using stock consideration, then the deal will most likely be accretive. If the P/E ratio of the acquirer is lower than that of the target then the deal will likely be dilutive.

In a transaction where a high P/E company acquires a low P/E company, the acquirer will pay less for each dollar of earnings than the market values its own earnings. Therefore, the impact of adding the target's net income to its own (the numerator of EPS) will more than offset the number of shares the acquirer will have to issue (the denominator of EPS) and EPS will increase. The opposite will be true when a low P/E company acquires a high P/E company.

Let's do a simple example. Suppose a company with a P/E ratio of 20x acquires a company with a P/E ratio of 10x. To keep the math easy, assume that both companies have earnings of $10,000 and 10,000 shares outstanding. (You can substitute any numbers of earnings and EPS and the analysis will show the same result.) Therefore, both companies currently have an EPS of $1.00 ($10,000 net income/10,000 fully diluted shares outstanding).

Based on these assumptions, we can calculate that the acquirer's stock will trade at $20 per share (P/E of 20 times $1.00 EPS) and the target's stock will trade at $10 (P/E of 10 times $1.00 EPS). The exchange ratio will therefore be equal to 0.5 ($10 target's share price/$20 acquirer's share price). The newly issued number of shares will be 5,000 (0.5 exchange ratio times target's 10,000 shares). So the new number of shares will be 15,000. Pro forma net income will be $20,000. Pro forma EPS will therefore be 20,000/15,000, or $1.33. We can easily see that this is higher than the $1.00 EPS prior to the transaction and thus the deal is accretive.

Keep in mind that we have purposely ignored such things like amortization, depreciation, and synergies. Obviously these adjustments will have an effect on pro forma EPS as well. We have also assumed that the transaction is a 100 percent stock transaction. Whether a cash transaction will be accretive or dilutive will depend on how the cash component is financed and the impact of interest expense to pro forma net income.

Full-Blown Merger Model In addition to an accretion/dilution analysis, investment bankers working on a live transaction will often create what we will call a full-blown merger model. Sometimes bankers working on an important M&A pitch will also build such a model. A full-blown merger model is an integrated cash flow model of the combined companies. The process of creating such a model involves creating separate cash flow models for both the acquirer and the target and then aggregating them into one model.

Once the model is built for the combined company, bankers can then run accretion/dilution and other analyses that are required, such as a detailed synergy analysis, and sensitivity analysis around various purchase assumptions (i.e., purchase price and acquisition premium) and the purchase consideration (i.e., stock versus cash). The merger model can help answer such questions as:

- What will the combined financial statements of the two companies be after a merger?
- What is the impact of synergies or integration costs?
- Can the buyer afford to purchase the company using debt?
- What is the optimal method to finance the purchase price?

Building a full-blown merger model is essentially a combination of three skills. The first, and most important, is building cash flow models in the manner in which we learned in Chapter 6. The second such skill is to create what we call a pro forma balance sheet, which we will discuss in the next chapter when we talk about LBO analysis. The third skill is the accretion/dilution analysis that we learned in this chapter.

Contribution Analysis

In addition to the accretion/dilution analysis and a full-blown merger model, bankers also perform various other common analyses when analyzing an M&A deal. One such analysis is known as a contribution analysis.

A contribution analysis shows how much the acquirer and the target will contribute to the combined company after the acquisition based on various metrics. For instance, if the acquirer's LTM revenue is $1 billion and the target's LTM revenue is $500 million, then we can easily see that the combined company will be made up of two-thirds the acquirer's revenue and one-third the target's revenue.

A contribution analysis, an example of which is in Exhibit 7.1, typically shows the contribution of each company graphically using such financial

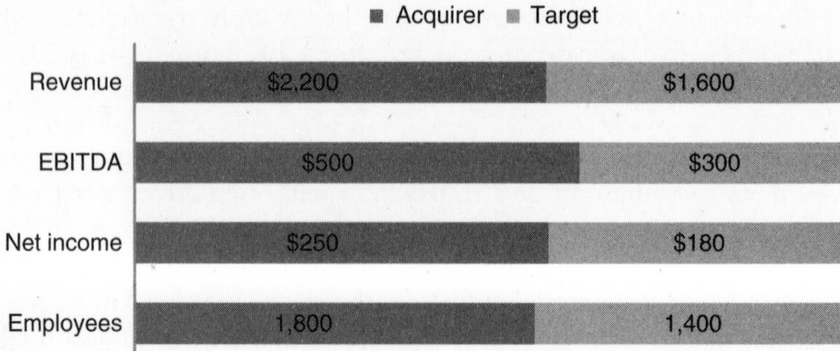

EXHIBIT 7.1 Example of a Contribution Analysis

metrics as revenue, EBITDA, and net income, as well as non-financial metrics such as the number of employees. An investment banker may also use important industry specific metrics such as the number of stores for retailers or the number of subscribers for telecom companies. Bankers typically exclude synergies and other adjustments. As such, the contribution analysis is typically a very easy analysis to perform.

Analysis at Various Prices (AVP)

Another type of analysis performed by bankers involved in an M&A transaction is what is known as an analysis at various prices, or AVP. The analysis at various prices is a simple analysis that shows the impact of different purchase prices on the acquisition premium and on various implied valuation multiples. For instance, suppose that a company's shares are currently trading at $20 and that a buyer is contemplating making an acquisition offer anywhere from $20 to $30 per share. Based on the AVP, the buyer could easily see that a $20 purchase price would imply a 0 percent acquisition premium, and a $30 purchase price would imply a 50 percent acquisition premium.

Further suppose that the target has 100 million fully diluted shares outstanding, net debt of $500 million, and LTM EBITDA of $350 million. Based on a $20 per share purchase price, the implied enterprise value would be $2.5 billion ($20 per share times 100 million shares plus $500 net debt) and the implied EV/LTM EBITDA multiple would be about 7.1x ($2.5 billion/$350 million). On the other hand, if we assume the buyer has to pay $30 per share, then enterprise value would be $3.5 billion ($30 per share times 100 million shares plus $500 million net debt) and the implied EV/EBITDA multiple would be 10.0x ($3.5 billion/$350 million).

Exhibit 7.2 shows an example of an AVP with a range of purchase prices and different implied valuation multiples.

EXHIBIT 7.2 Example of Analysis at Various Prices (AVP)

(*$ in millions*)						
Acqusition Price	$20.00	$22.00	$24.00	$26.00	$28.00	$30.00
Premium	0.0%	10.0%	20.0%	30.0%	40.0%	50.0%
Purchase Price (MVE)	$2,000	$2,200	$2,400	$2,600	$2,800	$3,000
Enterprise Value	$2,500	$2,700	$2,900	$3,100	$3,300	$3,500
LTM Multiples						
EV/Revenue	1.1x	1.2x	1.3x	1.4x	1.5x	1.6x
EV/EBITDA	7.1x	7.7x	8.3x	8.9x	9.4x	10.0x
P/E	12.5x	13.8x	15.0x	16.3x	17.5x	18.8x
Next Fiscal Year Multiples						
EV/Revenue	1.0x	1.1x	1.2x	1.3x	1.4x	1.5x
EV/EBITDA	6.6x	7.1x	7.7x	8.2x	8.7x	9.3x
P/E	11.7x	12.9x	14.0x	15.2x	16.4x	17.5x

END-OF-CHAPTER QUESTIONS

1. Why might one company want to acquire another company?
2. Explain the concept of synergies and provide some examples.
3. What are some of the differences between a merger and a tender offer?
4. What are some of the pros and cons of a stock versus asset purchase?
5. Do buyers generally prefer stock or asset deals?
6. Do sellers generally prefer stock or asset deals?
7. Walk me through a sell-side M&A process.
8. Would an investment bank prefer to be on the sell side of an M&A deal or the buy side?
9. What are some of the marketing documents that bankers create when working on a sell-side M&A transaction?
10. What analysis might be done for an M&A assignment?
11. Walk me through an accretion/dilution analysis.
12. What factors can lead to the dilution of EPS in an acquisition?
13. If a company with a low P/E acquires a company with a high P/E in an all-stock deal, will the deal likely be accretive or dilutive?
14. What is an analysis at various prices?
15. What is a contribution analysis?

Answers can be found at www.wiley.com/go/gutmann (password: investment).

CHAPTER 8

Leveraged Buyouts

In the last chapter we covered mergers and acquisitions, and discussed the various types of analysis that investment bankers typically perform when analyzing a prospective M&A transaction. In this chapter, we'll discuss a particular subset of M&A transactions: leveraged buyouts.

A leveraged buyout (LBO) is an acquisition of a company using a significant amount of debt to help fund the purchase. LBO transactions can be incredibly lucrative for the investment firms that execute LBO transactions, and in today's world, the funds that invest in LBOs are considered to be a core asset class of institutional investors such as pension funds and endowments. Leveraged buyouts are also highly rewarding for the investment banks that advise on such transactions given the substantial fees involved in raising the funds necessary to complete the deal.

As a prospective investment banker, there are several reasons why you should understand the basic concept of leverage buyouts and have a familiarity with LBO analysis. First, while not as frequently as valuation or M&A, the topic of leveraged buyouts can come up for discussion in the technical portion of investment banking interviews. Second, leveraged buyouts are the primary type of transaction on which you will work if you join a leveraged finance or financial sponsors group. But even bankers in M&A and industry groups will be called on to perform LBO analysis since it is frequently used as a valuation technique. Finally, as we discussed in Chapter 1, it is the goal of many a junior banker to exit investment banking for private equity. So for those of you who fit that bill, you might as well get a head start preparing not just for your banking career but for private equity recruiting, too!

This chapter will start with an explanation of why using substantial amounts of debt can be an advantage when making acquisitions. Next, we will discuss the main players in an LBO transaction, namely private equity firms, investment banks, and the types of companies that make good

LBO targets. Then we will move on to the actual LBO analysis that investment bankers frequently perform. We will talk about how to build an LBO model and then, based on that model, we will discuss how to measure the investment returns to the private equity firm making the acquisition, how to perform credit analysis, and how to utilize the model for purposes of valuation. Finally, we will conclude the chapter with a brief discussion of how the firms that execute LBOs think about and actually make their investment decisions.

OVERVIEW OF LBOS

Before we approach the analysis that bankers and private equity professionals perform when analyzing prospective LBO transactions, we need to first cover a few key topics.

We will start this section with a discussion of the rationale for using substantial amounts of debt when making acquisitions and the impact that such a transaction structure has on investor returns. Next we will talk about the key players involved in an LBO transaction, namely the private equity firm making the acquisition, the investment bankers advising on the transaction, and the kind of companies that make good LBO candidates (the target). Finally, we will discuss the cyclicality of LBO transactions and their dependence on the credit markets.

The Miracle of Leverage

We've already stated that private equity firms make acquisitions using a substantial amount of debt. In many walks of life, this concept is sometimes referred to as making purchases using "other people's money." Just as we did when we introduced the concept of enterprise value in Chapter 5, let's utilize a simple real estate example to illustrate the advantages of using debt. Keep in mind that in this context, leverage and debt are synonymous.

Consider buying a house that costs $1 million today. Just as we did previously, let's assume that we contribute a down payment of 10 percent of the purchase price ($100,000) and that we borrow the remainder ($900,000) in the form of a mortgage.

Three years from now we are a successful private equity mogul, and are ready to upgrade our meager living standards and move into a larger home. Let's assume we are able to sell our house for $1.3 million. To keep our analysis simple, let's assume that we made no mortgage principal payments over the three years, and let's ignore any transaction fees and taxes. How much money did we make?

EXHIBIT 8.1 Equity Gain in Housing Example

	Year 1 (Buying)	Year 3 (Selling)
House Price	$1,000,000	$1,300,000
Less: Mortgage	($900,000)	($900,000)
Equity Value	$100,000	$400,000
Percentage gain		300%

So the house increased in value from $1 million to $1.3 million, or an increase of $300,000. In percentage terms, the increase is 30 percent. Not too bad, right? But that's not the whole story. Look what happened to the equity that we put in (the original down payment), as shown in Exhibit 8.1.

As you can see from Exhibit 8.1, the money that we put in (our equity) increased from $100,000 to $400,000, or, in percentage terms, a 300 percent increase. Even though we only contributed 10 percent of the funds needed to make the purchase, we, as the equity holder receive *all* of the gains.

In fact, take a look at the chart in Exhibit 8.2 and notice the difference between the percentage increase in the house price and the percentage increase in our equity value as the house price continues to appreciate.

Of course, as economists are prone to say, there is no such thing as a free lunch. There is a downside to leverage, too. It does not take a huge drop in the house price for our equity to be wiped out. In our example, merely a

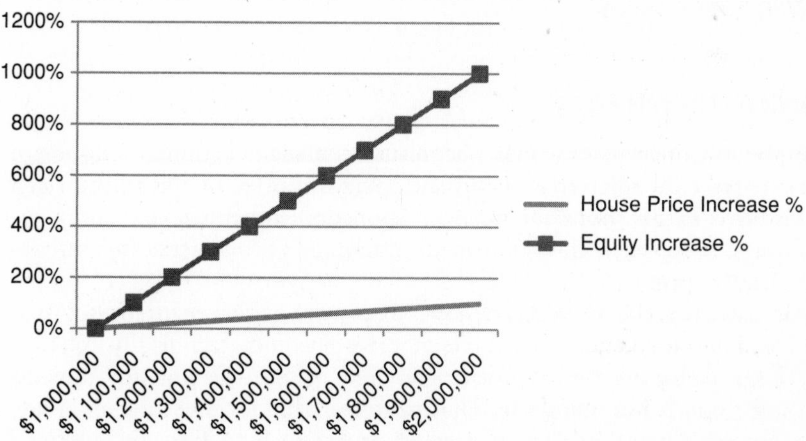

EXHIBIT 8.2 Comparison of the Increase in House Price and the Increase in Equity Value

10 percent drop in the price of the house, to $900,000, results in our equity being worthless. In fact, this is exactly what has happened to many homeowners in the past few years subsequent to the bursting of the real estate bubble in the United States and elsewhere.

However, the news here is not all bad. Due to the limited liability granted to equity holders, there is a fundamental asymmetry between gains and losses on equity. As we mentioned earlier, all of the gains in the house price are recognized by and flow to the equity holders. However, potential losses are limited to the amount of money equity holders have contributed. In our example, potential gains are unlimited as the house price appreciates, but losses can never be greater than $100,000. The worst that can happen is that we lose our entire $100,000 investment and walk away from the house (we turn in the keys). This asymmetry between unlimited gain and limited loss is another big advantage to using debt as a significant source of funding.

The exact same miracle of leverage concept applies to a leveraged buyout transaction. In fact, in many ways real estate is a good analogy for LBOs given the high leverage used in a typical real estate transaction (significantly higher than in a leveraged buyout). Using debt to help finance the purchase of a company reduces the amount of money that the acquirer must contribute to the deal (its equity contribution), which can lead to an outsized increase to the value of the acquirer's equity stake upon an exit. Of course, substantial amounts of debt raise the company's risk of bankruptcy, which typically results in the acquirer's equity being wiped out. However, just like with real estate, in this downside scenario known as a busted LBO, the acquirer's economic loss is limited to its equity contribution, though the acquirer's reputation as a prudent dealmaker and investor may suffer.

Overview of Private Equity

The investment firms that make acquisitions using substantial amounts of debt are typically referred to as private equity firms (sometimes abbreviated as PE firms or PE shops) or financial sponsors (sometimes, for short, just sponsors). In the early days of private equity, such firms were often referred to as LBO firms.

In actuality, the asset class known as private equity encompasses more than just leveraged buyouts. In fact, private equity technically refers to any large investment in a private company where the investor typically has some control or influence. That universe includes investments in venture capital, growth capital, distressed situations, and mezzanine capital. Some would even consider investments in real estate or infrastructure as a subset of private equity. However, when investment bankers use the term "private equity," they are nearly always referring to investment firms that do leveraged buyouts. Therefore, we will do the same. For the remainder of this chapter, when we refer to a private equity firm, we are referring specifically to a firm that engages in leveraged buyouts.

Private equity firms are typically small (at least compared with investment banks), prestigious, and usually privately held (though in recent years some of the larger firms have become public companies). Some of the largest and most recognized firms, which each have many billions of dollars under management include:

- Apollo Management.
- Bain Capital.
- The Blackstone Group.
- The Carlyle Group.
- KKR (Kohlberg Kravis and Roberts).
- TPG Capital.

These firms, sometimes referred to as large cap private equity funds or mega funds, tend, not unsurprisingly, to do the largest deals. Most private equity firms, however, operate in the middle market and do smaller deals. Just like with middle market investment banks, middle market PE firms often have an industry or geographic focus.

In order for private equity firms to make investments, they must first raise a pool of money from investors, referred to as raising a fund. The bulk of the money typically comes from institutional investors such as pension funds, insurance companies, and endowments, with additional money sometimes coming from wealthy individuals. The investors in a fund are known as the limited partners (LPs), whereas the private equity firm that manages the fund is referred to as the general partner (GP). Private equity firms, especially the larger ones, aim to raise a new investment fund every few years.

Once a fund is raised (technically the money from investors is considered committed capital and not actually remitted until needed), the aim is to make acquisitions. The companies being acquired (the target companies) might be public or private, healthy or distressed, or might be a division being sold from a larger entity. Most acquisitions are made with 30–40 percent of the funds being contributed by the limited partners of a fund in the form of equity and the rest being raised through various types of debt. The basic objective is to acquire a company, make operational improvements, help it to grow, increase its value, and then exit the investment in five to seven years (the sooner the better) through a sale or IPO.

Historically, most financial sponsors have targeted investment returns in excess of 20 percent on each investment. However, given the current extremely low interest rate environment (as of 2012), target returns for private equity investments should be lower. Moreover, there is some academic debate as to whether private equity as an asset class outperforms the overall equity markets (i.e., S&P 500), especially on a risk-adjusted basis over time. This is not surprising given the intense competition for acquisitions among private equity firms, especially in the middle market. The target companies in most leveraged buyouts are sold by investment bankers in competitive auction processes, like we discussed in Chapter 7. A competitive sales process implies that the ultimate acquirer is paying top dollar (often referred to as the winner's curse). The few PE firms that do have proprietary dealflow have huge advantages over those that do not.

Proponents of private equity also like to claim that private equity returns are much less volatile than other asset classes, especially equities. This is hard to fathom since finance theory tells us that highly levered small-cap stocks (most companies acquired in leveraged buyouts would be considered small cap if they were publicly traded) should be more volatile than the overall market. Private equity returns appear to be much less volatile than publicly traded stocks, only because PE investments are not actively traded and are not marked-to-market like stocks, but are valued only periodically by valuation professionals, a process that will smooth out volatility.

In addition to the debate over performance, private equity firms are also criticized for profiting from doing little more than using leverage to finance acquisitions (referred to as financial engineering). Whether the typical financial sponsor really adds operational value is certainly up for discussion. Industry professionals maintain that their firms have operational expertise that is helpful to their portfolio companies, that being privately held rather than publicly held encourages long-term performance, and that high level of debt service forces management to be disciplined. On the other hand, critics of private equity maintain that companies owned by private equity firms tend to lay off personnel in cost cutting moves, underinvest in growth, and generally are left in worse shape than they were prior to the buyout. Thus, the critics argue that private equity is in general hurtful to the economy.

Notwithstanding the debate over returns, volatility, and the ultimate value to society of leveraged buyouts, private equity tends to be extremely lucrative to the general partners (GPs). A typical fund is structured so that the GP is granted a 2 percent annual management fee on the amount of money raised and 20 percent of the profits on the exit of investments (carried interest). In addition, management of private equity firms typically receives transaction or advisory fees on each deal as well as ongoing monitoring fees for the companies in their portfolios. Moreover, private equity investors receive very favorable and controversial tax treatment because the profits on investments (the carried interest) are treated as capital gains rather than ordinary income and are taxed at a significantly lower rate.

Role of Investment Bankers

Investment bankers play a number of roles in connection with leveraged buyouts. Most significantly, bankers advise PE firms on acquiring companies. Bankers receive fees not simply for the M&A advice but more significantly for structuring, arranging, and sometimes underwriting the different types of debt necessary to complete the deal. Bankers also work for PE firms when PE firms are ready to exit their investments, either by selling in an auction process (sell-side M&A) or through an IPO.

The two investment banking groups that are most involved with leveraged buyouts are the financial sponsor coverage group and the leveraged finance group. While it varies from firm to firm, typically bankers in the financial sponsors group spend more time marketing to private equity firms whereas bankers in the leveraged finance do more of the transaction execution, especially arranging debt financing. In addition, bankers in M&A groups and industry coverage groups also have exposure to private equity firms when executing sell-side M&A transactions since PE firms are often prospective buyers.

Finally, it is worth mentioning that private equity firms tend to be the most demanding of investment banking clients. This is because most private equity professionals are former investment bankers. They know how to do the work that bankers do, and therefore have very high expectations for both work quality and turnaround time. Junior private equity professionals especially, having recently been investment banking analysts, are prone to highlight and enjoy their new role as the client and not the adviser to the client.

LBO Targets

So far in this chapter we have talked about the private equity firms that make acquisitions and the investment banks that advise the private equity firms. Now let's talk about the kinds of companies that make good leveraged buyout candidates. Keep in mind that to have a successful investment, the private equity firm must not overburden the company with debt so as to risk distress or bankruptcy. But it also desires to grow the value of the firm, which is a large part a function of revenue and profitability growth.

Given the amount of debt raised in a typical LBO, the most obvious criteria for an LBO candidate is one that has the ability to generate sufficient and steady cash flow to support a substantial amount of debt. The financial sponsor must have confidence that the company can afford to pay its interest expense each year. An ideal LBO target is in a non-cyclical industry, and has limited business and market risk, and a strong management team, all supporting the idea of strong and steady cash flows. It is also helpful for the target to have a high asset base for use as debt collateral.

Good LBO candidates also have limited need for ongoing investment such as capital expenditures. However, strong growth prospects are valuable, too, and since growth typically requires investment, the natural tradeoff between the two must be considered. Private equity firms also look for targets that have opportunities for significant cost reductions and efficiency gains. Also very attractive are companies that have opportunities to sell excess and nonessential assets so that the proceeds can be used to pay down debt.

Finally, keep in mind that while most private equity firms seek good companies with healthy operations and quality management teams, there are some private equity firms that do specialize in operational turnarounds and/or distressed situations.

Cyclicality of LBO Activity

Given that leveraged buyouts are dependent on the ability to raise substantial amounts of debt, it should be obvious that LBO activity is highly dependent on the health of the credit markets. In good economic times where credit is abundant, there tends to be significant numbers of LBO transactions. It is typical to see companies being acquired as part of a leveraged buyout to have post-transaction leverage ratios (debt/EBITDA) of 4.0x–6.0x or even higher. Higher available leverage will lead to higher purchase prices, which in turn positively influences stock market returns. In addition, in good times, LBOs can become a very meaningful percentage of overall M&A activity.

In boom (i.e., bubble) times, such as we experienced in 2006 and the first half of 2007, credit tends to be highly abundant and there is a very high level of LBO activity, including very large transactions. Leverage ratios can climb to 6.0x–7.0x or even higher, and some of the types of debt raised in transactions can have very one-sided borrowing terms that favor the company at the expense of the lenders.

Another indication of loose credit markets is when PE firms exit their investments very quickly or refinance deals within a year or two of the initial LBO transaction. Such refinancing transactions often result in a special dividend being paid to the private equity firm. Often in boom times, strategic buyers are priced out of deals since PE firms can afford to pay very high prices given the generous credit markets. Moreover, in times of frothy credit markets, LBO criteria tend to loosen considerably. For example, in the boom of 2006 and early 2007, nearly all publicly traded companies were considered to be possible LBO candidates.

In difficult times, credit is tight and LBOs are few. Private equity firms try to keep their employees busy by focusing on the operating performance of current portfolio companies. Sometimes, private equity firms will use their available capital to buy the debt of portfolio companies that banks have not been able to sell. PE firms desperate to make investments sometimes do non-control investments in public companies, referred to as PIPEs (private investment in public equity).

As of this writing (late 2012), the current private equity environment is rather peculiar. While high yield debt is booming, LBO activity is slow. However, PE firms are sitting on an enormous amount of commitments from funds that they raised during boom times, and this money has to be spent before the commitments expire. This access to money is known as dry powder. PE firms have an incentive to do deals so that they do not lose the fees (typically 2 percent) associated with managing the money or have difficulty raising future funds. Therefore, we are likely to see more LBO activity, and especially a lot of activity trading on the secondary market, which refers to PE firms buying from another PE firm. Of course, profligate acquisitions during uncertain economic times are likely to lead to subpar returns down the road.

LBO MODELING

Now that we have discussed the background of private equity and leveraged buyouts, we are ready to talk about the kind of analysis that bankers and private equity professionals perform when analyzing LBOs.

LBO models are built for a variety of circumstances and not only by the firm or advisers contemplating an LBO. Private equity firms and the investment bankers that advise them build LBO models for the purpose of analyzing potential investment returns. In addition, investment bankers advising on a sell-side M&A assignment often build LBO models to help get a sense for the value that a financial buyer might pay for the company being sold. Moreover, bankers advising a strategic buyer on a buy-side transaction might use an LBO analysis to analyze how much a competing buyer might bid should the competitor be a private equity firm. Finally, lenders and investors in the company's debt, such as banks and hedge funds, will want to analyze their returns and also be comfortable that the target company will be able to service its debt.

Specifically, there are three primary analyses for which an LBO model is useful:

1. What is the internal rate of return (IRR) to the private equity firm and to other equity holders?
2. How do the credit statistics look over time and do they improve?
3. How much is a company worth? (Valuation based on the LBO analysis is often considered the fourth valuation methodology.)

Steps for Creating an LBO Model

An LBO model is based on the type of integrated cash flow model that we learned how to build in Chapter 6, with some additional assumptions layered on and some additional analysis. Just as with an integrated cash flow model, an LBO model can be relatively simple and short, or highly detailed and complex. Either way, however, the concepts and the mechanics are the same.

Following are the basic steps needed in order to build an LBO model. Like we discussed in Chapter 6, it is very unlikely that you will ever be asked to list the six steps, but you should be able to walk an interviewer through the general process. Note that we will not discuss the final step since it is similar to what we covered in Chapter 6.

1. Input purchase and exit assumptions.
2. Input "sources" and "uses."
3. Create the pro forma balance sheet.
4. Project the three financial statements and other necessary schedules (with appropriate assumptions), stress-test, and check the model.
5. Perform the various LBO analyses, including the investment returns to the financial sponsor (and other equity holders), credit statistics, and valuation.
6. Run sensitivity analysis and any other output analysis.

Step 1: Purchase and Exit Assumptions

The first step in building our LBO model is to make assumptions for how much money the private equity firm will pay for the target and how the target will be valued when the private firm exits its investment. We generally refer to these as the purchase and exit assumptions. Remember the basic business model of a leveraged buyout is to purchase a company and then sell or IPO the company five or so years in the future.

Purchase Assumptions In a real LBO transaction, the purchase price will likely be negotiated between the buyer and the seller after extensive due diligence. However, for most LBO models that bankers build, we will need to make an assumption for the purchase price based on a valuation exercise. In a typical LBO analysis, we assume that the private equity firm purchases 100 percent of the target's equity (though, as we will discuss later, it will likely not keep all 100 percent). We have two choices for how to calculate purchase price, based either on a valuation multiple or based on a premium to the current stock price.

The first method is to estimate the purchase price using some valuation multiple, such as an LTM EBITDA multiple. This is generally what we would do when performing an LBO analysis on a privately held target or a division of a larger company. If we use this method, we are estimating enterprise value, and we need to calculate the equity value using the enterprise value formula (for simplicity, ignoring any preferred stock and noncontrolling interest):

$$\text{Equity Value} = \text{Enterprise Value} - \text{Debt} + \text{Cash}$$

The second method, useful for analyzing a potential LBO in a publicly traded company, is to estimate the purchase price based on some acquisition premium. For example, let's say that we think a buyer will need to pay a 25 percent premium in order for the target's board of directors and shareholders to agree to the deal. In this case, to do the deal the purchase price will need to be 25 percent above today's market capitalization.

Exit Assumptions There are two primary exit assumptions. The first is the timing of the exit and the second is the method with which we will use to calculate the value upon an exit. A typical LBO analysis assumes a five-year holding period, though this is one of the variables that we will often want to sensitize. A typical LBO analysis also assumes that the exit valuation is based on some multiple such as an EBITDA multiple, based on the last year's EBITDA. We call this the exit multiple.

A standard assumption is to assume that the EBITDA multiple implied by the purchase price is exactly equal to the EBITDA exit multiple. In other words, we are not forecasting any multiple expansion or contraction. However, if we think that the purchase multiple is abnormally or cyclically high or low, we may alter this assumption. We will always want to sensitize both the purchase and exit assumptions, as they have significant impact on our analysis.

Step 2: Sources and Uses

Once we have assumed the purchase and exit assumptions, the next step is to account for what are known as the transaction's sources and uses. Sources represent the various types of funds that will be used to effectuate the transaction. Uses are the different things for which the funds will be used. Even though we typically refer to these assumptions as "sources and uses," we will discuss uses first since, as we will see, the sources actually are dependent on the uses. However, keep in mind that in our LBO analysis, sources must exactly equal uses.

Uses of Funds The most significant requirement for funds in a typical LBO is to buy out all of the equity of the existing shareholders—in other words, for the purchase price. However, in order to consummate an LBO, funds need to be raised not only for just the purchase price but also for a number of other things. Investment banking and other transaction fees will have to be paid, and often some or all the target company's existing debt will need to be refinanced.

Purchase Price We have already discussed in the previous section the two different methods for estimating the purchase price. In our analysis, in the table of uses, we need only to link to the total purchase price assumption. If we have estimated purchase price on a per share basis using an acquisition premium then we need to multiply the per share purchase price by the number of fully diluted shares. When calculating fully diluted shares, we need to make sure to account for all in the money stock options based on the purchase price, not the current stock price, and we need to account for both the options that have vested already and those that have not, since all options will vest upon the consummation of the LBO.

Transaction Fees We will typically make some assumptions for the transaction fees. For example, we will assume that the investment bankers will receive an M&A fee equal to some percentage of the purchase price as well as a typically larger financing fee equal to a percentage of the debt being raised. There may be other fees as well such as those paid to consultants, accountants, or lawyers.

Existing Debt to Be Refinanced In a typical LBO transaction, some or all of the target's existing debt will need to be refinanced as part of the transaction. This is because it is often written into the credit agreements or bond indentures that debt will automatically mature upon such a transaction. To properly estimate the amount of existing debt that needs to be refinanced, we need to go through the credit agreements and indentures for the company's existing debt. As a rule of thumb, bank credit facilities will nearly always be refinanced, and bonds and other types of debt may or may not have to be refinanced, depending on the covenants in the bond indenture or credit agreement.

While this does not affect the analysis, it is interesting to note that the target's publicly traded debt that does not need to refinanced will often trade down following the announcement and subsequent consummation of a LBO. This is because in a typical LBO, the target is much more highly levered post-transaction than it was pre-transaction. For this reason, it is often said that LBOs are good for shareholders, since the shareholders typically receive an acquisition premium over the current share price, but bad for bondholders, since the company is now much riskier and will likely have a lower credit rating.

Sources of Funds Once we know the amount of funds needed to complete the LBO (the uses), we can consider the various sources of funds. There are three general categories of possible sources: existing cash from the target's balance sheet, new debt, and money contributed by the investment fund managed by the private equity firm.

Cash from the Balance Sheet If the target has excess cash on its balance sheet that it does not require for working capital or other ordinary operational functions, then we will likely want to use it as one of the sources of funds.

New Debt The largest source of funds in the transaction is typically new debt. Often new debt will make up 60–70 percent of the post-transaction capital structure. As is probably obvious, the magnitude of debt used to execute the transaction is exactly why this kind of transaction is referred to as a leveraged buyout. When contemplating the debt in our sources of funds table, there are really two basic questions that we must consider: How much debt can be raised? And what are the different types of debt that can be raised?

The capital markets will dictate the amounts and types of debt that can be raised. As we discussed earlier in this chapter, the amount of debt that can be raised for a leveraged buyout is highly dependent on the state of the credit markets. The private equity firm typically wants to leverage the transaction as much as possible (as much as the business's cash flow and the lenders will allow).

Investment bankers performing an LBO analysis will need to estimate the transaction's capital structure. Bankers working on live transactions will be able to get guidance from their firm's leveraged finance group, who should have a good idea of the market's current appetite for debt. Otherwise, bankers can examine recent LBO deals done in the same industry to estimate an appropriate capital structure.

As you might expect, one goal of raising transaction debt is to keep the overall blended cost of debt as low as possible. This implies maximizing the amount of secured debt such as bank debt and minimizing the amount of more expensive, unsecured debt. However, companies must also make sure that they can afford the required interest payments. Sometimes companies are actually better off sacrificing cheaper bank debt, which requires cash interest payments for more expensive debt that allows interest payments to be deferred for several years.

There are a number of different types of debt that will be part of a typical LBO capital structure. Most companies will raise senior secured debt in the form of a revolving credit facility and one or more term loans. This debt will typically be syndicated to a number of banks. In addition, companies may raise money through issuing high yield bonds as well as mezzanine debt.

Debt may be raised in the private markets (for example, from hedge funds or mezzanine funds) or in the public markets (through high-yield bonds). Often, unsecured lenders will also receive equity in the company in the form of warrants in order to meet the lender's required rate of return but still keep the company's required cash interest payments manageable. A typical LBO model will analyze the expected investment return to the lenders, who receive warrants, in addition to the return to the financial sponsor.

Equity Contribution from the PE Fund (Sponsor's Equity)

During normal credit markets, lenders will typically require the financial sponsor to provide equity comprising of approximately 30 to 40 percent of the company's capitalization. As we have said previously, the less the equity contribution from the sponsor, the higher the investment returns will be, other things equal. To figure out how much the sponsor must contribute to the deal is actually very easy, once we have made all of the other assumptions in our sources and uses table.

Recall that by definition uses must equal sources. In fact in our model, we expressly make them equal by setting sources to equal uses. Since we have already figured out our uses, at this point we also know our total sources. And because we have already figured out how much cash we will use from the balance sheet and how much debt we will raise, the only missing number is the equity contribution. This becomes the plug to make the equation work and represents the amount being funded by the private equity firm. Exhibit 8.3 shows an example of such a sources and uses table.

Step 3: The Pro Forma Balance Sheet

Once we have made all of our assumptions for our sources and uses table, the next step is create what we call the pro forma balance sheet. At the moment the transaction is effectuated, the balance sheet of the acquired company will change. This revised balance sheet is called the pro forma balance sheet. Note that this process is very similar to what is done for M&A modeling.

To create the pro forma balance sheet, we start with the balance sheet as it exists immediately prior to the transaction. If we are doing our analysis based on publicly available information, then we typically start with the latest available balance sheet from the most recent 10-K or 10-Q. We will typically set up three or four columns in our analysis: the original balance

EXHIBIT 8.3 Example of a Sources and Uses Table

Total Uses		Total Sources			
Uses		Capitalization	Amount Funded	EBITDA Multiple	% of Capitalization
Equity Purchase Price	$5,500.0	Available Cash	$250.0		
Debt Refinanced	1,500.0				
Transaction Fees @ 1.0%	55.0	Revolver	0.0	0.0x	0.0%
Financing Fees @ 2.0%	90.0	Term Loan	2,500.0	2.5x	36.3%
		Total Senior Debt	2,500.0	2.5x	36.3%
		Second Lien	500.0	0.5x	7.3%
		Unsecured Notes	1,500.0	1.5x	21.8%
		Total Debt	4,500.0	4.5x	65.3%
		Sponsor Equity	2,395.0		34.7%
Total Uses	$7,145.0	Total Sources	$7,145.0		100.0%

sheet, the adjustments (sometimes two columns: one for positive adjustments and one for negative ones), and the new (pro forma) balance sheet.

Following are many of the most common adjustments that need to be made when creating a pro forma balance sheet for an LBO analysis.

Cash If we assumed that excess cash will be used as a source of funds for the transaction, then we will need to reduce cash on the balance sheet by that same amount. We can link this adjustment to cash from the sources section of the sources and uses table. Remember to make the adjustment a negative number since we are reducing the cash balance.

Deferred Financing Fees Accounting rules allow the financing fee (though not the M&A transaction fee) to be amortized over time. You will need to add the deferred finance fee to the balance sheet by linking it to the uses section of the sources and uses table.

Goodwill Goodwill will like need to be created in the pro forma balance sheet. Just as we discussed in Chapter 2, goodwill is equal to the equity purchase price less the fair market value of the company's identifiable assets and liabilities.

Assuming no identifiable intangible assets other than the deferred financing fee and no changes to tangible asset value, we can calculate the adjustment to goodwill as the equity purchase price less the company's prior book value.

Existing Debt Existing debt that gets refinanced needs to be eliminated. This can be linked to the uses section of the sources and uses table.

New Debt New debt raised for the transaction needs to be added. This can also be linked to the sources section of the sources and uses table. As we discussed in Chapter 6, it makes modeling easier if each type of debt has its own row in the balance sheet.

Existing Equity Assuming that the sponsor is purchasing 100 percent of existing equity, all existing equity will be eliminated. So each line is adjusted to zero. This includes all equity accounts in the balance sheet; even retained earnings is set to zero.

New Equity New equity contributed by the financial sponsor needs to be added. This can also be linked from the sources section of the sources and uses table. You should also subtract from this figure the amount of the M&A transaction fee (but not the financing fee), which can also be linked to from the uses section of the source and uses table.

Balancing the Pro Forma Balance Sheet For each line item of the balance sheet, start with the most recent actual balance sheet, and then add and subtract any adjustments. The pro forma balance sheet should balance. If it does not balance, then there are one or more mistakes. Exhibit 8.4 shows an example of a pro forma balance sheet with the adjustments.

Step 4: Creating the Model

Once we have created our pro forma balance sheet, we are ready to actually create the forecasts of the three statements. We will not repeat the process in detail here, since it involves the same steps we learned in Chapter 6. We model the income statement, balance sheet, cash flow statement, debt schedule, and any other supporting schedules that we need. Remember that the debt schedule should have one section for each of the new types of debt raised in the acquisition.

It is important to keep in mind a few things when creating the model. The new pro forma balance sheet must be the balance sheet from which the projections are based. Remember to include any new amortization, including the amortization of deferred finance fees in the income statement and cash flow

EXHIBIT 8.4 Example of a Pro Forma Balance Sheet

	Actual	Adjustments		Pro forma
	12/31/12	+	–	12/31/12
ASSETS				
Current assets				
Cash and cash equivalents	$500.0		($250.0)	$250.0
Accounts receivable	850.0			850.0
Inventories	1,200.0			1,200.0
Deferred tax assets	50.0			50.0
Prepaid expenses and other	175.0			175.0
Total current assets	**2,775.0**			**2,525.0**
Property and equipment, gross	3,800.0			3,800.0
Less: accumulated depreciation	(1,500.0)			(1,500.0)
Property and equipment, net	2,300.0			2,300.0
Deferred tax assets	60.0			60.0
Goodwill	800.0	2,740.0	(800.0)	2,740.0
Intangible assets, net	300.0			300.0
Deferred financing fees		90.0		90.0
Other assets	250.0			250.0
Total assets	**6,485.0**			**8,265.0**
LIABILITIES AND STOCKHOLDERS' EQUITY				
Current liabilities				
Accounts payable	575.0			575.0
Income tax payable	75.0			75.0
Accrued expenses and other	400.0			400.0
Short-term debt (revolving credit facility)	0.0			0.0
Total current liabilities	**1,050.0**			**1,050.0**

(*continued*)

EXHIBIT 8.4 (*Continued*)

	Actual	Adjustments		Pro forma
	12/31/12	+	–	12/31/12
Existing long-term debt	1,500.0		(1,500.0)	0.0
Term loan		2,500.0		2,500.0
Second lien debt		500.0		500.0
Unsecured Notes		1,500.0		1,500.0
Other non-current liabilities	375.0			375.0
Total liabilities	**2,925.0**			**5,925.0**
Stockholders' equity				
Old equity	3,560.0		(3,560.0)	0.0
New equity		2,340.0		2,340.0
Total stockholders' equity	**3,560.0**			**2,340.0**
Total liabilities and stockholders' equity	**6,485.0**			**8,265.0**
Check	*0.000*			*0.000*

statement. Make sure to exclude existing debt that has been refinanced, as it no longer exists, and to include all new types of debt in all of the statements. Just like we did in Chapter 6, once the model is built, stress-test it, check it for mistakes, and analyze the assumptions to make sure they are realistic.

Step 5: LBO Analysis

Once we are confident that we have a solid working model that is based on the purchase assumptions, the sources and uses table, and the pro forma balance sheet, then we are ready to build and run the various LBO analyses. Remember that, broadly speaking, there are three types of analysis that bankers typically run based on the LBO model:

1. Investment returns to the financial sponsor and other equity investors.
2. Credit analysis.
3. Valuation.

Internal Rate of Return (IRR) Analysis The most important analysis based on the LBO is typically the investment returns to the private equity firm. We typically measure investment returns using the internal rate of return (IRR). Remember from Chapter 3 that the IRR reflects the annualized compounded percentage return rate based on the time-weighted cash flows. Also recall that IRR is calculated by solving for r in the following equation:

$$0 = \frac{CF_1}{(1+r)^1} + \frac{CF_2}{(1+r)^2} + \frac{CF_3}{(1+r)^3} + \frac{CF_4}{(1+r)^4} + \cdots + \frac{CF_t}{(1+r)^t}$$

Excel can easily calculate the IRR using the IRR or XIRR functions, as we mentioned in Chapter 3. The difference is that the IRR function assumes all cash flows are exactly one period apart, while the XIRR function is more powerful and allows cash flows at any dates. For LBO analysis, we typically use XIRR so we can be more precise with the timing of cash flows.

The financial sponsor's IRR analysis accounts for all cash flows to and from the financial sponsor (other than management fees):

- Initial equity investment.
- Any additional equity investments.
- Dividends.
- Proceeds from exit of investment (sale or IPO).

We need to make sure to account for the financial sponsor's ownership only. Typically, management will receive equity in the form of warrants, and unsecured lenders may also receive equity in the form of warrants. In fact, as part of our investment return analysis, we will typically also calculate the returns to unsecured lenders based on them receiving interest payments and equity value upon on exit due to the warrants.

Exhibit 8.5 shows an example of the investment returns to the financial sponsor based upon certain exit assumptions (also shown).

Multiple of Investment (MOI) Analysis In addition to the IRR, we often also show another measure of investment return called the multiple of investment (MOI). MOI equals the sponsor's equity value at exit divided by the sponsor's equity capital invested:

$$MOI = \frac{\text{Equity Value at Exit}}{\text{Equity Invested}}$$

EXHIBIT 8.5 Example of IRR Analysis

Exit Assumption	
Exit Date	12/31/2017
Transaction EBITDA Multiple	8.0x
2017 EBITDA	$1,250.0
Transaction Enterprise Value	**10,000.0**
Less: Debt	(2,500.0)
Plus: Cash	250.0
Less: Transaction Fees @ 1%	(100.0)
Equity Selling Price	7,650.0
Financial Sponsor Ownership %	95.0%
Financial Sponsor Sellout	$7,267.5

IRR Analyis						
	12/31/2012	**12/31/2013**	**12/31/2014**	**12/31/2015**	**12/31/2016**	**12/31/2017**
Sponsor Equity Investment	($2,395.0)					
Dividends		$0.0	$0.0	$0.0	$0.0	$0.0
Additional Investment		0.0	0.0	0.0	0.0	0.0
Financial Sponsor Sellout						7,267.5
Cash Flow to Sponsor	($2,395.0)	$0.0	$0.0	$0.0	$0.0	$7,267.5
IRR	**24.8%**					

Key Drivers of IRR A number of factors will affect the IRR to the financial sponsor. In fact, a common interview question is to be asked the various factors that might increase (or decrease) a private equity firm's IRR. Following are the important model drivers that will increase the sponsor's rate of return.

Reduce the Purchase Price Reducing the purchase price of the acquisition will increase the rate of return even if the exit multiple realized upon the investment exit is reduced accordingly to match the entrance multiple. Due to the nature of present value embedded in the IRR formula, the lower investment amount required by the financial sponsor more than offsets the lower exit amount on a present value basis.

Increase the Amount of Leverage Increasing the amount of debt used to finance the transaction, other things equal, reduces the amount of equity that the financial sponsor must contribute. This has a direct effect of increasing the IRR to the sponsor.

Increase the Exit Multiple Increasing the price for which the company sells when the PE firm exits its investment (i.e., increase the assumed exit multiple) results in the sponsor receiving more money upon exit, thus increasing returns.

Increase the Company's Growth Rate Increasing the company's growth rate in order to raise operating income, cash flow, or EBITDA in the projections will raise the enterprise value and equity value upon the sponsor's exit, thus increasing returns.

Decrease the Company's Cost Structure Decreasing the company's costs in order to raise operating income, cash flow, or EBITDA in the projections will also raise the enterprise value and equity value upon exit, also increasing the sponsor's returns.

Exit the Investment Sooner Other things equal, exiting the investment sooner will increase the sponsor's IRR due to the nature of present value.

IRR Sensitivity Analysis Just like we learned for the accretion/dilution analysis in Chapter 7, bankers will typically run sensitivity analysis on the private equity firm's IRR and MOI based on a number of variables, including:

- Purchase price.
- Exit multiple.

- Amount of debt raised.
- Operating growth rates (e.g., revenue growth).
- Operating costs (i.e., SG&A/revenue).

We can run this sensitivity analysis using Microsoft Excel's table functionality just as we did for the DCF in Chapter 5 and accretion/dilution analysis in Chapter 7, by having Excel vary two variables at a time. Note that in a very detailed LBO analysis, we might build our model with several scenarios using multiple sets of assumptions.

Analyzing Credit Statistics The second key type of analysis that is frequently performed when building an LBO model is credit analysis. Credit analysis is important to the investment banker, to the financial sponsor, and to the lenders in the transaction, all of which need to be confident that the company being acquired will be able to meet its ongoing interest obligations and also stay within the covenants of its credit agreements and indentures.

Obviously the company will be highly levered "out of the gate," but lenders will want to see the leverage come down over time. Therefore, it is important to analyze the credit statistics of the company for each year over the projection period and see the trends of various credit statistics. The key credit statistics typically analyzed include the debt to capitalization ratio, leverage ratios, and interest coverage ratios. In addition, industry-specific credit ratios may also be important.

Remember from our discussion of credit ratios in Chapter 4 that often a number of different calculations can be utilized for the various ratios.

Debt to Capitalization Ratio One of the easiest ratios to calculate is the debt to capitalization ratio. This ratio should decline through the projection period as debt is paid off.

Leverage Ratios Bankers typically calculate a number of different leverage ratios for each year of the projections. Leverage ratios should also decline over the projection period as debt is paid off, but also as EBITDA increases because of anticipated revenue growth or cost-cutting measures. Remember that bankers will often calculate leverage ratios using various proxies for cash flow including not just EBITDA, but also EBITDA less capital expenditures and other cash needs. The numerator of the leverage ratios may use total debt and/or net debt. Moreover, leverage ratios are sometimes also calculated for just certain types of debt just as senior debt or senior secured debt (i.e., senior debt/EBITDA).

Interest Coverage Ratio Just like leverage ratios, various interest coverage ratios will be calculated. Interest coverage ratios should increase over time through the projection period as EBITDA increases and as interest expense declines due to debt being retired or due to debt being refinanced at lower interest rates. Just as we use various metrics for the numerator, the denominator of the interest coverage ratio may use total interest expense, cash interest expense, and/or net interest expense.

LBO Valuation The third type of analysis performed by investment bankers building an LBO model is valuation. As we mentioned earlier in this chapter, an LBO analysis is sometimes considered the fourth primary valuation methodology in the context of an M&A assignment. Remember that an LBO valuation is used not only by bankers on the buy side of a deal to advise a client as to what price to pay, but also by bankers on the sell side of the deal to advise a client on how much various financial buyers might be able and willing to pay.

Required Assumptions In order to use the LBO model for purposes of valuation, bankers need to make four important assumptions. These assumptions are in addition to all of the operating assumptions, such as revenue growth and margins, that have already been built into the model. Note that with the exception of the required sponsor IRR, the other assumptions are the same as those that need to be made when analyzing the financial sponsor's rate of return. The four key assumptions are:

1. Amount of debt raised in the transaction.
2. Exit multiple.
3. Time until investment exit.
4. Required return (IRR) to the financial sponsor.

Amount of Debt Raised In the Transaction The first assumption that bankers need to make is the amount of debt that can be raised as part of the leveraged buyout. Bankers will typically assume that this is based on some appropriate leverage ratio commensurate with the current credit market conditions.

Exit Multiple The second key assumption to make is the exit multiple for which the company will be able to be sold for some years in the future. As we discussed earlier in the chapter when we covered the IRR analysis, a typical assumption is for the exit multiple to equal today's appropriate multiple. We often use an EV/LTM EBITDA multiple as the type of valuation multiple unless a more appropriate multiple is warranted based on the industry.

Time until Investment Exit The other assumption relating to the sponsor's exit from the investment is the timing. Typically, bankers assume that an exit will occur five years after the initial investment, but, like all assumptions, this one can be sensitized.

Financial Sponsor's Required IRR The final assumption is really the most important one. This is the minimum IRR required by the private equity firm for this investment or, alternatively, the sponsor's target IRR. Bankers will typically perform the LBO valuation analysis using a range of required IRRs.

Valuation Analysis By combining the LBO model with the four key assumptions just discussed, bankers can back into the amount of equity that the financial sponsor can afford to contribute as part of the purchase price. Once we have determined the sponsor's maximum equity contribution, we can easily calculate the implied purchase price and the enterprise value based on that implied purchase price. And, as we mentioned, bankers will typically sensitize several of the inputs to concluding a range of values.

As an example, let us assume that a private equity firm requires a 20 percent IRR in order to be interested in pursuing the acquisition. Further suppose that we have already built an operating model that shows $1 billion of EBITDA in the exit year, which will be five years from now. Let's also assume that the appropriate exit multiple will be 7x EBITDA and that, at the exit, the company will have $3 billion of net debt on its balance sheet. To keep our analysis simpler, assume that the private equity firm owns 100 percent of the equity of the company and assume no transaction fees upon an exit.

Based on these assumptions, we know that the company will be sold for $7 billion in five years. Given net debt of $3 billion, this implies that the sponsor's equity will be worth $4 billion upon exit. In order to calculate the amount of money that the sponsor can put into the deal, we can use the following formula:

$$\text{Investment Amount} = \frac{\text{Exit Amount}}{(1+\text{IRR})^{t}}$$

t = years until an exit.

Using our assumptions, we can calculate the sponsor's investment as:

$$\text{Investment Amount} = \frac{\$4 \text{ billion}}{(1+.2)^{5}} = \$1.6 \text{ billion}$$

Therefore, in order to generate a 20 percent IRR, the sponsor will need to invest approximately $1.6 billion.

Now, let's assume that the company's current EBITDA is $500 million and that the credit markets will allow a leverage ratio based on total debt to EBITDA of 4.0x. Therefore, $2 billion of debt will be able to be raised to help finance the transaction. To make our calculation easier, assume the company has no excess cash today and no existing debt, and let's also ignore transaction fees. We can now calculate an implied purchase price today of $3.6 billion ($2 billion of debt plus $1.6 billion of sponsor equity) based on a very simple LBO analysis and our key assumptions.

LBO CONCLUSIONS: DO WE DO THE DEAL?

As a conclusion to this chapter, let us consider one final idea. Suppose we work for a private equity firm contemplating an acquisition and we have completed our LBO analysis. How should we decide whether or not to do the deal?

On the one hand, we could make an easy decision and say that if our expected IRR is higher than our firm's target IRR then we should pursue the deal. Similarity, based on our LBO valuation, we could say that we can bid up to an amount that makes our expected IRR equal to our target IRR. While this is what finance theory may dictate, in the real world of private equity boardrooms, things are much more complicated.

The first question we need to ask is how comfortable we feel about the financial projections and the various assumptions underlying the LBO model. Are they realistic, or, more likely, overly optimistic? Do the projections assume significant cost reductions or higher revenue growth? Second, how do we feel about the level of risk inherent in the business? What would happen if we enter into a recession? What if the company loses a big customer? Will the company be able to support the debt level under any and all circumstances? Third, how do we feel about the exit multiple? Is it aggressive or conservative? And will there be sufficient buyer interest when it is time to exit? Are there strategic buyers that might pay a high price, or will the process be less competitive? Alternatively, will the company make a strong IPO candidate?

While IRR and valuation are important criteria when assessing whether to pursue an LBO transaction, often non-economic considerations play a crucial role as well. For example, sponsors might pay less attention to standalone returns if the target will be an add-on to another portfolio company. Or, perhaps the company being acquired will be used as a platform to then make bolt-on acquisitions.

Just as CEOs make acquisitions for lots of reasons other than purely maximizing shareholder value, as we discussed in Chapter 7, so do private equity firms. In fact, senior private equity professionals tend to have egos that dwarf even CEOs'. This can lead PE firms to pursue acquisitions to prevent competitors from making the same deal or to show a certain leadership position within the private equity industry. Moreover, often private equity firms make acquisitions of companies that are considered glamorous. Who really cares about investment returns when owning a company can get you invited to fashion shows or allow you to hobnob with celebrities? And in any case, if limited partners complain, they can just be invited along, too. Lastly, sometimes a private equity firm just has to put money to work so it does not lose significant management fees.

END-OF-CHAPTER QUESTIONS

1. What is an LBO?
2. Why do private equity firms do LBOs?
3. What makes a good LBO candidate?
4. What would be a bad LBO candidate?
5. What are key assumptions that go into making an LBO model?
6. What is an LBO model used for?
7. Walk me through an LBO model.
8. How do we use an LBO model for valuation?
9. How might we increase the IRR to a PE firm?
10. How do sources and uses work?
11. How do we create the pro forma balance sheet?
12. What are some considerations to whether a PE firm should do the deal?
13. What are some key credit statistics used when analyzing an LBO?

Answers can be found at www.wiley.com/go/gutmann (password: investment).

CHAPTER 9

Recruiting, Interviewing, and Landing the Job

So you've read through this book. You should have a good understanding of what investment bankers do and what you will do as a banker. You should feel comfortable with the fundamental principles of accounting and finance. You should be familiar with financial statement analysis. You should understand the importance of valuation and be able to talk about each of the three primary valuation methodologies. You should have a grasp of how to build an integrated financial model. And you should be able to converse about a banker's role in executing M&A and LBO transactions.

In short, you should now have the basic technical skills required of junior investment bankers. In fact, you are well on your way to becoming a banker. But learning the technical skills is relatively easy. Recruiting, on the other hand, is hard. Now you need to focus on the recruiting process. Now the real challenge begins.

In order to get interviews, you will need to make your resume stand out. You will need to start networking with investment banking professionals and set up informational interviews. Do that well and you will secure interviews. But of course, landing interviews is only half the battle.

You need to nail your interviews. As important as technical questions are in an interview, fit questions are even more important. You need to be able to walk through your resume, talk about your strengths, and have great answers for why you want to be an investment banker and why you are interested in a particular firm. Interview well, and you will convert those interviews into offers and you will be an investment banker.

In this final chapter we will talk about recruiting and interviewing. We will start with a discussion of what investment banks are looking for when hiring the two most junior-level positions, analysts and associates. Then we will talk about the recruiting process, including networking and informational interviews. Next we will move on to the interview process, where we will focus on the two main types of interview questions—fit and technical. Finally, we will wrap up the chapter, and the book, with a discussion of how to choose among multiple offers and how to start your career as a great junior investment banker.

WHAT ARE INVESTMENT BANKS LOOKING FOR?

Before we begin talking about the recruiting and interviewing processes, let's start with a discussion of what investment banks are looking for when they are hiring new bankers. In other words, on what factors will you be judged? We will focus on analysts and associates since those are the two most common entry points into the industry.

When an investment banker meets with a candidate, either at a networking event, in an informational interview, or in an actual interview, the banker has two questions in his or her mind. The first and more important question is: Would I, the banker, want this individual working for me? In other words, will he or she do a good job? Does this person have the right attitude? Does he or she have the requisite intellectual capabilities and possess the necessary technical foundation?

The second question is: Would I want to work with the candidate? This is what is known as the "airport test." If I were stuck with the candidate in an airport for five hours waiting for a delayed flight, would I enjoy his or her company, or would I want nothing to do with him or her? Would the candidate be fun to have a beer with or would the conversation be dreadfully boring?

We stated in Chapter 1 that junior bankers are essentially commodities. One of the implications of this fact is that most candidates from well-regarded undergraduate institutions and graduate business schools are intellectually capable of doing the job of an investment banker. It is attitude and work ethic that are differentiating. For the investment bank, the recruiting process is one of trying to identify the candidates that have the highest probabilities of being successful investment bankers, and weeding out those candidates who are less likely to succeed. In fact, the latter—eliminating candidates, is usually much easier for recruiters than the former.

In this section, we will discuss the specific criteria by which candidates for analyst and associate positions are measured and evaluated. I have listed these criteria in what I believe to be their general order of importance.

Prior Achievement

As we discussed in Chapter 1, junior investment bankers are expected to do excellent work under stressful conditions and long hours while maintaining a great attitude. To measure a candidate's likelihood of meeting these requirements, prospective bankers are judged on their achievements to date. Of course, you can mention in an interview how you are willing to work hard and your great attitude, but you need to be able to demonstrate and support those statements with what you have actually achieved over the course of your adult life so far.

For undergraduate students applying for analyst positions, one of the primary ways in which your achievements are measured is your grades. However, extracurricular activities and internships are important, too. For MBA students applying for associate positions, grades and extracurricular activities are less important, but your prior work experience and your professional achievements are paramount.

Grades There is a common misconception among undergraduate level candidates recruiting for analyst positions that the primary reason why grades and grade point average (GPA) are valued by bankers is to measure a candidate's intelligence or aptitude in certain subjects. This is not the case. Grades are used as a proxy for whether the candidate has the attitude, drive, and work ethic that it takes to be a good banker, not just the intellectual capabilities.

In order to get a 4.0 GPA, you need to get A's in all of your classes, not just the classes in your major and not just the finance classes that you liked or found interesting. To achieve a very high GPA means you did well even when you didn't like the class or the professor, even when you were feeling ill during the final, even when you just broke up with your boyfriend or girlfriend. This kind of perseverance and attitude are what makes a great investment banker, especially at the analyst level. As a banker, you need to do solid work even when you are sick or tired, even when you don't like your associate or VP, and even when you find the work incredibly boring.

Of course, it does not mean that you cannot succeed in the recruiting process if you have less-than-stellar grades, but you do face an uphill battle. A low GPA is a red flag to recruiters, possibly indicative of a weaker work ethic, poorer attitude, and less maturity. To overcome this handicap, you will need to have good explanations for why your grades are weaker than those of your peers. Perhaps your grades suffered because you worked a full-time job while you were in school or you had to take time off because of illness or family emergency, or if you played a sport at a high level. However, even with these valid explanations, you should expect some pushback from bankers through the recruiting process since, as an investment banker, you will be expected to do high quality work regardless of the circumstances.

Extracurricular Activities, Internships, and Work Experience In addition to grades, a candidate is judged on extracurricular activities, internships, and, in the case of MBA students, especially prior work experience. Just as with grades, bankers are looking for indications that you have worked hard, have excelled, and have shown an ability to manage many things at once.

As we just mentioned, it is great if you earned a high grade point average. However, if you received excellent grades while also holding a job and being a leader in various extracurricular activities, then that is even better. Do your extracurricular activities show leadership or any special awards or recognition? Have you made real time commitments, or did you just spend a couple of hours so you could pad your resume? Did you stick with things for a while or do things for a short period of time? All of these items help to demonstrate that you have the work ethic and attitude to be a great junior banker.

For MBA students, work experience is one of the most important criteria in showing that you have the right attitude and mentality. Did you work in a high-stress environment similar to banking, or has your work experience been more relaxed and laid back? Do you have experience dealing with difficult clients in challenging circumstances? Have you had real responsibilities, or were you always the most junior person on a project? Have you had to juggle multiple projects at one time? Did you get promoted, or were you stuck in the same position for three or four years? And did you win any awards or receive any recognition because of your work performance? These are the kinds of questions that will be asked of you, and the kinds of experiences that will help you demonstrate that you have what it takes to be an investment banking associate.

Interest in Being an Investment Banker

After achievement, the next most important criterion on which you will be evaluated is your interest and passion for being an investment banker. Remember that a recruiter's attitude is that most candidates from good schools are qualified to do the job. But the ones who want it the most will work the hardest. Moreover, at the associate level, those are also the candidates who are most likely to view investment banking as a career rather than just use banking as a learning experience and for the exit opportunities.

You will need to demonstrate your interest and your passion in a number of different ways. To a large extent, your interest level will be established by the answers you give in informational interviews and in interviews. As we will discuss when we get to interviewing, one of the most important questions you will be asked is why you want to be a banker. You will need to demonstrate that you are indeed highly interested and not just going through the motions, that you have done your homework, that you really know what you are getting into, and that you are you doing it for the right reasons.

In addition to your interview answers, your motivation will also be measured by how much time and effort you put into the recruiting process. You need to show this through the entire recruiting process. The more you network and the more people you meet, the more serious you are. Did you go to all the events? Did you reach out on your own to bankers to do informational interviews? Are you knowledgeable about the firm? All of these criteria will be used by the investment bank to evaluate you.

Finally, your level of interest will be measured by your knowledge of the technical skills of investment banking and of the industry in general. It is one thing to pay attention in your finance and accounting classes in school. However, as we have mentioned throughout the book, there are many differences to how things are actually done in investment banking. Demonstrating that you know how bankers do things (for example, how they value companies and how they build models) shows that you have gone above and beyond what you learn in school. This is especially true if you are not a business or finance major and have never taken finance or accounting classes. Obviously, having read this book, you should be in that position.

Intellectual Ability and Analytical Skills

Even though we have stated repeatedly that the job of an investment banker does not require extraordinary intellectual capabilities, you will still need to demonstrate at least a certain level of analytical skills and general smarts. Keep in mind that the goal of a recruiter or interviewer is not to find the most intelligent candidates necessarily, but to weed out those who do not have the abilities to do the job. This is especially true for analyst recruits.

You will be judged on your grades and grade point average, the quality of your undergraduate and/or graduate institution, the difficulty of your major, and your test scores such as the SAT or GMAT. At the undergraduate level, you may also be able to demonstrate your analytical skills through relevant extracurricular activities, school projects, or internships. At the associate level, your prior work experience can help you prove your merits, assuming your previous jobs required such skills. Lastly, to some extent, your intellectual capabilities and analytical skills will be tested by the technical questions that you will receive in the interview process.

Technical Knowledge

In addition to using technical knowledge to test whether you are serious about banking and have done your homework, bankers are also usually expected to come in with a proper foundation in finance and accounting. This will be measured mostly through the technical interview questions that you will be asked. However, to a certain extent, your technical knowledge will also be measured in general conversations and informational interviews that you have with bankers throughout the recruiting process. You need to sound knowledgeable about the work of a banker and should be informed about general investment banking activity and related current events.

All candidates are expected to have the basic finance and accounting knowledge, even liberal arts or engineering majors who have not taken any finance or accounting classes in school. There are enough resources (like this book!) that will give you that. Having said that, chances are you will be held to a higher standard as an undergrad business or finance major. For sure, MBA students are expected to have even a better technical skillset and base of knowledge than are undergraduates.

Communication Skills and Personality

Additional criteria on which candidates are evaluated are communications skills and general personality. To a large extent, being measured on such "softer" skills is a part of the airport test. Bankers want to know if you can hold a conversation—and, better yet, an interesting conversation. However, you are also judged on whether you have the skills and maturity to be presentable in front of a client. This is especially true for MBA candidates recruiting for associate positions. MBA students are also evaluated for whether they have the requisite people skills to be able to manage analysts, as well as the capabilities to develop leadership and sales skills that will make them an effective senior level banker down the road.

Obviously, these kinds of skills are easiest to assess in an interview setting. However, keep in mind that you will be appraised throughout the entire recruiting process and through all of the interactions you have with bankers at the firm and even the HR staff. Be thoughtful about how you present yourself throughout the networking process, at receptions, when doing informational interviews, and, of course, in actual interviews.

THE RECRUITING PROCESS

The recruiting process for most investment banks, including all of the bulge bracket banks and most of the larger boutiques, is highly formalized. There are various stages to the process, and your goal is to pass each stage. You should try to take each stage of the process one step at a time.

For instance, you will likely attend recruiting receptions and start networking with investment bankers. Your goal through this networking process is to get informational interviews. The goal of informational interviews is to be selected for first-round interviews. The goal of the first-round interview is to move onto to what is the second, and typically final, round of interviews. Finally, the goal of final-round interviews is to land an offer.

In this section, we will discuss the standard recruiting process for investment banking. We will start by covering some of the differences between recruiting for full-time positions and for summer internships. Then we will move on to a discussion of the on-campus recruiting process, for those of you who are at a target school for investment banks. Then we will discuss the recruiting process if you are not at a target school. Finally, we will talk about the recruiting process if you are trying to break into investment banking from another career or job. Note that this section is only meant to give you a general sense of the process. We will discuss each step in more detail later in the chapter.

Recruiting for Summer Internships

Most serious candidates for investment banking will start the recruiting process not for full-time investment banking positions but for summer internships. For undergraduate students, you will be seeking an investment banking internship for the summer between your junior and senior years. MBA students will be recruiting for an internship to take place between the first and second years of business school. Summer internships at reputable investment banks are always paid internships.

Especially in a challenging job market, securing a summer internship is almost mandatory for a candidate seeking an investment banking job. In fact, it has effectively become part of the formal recruiting process, especially since, in recent years, the majority of an investment bank's incoming analyst and associate classes have completed a summer internship at that bank.

The recruiting process for internship recruiting is very similar to the process for full-time recruiting. As we will discuss in greater detail later in the chapter, banks will come on campus for receptions, and you will need to network and do informational interviews. However, whereas interviews for full-time positions take place in the fall, interviews for summer internships generally occur in January and February. You also will usually have fewer total interviews at any given investment bank for summer internships than you will for full-time positions.

At the end of the summer, investment banks will typically offer a portion of the interns a full-time job. The percentage of interns given a full-time offer varies from year to year. First and foremost, the goal of doing a summer internship is to secure this full-time offer. But there are secondary goals as well. Doing the internship is a way to make sure that investment banking is really what you want to do after graduation. In addition, you want to learn as much as possible, gain as many skills as you can, and network with other bankers within the firm.

If you are not able to secure a summer internship in investment banking, or you decided that you wanted to be a banker too late to recruit for internships, all is not lost. You still have a shot at full-time recruiting. However, keep in mind that you are definitely at a disadvantage vis-à-vis candidates who have completed banking internships, and therefore you will have to work harder and likely put more effort into the full-time recruiting process. You will have to network more, and really demonstrate your desire and passion to be an investment banker. You will also have to be prepared to have a good answer for why you did not do an investment banking internship.

Off-Cycle Internships As we already mentioned, investment banking internships are very much a part of the full-time recruiting process. If, for whatever reason, you were not able to secure a summer internship in investment banking, then you may want to try to seek out an internship during the school year, which we sometimes refer to as an off-cycle internship. Doing such an internship helps demonstrate that you are very serious about investment banking, that you know what you are getting into, and that you possess some of the same skills that other candidates will have attained through the summer internship. It will also help to show that you can juggle both schoolwork and a job. However, make sure that your grades do not suffer as a result of the internship.

Typically, you will have to network your way into these kinds of opportunities. Most investment banks do not advertise or recruit on campus for such internships, though occasionally you may see a job posting through your school's job board. It is unusual for bulge bracket banks to offer off-cycle internships, so your best bet is to seek out boutique banks. Also note that some internships may be paid, and others may be unpaid.

Internships done during the school year are challenging. Given your schoolwork and other commitments, you may not have a lot of free time. Generally, such internships are only worth it to you if you can devote a significant amount of time to the firm, at least 20–30 hours per week, and on a set schedule. Otherwise, you are not likely to get to perform any "real" investment banking work, such as analytical work, and you will not get much out of the experience.

Recruiting for Full-Time Positions

Now that we have talked a little about the internship recruiting process, let us turn our attention to the full-time recruiting process. Remember that the internship and full-time recruiting processes are very similar, except for the recruiting calendar, so nearly all of what we will discuss here applies for internship recruiting as well. Let us start with the process of full-time recruiting for individuals enrolled at the schools at which investment banks recruit.

On-Campus Recruiting (OCR) All of the bulge bracket banks and most of the larger boutique banks typically come to a select number of undergraduate university and graduate business school campuses each year to recruit both analysts and associates. We refer to the schools at which investments banks recruit as target schools. Most bulge bracket banks will recruit at perhaps 10–15 undergraduate universities for investment banking positions and a smaller number of graduate business schools. Boutiques tend to recruit at a smaller number of schools. The process of recruiting with firms that come to campus is known as on-campus recruiting, sometimes abbreviated OCR.

Usually in the early fall, investment banks will come to campus for informational presentations and receptions in order to give students an opportunity to learn more about the firm and to meet some investment banking professionals. These events are also an opportunity for the bankers to begin to identify good potential candidates. Later in the fall, typically in late September and October, banks will hold first-round interviews on campus. Bankers will select most of the students who receive first-round interview slots, and it is often highly competitive for students to win places on the interview schedule. Some investment banks and some schools will leave a number of interview slots open to students who were not directly selected for an interview through a lottery or another mechanism.

Generally, students will have one or two 30-minute interviews. Second (and typically final) round interviews generally take place at the investment bank on what are known as "super days" (often occurring on a Friday or Saturday). Banks will normally pay for out-of-town candidates to travel to the bank and frequently hold a dinner for final-round candidates the night before the interviews.

During these super days, candidates can expect to have anywhere from four to 10 or more interviews of 30–45 minutes in length each. Banks often make their decisions very quickly with regard to whom they will offer full-time positions. Candidates are contacted accordingly, often that same day, with the good or bad news. If there are multiple super days over the course of a week or two, then candidates may have to wait longer.

Before we move away from the subject of on-campus recruiting, there is one more key point worth making. The recruiting process for candidates at target schools is a very formalized process. In essence, it is pretty much a game that follows a set of rules. If you play the game well—that is, if you put the necessary time and effort into the recruiting process—then you will get offers. If you play the game poorly, do not put in the time and effort, or do not take the process seriously, then you will not get offers.

Non-Target Recruiting While the majority of analysts and associate at bulge bracket and well-regarded boutique investment banks will have recruited from target schools, nearly all investment banks will also consider candidates from schools at which the bank does not recruit on campus. We often refer to such schools as non-targets. If you are at a non-target school, you need to be more proactive and work harder to get in the recruiting process. It will be more challenging but being successful recruiting from a non-target is absolutely achievable.

If you are interested in recruiting for investment banking and are at a non-target school then you should "cast a wide net." That is, consider a wide range of boutique banks and not just bulge bracket banks. Also make sure to reach out to firms that are headquartered or have offices in cities or regions near your school's campus. These firms may not have the name recognition of firms based in New York or other global financial centers, but they can often represent a great career in banking or a stepping stone to other firms. Moreover, firms outside of the major financial markets are often slightly less competitive for recruiting.

Once you have identified a list of banks in which you have interest, the first thing you need to do is to find out the recruiting process for students at non-target schools for each of those firms. Most investment banks will have a section on their web site that has information for candidates recruiting from non-target schools. Firms also often have an online application process. If there is no such information on an investment bank's web site, then contact the firm's human resources department to find out the process.

The key to landing an interview from a non-target school is networking. Applying online, while often a necessary step, will typically get you nowhere. You need to reach out to bankers at the firm and get your resume in front of those bankers. Try to find out if there are any alumni from your school who work at a particular bank. If so, definitely contact them early on in the process. Sometimes a banker coming from a non-target will be very active recruiting from that school. You may also want to try to attend an investment bank's reception that occurs at a target school located near yours. Lastly, if you have friends at target schools, ask them if they can help in any way, given the resources at their schools and given that they may have easier access to investment bankers. At the very least, they may help you get the names and e-mail addresses of some bankers that you can then contact.

If you put enough time and effort in the networking process, you should be able to land some first-round interviews. For students at non-target schools, sometimes first-round interviews will be held over the phone. Just like for students at target schools, if you successfully pass the first round of interviews, then you will be invited to the firm's offices for final-round interviews on a super day. Keep in mind that you are now on an even playing field with the candidates from target schools. In some cases you even have an advantage because you may have worked harder to get to this point. Do not feel badly for yourself or apologize for that fact that you do not attend the same Ivy League schools as other candidates. Once you get to final rounds, you have as good of a shot as anyone else.

Recruiting from Other Careers or Industries Most investment bankers enter the industry by recruiting directly out of either undergraduate schools or graduate business schools. However, occasionally firms do hire investment bankers from other jobs or careers. Unlike campus recruiting, this is a much less formalized recruiting process. It is also definitely a more difficult recruiting process, one that will require significant time and effort. However, it is possible to make the switch into investment banking. Generally you will have an easier time recruiting for boutique banks than for bulge bracket banks. You also have a greater chance of success if you are trying to switch into banking from a related area of finance or corporate law. If you are trying to make a complete career switch (say, from sales, engineering, or IT), then your work is cut out for you. Consider whether getting an MBA is a more likely path for you into investment banking.

Investment banks may have need for additional professionals throughout the year. However, probably the best time to recruit for an analyst position outside of the campus recruiting process is late summer and early fall. This is after most firms have paid out analyst bonuses and after some analysts may have resigned. Similarly, the best time to recruit for associate (or more senior-level) positions is in the beginning of the year through the spring, also after bonuses have been paid. Keep in mind that banks often institute hiring freezes toward the end of the calendar year. Having said all of this, if you are serious about making a switch into investment banking, you should network with bankers and pursue the process throughout the entire year.

Just like for non-target recruiting, in order to get interviews, you will need to get your resume in front of the right people. The right people are investment bankers and not HR professionals. You will need to network to meet bankers and do informational interviews. We will talk about the process of networking and informational interviews later in this chapter.

Assuming you have passed the first steps of networking and getting your resume into the hands of bankers, and that the firm has agreed to interview you, the next step is to schedule your first-round interview. You will typically have one or two back-to-back 30-minute interviews. If you are interviewing to be an analyst, you will often meet with associates and/or VPs and if you are interviewing for an associate position, you will probably meet with VPs and/or directors. At some banks, especially bulge brackets, one of the first-round interviewers might be someone from the HR department. Your first round will probably be a phone interview if you live far from the firm's offices.

If your first-round interviews go well, then you will be invited to meet with more investment bankers on site. In total, you might meet with anywhere from four to 12 or more bankers over one or two days. You will probably meet with bankers at all different levels, including the head of the group with which you are interviewing. If all goes well with the additional interview rounds, then someone, either an HR professional or a banker, will let you know that you will be receiving an offer.

RESUMES AND COVER LETTERS

Now that we have provided a general overview of the recruiting process, let us focus on some of the more tactical aspects of recruiting. In this section we will discuss resumes and cover letters. We purposely have not provided any templates or sample resumes and cover letters. You can find such things by searching the Internet, as well as find services that will help you write and/or provide feedback on your resume and cover letters.

Instead, our purpose is to give a general overview of what should be, and should not be, contained in resumes and cover letters. We will also talk about some of the common mistakes that candidates make in these documents. As we will discuss, it is crucial that your resume be tailored specifically for investment banking.

Resumes

Investment bankers will typically spend no more than about 30 seconds reviewing a candidate's resume. That is not a lot of time. In that amount of time, it is much easier for your resume to stand out in a negative way than in a positive way. So most importantly, you need to make sure that there is nothing in your resume that will get you eliminated from contention in those 30 seconds.

Aside from spotting glaring errors or a poorly formatted resume, a banker will look for certain things when reading a resume. A banker will look at your resume to see your name, where you go/went to school, your major if you are an undergraduate student, your grades, and your test scores. These facts will form a banker's first impression of you. Then a banker will quickly skim your resume to see your previous work experience, internships, and extracurricular activities. Finally, a banker may take a glance at the bottom of your resume, where you will typically list skills and interests.

Sometimes investment bankers who are involved in the recruiting process will have a stack of resumes to go through in order to pick out the candidates that merit first-round interviews from a particular school's resume drop. Let's say there are 100 resumes in the pile. Here's what typically happens. Ten resumes are strong enough that they immediately go in the yes pile. Twenty resumes have glaring errors or reflect weak candidates and go in the no pile. The remaining 70 or so resumes go in the maybe pile. Now the banker or bankers (sometimes there are multiple bankers doing this) have to try to pick out who should get an interview among the maybes. This is hard, because most resumes of candidates from the same school look alike and contain similar experiences.

Bankers will try to eliminate more resumes. Minor formatting error? That's a ding. Margins too large? Ding. Member of the management consulting and sales and trading clubs? Ding. No obvious finance experience? Ding. Too much entrepreneurial experience? Ding.

There are three goals you should keep in mind when creating the resume that you will use for investment banking recruiting. First, it has to be perfect. Obviously, there should be no typos, spelling mistakes, or grammatical mistakes, and you should usually avoid abbreviations. Your resume also needs to be formatted perfectly. For instance, make sure that all bullets line up properly, that fonts are consistent, and that all hyphens are the same length. We will discuss formatting your resume in greater detail shortly.

The second goal when creating your resume is to avoid, or at least try your best to minimize, the impact of what we call "red flags." Red flags are things on your resume that may lead whoever is reading your resume to believe that either you are not completely serious about investment banking or that you may not make a great investment banker. For example, if you list that you are a member of your school's management consulting club, sales and trading club, and marketing club, it may be taken as an indication that you are pursuing many different careers and are not very serious about banking. Also, if you emphasize the four businesses that you founded while in college, you may lead a recruiter to believe that you will leave banking after one year to pursue yet another entrepreneurial experience. Moreover, if you highlight too strongly the awards you have won for your stock-picking prowess, you may be indicating that you are really interested in asset management or working for a hedge fund.

Other obvious red flags including missing dates or gaps on your resume, a low GPA, or having transferred schools more than once. Some of these are unavoidable on your resume. You cannot lie about your GPA or make up work experience to fill gaps. If you do have such red flags on your resume, be prepared to address them in an interview.

The third goal to keep in mind when crafting your resume is to, as best you can, differentiate your resume from other candidates by highlighting your experiences that are relevant to investment banking, demonstrating your knowledge of investment banking, and showing a high level of interest in being an investment banker. We will talk about how to "bankify" your resume in the work experience section shortly.

Creating Your Resume In this section, we will discuss how to put together a resume to be used for investment banking recruiting. We will start with some basic formatting issues and then discuss each of the major sections that should be included in a resume.

If you are recruiting for industries or jobs in addition to investment banking, then you should have multiple versions of your resume. Each version will likely be very similar, but you will want to have a resume that it is specifically used for investment banking recruiting. Make sure that you are well organized and send the appropriate version of your resume to whichever type of job you are applying. Also, if you are e-mailing your resume to a firm, do not save the filename as "resume_investmentbanking." Doing this is a red flag and may lead a recruiter to believe that you also have other versions of your resume, such as "resume_trading" and "resume_consulting."

Formatting Your Resume That your resume should be formatted nicely and perfectly is true regardless of the job or industry to which you are applying. However, given the importance that investment banks place on formatting, and given the attention to detail that most investment bankers possess, bankers are much more likely to find formatting mistakes on your resume and to penalize you for having them. Don't get rejected for having such errors on your resume. Following are some general tips and guidelines for formatting your resume. Most of these suggestions reflect common sense and are applicable to a resume used for a job search in any industry.

Resumes used for investment banking recruiting should not be longer than one page. (For other industries, multi-page resumes might be acceptable, but not for banking.) If you are an experienced investment banker then you can also include a separate list of transactions on which you have worked (a deal list). However, prospective bankers recruiting from school should only submit a resume and not a deal list, even if you have worked on a few transactions in an internship. Until you can fill up a full page of transactions, you are much better off including a few examples of transactions directly in your resume.

A resume is not a piece of art. It should not look creative. While you want to differentiate the content of your resume from your peers, you do not want to differentiate your resume by its formatting. When you print, print on white, not colored paper. Use a standard font. Make sure everything is lined up perfectly. Your resume should look clean. It should not appear too crowded and it should not appear too empty. Margins should be symmetric, top and bottom, left and right, both neither too small nor too large.

If your school has a standard template for a resume, you probably want to use it, or at least use it as a guideline. Your name and contact information should go in the header of the resume, and your resume should be divided into sections, each with a section header.

Your resume should have a certain order. If you are still in school, your education should be listed before your experience. Once you are out of school, your experience should come before your education. Skills, interests, and other materials should be at the bottom. You should *not* include an objective statement or summary at the top, and you should *not* include the statement "References available upon request" at the bottom.

Education Generally if you are currently a student, the first section of your resume should be the education section. If you are already in the workforce, then education should come at the bottom of your resume, below your work experience. In this section, you should list the undergraduate and graduate institutions that you have attended, along with the applicable dates and the degrees that you have received or anticipate receiving. You should also include your major(s), minor(s), and/or concentrations(s), and any awards or recognitions you have received from the school such as Dean's List. You can also include GPA and test scores, which we will discuss shortly.

If you want, you can also include any relevant coursework in your education section. However, make sure to only include courses that are relevant to investment banking, such as advanced finance courses. You should not include basic accounting or finance courses if you are a business major or MBA student. However, if you are a liberal arts, science, or engineering student, then by all means include any classes you have taken that are relevant, including accounting or finance 101. If you are applying to work in a specific coverage group, you can also include coursework relevant to that group. For example, if you are applying to work in a healthcare coverage group, certainly list the fact that you have taken pre-med classes.

In addition to degrees and classes you have taken at school, you can include awards or recognition you have received for special projects or extracurricular activities. Otherwise, you can include such things in the skills and interest section at the bottom of your resume. If you have taken any classes or seminars relevant to investment banking, such as a two-day valuation or modeling class, you can list them in this section as well.

GPA Generally, if your undergraduate GPA is a 3.5 or above (on a 4.0 scale), and you are currently a student or have graduated within the last few years, then you should include your GPA. If you are an undergraduate student applying for analyst positions and your GPA is not on your resume, bankers will assume it is poor. So you may want to include anything above a 3.0. If your GPA in your major was better than your overall GPA, then include that, too. If you are more than one or two years out of school, you do not need to include your undergraduate GPA, but you can if you want to. However, do not be surprised if you are asked about it in an interview.

Listing grades on a resume is generally less important for MBA students, especially since some of the top business schools have grade non-disclosure policies. Moreover, you may have not even completed one full semester of classes when the summer internship recruiting receptions begin in the late fall of your first year. However, if your school does permit grades to be disclosed and your GPA is strong, then list it. If you are not permitted to or do not want to list grades, then you can mention any distinctions that you have received, such as Dean's List.

Test Scores If you are still in school or not more than a couple of years out of school, and your test scores are very good than you should include them. Generally above a 2100 for the SAT or a 700 for GMAT is worth mentioning on your resume. As with grades, if you are currently a student and do not include your relevant test scores, then some bankers looking at your resume will assume you scored below these thresholds. However, once you are more than a couple of years out of school, it is much less common to include test scores, regardless of how high you scored. However, just like with grades, don't be surprised if you are asked about your test scores in an interview.

Work Experience The work experience section of your resume should list all of your jobs and significant internships from the time you were in college through today, in reverse chronological order (i.e., the most recent work experience at the top of the page). It is very important not to leave gaps in your resume. As we mentioned earlier, gaps are considered red flags. You should also include the starting and ending dates you worked at each job, using either months and years or just years.

As you would do for any resume, under each job or internship, you should have a number of bullets providing details of your work experience. Generally, you should have at least two or three bullets for each job, and no more than five or six. It also usually makes sense for recent jobs or internships to have more bullets than less recent ones. Each bullet should have between one and three lines of text. You resume will look better if you try to mix long and short bullets within the same work experience section and, of course, you should begin each bullet with a verb.

As we mentioned earlier in this chapter, one of the goals of your resume is to highlight skills and experiences that are relevant to investment banking. Doing this will help you in a least three ways. First, it tells the reader of your resume that you have the kinds of skills required of investment bankers. Second, it demonstrates that you are aware of the kinds of skills that are used in banking and are therefore knowledgeable about the industry. Third, using investment banking–related terminology will catch the attention of the banker looking at your resume. All of these things will help differentiate your resume from those of your peers.

Make sure to put the most relevant bullets toward the top of each section, even if those tasks were not the most important to your job. A banker may only skim the first two or three bullets and never get to bullets four or five. Remember, the purpose of a resume is not simply to provide a list of your skills and experiences, but to market you and your candidacy for a particular job.

Moreover, when you write about your skills and experiences, make sure to include some details. Details also help differentiate your resume and make it more interesting to read. For example, do not just state that you did analysis in a job. Talk about the type of analysis. What type of company were you analyzing? What industry? What metrics did you use? Where did your assumptions come from? Did you do any due diligence?

Similarly, do not merely say that you performed a valuation on a company. What was the purpose of the valuation? What methodologies did you use? Did you also build a projection model? Even if you never built a financial model yourself, perhaps you "reviewed" a financial model. Make sure to use appropriate investment banking terminology to describe your experiences.

While finance-related skills are the most relevant skills to highlight in your resume, you should also emphasize non-technical experiences that are similar to what your experiences will be like as an analyst or associate. Draw attention to tasks and experiences where you worked on multiple projects at once or had projects with tight deadlines, where you dealt with or presented to clients, and where you managed junior staff.

Skills, Interests, and Other The bottom section of a typical resume is a section entitled "skills and interests," "additional," or something similar. Sometimes candidates will make these into two separate sections, which is fine. If you did not include them in your education section, you can also include any awards, recognition, and certifications that you have received in this section. For instance, it is worth mentioning if you are a CFA charter holder or have passed at least one level of the CFA, or if you hold any relevant regulatory licenses relevant to investment banking. In the United States especially, if you are a foreign student but have U.S. work authorization, a green card, or U.S. citizenship, then it is worth mentioning that on your resume as well.

Skills If you have real skills then include them. Keep in mind, however, if they are not relevant to investment banking then they will not help you at all. Language skills especially (except Latin) should be included, as they might actually one day be relevant to your investment banking job. However, do not state that you speak French fluently if all you can do is say "bonjour," "merci," and "croissant." You can list basic French or intermediate French, but do not misrepresent your level of fluency. You never know if your interviewer will also speak that language and decide to test your fluency.

Computer skills are fine to list if they include real computer skills (e.g., programming languages) but you do not need to list basic computer skills such as Microsoft Word or Excel. It is pretty much assumed that you are familiar with such software. If you have strong familiarity with some of the specialized data sources used by investment bankers such as a Bloomberg terminal, FactSet, or Capital IQ, then you should list them as well.

Interests Include interests that are interesting. It does not help you one bit to say that you like to travel, eat, and read. Pretty much everyone likes to travel, eat, and read, too. Instead, mention the types of books you enjoy reading, or state that you have traveled to over 40 countries (only if it's true, of course). And if you do list reading as an interest, make sure to be able to cite and discuss a few books that you have recently read, preferably ones that make you seem intelligent and worldly, but not ones that sound like you are trying too hard to impress.

Finally, keep in mind that what you include in your skills and interests section rarely hurts you, but they rarely help you, either. If they are especially unique or differentiating they can spark some conversation in an interview. However, if you are running out of space on your resume (remember that it must fit on one page), then this section is generally the first section to be removed or shortened.

Knowing Your Resume Before we leave the subject of resumes, there are two very important points worth stressing. First, when you are preparing for an interview, make sure that you are familiar with and can speak about every single thing on your resume. Anything on your resume is fair game in an interview. This point cannot be overstated. Do not put something on your resume if you cannot talk about it in an interview. Some interviewers will pick a random bullet point and ask you to discuss it. You will lose many points if your reply is, "Well, that was five years ago and I really don't remember."

Secondly, do not lie about anything or embellish your experiences on your resume. Your resume is a marketing document, and you do want to market yourself strongly, and emphasize your strengths and your relevant experiences. However, good interviewers will catch on quickly if you have misrepresented yourself. Plus, even if you do fool your interviewers, at almost all investment banks, your offer will be subject to a serious background check.

Cover Letters

Most of the time when you submit your resume through an online application process, or through a resume drop at your school, you will be required to include a cover letter. If you are applying to a position via e-mail, generally the e-mail can be your cover letter unless a firm's instructions specifically state otherwise. Needless to say, cover letters are not very important to the investment banking recruiting process and are, in fact, rarely read by bankers or recruiters. However, since they are often required we will discuss them briefly.

Cover letters almost never help your cause, but they can hurt you. First of all, keep in mind that cover letters much more frequently contain typos and other simple errors than do resumes. Candidates tend to obsess over a resume, reading it over dozens of time, and having friends and family edit and review it. Cover letters, on the other hand, are often written quickly and without much review. Make sure to read over your cover letters carefully and check them for errors. Also, ensure that you put the correct firm's name in your cover letter. Many students use the same cover letter applying for multiple banks and forget to search and replace the name of the firm. It does not look good if you send a letter to Morgan Stanley saying how much you really want to work at Goldman Sachs.

The next piece of advice may go against what you have been told by your career services department at school, or what you have read in other career or recruiting guides or web sites. For investment banking positions, keep your cover letters very short. They should be not much more than one paragraph and certainly not an entire page. Basically, in one sentence, state the job you are applying for or how you heard about it. Mention that you have enclosed or attached your resume. Then in not more than two or three sentences mention some relevant facts about yourself that indicate your interest in the position. Lastly, thank them and tell them how they can reach you or that you will follow up. That's it.

Common Cover Letter Mistakes Aside from simple typos and making a cover letter too long, there are a number of other mistakes that candidates for investment banking positions often make when authoring cover letters. First and foremost, you do not need to restate your entire resume. Anybody reading your cover letter will also have your resume.

Second, while it is okay to highlight something positive about the firm to which you are applying that supports your interest, do not go overboard with your compliments. Do not say things like, "I know that your firm has the smartest people and the most dealflow, and is the most awesome place to work!" Also do not state that the company for which you are applying is the best company in the world. If you have a concrete reason why you want to work at that bank then say so in one sentence, but if you go too far, you come off sounding naive. This is especially true since most investment banks (especially bulge bracket banks) are pretty much the same anyway.

While you need to be careful complimenting the firm, you also need to make sure that you do not go too far stating how great you are. Just about everyone applying to investment banking is smart, hardworking, enthusiastic, and so forth. The reader will judge these traits by your resume; by where you went to school; and by your degrees, GPA, test scores, and prior work experience or internships. Saying these things, at best, adds nothing to your cover letter. At worst, you run the risk that the interviewer will look at your resume and not agree with you or that you will come across as arrogant and conceited.

Finally, do not state in your cover letter how the firm is going to benefit by letting you work there. And regardless of your skills, if you are not already an investment banker, don't state that you will hit the ground running as a first-year investment banking analyst or associate. Remember, to an investment bank, you are just one more potential generic analyst or associate. No analyst or associate new to banking is going to be able to contribute significantly for months, so to state otherwise makes you once again seem inexperienced about the industry.

NETWORKING AND INFORMATIONAL INTERVIEWS

Regardless of whether or not you are seeking an investment banking position through the on-campus recruiting process, networking will play a crucial role in determining your success in securing first-round interviews. And if you are not at a target school, or are trying to break into the industry from another job, networking is that much more important.

For students participating in on-campus recruiting, the first step in the networking process is to attend recruiting receptions. The second step for the students from target schools, and the first step for everyone else, is to reach out directly to bankers. The final stage of the networking process is setting up informational interviews. In this section, we will discuss each of these three aspects of the networking process. We will also briefly review the usefulness (or lack thereof) of headhunters to aspiring bankers.

Recruiting Receptions

The networking process for students participating in on-campus recruiting typically kicks off with recruiting receptions. Usually in the fall, investment banks will come to the campuses of target schools and make a presentation to students. Sometimes presentations will be held off campus at a restaurant, bar, or hotel. Some investment banks will hold combined presentations at undergraduate universities for both juniors recruiting for summer internships and seniors recruiting for full-time positions, while others will opt to hold separate presentations at different times of the year. Similarly for MBA students, some banks will present to both first-year and second-year students, while other banks will present separately.

In addition, some investment banks will choose to hold one large reception for students interested in any functional area of the bank (i.e., investment banking, sales and trading, asset management, and private wealth management), while other banks will host a separate presentation for just investment banking. Finally, note that sometimes receptions are open to all students at a school who RSVP, while others are only open to a select number of students invited by the investment bank.

These receptions will usually begin with a senior member of the bank making a formal presentation. Investment banks take recruiting very seriously and sometimes even the bank's CEO will give the presentation, especially if the CEO is an alumnus of the school. The presentation may include a video or a slide show, and will usually talk about the history of the bank, the strengths of the bank, and the structure of the bank; highlight recent high profile transactions for which the bank was involved; and discuss the recruiting process. From the bank's perspective, the goal of the presentation is to market itself and to attract the best students. Often the formal presentation will end with some time for students to ask questions.

After the prepared presentation, professionals from the firm will spread out to different spots in the room so students can ask questions individually. Typically there will be bankers present from different groups and from all levels (analyst through MD for undergraduate presentations, associate through MD for MBA presentations). There will usually be a number of students congregating around each banker, especially at the beginning of this phase of the reception. Staff from the human resources department will also be in attendance to make sure that the event runs smoothly and to answer questions.

Goals of the Recruiting Receptions Your goal at these receptions is threefold. First, you want to show your interest in the firm by attending. Make sure that your name is listed and checked off on the bank's signup sheet and that you get credit for attending. Banks do often keep track of which students attend, and missing a presentation at your school can definitely hurt your candidacy.

The second reason for attending these receptions is to learn more about the firm. By listening to the corporate presentation and by meeting some bankers, you should gain some insight as to whether you have an interest in working for that particular firm. You may be able to get a taste of the firm's culture, its strengths, and the type of people that work at the firm. You will also frequently learn about the recruiting process, including key dates and deadlines, the firm's hiring needs, whether the firm recruits directly into groups, and how to go about recruiting for different geographic offices.

One of the most important questions that you will be asked in interviews is why you are interested in working for the firm with which you are interviewing. We will discuss this question further when we talk about interviewing later in the chapter. The information that you can gain from both the presentation and talking with bankers at these receptions will help you to answer this interview question. Try to remember how the firm markets itself to students and how it tries to differentiate from other investment banks. What factors are stressed in the corporate presentation? How does the bank market to its clients or prospective clients? What groups or products does the firm emphasize? Understanding the way in which the bank promotes itself to you will allow you to talk about why you are interested in working there, and ultimately help you sell yourself to the bank in your interviews.

The third, and most important, goal of attending these recruiting receptions is to network with bankers after the formal presentation. You should try to meet with a few professionals, ask a few questions of them, and then ask for a business card. In the days following the event, you will then follow up with the bankers whom you met to ask for informational interviews, which we will discuss shortly.

Many students make the mistake when chatting with bankers of trying too hard to make a great impression. Your objective is not to be memorable.

A banker will meet with many students, and generally the most memorable students are those who behaved poorly or asked silly questions. Students who ask questions that are very technical or involve something about the firm they read about recently in the newspaper usually wind up sounding unsophisticated about the investment banking industry. You should also not be asking very basic questions such as, "What does an investment banker do?" or "How many hours do you work?" You should have already done your basic homework about the industry before attending any of the receptions.

Instead, your objective is to learn a little bit more about the firm and to get business cards. You are much better off asking more personal questions of the banker, such as why the banker chose to work for that firm, or what the banker likes about that firm, or what kind of deals the banker is currently executing. (Later in this chapter in the section on interviewing, I have listed a number of questions that can be asked of the interviewer in an interview. All of those questions can be safely used in a recruiting reception as well.)

Tips for Recruiting Receptions Following are some additional tips to keep in mind when attending a firm's recruiting reception and chatting with the firm's investment bankers after the presentation:

- Dress formally (i.e., suit and tie for men, suit for women) for these events, unless the firms specifies otherwise.
- Do not drink too much alcohol if it is offered.
- Offer to get the banker a drink. Often bankers will not have time to get to the bar because they are being inundated with student questions.
- Stay until the end when the crowd thins out. You may have more opportunity for one-on-one time with a banker and a better chance to be remembered.
- Do not be annoying and monopolize a banker's time. Ask one or two questions, and ask politely for a business card. Then move on to another banker or listen to your fellow students' questions. Do not demand a business card.
- Be respectful of both the bankers and your fellow students.
- Talk to bankers all levels, not only managing directors. You do not know who is going to be making the decisions about first-round interviews.
- Sometimes bankers get bored of answering the same questions over and over and instead will ask you a question. Be prepared to give a quick background about yourself and to answer the questions of why you are interested in investment banking and why you are interested in this particular firm.
- If you were not able to get a business card for someone with whom you spoke, try following up with the HR department to ask for a banker's e-mail address.

Reaching Out to Bankers and Networking

For students recruiting for banking positions through the OCR process, your first opportunity to meet with bankers will likely be through the recruiting receptions. However, you still should try to network with and contact additional bankers on your own. For everyone else, this networking process is even more important. Networking is a time-consuming process and certainly not always fun. You will receive rejections, and your ego will get bruised. Networking is especially hard for individuals who have less outgoing personalities. However, if you are serious about recruiting for investment banking, you need do it, and you need to do it well.

When you contact investment bankers, remember that your goal is to ask for informational interviews. If a banker likes you and is able to help you then you will be able to translate informational interviews into actual interviews. Generally if you e-mail someone in the industry, you do not have to include your resume in your first e-mail. Usually, they will ask for it. However, if you find that you are not getting many responses to your e-mails then try including your resume. Keep in mind that many bankers are busy and not everyone will respond to you. Be organized about who you contact and try not to get too discouraged.

In your e-mail or phone call you should ask if you can meet with that person. You don't have to use the words "informational interview," but do not be shy about asking for a meeting. You can say something like, "I'd love to come to your office to meet you and to learn a little bit more about your firm or your group." Make sure that you are polite and respectful when making such a request, and also do not forget to highlight your level of interest in the firm. If a banker is noncommittal about a meeting, then try suggesting two or three dates that work for you.

Who to Contact One of the first things you should do is contact any friends, family, or acquaintances who are in the industry. If they are bankers, then obviously ask if you can meet them and how they can help you get interviews. If they work for investment banks or similar financial institutions but are not bankers themselves, then ask them to look at your resume and to pass it on to any bankers who might be able to help you. At the very least, ask anyone you know if they can pass on your resume to HR. Without a doubt, you have a much better chance of obtaining an interview if a banker passes your resume to HR than you do sending it to HR directly yourself.

In addition to friends and family, make sure to network with your peers at school. In fact, peers represent one of the most underutilized resources. Talk to classmates who might have done internships in investment banking. If you are a junior then don't forget to utilize the seniors for networking opportunities. Similarly, if you are a first-year MBA student, make sure to take advantage of the second-year students. If your school has an investment banking or finance club, then talk to the leadership of the club about networking opportunities. Such a club may be able to put you in touch with investment bankers and may even hold their own networking events with professionals.

After your peers, make sure to reach out to your alumni network. Almost all schools have them, and almost all schools (undergrad and MBA) have alumni on Wall Street. Talk to alumni, ask about job openings, ask for advice, and ask for informational interviews. While you will not have a 100 percent success rate, most students find that alumni tend to be very helpful to students. This is especially true at non-targets schools. Senior professionals who are alums of non-target schools are understanding of the challenges you face and are often more apt to help. If you are an MBA student, don't forget about your undergraduate alumni network as well.

Once you've exhausted your family, friends, peers, and alumni network, try cold calling or e-mailing bankers. You will have the lowest success rate doing this, but remember it may only take one good meeting to land an informational interview and one good informational interview to score an interview. Do not just focus on bulge bracket banks but also reach out to professionals at boutique banks. Use Internet resources such as LinkedIn to find bankers who work at firms in which you are interested.

Finally, be aware of any of cultural sensitiveness depending on the region for which you are recruiting. For example, it is perfectly acceptable to cold call a managing director in New York. (They may or may not respond, of course.) However, to reach out to an MD in Asia, for instance, you generally need someone to make an introduction on your behalf.

Informational Interviews

As we have said repeatedly, the goal of networking is to land informational interviews. You should treat informational interviews as if they are real interviews and prepare accordingly. Even if they are not officially part of a bank's recruiting process (though for some banks they are), you should think of them as your first round of interviews.

When you request a meeting with an investment banker, the banker may invite you to his or her office for the meeting or suggest meeting at a coffee place or somewhere similar. If you do not live in the general vicinity of the firm's offices, then informational interviews are likely to be held over the phone. Most informational interviews last about 30 minutes.

Unlike interviews, which usually follow the same general format regardless of the bank and the interviewer, there is less consistency with informational interviews. Some bankers will ask you the standard fit questions that you are likely to receive in an interview, such as:

- Tell me about your background. Walk me through your resume.
- Why do you want to be an investment banker?
- Why do you think you will make a great investment banker?
- Why are you interested in this firm?

We will discuss how to tackle these kinds of questions later in this chapter when we cover interviewing. You are much less likely to get technical questions in informational interviews than you are in real interviews, though it is not impossible. Some bankers will not ask you any questions at all, and instead will allow you to ask 30 minutes of questions. We will also discuss some of the questions that you can ask a banker when we cover interviewing. In summary, you need to be prepared to both answer the common interview questions but also to ask the banker a good many questions.

If you feel like the informational interview went well, then you should ask for other names of bankers that you should speak with. This is a great way to expand your networking efforts with that firm. Make sure to always reiterate how interested you are in working for that firm. Moreover, do not be shy about asking direct questions about the interview process or the firm's hiring needs. Ask if the banker has any suggestions for how you can be successful through the recruiting process. You can also ask for feedback, something that is much more difficult to do in real interviews.

After the informational interview, you should send a thank you e-mail to the person with whom you met. Especially if you met a banker early in the recruiting process, you should also follow up periodically with an e-mail to keep the contact "warm." Lastly, if you are invited for an interview, it is a good idea to contact anyone you did informational interviews with to let them know that you received an interview and to thank them again. You never know if they will give you a few insights into, or tips about the interview process.

Headhunters

Before we leave the topic of networking and the different ways in which you can reach out to investment bankers, let us briefly mention headhunters, also referred to as executive recruiting firms or executive search firms. Headhunters are generally only useful for individuals trying to switch from one investment bank to another (lateral moves) or from investment banking to buy-side jobs such as private equity or hedge funds. Headhunters are very unlikely to be helpful to candidates trying to break into investment banking, and they rarely work with students. Finally, it is also important to understand that executive search firms get retained by and paid by the investment banks when they place people at those firms. Candidates should never, ever pay for the services of a search firm.

INTERVIEWING

Without a doubt, the most important part of the recruiting process is the interviews. As we mentioned earlier in the chapter, if you are interviewing as part of the standard investment banking recruiting process, you will likely have two rounds of interviews. Generally, you will have one or two first-round interviews. If you pass through the first round, you will be invited back for more interviews. You may wind up meeting with anywhere from four to ten or even more bankers in subsequent round(s). Most interviews are scheduled for 30 minutes and occasionally for 45 minutes. The majority of interviews will be one-on-one—that is, you and one investment banker. Some firms do prefer two-on-one interviews, with you and two bankers. In this situation, don't be surprised if the two bankers play the game of "good cop, bad cop," with one being more friendly and one challenging your answers.

Nearly all interview questions can be segregated into two types. The first type is what we call fit questions or qualitative questions. The second type is technical questions. In most interviews, you will be asked a combination of both types of questions. However, in other instances, a series of interviews might have one or two purely technical questions and the rest solely fit. Furthermore, it is worth noting that interviews with senior bankers are much less likely to be technical than are interviews with analysts, associates, or VPs.

The primary use of fit questions is for the interviewer to make an assessment of whether you have the right attitude, skillset, and desire to be a successful investment banker. Most importantly, interviewers will want to understand why you want to be a banker, why you wish to work at this firm, and whether you are someone they would want working for them. The secondary purpose of fit questions is to assess whether you are someone they would want to work with.

Technical questions test your knowledge of subjects relevant to investment banking such as accounting, finance, and valuation (namely, the subjects covered in Chapters 2 through 8 of this book). To some extent, the types of technical questions will likely vary based on your background and the role for which you are interviewing. For example, students with finance or accounting degrees who are interviewing for analyst jobs will likely get asked a greater number of technical questions than students who do not have finance/accounting degrees.

Similarly, MBA students interviewing for associate positions can expect technical questions with greater complexity and real-world application than analyst applicants. Interviewees with banking experience should expect questions about their deal experience, which may come in addition to, or in lieu of, traditional "textbook" technical questions.

However, keep in mind that pretty much everyone recruiting for investment banking positions is expected to know the basics of finance and accounting, even liberal arts, science, or engineering majors who have never taken such classes in school. Remember that one of the reasons that technical questions are asked is to evaluate your seriousness about investment banking and see if you have done your homework about the industry.

Preparing for Interviews

Interviewing is a skill. As with most skills, the best way to improve your interviewing skills is to practice. You want to get to the point where you can be comfortable answering interview questions but without sounding too rehearsed in your answers.

You should practice walking through your resume and telling your story. You should also practice answering some of the common interview questions, both fit and technical. In addition, it can be very helpful to do mock interviews with friends, with family, and with peers. If there is an investment banking or finance club at your school, you may be able to schedule mock interviews with members of the club. Furthermore, the career services department of your school may offer mock interviews and interview prep sessions.

You can also practice in front of a mirror, in the shower, or any other method that works for you. You may even want to videotape yourself practicing (though probably not in the shower) so you can really evaluate how you look and how you sound answering common interview questions. If you have the opportunity to schedule interviews with a number of firms, schedule the less-desirable firms first and use those as rehearsals.

Scheduling Interviews

If you are interviewing through the on-campus recruiting process then you may be given the opportunity to choose your interview slot. Students sometimes overthink this decision. The most important factor when selecting an interview slot is to schedule an interview when you are most likely to be at your best. If you are not a morning person, then try to avoid a 9:00 AM interview. If you tend to get sleepy after lunch, then don't take an early afternoon slot.

It is impossible to predict how the interview slot will affect a banker's assessment of you, if at all. Some interviewers will continue to raise the bar higher as the day goes along. Other bankers are more likely to remember you if you are one of the final candidates. The only suggestion I will make is to try to avoid the last slot before an interviewer's lunch break. A hungry interviewer probably does judge a candidate in a slightly harsher manner.

General Interview Tips

In this section we will cover some very general and basic interview tips. The majority of these guidelines apply to interviews for all fields, not just investment banking, and most also reflect common sense. First, make sure you are on time for your interview. You should be a few minutes early, but not too early, and certainly do not be late. Also make sure to dress conservatively. That means a suit and tie for men and a pant or skirt suit for women. Bring several copies of your resume with you in case an interviewer does not already have it or cannot find it.

One thing that many candidates worry about is their nerves. It is okay to be nervous in an interview. In fact, almost everybody, at every level, is at least a little bit nervous in an interview setting. It is, after all, a stressful situation. And always remember, at some point, the person who is interviewing you was on your side of the table. However, you also cannot be too nervous. If you sweat profusely or have trouble speaking without nervous stuttering, then that is a problem. To a certain extent, interviewing skills are similar to the types of skills you will need to speak to or be questioned by a client or a senior banker. Therefore, being too nervous will be held against you, as it may be a sign that you won't be able to be put in front of a client or be able to deal with the stressful situations you will encounter as a banker. The more practice you have interviewing, the more comfortable you will be.

In addition, you should bear in mind that, in an interview, often how you say things is as important as what you say. This includes your body language and general demeanor. As best you can, you should be friendly and engaging, confident yet respectful, sincere and passionate. You should not be arrogant, even if your interviewer is, nor should you be apologetic about your grades or work experiences or if you miss a technical question. It is okay to pause and think for a short amount of time before your answer and politely ask for clarification if you do not understand the question. Never answer a question by saying, "Good question." Shake hands confidently when you enter the interview, and don't forget to thank your interviewer for his or her time when you exit.

Finally, keep in mind that especially for super days, you need to keep up your energy level for the entire day. This is hard, as interviews are draining. If possible, try to take a few minutes to compose yourself between interviews. Bathroom breaks can also help you if you need a few minutes to regroup. If you have a poor interview, put it behind you and move on. Moreover, make sure your answers are consistent throughout all of the interviews.

Qualitative (Fit) Interview Questions

In this section we will discuss some of the most common fit questions. In nearly all of your interviewers you will be asked some variation of each of these questions. Never forget that as important as technical questions are, fit questions are more important. It is possible to receive a job offer without acing the technical portion of an interview. However, you will definitely not receive an offer unless you perform very well on the qualitative portion.

Following are the most common fit questions. The first three are by far the most important, and you will be asked them in almost every interview and in many informational interviews as well. Keep in mind that there are often variations of these questions, especially the ones about your strengths and weaknesses.

Walk Me through Your Resume Most interviews will start off with the interviewer asking you to "walk me through your resume" or "tell me about your background." This is the most important question that you will be asked. Plan to spend no more than about three minutes telling your story. This might be your only opportunity to talk about yourself and sell your story the way you want. These few minutes will also set the tone for the remainder of the interview. Market yourself well, and you can turn the interviewer to your side. Do a poor job of telling your story and your interview is much more likely to aggressively challenge every qualitative answer that you give.

You should talk about your experiences in chronological order so that your interviewer can easily follow along with your resume as you speak. If you want, you can start off with you where you were born or where you grew up. Most candidates, however, begin with where they went to university. You should not be reading from or referring to your resume when you do this. Also be prepared for some interviewers to interrupt you and ask you questions. Others will hold off asking questions until you are finished. In addition, make sure to look for cues from the interviewer. If your interviewer seems engaged and interested, then you can go ahead and give more detail. If, on the other hand, they look bored then you are best advised to speed things up.

When you talk about your background you are telling a story. You are not simply listing facts. Your story should be interesting and compelling, but you also need to tell it in a way so that the choices you have made in your life make sense. Why did you pick your particular school? Why did you select your major or field of study? Why did you choose each job or internship? You need to explain your decisions so that it seems natural that one experience leads to the next. We refer to this as weaving a thread through your experiences, or connecting the dots of you resume.

Equally important, your narrative should also begin to answer two crucial questions: why you want to be an investment banker and why you are going to be a good investment banker. As you walk an interviewer through your adult and professional life, you should highlight experiences that have led you to investment banking, and the skills and achievements that are relevant to banking.

For instance, you might mention that you first got interested in the industry because of a class that you took freshman year that was taught by an adjunct professor who was also a practicing investment banker. Or, you might point out that in a previous job as a consultant, you worked on a project relating to an M&A deal. Even though you did not play a finance role, working on this project made you realize that the work that you did was very similar to what a banker does.

Before we move on from the "walk through the resume" interview question, we need to discuss one last matter. Recall that when we covered resumes, we talked about avoiding red flags. Here, too, it is paramount that you tell a story that does not raise any red flags in the mind of the interviewer. The biggest red flag for an interviewer is if your story just does not make sense—that is, if your decisions seem random and unconnected.

In addition, if you do have unavoidable red flags on your resume, try to be proactive by addressing them in your story. For instance, if you transferred schools, have a good reason why. If you have a low GPA and there is a good reason for it, explain that reason. Try to take the red flags off the table and address them on your terms. If you wait for your interviewer to ask about them, you will have a much tougher time and you will run the risk of coming across as apologetic or sounding like you are making excuses.

Why Do You Want to Be an Investment Banker? After "Walk me through your resume," "Why do you want to be an investment banker?" is the most important question you will be asked. If you do not answer this question well, your odds of passing through to the next interview round or getting an offer are very slim.

There are a number of generic answers to the "why banking" question that you can use, and we will discuss many of them. However, the crucial key to answering this question convincingly is to support each generic response with examples from your life. Generally, you should choose two or three of the stock reasons, and have one or two supporting examples from your life for each. You can use stories relating to your work experience, internships, extracurricular activities, or school.

Bear in mind that you need to make a very strong case that you want to be an investment banker and, hence, your responses to this question must be specific to investment banking. For instance, it is not good enough to merely say that you want to be a banker so you can give advice to companies. You are not differentiating banking from management consulting. Similarly, simply stating that you want to be an investment banker because you enjoy your finance classes will not convince an interviewer that perhaps you would prefer banking over sales and trading or asset management.

Also consider that in order to answer this question well, you will need to differentiate your answers from other candidates. Chances are, you are competing for job offers with other students from your school or from schools of comparable quality. Many of those students will also have similar grades and test scores to you, as well as the same kinds of internships and work experience. When you practice answering the "why banking" question, think about if one of your classmates could give the exact same answer. If the answer is yes, then your response is not good enough. You need to differentiate it more.

Before we discuss some of the good generic answers to this question, let's talk about some of the dumb ones. Hopefully that these are bad answers is obvious to you.

Do not state that you want to be an investment banker to make a lot of money. Yes, everyone knows that the primary reason to be a banker is for the money. But no, you cannot say that in an interview. Secondly, do not say that you want to be a banker because you don't need sleep and love working all night. No matter how little sleep you think you need, nobody enjoys working on a pitchbook at 3:00 AM. Nobody. Lastly, do not say that you want to be an investment banker so that you can advise CEOs. Even managing directors do not really advise CEOs, as we spoke about at the end of Chapter 1. Certainly, analysts and associates do not. Do not give an answer that makes you seem naive about the industry or indicates that you have no idea about what your life will be like as an investment banker.

Following are some examples of some of the good generic answers that you can use when posed with the question "Why do you want to be an investment banker?" I cannot stress enough that you need to support these answers with concrete examples from your experiences. Keep in mind that this is not an exhaustive list of every answer you can use to help you respond to this interview question. There are many others.

I did an investment banking internship over the summer and I really enjoyed it. If you are applying for a full-time investment banking position and you did a summer internship, then this is probably the best answer that you can give. Having worked in the industry already, even only for a few months, shows that you know what the work is like and what the lifestyle is like. Make sure to give a few examples of what specifically you liked about your internship.

I like the people I've met through the recruiting process, and I feel like I will fit in and that my personality is a great match for banking. This answer tries to make the point that you have the right personality to be an investment banker and reiterates that you have put the time and effort into the recruiting process by going to receptions and doing informational interviews. Be prepared to give the names of the people you have met and to talk about the events you attended. Also be able to explain the relevant kinds of personality traits you possess.

I've always enjoyed the aspects of my past jobs or classes in school that involved corporate finance. This is a lot stronger of an answer if some of your work experience involved corporate finance. In that case, you can state that you like the work of a banker. Be able to talk about specific projects or tasks from your work experience. Try to make them sound as relevant as you can to the kind of work a junior banker performs, especially analytical work.

If you are referring only to your classes in school, make sure that you sound passionate and knowledgeable about finance. Anybody who has taken finance classes can give this answer, so if you do use it, you had better also do well on the technical interview questions.

I like the fast-paced environment of investment banking as I have always excelled in pressure situations. This is a good answer as long as you can give specific examples from past jobs, internships, or school where you did well under pressure and significant time constraints. Make sure that the examples are really comparable to the kind of environment that you will experience as a banker.

I am excited to be able to work on many projects at the same time. Similar to the last response, make sure you that you can give relevant examples where you thrived working on many projects at once. Do not use as an example the fact that one semester you had three final exams in one day. Any student could say this, so it is not sufficiently differentiating.

I can't wait to be in an environment where I can take a lot of responsibility. Make sure you can give examples where you have stepped up and taken a lot of responsibility. However, you do need to be a little bit careful with this one. As an analyst or associate, you are the junior members of the deal team. Your job is to shut up and do the work. While you will have a lot of responsibility to make sure that the work gets done, you will not be the one making important decisions. In other words, do not place too much emphasis on your leadership skills or initiative.

I can't wait to be in an environment where I'll always be learning. This one is okay, especially for an analyst candidate. However, keep in mind that you are not being hired to learn. You are being hired to work. Saying that you are there to learn can make it seem like you really just want to be there for two years and then go take that knowledge somewhere else, like private equity. It is okay for an analyst to give that impression because you are only expected to be at the firm for two years, but it is a little dangerous for an associate candidate. In any case, if you use this response, be prepared to discuss what exactly it is that you think you will learn as a banker. Your response will help an interviewer evaluate whether or not you really understand the work of an investment banker.

Even though I know I'll be playing a junior role for a number of years, I like that ultimately I will be able to help advise senior management of companies. This answer is better for an associate candidate since you are being judged on whether you might be a managing director someday. This response also shows that you are thinking long term, which is good. It also shows that you are not inexperienced enough to think that you will be advising CEOs as a first-year associate. Be prepared to discuss the kinds of advice that bankers provide to their clients.

I enjoy reading about M&A transactions in the newspaper. This answer is okay as long as it is used in conjunction with other responses. It shows that you care enough about investment banking to follow the news about it. Of course, make sure that you can talk about what is going on in the finance world and be able to discuss any important recent transactions that have been in the news.

Why Do You Want to Work at Our Firm? The third most important question that you will be asked in an interview is why you want to work at the bank for which you are interviewing. Remember that you will often also be asked this question in informational interviews as well. This can be a difficult question to answer since, as we discussed in Chapter 1, it can be tough to differentiate among banks, especially between the bulge brackets.

To answer this question well, you first need to demonstrate that you know a little bit about the investment bank. Nobody will expect you to be an expert, but you should have some insights into the firm's strengths, whether that be particular industry groups, products, or geographic regions. It also helps to be aware of a few recent transactions on which the bank advised.

If you attended a firm's presentation at a recruiting reception, then remember how the bank marketed itself. When you met with investment bankers through the networking and informational interview process and at previous interviews, recall some of the answers they gave you for why they chose to work at this particular firm or why they like working there. You should try to recycle these answers as your own. In addition, prior to your interviews, you should try to talk to fellow students from your school who have worked or interned at the firm who might be able to give you some insights into the firm's strengths and its culture, which you can also use as ammunition for this question.

For instance, if in a corporate presentation or on its web site, a bulge bracket bank emphasized its global presence, then one of your answers to this question can be how you want to work for a bank that has such a global presence so you can work on lots of cross-border transactions. Or, if some of the bankers that you met told you that they like working at the firm because of its strong team-oriented culture and because most bankers have a long tenure, then by all means, talk about how these things are important to you. If you are interested in a particular industry group and the firm is particularly strong in that area, then certainly mention that, too.

Moreover, you can, and should, always mention that you want to work for a bank because you like the people you have met so far in the process. Talk about how you have a similar personality and feel like you will fit in. However, just make sure you sound sincere when you say this, and be prepared to name some of the people with whom you have met.

Finally, when interviewing with boutique banks, there are certain canned answers that you can usually provide. Most boutique banks describe their culture as entrepreneurial, and talk about how junior bankers will have more responsibility and more exposure to senior bankers and to clients. Moreover, the training programs at boutique banks tend to be shorter than at bulge bracket banks and the deal teams smaller. So for boutiques, you can answer this question by stating that you are specifically attracted to the firm because you will be able to take more responsibility sooner and because you are the type of person that learns quickly on your own.

What Are Your Strengths? You will almost always be asked some variation of the "strength" question in an interview, though not frequently as direct as "What are you strengths?" Examples of such alternatives include:

- What would your friends, professors, classmates, or coworkers say about you if I asked?
- What would your boss say about you?
- Why should we hire you?
- Why are you a better candidate than your peers?
- What should we know about you that I haven't already asked?
- Tell me about yourself. (This is different from the "walk me through your resume/tell me about your background" question.)

Before you think about how to answer this question, first recall some of the criteria from Chapter 1 about what makes a good analyst or associate:

- Attitude.
- Analytical skills.
- Attention to detail.
- Ability to work hard.
- Ability to learn quickly.
- Communication and management skills (especially for an associate).
- Finance/accounting knowledge.

The key to the strength question is to talk about this list of criteria but to have examples from your past experiences that support the reasons that you choose. For instance, state that you have strong analytical skills and give one or two examples from a past job or from school that support your strong analytical skills. Be very careful using strengths that are not supported by your resume or by what you have already said in the interview. For example, do not say you have strong finance skills if you have messed up on your technical interview questions. Similarly, do not say you have a strong work ethic if your GPA is a 2.5.

In addition to this list of what makes a good banker, there is one other strength that you should always try to mention. Emphasize how passionate and interested you are about being an investment banker and about working for this firm. Just make sure you sound genuine when saying this.

What Are Your Weaknesses? The "weakness" question is one of the hardest questions asked in any interview for any job. Just as with the strength question, you won't often be asked, "What are your weaknesses?" but you will frequently some variation of the question. For instance:

- What skills do you need to improve?
- What is your weakest skill?
- Name something negative that a classmate, professor, or colleague would say about you.
- What do your performance reviews tell you that you need to work on?
- What do you think your biggest challenge will be as an investment banker?
- Tell me three of your weaknesses.

First of all, no matter how smart you are, and no matter how hardworking, you cannot state that you have no weaknesses. You have two choices for how to approach this question. The first is to give what we call a "bullshit" answer. This is where you try to turn a weakness into a strength. Sometimes this will work, but if you have a savvy interviewer, he or she may call you out on your answer and ask you for a real weakness (or if you are really unlucky, for three real weaknesses). Examples of these kinds of answers include:

- Sometimes I am so focused or work so hard that I can tune out other aspects of my life.
- I tend to get frustrated by peers or colleagues who don't show the same commitment that I do or have the same work ethic that I have.
- I think my skills are very strong compared to my peers, but as I am new to investment banking I naturally need more experience.

Your second choice is the better one, which is to give a real weakness but one that will not have any significant impact on your ability to be a great investment banker. Obviously do not give a weakness that implies that you are not very smart, that your analytical skills are poor, or that your work ethic stinks. Some examples of innocuous replies include:

- My analytical skills are really strong but my writing skills could be a little better. (It is always nice to remind the interviewer of a strength in your answer, too.)
- I am not a great networker, though it is something that I have worked to improve while in business school.
- I think that my communication skills are generally strong but I am not so comfortable with public speaking. I hope to have a chance to work

on this skill as I become a more senior banker and have the opportunity to pitch to clients.

- For a foreign student: I have worked really hard to improve my English (or any language) skills, but they can always get better.

Where Do You See Yourself in Five Years? You may be asked such a question about your long-term career plans. If you are applying for an analyst position then your answer really does not matter very much since the typical investment bank's analyst program is for two years. You can reply with an answer such as, "I really don't know but right now I am totally focused on the prospects of working really hard for the next two years, getting excellent deal experience, learning an amazing amount, and being a great analyst. We'll see what happens after that."

If, however, you are applying for an associate position then you need to give a different answer. Remember that associates are evaluated partially on their likelihood of them becoming senior investment bankers. Therefore you should demonstrate at least a medium-term commitment to investment banking. You do not have to say that you know with 100 percent certainty that you want to be an investment banker for the rest of your life. Nobody will believe you, anyway. But you should say something like, "I definitely see myself being a banker for the long term. Right now I am focused on being a great associate, getting strong deal experience, and building up my skillset so that I can be an effective adviser down the road when I am hopefully an MD."

With What Other Investment Banks Are You Interviewing? This is one of the questions that students tend to overestimate in its importance and therefore get tripped up in an interview. To some extent, the interviewer is trying to size up its competition and to get a sense for how attractive a candidate you are based on the number of interviews you have and with what firms. However, at this point in the interview, you will probably have already been asked why you are interested in this particular firm. As long as you gave a strong answer to that question, then this question should not have much of an impact on how you are judged.

If you are interviewing with a number of investment banks, then list a few of them that are similar to the bank with which you are interviewing. For example, if you receive this question in a bulge bracket interview, try to list a few other bulge bracket firms. Just try not to list Goldman Sachs first since it is almost every prospective banker's first choice (but definitely include it if you do indeed have an interview). If you are interviewing with a boutique, list a few other boutiques of similar levels of prestige.

If this is the only bulge bracket firm for which you are interviewing then just list the other firms for which you do have interviews and reiterate that you are very interested in this firm. Don't worry so much that the banks are different. Finally, if this is your only investment banking interview, try to say something like, "I'm talking to a number of firms right now" and hope the interviewer moves on. If the interviewer presses you for an answer then be honest and say that this is your only interview right now and reiterate how much you want to work here.

For What Other Types of Jobs or Industries Are You Interviewing? When posed with this question, you definitely need to be careful with your answer. Investment banks really want you to be focused on investment banking. If you mention that you are also interviewing for management consulting and for marketing positions, then it shows that you are probably not committed to investment banking. If you are not fully committed, then you will probably not be willing to make the sacrifices that bankers need to make.

In short, it is always better to state that you are focused exclusively on investment banks. Having said that, interviewers will understand that you do need a job, and since you may be asked with what other firms you are interviewing, you may need to need to disclose the fact that you are pursuing other fields as well. It is much better if these jobs are in the finance industry and in a related area to investment banking. Make sure, however, that you emphasize that investment banking is your top priority. You should be okay if you say something like, "Investment banking is by far my top priority, but I am also interviewing with a couple of firms for equity research or asset management as a backup."

In What Investment Banking Groups Are You Interested? As we discussed in Chapter 1, some investment banks (typically boutiques) hire junior bankers as generalists, while other banks (especially bulge brackets) hire analysts and associates directly into groups or have them do rotational programs before choosing a group. If you are interviewing with a firm that hires bankers straight into groups or does a rotational program, you will almost certainly be asked about your group preference. You may even get this question during the networking and informational interview process.

If you have a strong preference for one or more groups then you should articulate that preference and have one or two good reasons for your choices. Usually the best reasons are based on your prior internships, work experience, or field of study. For example, if you are a pre-med student, it will be easy for you to justify your interest in a healthcare group. If you are an MBA student and previously worked as an engineer in the oil and gas industry, then you should be able to rationalize your desire to join an energy group without difficulty. If you cannot point to work or school experiences then make sure you are at least passionate about the group or industry.

If you do not have a strong preference for a particular group, then you should still be prepared to give one or two groups for which you would be interested. It is perfectly fine to state that what is most important to you is to be an analyst or associate at your firm and that you would be happy wherever you are placed. In fact, this kind of answer shows you have the right attitude.

However, if you are knowledgeable about investment banking, you should be able to come up with a few reasons for preferring one or two groups. Perhaps you have an interest in a particular industry or perhaps that industry has seen a lot of M&A activity recently. Remember you do not need to have any expertise in a particular industry in order to be a successful investment banker in that coverage group. If you met a few bankers who work in a particular group, you can always say that you are attracted to that group because of the people and that you think you will fit in well there.

Finally, be aware that you should be careful giving the answer of certain groups as your preference, especially when recruiting for associate positions. Specifically, these groups are M&A, leveraged finance, and financial sponsors. If you do not have a good reason to justify your preference then your response is often taken as a sign that you really just want to use investment banking as a stepping stone to private equity, since these three groups are often thought to provide the strongest exit opportunities.

What Are Your Interests or Hobbies? Often in an interview you will be asked about your interests or hobbies, or asked, "What do you like to do when you are not working or in school?" This is a very easy question. Just like we discussed when we covered the interests section of the resume, try to demonstrate that you are an interesting person. You should be able to talk about one or two interests or hobbies, aside from being your fraternity's beer pong champion or growing marijuana in your dorm room. Also, do not use any examples of interests that are bizarre and make you sound like a weird person. Additionally, it is usually better to not mention interests or hobbies that are related to politics or religion.

Finally, you should be a little bit careful about being too passionate about a hobby or interest. Remember that as a junior banker you will not have any time whatsoever to pursue these interests. If you mention how you can't live without a certain pursuit, you may give the impression that you are either not knowledgeable about the kind of lifestyle that you will have as a banker or, worse, not willing to make the sacrifices.

Do You Have Any Questions for Me? Nearly all interviews will end with you being given an opportunity to ask a few questions of the interviewer. Generally you will have approximately five minutes to ask questions. This is a chance for you to learn a little bit more about the firm and the position for which you are interviewing. However, like everything else in an interview, you are still being judged by the questions you ask.

You should never say that you do not have any questions, even if this is your seventh interview with the firm and all of your questions have already been answered. Therefore, as part of your interview preparations, you should always have a few questions in mind that you can ask an interviewer. Just as we discussed in the section on networking and recruiting receptions, you should not try too hard to ask "smart" questions about finance or about a specific investment banking transaction. You are much better off trying to turn this portion of the interview into more of a conversation rather than a question and answer session. Most people like talking about themselves, so try to get the interviewer talking about him- or herself with your questions.

One thing you should be wary of is asking about a firm's culture, lifestyle, or work hours. A question on these topics is often received as an indication that you are not willing to work hard or do not understand the sacrifices you will need to make as a banker. However, it is acceptable to ask about culture or lifestyle if your interviewer has already brought it up in the interview. Moreover, you should never ask about topics such as compensation, benefits, or vacation days. Wait until you have an offer in hand to discuss these kinds of issues.

Following are a few sample questions that are generally safe to ask most interviewers:

- How long have you been with the bank, and how has your experience been?
- What do you like best about working here? Worst?
- What made you choose to work for this firm?
- What made you choose this particular group?
- How do you compare working here with other investment banks at which you have worked?
- On what types of deals are you currently working?
- How is the level of dealflow right now?
- Can you tell me about your training program?
- How do analysts/associates in you firm/group get staffed?
- In your opinion, what makes a good analyst/associate?
- What are some things that you wished you knew or you wished someone told you before you became a banker?

- Do you have a sense for how many analysts/associates your firm/group will be hiring this year?
- Do you have any recommendations for specific classes or professors that I should take (especially if the interviewer is a recent alum of your school)?

Lastly, there is one additional type of question which you can ask an interviewer, but you need to be a little bit careful doing so. You may be able to ask for some feedback on your interview performance. If you feel like the interview went very poorly, then it cannot hurt to ask for some feedback that might help you in future interviews. If, on the other hand, you feel like the interview went well, then your interviewer may have some incentive to help you move further in the process. In this instance, you may want to ask a question, such as, "I am really highly interested in working here. Do you have any advice for me going forward?" If you do not have a strong feeling about the interview, then it is probably best not to ask for such feedback or advice.

Technical Interview Questions

The second category of interview question that you will be asked in investment banking interviews is technical questions. Recall from earlier in this chapter that there are at least three primary reasons that technical questions are asked in banking interviews. The obvious reason is to evaluate your technical skills and knowledge to determine if you will be able to do the job if you are hired. The second reason is to test your interest level for banking, to see if you put forth the effort to learn some of the investment banking skills that are not typically taught in school. The third reason is to see how you handle stress.

As we stated in the introduction to the book, nearly all of the topics that you are likely to encounter in technical interview questions have been covered in this book. Moreover, most of the specific interview questions that you are likely to be asked have also been covered in the end-of-chapter questions. If you feel comfortable with the content contained in each chapter, then you should feel well prepared for the technical portion of an investment banking interview.

Before we discuss the specific categories of technical questions that you will likely encounter, let us cover some strategies for answering these kinds of questions in interviews. First, suppose that you do not know the answer to a technical question. In this case, what should you do?

If you have no idea of the answer of a technical question, you should say so. Politely say that you don't know or don't remember or would have to think about it. Since technical questions are designed to test your ability to handle stress, you will generally score more points in an interview if you calmly, coolly, and matter of factly state that you do not know an answer rather than fumbling around for 10 minutes trying to figure it out. If you know part of the answer, by all means state the part that you do know first and then the part that you don't know.

Another issue that candidates often wonder is if you should ask your interviewer for the correct response to a technical question. Generally, if you have no idea about the answer to the question posed, then you should just move on. However, if you make a valid attempt and are told that you got the answer wrong, then it probably makes sense to ask for the correct answer. You never know if you will be asked the same question again in a later interview, so you might as well get it right the second time. The only time that you should not ask the interviewer for the answer is if you think the interviewer doesn't know the correct answer. (Yes, bankers sometimes ask questions to which they don't know the answer.) If the interviewer doesn't know, then he or she is just going to look stupid, and making the interviewer look stupid will never help your cause.

General Business or Finance Questions As we mentioned earlier in this chapter, if you come from a liberal arts, engineering, or any other non-business/finance/accounting background, you will still likely get asked the same questions as everyone else. However, you may get some more general business questions to that test to see if you have a general interest in business and finance, and investment banking. For example:

- Do you follow the stock market?
- What is the current level of the Dow Jones Industrial Average? The S&P 500?
- What is the current level of interest rates? What is the current yield on a 10-year Treasury bond?
- What do you think about the strength of the economy right now?
- Where do you think the economy will be a year from now?
- What do you think that the Federal Reserve is going to do in the near future?
- Tell me something about finance or the economy that is affecting markets today.
- Talk about a company or a stock that you follow or recommend.
- Tell me about a recent M&A transaction that you've read about.

Accounting and Financial Statement Analysis Some of the technical questions that you are likely to be asked in interviews will be on the subject of accounting and financial statement analysis. We covered these topics in Chapters 2 and 4.

It is not very common, though not unheard of either, for you to be asked very basic questions about accounting definitions. For instance, you will probably not be asked, "What is a balance sheet?" or "What are costs of goods sold?" You are more likely to be asked about some of the slightly more advanced accounting topics, such as deferred taxes, leases, and goodwill. You should also be prepared to answer questions about calculating some of the key metrics used for financial statement analysis, and especially about how to interpret them.

The most common question asked about accounting and financial statement analysis refers to the interactions between the three financial statements. We discussed this in detail at the end of Chapter 2. In fact, one of the most frequently asked technical questions of all is "How would $10 of depreciation expense impact each of the three financial statements?" Make sure you can comfortably walk an interviewer through these impacts in your head. You will usually not be afforded the opportunity to do this using a piece of paper.

Finance General finance questions represent another common subject of technical interview questions. We covered this topic in Chapter 3. You should be comfortable with the basic present value formulas, understand the inverse relationship between interest rates and bond prices, and be able to talk about NPV and IRR. You should also understand capital structure and the various pros and cons of issuing debt versus issuing equity. Also make sure you understand why debt is a less expensive form of capital than equity. In addition, you should understand the various assumptions that go into a Black-Scholes model for valuing options and warrants, and how a change of each assumption will affect the value of a call or put option.

Valuation As we mentioned in the introduction to Chapter 5, valuation is the topic of more investment banking technical questions than any other subject. In fact, "How do you value a company?" and "Walk me through a DCF" might be the two most commonly asked of all technical questions.

You should be prepared to discuss how bankers value companies and to walk through each of the three valuation methodologies. Be prepared to answer how you use the three methodologies to conclude value, and the pros and cons of each technique. Know the concept of enterprise value, how to calculate it, and how it differs from equity value. Be able to talk about various valuation multiples as well as how to calculate the weighted average cost of capital, and the cost of equity using the CAPM formula. Make sure you understand the concept of beta and the reasons for levering and unlevering beta. Lastly, make sure you can mention and talk about some additional valuation methodologies in addition to the three primary ones.

Mergers and Acquisitions (M&A) Mergers and acquisitions, the subject of Chapter 7, represents one of the more advanced investment banking topics that we have discussed. As such, you are more likely to be asked questions pertaining to M&A if you are an MBA student recruiting for an associate position than an undergraduate student recruiting for an analyst position. Having said that, everything is fair game in an interview, so it is worth being familiar with M&A regardless of your situation.

You should be prepared to talk about why companies make acquisitions and discuss the topic of synergies. Demonstrating that you know enough to walk through the basic M&A sell-side process can also differentiate you from other, less-knowledgeable candidates. However, the most important M&A topic to know is the accretion/dilution analysis. You should be able to walk through the process for performing such an analysis and understand what factors contribute to whether a transaction will be accretive or dilutive.

You should make sure you can answer a variation of the most common M&A–related question: "If a company with a P/E ratio of x acquires a company with a P/E ratio of y in a stock transaction, is this deal likely to be accretive or dilutive?" Finally, if you are recruiting for an M&A group or a boutique bank that focuses on M&A, you should also be able to talk about some of the pros and cons of a tender offer versus merger and a stock versus asset transaction.

Leveraged Buyouts (LBOs) As with M&A, interview questions pertaining to leveraged buyouts are more likely to be encountered by prospective associates than by analyst candidates. Moreover, they are especially likely if a candidate is recruiting for a leveraged finance or financial sponsors group.

As we covered in Chapter 8, you should understand the benefits of using leverage in an acquisition and be able to converse about the various types of debt used in a typical LBO, as well as what makes an attractive LBO target. You should also be able to walk an interviewer through a basic LBO model and understand how the model is used to measure the anticipated investment returns to the financial sponsor and what the various factors that impact IRR are. Finally, be prepared to discuss some of the key credit ratios useful for measuring leverage and how the LBO analysis can be used to help value a company.

Financial Modeling Different from all of the other topics covered in the technical chapters of the book, financial modeling, which we discussed in

Chapter 6, is a much less likely topic of technical interview questions. If you are interviewing for a private equity firm or certain small boutique investment banks, you may face an actual financial modeling test, where you are asked to build a model in a short time frame. For bulge bracket banks and most boutiques, however, this is highly unlikely.

On the other hand, financial modeling underlies the kind of analysis bankers perform when creating discounted cash flow analyses, as well as M&A and LBO models. Being able to speak about building financial models the way that investment bankers build them can help you differentiate your candidacy by showing you really understand the work of a junior investment banker.

Questions about Your Deal Experience If you are an experienced investment banker, have done an investment banking internship, or have some experience in a field very related to investment banking, you will usually get questions about your transaction experience, in addition to or even in lieu of standard technical questions. You should be prepared to walk through some of the deals on which you have worked. It is very important to make sure that you can speak about any such deal or project that you have listed on your resume. Some interviewers may select a random transaction or project from your resume and ask you to talk about it.

It is also important that you are able to discuss some of the technical aspects of the deal. For example, if you mentioned on your resume or in an interview that you performed a valuation analysis for a deal, make sure that you can talk about the comparable companies that you used as well as the relevant multiples. If, for instance, you stated that you built a financial model for a project, then be sure that you can recollect the key drivers and assumptions that you used for the model.

Brainteasers

It is unusual to be asked brainteasers in investment banking interviews, though it is more common when recruiting for other areas of finance. If you are going to be asked brainteasers, it is more likely recruiting for an analyst than an associate position, and more likely at a boutique bank than a bulge bracket. In this section, we have listed a few of the most common brainteasers asked in interviews (not just finance interviews). You can find additional examples of common brainteasers on my web site (www.ibankingfaq.com) and also by doing a quick Internet search.

Keep in mind two things if you are faced with brainteasers. The first thing is that the obvious answer to a brainteaser is nearly always incorrect. Second, most brainteasers are not designed to require a lot of math. So if you find yourself having to make difficult calculations, that is an indication that there is probably an easier way to answer the question. Note, however, this is not the case when interviewing for certain hedge funds or for highly quantitative positions where difficult math can be part of the interview process.

Finally, I will share with you one additional piece of advice when confronted with a brainteaser. It is a risky strategy but can work for you if you are willing to take the risk. Before the interviewer even finishes asking the question, or immediately thereafter, state with confidence that you are familiar with this particular brainteaser, even if you are not. Only try this if you have no idea how to answer the question and therefore have little to lose. If you get lucky, the interviewer might not make you answer it and may not have an alternative brainteaser to ask you. Of course, the interviewer may still ask you to answer it or may call your bluff.

Following are five of the most commonly asked brainteasers.

What is the angle between the hour-hand and minute-hand of a clock at 3:15? This is probably the most commonly asked brainteaser of them all. The obvious answer is a zero angle between the hour-hand and minute-hand at 3:15. But of course, the obvious answer is wrong. At quarter past the hour, the minute-hand is exactly at 3 but the hour-hand has moved one-fourth of the way between 3 and 4. Since there are 12 hours on a clock, the difference between the two hands is 1/48th (1/4 times 1/12). And since there are 360 degrees in a circle, the angle between the two hands is 360 divided by 48, or 7.5 degrees.

You are given a three-gallon jug and a five-gallon jug. How do you use them to get four gallons of liquid? There is more than one way to answer the question, but here is one solution. Fill the five-gallon jug completely. Pour the contents of the five-gallon jug into the three-gallon jug, leaving two gallons of liquid in the five-gallon jug. Next, dump out the contents of the three-gallon jug and pour the contents of the five-gallon jug into the three-gallon jug. At this point, there are two gallons in the three-gallon jug. Fill the five-gallon jug and then pour the contents of the five-gallon jug into the three-gallon jug until the three-gallon jug is full. You will have poured one gallon, leaving four gallons in the five-gallon jug.

What is the sum of numbers from 1 to 100? Remember that brainteasers are not usually designed to test your math ability, so there must be a shortcut to this type of question. Indeed there is. The trick here is to know that the sum of numbers from 1 to 100 is made up of exactly 50 pairs of numbers that each total to 101 (i.e., 1 + 100, 2 + 99, 3 + 98). Hence, 50 multiplied by 101 equals 5,050.

You have a 10 × 10 × 10 cube made up of 1 × 1 × 1 smaller cubes. The outside of the larger cube is completely painted red. On how many of the smaller cubes is there any red paint? First, note that the larger cube is made up of 1,000 smaller cubes. The easiest way to think about this is: How many cubes are *not* painted? The 8 × 8 × 8 inner cubes are not painted, which equals 512 cubes. Therefore, 1,000 – 512 = 488 cubes that have some paint. Alternatively, we can calculate this by saying that two 10 × 10 sides are painted (200) plus two 10 × 8 sides (160) plus two 8 × 8 sides (128): 200 + 160 + 128 = 488.

A car travels a distance of 60 miles at an average speed of 30 mph. How fast would the car have to travel the same 60 mile distance home to average 60 mph over the entire trip? Here, the obvious answer is 90 mph, but of course that is not right. This is actually a trick question! The first leg of the trip covers 60 miles at an average speed of 30 mph. So, this means the car traveled for two hours (60/30). In order for the car to average 60 mph over 120 miles, it would have to travel for exactly two hours (120/60). Since the car has already traveled for two hours, it is impossible for it to average 60 mph over the entire trip.

After the Interview

In this section, we'll talk about what happens after the interview. We will start with a brief discussion of some indications that you may have fared well in your interview, or fared poorly. We will also talk about the thank-you notes that you should send your interviewer and a little bit about how firms decide to which candidates to make offers.

Signs that an Interview Has Gone Well There are some general indications that your interview may have gone well. However, it is very important to keep in mind that you cannot always tell. Some interviewers have very good poker faces and often your initial reaction, whether positive or negative, proves to be erroneous.

Often, it is a good sign if your interview lasts significantly longer than its allotted time, which is typically 30 minutes. This is especially true if you are interviewing with a relatively senior investment banker. Another very positive sign is when the banker with whom you are interviewing ceases to ask you questions and starts telling you about the benefits of the firm. This is known as switching into sell mode, and generally indicates that the banker thought highly of you and wants you to work there. Similarly to your interview going long on time, this is an especially strong indication if your interviewer is a managing director.

A third, though less significant, sign of interest is if you are asked about the other banks with which you are interviewing, and more importantly if you are asked how far along you are in the recruiting process with those banks and if you have any offers yet. Finally, you can often tell if you had a good interview if it felt more like a conversation than a formal question and answer session.

Signs that an Interview Has Gone Poorly Just as we stated previously, some interviewers are hard to judge, so do not place too much stock in some of the following indications. More importantly, if you do feel like an interview went poorly and you have additional interviews that day, try your hardest not to let that poor interview get you down. As best you can, snap back and gear yourself up for the remaining interviews.

Generally, it is a bad sign if an interview lasts for less than its scheduled time. Another negative indication is if you are not given the chance to ask any questions of the interviewer at the end of the meeting or if the meeting ends very abruptly. Also, often the interviewer's facial and body reactions will give you clues that he or she does not like your answers or is not "buying your story." Similarly, it is a negative sign if your interviewer focuses for a long time on a particular red flag, such as a low GPA or having been terminated from a previous job.

Thank-You Notes While it usually will not make or break your candidacy, you should send a thank-you e-mail to each interviewer within 24 hours of your interview. There is no need for a handwritten note. Thank-you notes need not be more than two sentences long. Thank your interviewer for his or her time and reiterate your strong interest in working for the firm. If you are able to, try to mention one topic that came up in the interview. However, do not worry too much if you cannot do this. Additionally, if you had multiple interviews, you should make each thank-you e-mail slightly different, even if it just means the wording is varied.

Candidates tend to write these thank-you e-mails at the end of a long day of interviews. As such, they are often written quickly and contain basic typos or grammatical mistakes. Make sure that you read them carefully before you hit send. You do not want to end a great day of interviews with a silly mistake in a thank-you e-mail. Lastly, do not expect to receive a response to your e-mail. In fact, whether you receive a response is rarely indicative of how you fared in your interviews, so do not read too much into it. Some investment bankers will respond out of courtesy to all applicants. Others never respond regardless of how well you performed in your interview.

The Interview Response Once the interview is finished, you will usually hear back within a few days, sometimes even the same day. At most you should hear within a week. If you do not hear back within a week, you should politely follow up. Often boutique banks have only one super day and will make verbal offers the same day. Bulge bracket banks usually have multiple super days. Sometimes the strongest candidates will receive offers the same day, while others will be put on hold until all of the super days have been completed. At other firms, each candidate will have to wait until all super days are finished.

How banks decide who to make offers to also varies from firm to firm. Usually every interviewer will have to fill out an evaluation form on each candidate they interviewed that day. As part of the evaluation form, often interviewers have to assign a numerical score so each candidate can be ranked. At the end of the day of interviews, all of the interviewers will gather in a conference room to discuss who moves on to the final round (in the case of a first-round interview) or who should receive an offer (in the case of a super day interview). This process can certainly be contentious. Most firms require a consensus, and some firms even mandate a unanimous decision. However, sometimes having a senior banker be very supportive of a candidate can override a few no's from more junior bankers.

Rejection and Interview Feedback If you get rejected after an interview, try to get some feedback. Feedback can be incredibly helpful when preparing for future interviews. Unfortunately, most firms will not give any feedback, but it cannot hurt to ask. You can try reaching out to any good contacts you had at the firm or any banker with whom you had a strong informational interview or real interview during the recruiting process, and asking for feedback. Sometimes a banker may be able to ask around and find out why you were rejected.

Whatever you do, do not be belligerent with anyone from the firm, including the HR professionals, and do not "burn the bridge." Accept the bad news professionally and move on. Moreover, try not to take the rejection too personally. Even the best candidates do not have a 100 percent success rate in interviews.

It is also worth continuing to keep in contact with some of the bankers you met through the recruiting process. You may even want to e-mail them to let them know that you are disappointed that you did not receive an offer but that you would still like to keep in touch. Plenty of bankers have been rejected for summer internships but have received offers the next year for full-time positions. Similarly, you never know if you will wind up trying to make a lateral switch a few years down the road to a firm with which you had previously interviewed.

RECEIVING AN OFFER AND BEING A BANKER

Applicants who are being offered positions will usually receive a phone call from an investment banker to let them know and give congratulations.

Make sure you show your excitement and enthusiasm. A formal offer package will then follow in the mail. The offer package will include salary, signing bonus, and a host of HR documents. Most of the time, an investment banking offer will have an expiration date, known as an exploding offer. Banks use exploding offers to pressure candidates to accept and to try to prevent candidates from using the offer as negotiating leverage with another investment bank or other institution.

Before an offer does expire, many firms will invite you to what is known as a sell day, where you have an opportunity to meet with bankers in a relaxed environment. Often you will be taken out to a nice dinner and "wined and dined." This is your chance to get further insight into the firm's culture and to get to know some of your potential colleagues better. From the bank's perspective, the purpose of the sell day is to help encourage you to accept their job offer.

If you receive a job offer from a firm that does not have such a sell day, you are certainly free to request a meeting with a couple of bankers in order to help make your decision. Banks are usually happy to oblige and will often set up a lunch for you with a number of bankers.

Finally, keep in mind that your offer will almost certainly be subject to you passing a basic background check and drug test. For undergraduate and MBA candidates, banks will often also request transcripts.

Selecting Among Multiple Offers

Let's assume you are fortunate enough to receive job offers from multiple investment banks. In this section we will discuss some of the criteria that you should consider when making your decision of which offer to accept. We will start by talking about some of the factors when choosing between bulge bracket and boutique investment banks and then cover issues relating to group selection.

Bulge Bracket Banks vs. Boutique Banks In Chapter 1 of the book, we spoke of some of the differences between bulge bracket banks and boutique banks. Here we will discuss some of the issues you should consider when contemplating starting your investment banking career at a bulge bracket bank versus a boutique bank.

Bulge bracket banks have some advantages. First, they tend to have larger brand recognition, especially globally, than do nearly all boutique banks. Second, you tend to get a broader experience at bulge bracket banks than you do at boutiques. For example, you may work on an IPO one day, a debt issuance the next day, and be pitching a public sell-side M&A deal the third day. You will also get exposure to a larger breadth of financial services and products. Your experience at a boutique bank tends to be narrower. Moreover, bulge bracket banks tend to have longer training programs during the summer and more ongoing training during the rest of the year. They also often have more support services than do boutique banks. Finally, it tends to be easier to make a lateral move from a bulge bracket bank to a boutique than the other way around.

Boutiques, on the other hand, have some of their own advantages. As stated earlier in this chapter, you often get more responsibility at a junior level. You also will likely have more exposure to clients and to senior investment bankers. You will probably attend more pitches and more meetings. Some, though not all, boutiques have more relaxed cultures and better lifestyles. Boutique banks also tend to be less volatile with hiring and firing. So, you may have better job security at a boutique than at a bulge bracket bank. Finally, since many boutiques are privately held (unlike the large financial institutions), you are more likely to be paid your bonus in cash, rather than stock.

Choosing among Groups If you have multiple job offers for different investment banking groups then there is an additional set of considerations that you need to contemplate. In this section, we will discuss some of the issues for choosing among product groups and industry coverage groups. First, keep in mind that just like with banks, different groups may have their own cultures, reputations, politics, and varying levels of dealflow.

As we mentioned in Chapter 1, there is some truth to the perception that product groups such as M&A, leveraged finance, and restructuring can lead to better deal experience, more modeling experience, and better exit opportunities. These groups also sometimes have somewhat longer work hours and a slightly tougher lifestyle. Remember, though, that these generalizations will only hold true if there is sufficient market activity for the particular product. In short, there are probably some advantages to being in one of these groups as an analyst, especially someone considering recruiting for private equity positions. Finally, note that restructuring groups can lead to not only to private equity exit opportunities but to distressed buy-side jobs. No other group is likely to provide such opportunities.

There are two primary advantages to industry coverage groups. The first is that you are not subject to market conditions for one particular product. Even more importantly, because bankers in industry groups tend to do much more marketing, investment bankers tend to form relationships with clients sooner in a product group, and these relationships tend to be stronger. If you are a prospective associate contemplating a long-term career in investment banking, then the sooner you start making client relationships the better.

Additional Criteria for Making a Decision In addition to the issues surrounding the decision to go to a bulge bracket or a boutique bank and selecting a bank based on a particular group, there are a variety of factors that you should consider when selecting the firm for which to work.

Dealflow Dealflow should be the most important consideration when choosing an investment bank, especially at the junior levels. While you will learn a lot doing pitches, you need to have live transaction experience in order to build your career as a banker or to maximize your exit opportunities into buy-side jobs such as private equity or hedge funds. Moreover, at the analyst level, dealflow generally correlates highly with modeling experience, which is especially important when recruiting for private equity positions. There is one additional reason why you should favor banks that have or are likely to have more dealflow: Firms with strong dealflow are much less likely to lay off bankers and therefore provide a higher certainty of job security.

Reputation Many candidates choose offers because of the name of the firm. Having a well-recognized name on your resume provides some prestige and boosts your ego, and also can lead to more opportunities for you in the future. For the most part, bulge bracket banks have a similar degree of prestige and reputation, the exception being Goldman Sachs, which is a step above. There is, however, much more diversity when talking about boutique banks.

Culture and Lifestyle Bulge bracket banks are also pretty similar from a lifestyle and culture standpoint; however, boutiques can vary somewhat. Some banks are sweatshops; others have slightly more relaxed cultures with less face time and fewer hours. When deciding among boutique banks, the culture of the firm should enter into your thought process.

People As an investment banker, you will spend a lot of time in the office and a lot of time with your colleagues. Obviously, it helps to like the people with whom you work. Even though bankers, especially senior bankers, tend to have very similar personalities and personality traits, if you like the people better at one firm more than another, then that is certainly important.

Compensation At the analyst and associate levels, compensation varies little at the bulge brackets and top boutiques. Generally, at the junior levels of banking, compensation is not a reason to select one bank over another (though it certainly can be at the more senior levels of banking). The one exception is how you get paid. Starting at the associate level, public companies are more likely to pay a large percentage of your compensation in stock rather than in cash.

Geography If you are considering offers from firms located in different cities, then, other things equal, you should consider where you would be happier living. For instance, suppose you have offers at a technology-focused boutique bank in San Francisco and a tech group of a bulge bracket bank based in New York. Certainly you should consider factors such as dealflow, reputation, and culture. However, if you grew up on the west coast, if your family is on the west coast, and if you generally prefer the culture of Northern California over New York, then your answer should be pretty clear. Even though you will spend most of your waking hours at the office as a junior banker, do not underestimate the importance of being happy with your life outside of work.

Starting Your Investment Banking Career In this final section, we will briefly talk about some of the things you can do to prepare yourself for your investment banking career and for being a great analyst or associate. First of all, once you have accepted an offer, relax. Rediscover your social life, take the classes that you want, travel, and spend time with family. Don't completely blow off your classwork (remember you still need to graduate), but enjoy your life while you can. It will change as soon as you start working. Finally, don't worry about brushing up on your technical skills or finance knowledge at this point. You've passed the test. The rest, you can and will learn on the job.

Summer Interns If you are going to be a summer intern, either at the analyst or associate level, remember that your primary goal is to secure a full-time offer. Work as hard as you can and have a great attitude. Make sure that you are proactive. Ask how you can help and don't wait for bankers to come to you. You want to do as much work as possible during your summer internship, both to gain experience but also so that you have a number of supporters when it comes time for the firm to decide to whom to give full-time offers.

Analysts If you are going to be a full-time analyst, be prepared to give up your life. You want to get as much deal experience and as much modeling experience as possible, especially if you are expecting to recruit for private equity positions. Just like being an intern, have a great attitude and be proactive. Try never to turn down work or staffing assignments. Moreover, remember that the best analysts do not wait to be asked to do work by their associates or VPs. They do the work before they are asked. And they do it perfectly.

Associates If you are going to be an associate, expect your life especially the first year to be similar to that of an analyst's. Don't think that you know everything just because you have an MBA from a fancy school. Things are very different in the real world than they were in business school. For many of you, business school was a vacation from the real world. Now you need to remember how to work hard again.

Never forget that you are useless at the beginning. Defer to the more senior analysts who actually know what they are doing. Over time, you will learn and you can take over the role of managing an analyst. As much as you can the first year, do the work yourself. Spread the comps, and build the models. You will move up the learning curve faster and gain the respect of the better analysts. And just like for analysts, be proactive and agreeable when dealing with senior bankers and your staffer. Start forming relationships internally with senior bankers and with clients.

CONCLUSIONS

We have covered a lot of ground in this book. My goal in writing this book was to prepare you to be an investment banker. I tried to provide you with not only an overview of the concepts and the technical skills needed to do the work of a junior banker, but also the knowledge required to be successful in the recruiting and interviewing process.

You should now have a good understanding of what it takes to be an investment banker. You know what investment banks are looking for in candidates. You are aware of what the lifestyle will be like and what the work will be like. You know what you are getting into. You are familiar with the core concepts and principles of finance and accounting, and you understand the basics of valuation and financial modeling. You can speak intelligibly about M&A and LBOs. You know what you need to do to network and to secure interviews. You know how to prepare for those interviews.

Investment banking is not for everyone. You will have to sacrifice a lot in order to be successful in the recruiting process. You will have to sacrifice a lot more to be a successful banker. But if it is want you want to do, make it happen. Be an investment banker.

Good luck!

Further Reading

Rather than provide a detailed bibliography of books and articles relating to investment banking, I thought it would be more helpful to provide a small list of resources that you can use to learn even more about investment banking.

To learn more about life as an investment banker

Monkey Business: Swinging Through the Wall Street Jungle by John Rolfe and Peter Troob

Monkey Business, written by two former investment bankers, is a somewhat embellished but not inaccurate depiction of life as an investment banking associate. It was written during the boom years of the late 1990s but is still relevant today.

The Accidental Investment Banker: Inside the Decade that Transformed Wall Street by Jonathan A. Knee

The Accidental Investment Banker provides a good overview of the investment banking industry from the perspective of a senior investment banker.

To learn more about the technical skills used in investment banking

Investment Banking: Valuation, Leveraged Buyouts, and Mergers and Acquisitions (Wiley Finance) by Joshua Rosenbaum and Joshua Pearl

Investment Banking is a good follow-up to this book. It covers the primary valuation methodologies like we did, but is more geared toward how to do the work rather than the underlying concepts. It is also provides a more detailed overview of the sell-side M&A process, and an excellent and much more detailed overview of LBO analysis.

Investment Valuation: Tools and Techniques for Determining the Value of Any Asset (Wiley Finance) by Aswath Damodaran

There are lots of books in the marketplace that cover valuation from a more detailed and theoretical standpoint, but Damodaran's are the best.

Microsoft Excel

If you are looking for a book on Microsoft Excel, I recommend anything by John Walkenbach.

Web sites about investment banking

www.ibankingfaq.com (my own web site)

www.wallstreetoasis.com

www.mergersandinqusitions.com

epicureandealmaker.blogspot.com

Self-study training

Ibankingfaq Self Study Financial Modeling

Breaking into Wall Street

Training the Street

Wall Street Prep

Live investment banking training classes

Adkins Matchett & Toy

Investment Banking Institute

Training the Street

Wall Street Prep

About the Author

Andrew Gutmann is the creator of www.ibankingfaq.com, one of the most widely visited web sites focused on the topic of investment banking. He has taught finance and investment banking classes for a number of institutions, including at the Institute for Finance, the firm that he founded. For the past five years, he has also been a career coach at Columbia Business School, where he advises and mentors MBA and Executive MBA students interested in investment banking careers.

Andrew was a senior vice president at Asgaard Capital, a vice president in the M&A group of HSBC, and an associate at Houlihan Lokey. He has led or helped execute M&A, restructuring, and capital-raising transactions for clients in multiple business sectors, including consumer/retail, energy, financial services, industrials, real estate, technology, and telecommunications. In addition to the time he has spent as an investment banker, Andrew has also been involved in a number of entrepreneurial ventures. He is currently the founder of igokids, a New York–based tech startup. Andrew earned his B.A. in economics from The Johns Hopkins University and his M.B.A. from Columbia Business School.

About the Companion Website

The companion website contains solutions to the end of chapter questions in the book. To access the site, go to www.wiley.com/go/gutmann (password: investment).

Index

I